The Little Oxford
Dictionary of Quotations

The Little Oxford Dictionary of **Quotations**

SECOND EDITION

Edited by Susan Ratcliffe
with Helen Rappaport

OXFORD
UNIVERSITY PRESS

OXFORD
UNIVERSITY PRESS

Great Clarendon Street, Oxford OX2 6DP

Oxford University Press is a department of the University of Oxford.
It furthers the University's objective of excellence in research, scholarship,
and education by publishing worldwide in

Oxford New York

Athens Auckland Bangkok Bogotá Buenos Aires Calcutta
Cape Town Chennai Dar es Salaam Delhi Florence Hong Kong Istanbul
Karachi Kuala Lumpur Madrid Melbourne Mexico City Mumbai
Nairobi Paris São Paulo Shanghai Singapore Taipei Tokyo Toronto Warsaw

with associated companies in Berlin Ibadan

Oxford is a registered trade mark of Oxford University Press
in the UK and in certain other countries

Published in the United States
by Oxford University Press Inc., New York

British Library Cataloguing in Publication Data
Data available

Library of Congress Cataloging in Publication Data
Data available
ISBN 0–19–866266–1

10 9 8 7 6 5 4 3

Typeset in Nimrod and Arial
by Interactive Sciences Ltd, Gloucester
Printed in Spain
by Bookprint S.L., Barcelona

Contents

Foreword to the Second Edition   vii

Foreword to the First Edition   viii

List of Themes   xi

The Little Oxford Dictionary of Quotations   **1**

Index of Authors   459

Foreword to the Second Edition

'He that will not apply new remedies must expect new evils, for time is the greatest innovator' said Francis Bacon. A dictionary of quotations must expect to find time looking over its shoulder, as new expressions pass into the language, or older ones suddenly acquire new resonances. In this second edition of *The Little Oxford Dictionary of Quotations*, Eric Cantona's comments on seagulls join Kipling and Shakespeare at **News and Journalism**, while Hillary Clinton's views on baking cookies join Dr. Johnson and Queen Victoria at **Woman's Role**.

In compiling this edition it has been possible to draw on a greatly enhanced range of material, both old and new. In the years since publication of the first edition, there has been a considerable expansion of the Oxford Bank of New Quotations. Not only has a new edition of the parent volume *The Oxford Dictionary of Quotations* appeared, but so too have entirely new dictionaries of political, literary, and twentieth-century quotations, amongst others. New additions include classic quotations from non-Western cultures, such as Confucius on **Teaching** or **Human Nature**, and Lao Tzu on **Beginnings**, and historical quotations which have acquired new relevance (Napoleon: 'I want the whole of Europe to have one currency'). More recent quotations which have become well-known, such as Tony Blair's 'Education, education, education' and Diana, Princess of Wales's aspiration to be a 'queen in people's hearts', have also earned a place.

To make it easier to find quotations, the order of the authors within the themes has been changed from chronological to alphabetical. This also increases the element of serendipity, the sense of a variety of viewpoints across the years: Samuel Beckett on **Time** is followed by the Bhagavad Gita and Michael Portillo on **Careers** by Shakespeare. New themes have been added, some for topical subjects such as **Drugs**, where authors range from Thomas De Quincey to Noel Gallagher, and **Computers** (Timothy Leary: 'The PC is the LSD of the 1990's'). Elsewhere, **Photography** includes practitioners such as David Bailey and those for whom it is 'a moment of embarrassment and a lifetime of pleasure' (Tony Benn). At **The Presidency**,

Eisenhower thought that 'No easy problems ever come to the President of the United States', but George Bush has solved one problem at least: 'I'm President of the United States, and I'm not going to eat any more broccoli!' Perhaps he had been listening to Isaac Asimov at **Health and Fitness**: 'The first law of dietetics seems to be: if it tastes good, it's bad for you'.

Revising this dictionary would not have been possible without the help of many people, and I should like to thank Elizabeth Knowles, Managing Editor of Quotations Dictionaries, for her help and advice at all stages, Muriel Summersgill for data capture, and Kim Allen and Carolyn Garwes for proofreading. In addition, I should like to acknowledge the contributions made to the first edition by Ralph Bates and Marie G. Diaz for library research, and by Sandra Vaughan and Katie Weale for data assembly and capture.

Finally, Pete Seeger may be right in saying that 'Education is when you read the fine print, experience is what you get when you don't', but I hope that this collection will at least offer some of the experiences and ideas of many different people over three thousand years, if only because, in the words of Dorothy L. Sayers, 'it saves original thinking'.

Susan Ratcliffe

Oxford, 2000

Foreword to the First Edition

The Little Oxford Dictionary of Quotations is a collection which casts a fresh light on even the most familiar sayings. It is organized by themes, such as **Action**, **Liberty**, and **Memory**, and within each theme the quotations are arranged in date order, so that the interplay of ideas down the centuries becomes apparent. It is intended for the reader who is searching for quotations on a specific subject, the reader who remembers the sense of a quotation but not the precise words, and, of course, the browser.

The themes have been chosen to reflect as wide a range of

subjects as possible, concentrating on the general rather than the specific. A few themes have a slightly different character: thus **People** and **Places** cover quotations about many different individual people and places, while **Political Comment** and **Wars** include quotations relevant to specific events. The length of the sections reflects to some extent the preoccupations of people throughout history, ranging from short ones such as **Advice** to the many and varied comments on **Life** and **Love**. Where subjects overlap, the reader is directed to related themes at the head of the section; for example, at **Death**: see also **Epitaphs**, **Last Words**, **Murder**. An author index is provided to help readers wishing to trace a particular quotation or seeking quotations from specific individuals.

Within each theme, the aim is to take in a variety of viewpoints, including both the most familiar quotations and some less well-known or perhaps new material. So within **News and Journalism**, along with C. P. Scott's classic 'Comment is free, but facts are sacred', we have Tom Stoppard's gloss 'Comment is free but facts are on expenses' and more recently Lord MacGregor on 'journalists dabbling their fingers in the stuff of other people's souls'. This book contains some one hundred quotations which have not previously appeared in any dictionary of quotations. These new quotations appear, for example, under the themes **Environment** (... all that remains/For us will be concrete and tyres'), **Men and Women** ('Whereas nature turns girls into women, society has to make boys into men'), and **Science** ('The aim of science is not to open the door to infinite wisdom, but to set a limit to infinite error').

The chronological ordering within each theme enables the quotations to 'talk' to one another, shedding new light on each. Thus we have Samuel Johnson telling us 'Change is not made without inconvenience, even from worse to better', followed by Voltaire: 'If we do not find anything pleasant, at least we shall find something new'. Much of the cross-referencing required by an alphabetical arrangement of authors becomes redundant: Ralegh's line written on a window-pane 'Fain would I climb, yet fear I to fall' is now immediately followed by Elizabeth I's reply 'If thy heart fails thee, climb not at all.'

The quotations have been classified by their subject rather

than by keywords in the text. For example, Tom Lehrer's 'It is sobering to consider that when Mozart was my age he had already been dead for a year' is essentially about **Achievement** rather than **Music** or **Death**, and has been placed accordingly. As far as possible each quotation has been included only once, but a few, such as Pope's 'To err is human, to forgive divine' plainly had a place in two sections.

A short source reference is given for each quotation, usually including its date. Where the date is uncertain or unknown, the author's date of death has been used to determine the order within a theme. The quotations themselves have been kept as short as possible: contextual information has occasionally been added to the source note, and related but less well-known and well-expressed versions have generally been excluded. Owing to constraints of space, foreign language originals have been given only where they are well-known or where translations differ. Such information, including full finding references, can be found in *The Oxford Dictionary of Quotations*.

We are always grateful to those readers who write to us with their comments, suggestions, and discoveries, and we hope this tradition will continue. *The Little Oxford Dictionary* draws largely on the work done for the fourth edition of *The Oxford Dictionary of Quotations*, and therefore owes a substantial debt to all those involved in the preparation of that volume. None the less, this book has its own identity, and the editor's chief pleasure as it took shape has been in listening to diffent voices speaking to each other across the ages: ' "What is the use of a book," thought Alice, "without pictures or conversations?" '

Susan Ratcliffe

Oxford, March 1994

List of Themes

Absence

Achievement and Endeavour

Acting and the Theatre

Action

Advertising

Advice

Alcohol

Ambition

America and Americans

Anger

Animals

Apology

Architecture

Argument

The Army

Art

Australia

Beauty

Beginnings and Endings

Behaviour

Belief and Unbelief

The Bible

Biography

Birds

Birth

The Body

Books

Bores and Boredom

Britain

Broadcasting

Bureaucracy

Business and Commerce

Canada

Careers

Cats

Censorship

Certainty and Doubt

Chance

Change

Character

Charm

Children

Choice

Christmas

The Church

The Cinema

Civilization

Class

Commerce see Business and Commerce

Computers

Conscience

Conversation

Cooperation

The Country and the Town

Courage

Crime and Punishment

Crises

Critics and Criticism

Cruelty

Custom and Habit

Cynicism

Dance

Day and Night

Death

Democracy

Despair see Hope and Despair

Determination

Diaries

Diplomacy

Discontent see Satisfaction and Discontent

Discoveries see Inventions and Discoveries

Dogs

Doubt see Certainty and Doubt

Drawing see Painting and Drawing

Dreams see Sleep and Dreams

Dress

Drink see Food and Drink

Drugs

Economics

Education

Endeavour *see Achievement and Endeavour*

Endings *see Beginnings and Endings*

Enemies

England and the English

Environment

Envy and Jealousy

Epitaphs

Equality

Europe and Europeans

Evil *see Good and Evil*

Experience

Failure *see Success and Failure*

Fame

The Family

Fate

Fear

Fitness *see Health and Fitness*

Flowers

Food and Drink

Fools and Foolishness

Forgiveness

France and the French

Friendship

The Future

Gardens

The Generation Gap

Genius

Gifts and Giving

God

Good and Evil

Gossip

Government

Greatness

Habit *see Custom and Habit*

Happiness

Hatred

Health and Fitness

The Heart

Heaven and Hell

Heroes

History

The Home and Housework

Honour

Hope and Despair

The Human Race

Human Rights

Humour

Hypocrisy

Idealism

Ideas

Idleness

Ignorance

Imagination

Indifference

Intelligence and Intellectuals

Inventions and Discoveries

Ireland and the Irish

Jealousy *see Envy and Jealousy*

Journalism *see News and Journalism*

Justice

Knowledge

Language

Languages

Last Words

The Law and Lawyers

Leadership

Leisure

Letters and Letter-writing

Liberty

Libraries

Lies and Lying

Life

Life Sciences

Literature

Living

London

Love

Madness

Majorities *see Minorities and Majorities*
Management
Manners
Marriage
Mathematics
Meaning
Medicine
Meeting and Parting
Memory
Men
Men and Women
Middle Age
The Mind
Minorities and Majorities
Misfortune
Mistakes
Moderation
Money
Morality
Murder
Music
Musicians

Nature
News and Journalism
Night *see Day and Night*

Old Age
Opening Lines
Optimism and Pessimism

Painting and Drawing
Parents
The Past
Patriotism
Peace
People
Perfection
Pessimism *see Optimism and Pessimism*
Philosophy
Photography
Places
Pleasure
Poetry
Poets
Political Comment
Political Parties
Politicians
Politics
Pollution
Poverty
Power
Practicality
Praise
Prayer
Prejudice
The Present
The Presidency
Pride
Progress
Punishment *see Crime and Punishment*

Quotations

Race
Reading
Reality
Religion
Revenge
Revolution and Rebellion
Royalty

Satisfaction and Discontent
Science
Scotland and the Scots
The Sea
The Seasons
Secrets
The Self
Self-Knowledge
Sex
Shakespeare
Sickness
Silence
Singing
The Skies
Sleep and Dreams
Society
Solitude
Sorrow
Speech and Speeches
Sport
Statistics
Style
Success and Failure
Suffering
The Supernatural

Taxes
Teaching
Technology
Temptation
The Theatre *see Acting and the Theatre*
Thinking
Time
Titles
The Town *see The Country and the Town*
Transience
Transport

Travel
Trust and Treachery
Truth
The Twentieth Century

Unbelief *see Belief and Unbelief*
The Universe

Vice *see Virtue and Vice*
Violence
Virtue and Vice

Voting

Wales
War
Wars
Wealth
Weather
Woman's Role
Women
Words
Work
Writers
Writing

Youth

Absence

1 When I came back to Dublin, I was courtmartialled in my
absence and sentenced to death in my absence, so I said
they could shoot me in my absence.
Brendan Behan 1923–64: *Hostage* (1958)

2 The Lord watch between me and thee, when we are absent
one from another.
Bible: Genesis

3 The heart may think it knows better: the senses know that
absence blots people out. We have really no absent friends.
Elizabeth Bowen 1899–1973: *Death of the Heart* (1938)

4 The absent are always in the wrong.
Philippe Néricault Destouches 1680–1754: *L'Obstacle
imprévu* (1717)

5 Absence diminishes commonplace passions and increases
great ones, as the wind extinguishes candles and kindles
fire.
Duc de la Rochefoucauld 1613–80: *Maximes* (1678)

6 Most of what matters in your life takes place in your
absence.
Salman Rushdie 1947– : *Midnight's Children* (1981)

Achievement and Endeavour

See also **Ambition**

1 That's one small step for a man, one giant leap for
mankind.
Neil Armstrong 1930– : landing on the moon, 21 July
1969 (interference in transmission obliterated 'a')

2 Madam, if a thing is possible, consider it done; the
impossible? that will be done.
Charles Alexandre de Calonne 1734–1802: in J.
Michelet *Histoire de la Révolution Française* (1847); better

known as the US Armed Forces' slogan: 'The difficult we
do immediately; the impossible takes a little longer'

3 Now, *here*, you see, it takes all the running *you* can do, to
keep in the same place. If you want to get somewhere else,
you must run at least twice as fast as that!
Lewis Carroll 1832–98: *Through the Looking-Glass* (1872)

4 The danger chiefly lies in acting well;
No crime's so great as daring to excel.
Charles Churchill 1731–64: *An Epistle to William
Hogarth* (1763)

5 None climbs so high as he who knows not whither he is
going.
Oliver Cromwell 1599–1658: attributed

6 The trouble with fulfilling your ambitions is you think you
will be transformed into some sort of archangel and you're
not. You still have to wash your socks.
Louis de Bernières 1954– : in *Independent* 14 February
1999

7 There must be a beginning of any great matter, but the
continuing unto the end until it be thoroughly finished
yields the true glory.
Francis Drake *c.*1540–96: dispatch to Sir Francis
Walsingham, 17 May 1587

8 The distance is nothing; it is only the first step that is
difficult.
Mme Du Deffand 1697–1780: commenting on the legend
that St Denis, carrying his head in his hands, walked
two leagues; letter to Jean Le Rond d'Alembert, 7 July
1763

9 If a man write a better book, preach a better sermon, or
make a better mouse-trap than his neighbour, tho' he build
his house in the woods, the world will make a beaten path
to his door.
Ralph Waldo Emerson 1803–82: attributed to Emerson
in S. Yule *Borrowings* (1889), but claimed also by Elbert
Hubbard

10 *Parturient montes, nascetur ridiculus mus.*
Mountains will go into labour, and a silly little mouse will
be born.
   Horace 65–8 BC: *Ars Poetica*

11 Had I been a man I might have explored the Poles, or
climbed Mount Everest, but as it was, my spirit found
outlet in the air.
   Amy Johnson 1903–41: Margot Asquith (ed.) *Myself
   When Young* (1938)

12 I had done all that I could; and no man is well pleased to
have his all neglected, be it ever so little.
   Samuel Johnson 1709–84: letter to Lord Chesterfield,
   7 February 1755

13 It is sobering to consider that when Mozart was my age he
had already been dead for a year.
   Tom Lehrer 1928– : in N. Shapiro (ed.) *An Encyclopedia
   of Quotations about Music* (1978)

14 Because it's there.
   George Leigh Mallory 1886–1924: on being asked why
   he wanted to climb Mount Everest; in *New York Times*
   18 March 1923

15 Things won are done; joy's soul lies in the doing.
   William Shakespeare 1564–1616: *Troilus and Cressida*
   (1602)

16 *Non omnia possumus omnes.*
We can't all do everything.
   Virgil 70–19 BC: *Eclogues*

Acting and the Theatre

See also **The Cinema**, **Shakespeare**

1 Tragedy is thus a representation of an action that is worth
serious attention, complete in itself and of some amplitude
. . . by means of pity and fear bringing about the purgation
of such emotions.
   Aristotle 384–322 BC: *Poetics*

2 I go to the theatre to be entertained, I want to be taken out of myself, I don't want to see lust and rape and incest and sodomy and so on, I can get all that at home.
   Alan Bennett 1934– : Alan Bennett et al. *Beyond the Fringe* (1963) 'Man of Principles'

3 There's no business like show business.
   Irving Berlin 1888–1989: title of song (1946)

4 Things on stage should be as complicated and as simple as in life. People dine, just dine, while their happiness is made and their lives are smashed. If in Act 1 you have a pistol hanging on the wall, then it must fire in the last act.
   Anton Chekhov 1860–1904: attributed; Donald Rayfield *Anton Chekhov* (1997)

5 To see him act is like reading Shakespeare by flashes of lightning.
   Samuel Taylor Coleridge 1772–1834: on Edmund Kean; *Table Talk* (1835) 27 April 1823

6 Just say the lines and don't trip over the furniture.
   Noël Coward 1899–1973: advice on acting, in D. Richards *The Wit of Noël Coward* (1968)

7 Actors are cattle.
   Alfred Hitchcock 1899–1980: in *Saturday Evening Post* 22 May 1943

8 Let's not get too precious about it: actors are not heart surgeons or brain surgeons. We are just entertaining people.
   Malcolm McDowell 1943– : in *Mail on Sunday* 14 May 2000

9 Acting is a masochistic form of exhibitionism. It is not quite the occupation of an adult.
   Laurence Olivier 1907–89: in *Time* 3 July 1978

10 She ran the whole gamut of the emotions from A to B.
   Dorothy Parker 1893–1967: of Katherine Hepburn on the first night of *The Lake* (1933); attributed

11 Acting is merely the art of keeping a large group of people from coughing.
  Ralph Richardson 1902–83: in *New York Herald Tribune* 19 May 1946

12 Suit the action to the word, the word to the action.
  William Shakespeare 1564–1616: *Hamlet* (1601)

13 It's a sound you can't get in the movies or television . . . the sound of a wonderful, deep silence that means you've hit them where they live.
  Shelley Winters 1922– : in *Theatre Arts* June 1956

Action

1 Every honourable action has its proper time and season, or rather it is this propriety or observance which distinguishes an honourable action from its opposite.
  Agesilaus 444–400 BC: Plutarch *Lives* 'Agesilaus'

2 But men must know, that in this theatre of man's life it is reserved only for God and angels to be lookers on.
  Francis Bacon 1561–1626: *The Advancement of Learning* (1605)

3 Enough of talking—it is time now to do.
  Tony Blair 1953– : on taking office as Prime Minister; Downing Street, 2 May 1997

4 The world can only be grasped by action, not by contemplation . . . The hand is the cutting edge of the mind.
  Jacob Bronowski 1908–74: *The Ascent of Man* (1973)

5 It is in vain to say human beings ought to be satisfied with tranquillity: they must have action; and they will make it if they cannot find it.
  Charlotte Brontë 1816–55: *Jane Eyre* (1847)

6 Oh that thou hadst like others been all words,
  And no performance.
  Philip Massinger 1583–1640: *The Parliament of Love* (1624)

7 They also serve who only stand and wait.
   John Milton 1608–74: 'When I consider how my light is spent' (1673)

8 Think nothing done while aught remains to do.
   Samuel Rogers 1763–1855: 'Human Life' (1819)

9 If it were done when 'tis done, then 'twere well
   It were done quickly.
   William Shakespeare 1564–1616: *Macbeth* (1606)

10 Nothing is ever done in this world until men are prepared to kill one another if it is not done.
   George Bernard Shaw 1856–1950: *Major Barbara* (1907)

....

Advertising
....

1 A good poster is a visual telegram.
   A. M. Cassandre 1901–68: attributed

2 It is not necessary to advertise food to hungry people, fuel to cold people, or houses to the homeless.
   J. K. Galbraith 1908– : *American Capitalism* (1952)

3 Promise, large promise, is the soul of an advertisement.
   Samuel Johnson 1709–84: *The Idler* 20 January 1759

4 Society drives people crazy with lust and calls it advertising.
   John Lahr 1941– : in *Guardian* 2 August 1989

5 Advertising may be described as the science of arresting human intelligence long enough to get money from it.
   Stephen Leacock 1869–1944: *Garden of Folly* (1924)

6 Half the money I spend on advertising is wasted, and the trouble is I don't know which half.
   Viscount Leverhulme 1851–1925: D. Ogilvy *Confessions of an Advertising Man* (1963)

7 Good wine needs no bush,
   And perhaps products that people really want need no hard-sell or soft-sell TV push.
   Why not?

Look at pot.
   Ogden Nash 1902–71: 'Most Doctors Recommend or
   Yours For Fast, Fast, Fast Relief' (1972)

8 The consumer isn't a moron; she is your wife.
   David Ogilvy 1911– : *Confessions of an Advertising Man*
   (1963)

9 Advertising is the rattling of a stick inside a swill bucket.
   George Orwell 1903–50: attributed

Advice

1 It was, perhaps, one of those cases in which advice is good
   or bad only as the event decides.
   Jane Austen 1775–1817: *Persuasion* (1818)

2 Well, if you knows of a better 'ole, go to it.
   Bruce Bairnsfather 1888–1959: *Fragments from France*
   (1915)

3 Advice is seldom welcome; and those who want it the most
   always like it the least.
   Lord Chesterfield 1694–1773: *Letters to his Son* (1774) 29
   January 1748

4 Get the advice of everybody whose advice is worth
   having—they are very few—and then do what you think
   best yourself.
   Charles Stewart Parnell 1846–91: Conor Cruise
   O'Brien *Parnell* (1957)

5 After all, when you seek advice from someone it's
   certainly not because you want them to give it. You just
   want them to be there while you talk to yourself.
   Terry Pratchett 1948– : *Jingo* (1997)

6 I always pass on good advice. It is the only thing to do with
   it. It is never of any use to oneself.
   Oscar Wilde 1854–1900: *An Ideal Husband* (1895)

Alcohol

See also **Food and Drink**

1 Let's get out of these wet clothes and into a dry Martini.
   Anonymous: line coined in the 1920s by Robert
   Benchley's press agent and adopted by Mae West in
   Every Day's a Holiday (1937 film)

2 One reason why I don't drink is because I wish to know
   when I am having a good time.
   Nancy Astor 1879–1964: in *Christian Herald* June 1960

3 When the wine is in, the wit is out.
   Thomas Becon 1512–67: *Catechism* (1560)

4 Wine is a mocker, strong drink is raging.
   Bible: Proverbs

5 I have taken more out of alcohol than alcohol has taken
   out of me.
   Winston Churchill 1874–1965: Quentin Reynolds *By
   Quentin Reynolds* (1964)

6 And malt does more than Milton can
   To justify God's ways to man.
   A. E. Housman 1859–1936: *A Shropshire Lad* (1896)

7 If merely 'feeling good' could decide, drunkenness would
   be the supremely valid human experience.
   William James 1842–1910: *Varieties of Religious
   Experience* (1902)

8 Claret is the liquor for boys; port, for men; but he who
   aspires to be a hero must drink brandy.
   Samuel Johnson 1709–84: in James Boswell *Life of
   Johnson* (1791) 7 April 1779

9 O for a beaker full of the warm South,
   Full of the true, the blushful Hippocrene,
   With beaded bubbles winking at the brim,
   And purple-stainèd mouth.
   John Keats 1795–1821: 'Ode to a Nightingale' (1820)

10 You're not drunk if you can lie on the floor without
holding on.
> **Dean Martin** 1917–95: in P. Dickson *Official Rules* (1978)

11 Candy
Is dandy
But liquor
Is quicker.
> **Ogden Nash** 1902–71: 'Reflections on Ice-breaking' (1931)

12 I'm only a beer teetotaller, not a champagne teetotaller.
> **George Bernard Shaw** 1856–1950: *Candida* (1898)

13 I'm not so think as you drunk I am.
> **J. C. Squire** 1884–1958: 'Ballade of Soporific Absorption'
> (1931)

14 It's a naïve domestic Burgundy without any breeding, but I
think you'll be amused by its presumption.
> **James Thurber** 1894–1961: cartoon caption in *New
> Yorker* 27 March 1937

15 The lips that touch liquor must never touch mine.
> **George W. Young** 1846–1919: title of verse (*c.*1870)

Ambition

See also **Achievement and Endeavour**

1 My desire to get here [parliament] was like miners' coal
dust, it was under my fingers and I couldn't scrub it out.
> **Betty Boothroyd** 1929– : Glenys Kinnock and Fiona
> Millar (eds.) *By Faith and Daring* (1993)

2 *Aut Caesar, aut nihil.*

Caesar or nothing.
> **Cesare Borgia** 1476–1507: motto inscribed on his sword

3 Ah, but a man's reach should exceed his grasp,
Or what's a heaven for?
> **Robert Browning** 1812–89: 'Andrea del Sarto' (1855)

4 Well is it known that ambition can creep as well as soar.
   Edmund Burke 1729–97: *Third Letter . . . on the Proposals for Peace with the Regicide Directory* (1797)

5 [I] had rather be first in a village than second at Rome.
   Julius Caesar 100–44 BC: Francis Bacon *Advancement of Learning*, based on Plutarch *Parallel Lives*

6 All ambitions are lawful except those which climb upwards on the miseries or credulities of mankind.
   Joseph Conrad 1857–1924: *Some Reminiscences* (1912)

7 At the age of six I wanted to be a cook. At seven I wanted to be Napoleon. And my ambition has been growing steadily ever since.
   Salvador Dali 1904–89: *The Secret Life of Salvador Dali* (1948)

8 If thy heart fails thee, climb not at all.
   Elizabeth I 1533–1603: line after Walter Ralegh, written on a window-pane

9 Hitch your wagon to a star.
   Ralph Waldo Emerson 1803–82: *Society and Solitude* (1870)

10 The worst fault of the working classes is telling their children they're not going to succeed, saying: 'There is life, but it's not for you.'
   John Mortimer 1923– : in *Daily Mail* 31 May 1988

11 Fain would I climb, yet fear I to fall.
   Walter Ralegh c.1552–1618: line written on a window-pane, in Thomas Fuller *Worthies of England* (1662)

12 When that the poor have cried, Caesar hath wept; Ambition should be made of sterner stuff.
   William Shakespeare 1564–1616: *Julius Caesar* (1599)

13 The world continues to offer glittering prizes to those who have stout hearts and sharp swords.
   F. E. Smith 1872–1930: Rectorial Address, Glasgow University, 7 November 1923

14 There is always room at the top.
   Daniel Webster 1782–1852: on being advised against joining the overcrowded legal profession (attributed)

America and Americans

See also **Places**

1 California is a fine place to live—if you happen to be an orange.
   Fred Allen 1894–1956: in *American Magazine* December 1945

2 A Boston man is the east wind made flesh.
   Thomas Gold Appleton 1812–84: attributed

3 Good Americans, when they die, go to Paris.
   Thomas Gold Appleton 1812–84: Oliver Wendell Holmes *The Autocrat of the Breakfast-Table* (1858)

4 America! America!
   God shed His grace on thee
   And crown thy good with brotherhood
   From sea to shining sea!
   Katherine Lee Bates 1859–1929: 'America the Beautiful' (1893)

5 The microwave, the waste disposal, the orgasmic elasticity of the carpets, this soft resort-style civilization irresistibly evokes the end of the world.
   Jean Baudrillard 1929– : *America* (1986)

6 God bless America,
   Land that I love,
   Stand beside her and guide her
   Thru the night with a light from above.
   Irving Berlin 1888–1989: 'God Bless America' (1939)

7 Go West, young man, and grow up with the country.
   Horace Greeley 1811–72: *Hints toward Reforms* (1850)

8 This land is your land, this land is my land,
   From California to the New York Island.
   From the redwood forest to the Gulf Stream waters
   This land was made for you and me.
   Woody Guthrie 1912–67: 'This Land is Your Land' (1956 song)

9 Don't forget the Western is not only the history of this
country, it is what the Saga of the Nibelungen is for the
European.
> **Fritz Lang** 1890–1976: Peter Bogdanovich *Fritz Lang in
> America* (1967)

10 Give me your tired, your poor,
Your huddled masses yearning to breathe free.
> **Emma Lazarus** 1849–87: 'The New Colossus' (1883);
> inscribed on the Statue of Liberty, New York

11 Europe is the unfinished negative of which America is the
proof.
> **Mary McCarthy** 1912–89: *On the Contrary* (1961)
> 'America the Beautiful'

12 There can be no fifty-fifty Americanism in this country.
There is room here for only 100 per cent. Americanism,
only for those who are Americans and nothing else.
> **Theodore Roosevelt** 1858–1919: speech in Saratoga, 19
> July 1918

13 I like to be in America!
OK by me in America!
Ev'rything free in America
For a small fee in America!
> **Stephen Sondheim** 1930– : 'America' (1957 song)

14 Overpaid, overfed, oversexed, and over here.
> **Tommy Trinder** 1909–89: of American troops in Britain
> during the Second World War (associated with Trinder,
> but probably not original)

15 America is a vast conspiracy to make you happy.
> **John Updike** 1932– : *Problems* (1980) 'How to love
> America and Leave it at the Same Time'

16 The United States themselves are essentially the greatest
poem.
> **Walt Whitman** 1819–92: *Leaves of Grass* (1855)

17 America is God's Crucible, the great Melting-Pot where all
the races of Europe are melting and re-forming!
> **Israel Zangwill** 1864–1926: *The Melting Pot* (1908)

Anger

1 Anger makes dull men witty, but it keeps them poor.
   Francis Bacon 1561–1626: 'Baconiana' (1859), often
   attributed to Queen Elizabeth I

2 A soft answer turneth away wrath.
   Bible: Proverbs

3 The tigers of wrath are wiser than the horses of
   instruction.
   William Blake 1757–1827: *The Marriage of Heaven and
   Hell* (1790–3) 'Proverbs of Hell'

4 Beware the fury of a patient man.
   John Dryden 1631–1700: *Absalom and Achitophel* (1681)

5 *Ira furor brevis est.*
   Anger is a short madness.
   Horace 65–8 BC: *Epistles*

6 When angry, count four; when very angry, swear.
   Mark Twain 1835–1910: *Pudd'nhead Wilson* (1894)

Animals

See also **Cats**, **Dogs**

1 All things bright and beautiful,
   All creatures great and small,
   All things wise and wonderful,
   The Lord God made them all.
   Cecil Frances Alexander 1818–95: 'All Things Bright
   and Beautiful' (1848)

2 I'm not over-fond of animals. I am merely astounded by
   them.
   David Attenborough 1926– : in *Independent* 14 January
   1995

3 Old pond,
   leap-splash—

a frog.
Matsuo Basho 1644–94: translated by Lucien Stryk

4 The question is not, Can they reason? nor, Can they talk? but, Can they suffer?
Jeremy Bentham 1748–1832: *Principles of Morals and Legislation* (1789)

5 A righteous man regardeth the life of his beast: but the tender mercies of the wicked are cruel.
Bible: Proverbs

6 Tiger Tiger, burning bright,
In the forests of the night;
What immortal hand or eye,
Could frame thy fearful symmetry?
William Blake 1757–1827: 'The Tiger' (1794)

7 A four-legged friend, a four-legged friend,
He'll never let you down.
J. Brooks: 'A Four Legged Friend' (1952 song); sung by Roy Rogers about his horse Trigger

8 Wee, sleekit, cow'rin', tim'rous beastie,
O what a panic's in thy breastie!
Robert Burns 1759–96: 'To a Mouse' (1786)

9 I am fond of pigs. Dogs look up to us. Cats look down on us. Pigs treat us as equals.
Winston Churchill 1874–1965: attributed, in M. Gilbert *Never Despair* (1988)

10 Animals, whom we have made our slaves, we do not like to consider our equal.
Charles Darwin 1809–82: Notebook B (1837–8)

11 Nature's great masterpiece, an elephant,
The only harmless great thing.
John Donne 1572–1631: 'The Progress of the Soul' (1601)

12 'Twould ring the bells of Heaven
The wildest peal for years,
If Parson lost his senses
And people came to theirs,
And he and they together
Knelt down with angry prayers
For tamed and shabby tigers

And dancing dogs and bears,
And wretched, blind, pit ponies,
And little hunted hares.
Ralph Hodgson 1871–1962: 'Bells of Heaven' (1917)

13 I hate a word like 'pets': it sounds so much
Like something with no living of its own.
Elizabeth Jennings 1926– : 'My Animals' (1966)

14 The cow is of the bovine ilk;
One end is moo, the other, milk.
Ogden Nash 1902–71: 'The Cow' (1931)

15 It ar'n't that I loves the fox less, but that I loves the 'ound
more.
R. S. Surtees 1805–64: *Handley Cross* (1843)

Apology

1 Very sorry can't come. Lie follows by post.
Lord Charles Beresford 1846–1919: telegraphed
message to the Prince of Wales, on being summoned to
dine at the eleventh hour

2 Never make a defence or apology before you be accused.
Charles I 1600–49: letter to Lord Wentworth,
3 September 1636

3 As I waited I thought that there's nothing like a confession
to make one look mad; and that of all confessions a written
one is the most detrimental all round. Never confess!
Never, never!
Joseph Conrad 1857–1924: *Chance* (1913)

4 Never complain and never explain.
Benjamin Disraeli 1804–81: in J. Morley *Life of
Gladstone* (1903)

5 The most important thing a man can learn—the
importance of three little words: 'I was wrong.' These
words will get you much further than 'I love you.'
Charlton Heston 1924– : in *Independent* 21 July 1999

6 Several excuses are always less convincing than one.
  Aldous Huxley 1894–1963: *Point Counter Point* (1928)

7 It is a good rule in life never to apologize. The right sort of
  people do not want apologies, and the wrong sort take a
  mean advantage of them.
  P. G. Wodehouse 1881–1975: *The Man Upstairs* (1914)

Architecture

1 A monstrous carbuncle on the face of a much-loved and
  elegant friend.
  Charles, Prince of Wales 1948– : speech on the
  proposed extension to the National Gallery, London,
  30 May 1984

2 Light (God's eldest daughter) is a principal beauty in
  building.
  Thomas Fuller 1608–61: *The Holy State and the Profane
  State* 'Of Building'

3 A house is a machine for living in.
  Le Corbusier 1887–1965: *Vers une architecture* (1923)

4 Less is more.
  Mies van der Rohe 1886–1969: P. Johnson *Mies van der
  Rohe* (1947)

5 God is in the details.
  Mies van der Rohe 1886–1969: in *New York Times* 19
  August 1969

6 You should be able to read a building. It should be what it
  does.
  Richard Rogers 1933– : lecture, London, March 1990

7 Architecture in general is frozen music.
  Friedrich von Schelling 1775–1854: *Philosophie der
  Kunst* (1809)

8 Form follows function.
  Louis Henri Sullivan 1856–1924: *The Tall Office Building
  Artistically Considered* (1896)

9 Well building hath three conditions. Commodity, firmness, and delight.
   Henry Wotton 1568–1639: *Elements of Architecture* (1624)

10 The physician can bury his mistakes, but the architect can only advise his client to plant vines—so they should go as far as possible from home to build their first buildings.
   Frank Lloyd Wright 1867–1959: in *New York Times* 4 October 1953

....

Argument

....

1 You cannot argue with someone who denies the first principles.
   Auctoritates Aristotelis: a compilation of medieval propositions

2 It is better to dwell in a corner of the housetop, than with a brawling woman in a wide house.
   Bible: Proverbs

3 Making noise is an effective means of opposition.
   Joseph Goebbels 1897–1945: Ernest K. Bramsted *Goebbels and National Socialist Propaganda 1925–45* (1965)

4 It takes in reality only one to make a quarrel. It is useless for the sheep to pass resolutions in favour of vegetarianism, while the wolf remains of a different opinion.
   Dean Inge 1860–1954: *Outspoken Essays: First Series* (1919)

5 Conflicts, like living organisms, had a natural lifespan. The trick was to know when to let them die.
   Ian McEwan 1948– : *Enduring Love* (1998)

6 The Catholic and the Communist are alike in assuming that an opponent cannot be both honest and intelligent.
   George Orwell 1903–50: in *Polemic* January 1946

7 Who can refute a sneer?
   William Paley 1743–1805: *Principles of Moral and Political Philosophy* (1785)

8 The argument of the broken window pane is the most valuable argument in modern politics.
  Emmeline Pankhurst 1858–1928: G. Dangerfield *The Strange Death of Liberal England* (1936)

9 I am not arguing with you—I am telling you.
  James McNeill Whistler 1834–1903: *The Gentle Art of Making Enemies* (1890)

The Army

See also **War**, **Wars**

1 Lions led by donkeys.
  Anonymous: associated with British soldiers during the First World War, and attributed to Max Hoffman (1869–1927) in Alan Clark *The Donkeys* (1961); this attribution has not been traced elsewhere, and the phrase is of much earlier origin

2 *C'est magnifique, mais ce n'est pas la guerre.*
It is magnificent, but it is not war.
  Pierre Bosquet 1810–61: on the charge of the Light Brigade at Balaclava, 25 October 1854

3 The sergeant is the army.
  Dwight D. Eisenhower 1890–1969: attributed

4 Old soldiers never die,
They simply fade away.
  J. Foley 1906–70: 'Old Soldiers Never Die' (1920 song); possibly a 'folk-song' from the First World War

5 O it's Tommy this, an' Tommy that, an' 'Tommy, go away';
But it's 'Thank you, Mister Atkins,' when the band begins to play.
  Rudyard Kipling 1865–1936: 'Tommy' (1892)

6 Remember that there is not one of you who does not carry in his cartridge-pouch the marshal's baton of the duke of Reggio; it is up to you to bring it forth.
  Louis XVIII 1755–1824: speech to Saint-Cyr cadets, 9 August 1819

7 When I was in the military, they gave me a medal for
killing two men and a discharge for loving one.
   Leonard Matlovich d. 1988: attributed

8 An army marches on its stomach.
   Napoleon I 1769–1821: attributed, but probably
   condensed from a long passage in E. A. de Las Cases
   Mémorial de Ste-Hélène (1823) 14 November 1816

9 What passing-bells for these who die as cattle?
Only the monstrous anger of the guns.
   Wilfred Owen 1893–1918: 'Anthem for Doomed Youth'
   (written 1917)

10 They dashed on towards that thin red line tipped with
steel.
   William Howard Russell 1820–1907: of the Russians
   charging the British, in *The British Expedition to the
   Crimea* (1877). Russell's original dispatch to *The Times*,
   14 November 1854, reads 'That thin red streak tipped
   with a line of steel'

11 If I were fierce, and bald, and short of breath,
I'd live with scarlet Majors at the Base,
And speed glum heroes up the line to death.
   Siegfried Sassoon 1886–1967: 'Base Details' (1918)

12   A soldier,
Full of strange oaths, and bearded like the pard,
Jealous in honour, sudden and quick in quarrel,
Seeking the bubble reputation
Even in the cannon's mouth.
   William Shakespeare 1564–1616: *As You Like It* (1599)

13 When the military man approaches, the world locks up its
spoons and packs off its womankind.
   George Bernard Shaw 1856–1950: *Man and Superman*
   (1903)

14 The British soldier can stand up to anything except the
British War Office.
   George Bernard Shaw 1856–1950: *The Devil's Disciple*
   (1901)

15 Theirs not to make reply,
Theirs not to reason why,

Theirs but to do and die:
Into the valley of Death
Rode the six hundred.
Alfred, Lord Tennyson 1809–92: 'The Charge of the
Light Brigade' (1854)

16 As Lord Chesterfield said of the generals of his day, 'I only
hope that when the enemy reads the list of their names, he
trembles as I do.'
Duke of Wellington 1769–1852: letter, 29 August 1810
(usually quoted 'I don't know what effect these men will
have upon the enemy, but, by God, they frighten me')

....

Art
....

See also **Painting and Drawing**

1 Art is born of humiliation.
W. H. Auden 1907–73: in Stephen Spender *World Within
World* (1951)

2 Art is meant to disturb, science reassures.
Georges Braque 1882–1963: *Le Jour et la nuit: Cahiers
1917–52*

3 The history of art is the history of revivals.
Samuel Butler 1835–1902: *Notebooks* (1912)

4 Art for art's sake, with no purpose, for any purpose
perverts art. But art achieves a purpose which is not its
own.
Benjamin Constant 1767–1834: *Journal intime*
11 February 1804

5 Art is vice. You don't marry it legitimately, you rape it.
Edgar Degas 1834–1917: in P. Lafond *Degas* (1918)

6 I always said God was against art and I still believe it.
Edward Elgar 1857–1934: letter to A. J. Jaeger, 9 October
1900

7 The artist must be in his work as God is in creation,
invisible and all-powerful; one must sense him everywhere
but never see him.
   Gustave Flaubert 1821–80: letter to Mlle Leroyer de
   Chantepie, 18 March 1857

8 In art the best is good enough.
   Johann Wolfgang von Goethe 1749–1832: *Italienische
   Reise* (1816–17) 3 March 1787

9 The proletarian state must bring up thousands of excellent
'mechanics of culture', 'engineers of the soul'.
   Maxim Gorky 1868–1936: speech at the Writers'
   Congress 1934

10 Art is not a mirror but a hammer.
   John Grierson 1888–1972: H. Forsyth Hardy (ed.)
   Grierson on Documentary (1946, 1966)

11 Life is short, the art long.
   Hippocrates c.460–357 BC: *Aphorisms*, often quoted as
   '*Ars longa, vita brevis*', after Seneca *De Brevitate Vitae*

12 It's amazing what you can do with an E in A-level art,
twisted imagination and a chainsaw.
   Damien Hirst 1965– : after winning the 1995 Turner
   Prize; in *Observer* 3 December 1995

13 We work in the dark—we do what we can—we give what
we have. Our doubt is our passion and our passion is our
task. The rest is the madness of art.
   Henry James 1843–1916: 'The Middle Years' (1893)

14 The artist, like the God of the creation, remains within or
behind or beyond or above his handiwork, invisible,
refined out of existence, indifferent, paring his fingernails.
   James Joyce 1882–1941: *A Portrait of the Artist as a
   Young Man* (1916)

15 It's clever, but is it Art?
   Rudyard Kipling 1865–1936: 'The Conundrum of the
   Workshops' (1892)

16 God help the Minister that meddles with art!
Lord Melbourne 1779–1848: in Lord David Cecil *Lord M*
(1954)

17 The marble not yet carved can hold the form
Of every thought the greatest artist has.
Michelangelo 1475–1564: Sonnet 15

18 I don't know what art is, but I do know what it isn't.
Brian Sewell: in *Independent* 26 April 1999

19 The true artist will let his wife starve, his children go
barefoot, his mother drudge for his living at seventy,
sooner than work at anything but his art.
George Bernard Shaw 1856–1950: *Man and Superman*
(1903)

Australia

1 True patriots we; for be it understood,
We left our country for our country's good.
Henry Carter d. 1806: prologue, written for, but not
recited at, the opening of the Playhouse, Sydney, New
South Wales, 16 January 1796, when the actors were
principally convicts; previously attributed to George
Barrington (b. 1755)

2 Australia is a huge rest home, where no unwelcome news
is ever wafted on to the pages of the worst newspapers in
the world.
Germaine Greer 1939– : in *Observer* 1 August 1982

3 And her five cities, like teeming sores,
Each drains her: a vast parasite robber-state
Where second-hand Europeans pullulate
Timidly on the edge of alien shores.
A. D. Hope 1907– : 'Australia' (1939)

4 Australia is a lucky country run mainly by second-rate
people who share its luck.
Donald Richmond Horne 1921– : *The Lucky Country:
Australia in the Sixties* (1964)

5 Australia has a marvellous sky and air and blue clarity,
and a hoary sort of land beneath it, like a Sleeping
Princess on whom the dust of ages has settled.
   D. H. Lawrence 1885–1930: letter to Jan Juta, 20 May
   1922

6 What Great Britain calls the Far East is to us the near
north.
   Robert Gordon Menzies 1894–1978: in *Sydney Morning
   Herald* 27 April 1939

7 The crimson thread of kinship runs through us all.
   Henry Parkes 1815–95: on Australian federation; speech,
   Melbourne, 6 February 1890

8 Australia is the flattest, driest, ugliest place on earth. Only
those who can be possessed by her can know what secret
beauty she holds.
   Eric Paul Willmot 1936– : *Australia The Last
   Experiment* (1987)

Beauty

1 There is no excellent beauty that hath not some
strangeness in the proportion.
   Francis Bacon 1561–1626: *Essays* (1625) 'Of Beauty'

2 Consider the lilies of the field, how they grow; they toil
not, neither do they spin:
And yet I say unto you, That even Solomon in all his glory
was not arrayed like one of these.
   Bible: St Matthew

3 If you get simple beauty and naught else,
You get about the best thing God invents.
   Robert Browning 1812–89: 'Fra Lippo Lippi' (1855)

4 She walks in beauty, like the night
Of cloudless climes and starry skies;
And all that's best of dark and bright
Meet in her aspect and her eyes.
   Lord Byron 1788–1824: 'She Walks in Beauty' (1815)

5 And she was fayr as is the rose in May.
  Geoffrey Chaucer c.1343–1400: *The Legend of Good Women* 'Cleopatra'

6 When a woman isn't beautiful, people always say, 'You have lovely eyes, you have lovely hair.'
  Anton Chekhov 1860–1904: *Uncle Vanya* (1897)

7 *I never saw an ugly thing in my life*: for let the form of an object be what it may,—light, shade, and perspective will always make it beautiful.
  John Constable 1776–1837: C. R. Leslie *Memoirs of the Life of John Constable* (1843)

8 Beauty is mysterious as well as terrible. God and devil are fighting there, and the battlefield is the heart of man.
  Fedor Dostoevsky 1821–81: *The Brothers Karamazov* (1879–80)

9 He was afflicted by the thought that where Beauty was, nothing ever ran quite straight, which, no doubt, was why so many people looked on it as immoral.
  John Galsworthy 1867–1933: *In Chancery* (1920)

10 Is it too much to ask that women be spared the daily struggle for superhuman beauty in order to offer it to the caresses of a subhumanly ugly mate?
  Germaine Greer 1939– : *The Female Eunuch* (1970)

11 All things counter, original, spare, strange;
  Whatever is fickle, freckled (who knows how?)
  With swift, slow; sweet, sour; adazzle, dim;
  He fathers-forth whose beauty is past change:
  Praise him.
  Gerard Manley Hopkins 1844–89: 'Pied Beauty' (written 1877)

12 Beauty is no quality in things themselves. It exists merely in the mind which contemplates them.
  David Hume 1711–76: 'Of the Standard of Taste' (1757)

13 'Beauty is truth, truth beauty,'—that is all
  Ye know on earth, and all ye need to know.
  John Keats 1795–1821: 'Ode on a Grecian Urn' (1820)

14 A thing of beauty is a joy for ever:
  Its loveliness increases; it will never

Pass into nothingness.
    John Keats 1795–1821: *Endymion* (1818)

15 The Lord prefers common-looking people. That is why he makes so many of them.
    Abraham Lincoln 1809–65: attributed

16 At some point in life the world's beauty becomes enough. You don't need to photograph, paint or even remember it. It is enough.
    Toni Morrison 1931– : *Tar Baby* (1981)

17 Beauty is handed out as undemocratically as inherited peerages, and beautiful people have done nothing to deserve their astonishing reward.
    John Mortimer 1923– : in *Observer* 21 March 1999

18 A beautiful face is a mute recommendation.
    Publilius Syrus 1st century BC: *Sententiae*

19 Remember that the most beautiful things in the world are the most useless; peacocks and lilies for instance.
    John Ruskin 1819–1900: *Stones of Venice* vol. 1 (1851)

20 I always say beauty is only sin deep.
    Saki (H. H. Munro) 1870–1916: *Reginald* (1904)

21 Shall I compare thee to a summer's day?
Thou art more lovely and more temperate:
Rough winds do shake the darling buds of May,
And summer's lease hath all too short a date.
    William Shakespeare 1564–1616: sonnet 18 (1609)

22 Beauty is all very well at first sight; but who ever looks at it when it has been in the house three days?
    George Bernard Shaw 1856–1950: *Man and Superman* (1903)

23 The beauty myth moves for men as a mirage; its power lies in its ever-receding nature. When the gap is closed, the lover embraces only his own disillusion.
    Naomi Wolf 1962– : *The Beauty Myth* (1990)

Beginnings and Endings

1 It ain't over till it's over.
> **Yogi Berra** 1925– : comment on National League
> pennant race, 1973, quoted in many versions

2 In the beginning God created the heaven and the earth.
And the earth was without form, and void; and darkness
was upon the face of the deep.
> **Bible**: Genesis

3 'Begin at the beginning,' the King said, gravely, 'and go on
till you come to the end: then stop.'
> **Lewis Carroll** 1832–98: *Alice's Adventures in Wonderland*
> (1865)

4 Now this is not the end. It is not even the beginning of the
end. But it is, perhaps, the end of the beginning.
> **Winston Churchill** 1874–1965: speech at the Mansion
> House, London, 10 November 1942

5 The party's over, it's time to call it a day.
> **Betty Comden** 1919– and **Adolph Green** 1915– : 'The
> Party's Over' (1956 song)

6 The opera ain't over 'til the fat lady sings.
> **Dan Cook**: in *Washington Post* 3 June 1978

7 This is the way the world ends
Not with a bang but a whimper.
> **T. S. Eliot** 1888–1965: 'The Hollow Men' (1925)

8 What we call the beginning is often the end
And to make an end is to make a beginning.
The end is where we start from.
> **T. S. Eliot** 1888–1965: *Four Quartets* 'Little Gidding'
> (1942)

9 All this will not be finished in the first 100 days. Nor will it
be finished in the first 1,000 days, nor in the life of this
Administration, nor even perhaps in our lifetime on this
planet. But let us begin.
> **John F. Kennedy** 1917–63: inaugural address,
> 20 January 1961

10 Are you sitting comfortably? Then I'll begin.
   Julia Lang 1921– : *Listen with Mother* (BBC radio
   programme for children, 1950–82)

11 A tower of nine storeys begins with a heap of earth.
   The journey of a thousand *li* starts from where one stands.
   Lao Tzu *c*.604–*c*.531 BC: *Tao-te Ching*

12 In my end is my beginning.
   Mary, Queen of Scots 1542–87: motto

13 Ring out the old, ring in the new,
   Ring, happy bells, across the snow:
   The year is going, let him go;
   Ring out the false, ring in the true.
   Alfred, Lord Tennyson 1809–92: *In Memoriam A. H. H.*
   (1850)

14 They think it's all over—it is now.
   Kenneth Wolstenholme: television commentary in
   closing moments of the World Cup Final, 30 July 1966

Behaviour

See also **Manners**

1 When I go to Rome, I fast on Saturday, but here [Milan] I
   do not. Do you also follow the custom of whatever church
   you attend, if you do not want to give or receive scandal.
   St Ambrose *c*.339–97: letter to Januarius, tr. Sr W.
   Parsons; usually quoted 'When in Rome, do as the
   Romans do'

2 Private faces in public places
   Are wiser and nicer
   Than public faces in private places.
   W. H. Auden 1907–73: *Orators* (1932)

3 In necessary things, unity; in doubtful things, liberty; in
   all things, charity.
   Richard Baxter 1615–91: motto

4 In short, he was a perfect cavaliero,
And to his very valet seemed a hero.
   Lord Byron 1788–1824: *Beppo* (1818)

5 Caesar's wife must be above suspicion.
   Julius Caesar 100–44 BC: oral tradition, based on
   Plutarch *Parallel Lives*

6 He was a verray, parfit gentil knyght.
   Geoffrey Chaucer c.1343–1400: *The Canterbury Tales*
   'General Prologue'

7 *O tempora, O mores!*
   Oh, the times! Oh, the manners!
   Cicero 106–43 BC: *In Catilinam*

8 I believe we should all behave quite differently if we lived
in a warm, sunny climate all the time.
   Noël Coward 1899–1973: *Brief Encounter* (1945)

9 The courtiers who surround him [Louis XVIII] have
forgotten nothing and learnt nothing.
   General Dumouriez 1739–1823: *Examen impartial d'un
   Écrit . . . de Louis XVIII* (1795)

10 Imitation lies at the root of most human actions. A
respectable person is one who conforms to custom. People
are called good when they do as others do.
   Anatole France 1844–1924: *Crainquebille* (1923)

11 I get too hungry for dinner at eight.
I like the theatre, but never come late.
I never bother with people I hate.
That's why the lady is a tramp.
   Lorenz Hart 1895–1943: 'The Lady is a Tramp' (1937
   song)

12 They [the *Letters* of Lord Chesterfield] teach the morals of
a whore, and the manners of a dancing master.
   Samuel Johnson 1709–84: James Boswell *Life of
   Johnson* (1791) 1754

13 *Tout comprendre rend très indulgent.*
   To be totally understanding makes one very indulgent.
   Mme de Staël 1766–1817: *Corinne* (1807)

··

Belief and Unbelief

··

1 The Sea of Faith
Was once, too, at the full, and round earth's shore
Lay like the folds of a bright girdle furled.
But now I only hear
Its melancholy, long, withdrawing roar.
   Matthew Arnold 1822–88: 'Dover Beach' (1867)

2 A little philosophy inclineth man's mind to atheism, but
depth in philosophy bringeth men's minds about to
religion.
   Francis Bacon 1561–1626: *Essays* (1625) 'Of Atheism'

3 Every time a child says 'I don't believe in fairies' there is a
little fairy somewhere that falls down dead.
   J. M. Barrie 1860–1937: *Peter Pan* (1928)

4 A faith is something you die for; a doctrine is something
you kill for: there is all the difference in the world.
   Tony Benn 1925– : in *Observer* 16 April 1989

5 Lord, I believe; help thou mine unbelief.
   Bible: St Mark

6 Of course not, but I am told it works even if you don't
believe in it.
   Niels Bohr 1885–1962: when asked whether he really
   believed a horseshoe hanging over his door would bring
   him luck, *c.*1930; A. Pais *Inward Bound* (1986)

7 Why, sometimes I've believed as many as six impossible
things before breakfast.
   Lewis Carroll 1832–98: *Through the Looking-Glass* (1872)

8 I do not consider it an insult, but rather a compliment to
be called an agnostic. I do not pretend to know where
many ignorant men are sure—that is all that agnosticism
means.
   Clarence Darrow 1857–1938: speech at trial of John
   Thomas Scopes, 15 July 1925

9 The dust of exploded beliefs may make a fine sunset.
   Geoffrey Madan 1895–1947: *Livre sans nom: Twelve
   Reflections* (1934)

10 *Que sais-je?*

What do I know?
   Montaigne 1533–92: *Essais* (1580) on the position of the
   sceptic

11 *We can believe what we choose.* We are answerable for what
we choose to believe.
   Cardinal Newman 1801–90: letter to Mrs William
   Froude, 27 June 1848

12 It is necessary to the happiness of man that he be mentally
faithful to himself. Infidelity does not consist in believing,
or in disbelieving, it consists in professing to believe what
one does not believe.
   Thomas Paine 1737–1809: *The Age of Reason* pt. 1 (1794)

13 Man is a credulous animal, and must believe *something*; in
the absence of good grounds for belief, he will be satisfied
with bad ones.
   Bertrand Russell 1872–1970: *Unpopular Essays* (1950)

14 There lives more faith in honest doubt,
Believe me, than in half the creeds.
   Alfred, Lord Tennyson 1809–92: *In Memoriam A. H. H.*
   (1850)

15 *Certum est quia impossibile est.*

It is certain because it is impossible.
   Tertullian AD *c.*160–*c.*225: *De Carne Christi*, often quoted
   '*Credo quia impossibile* [I believe because it is
   impossible]'

....

The Bible
....

1 There's a great text in Galatians,
Once you trip on it, entails
Twenty-nine distinct damnations,
One sure, if another fails.
   Robert Browning 1812–89: 'Soliloquy of the Spanish
   Cloister' (1842)

2 Here is wisdom; this is the royal Law; these are the lively
　Oracles of God.
　　Coronation Service 1689: The Presenting of the Holy
　　Bible

3 We have used the Bible as if it was a constable's
　handbook—an opium-dose for keeping beasts of burden
　patient while they are being overloaded.
　　Charles Kingsley 1819–75: *Letters to the Chartists*

4 The English Bible, a book which, if everything else in our
　language should perish, would alone suffice to show the
　whole extent of its beauty and power.
　　Lord Macaulay 1800–59: 'John Dryden' (1828)

5 I know of no book which has been a source of brutality
　and sadistic conduct, both public and private, that can
　compare with the Bible.
　　Reginald Paget 1908–90: in *Observer* 28 June 1964

6 The devil can cite Scripture for his purpose.
　　William Shakespeare 1564–1616: *The Merchant of
　　Venice* (1596–8)

7 LORD ILLINGWORTH: The Book of Life begins with a man
　and a woman in a garden.
　MRS ALLONBY: It ends with Revelations.
　　Oscar Wilde 1854–1900: *A Woman of No Importance*
　　(1893)

Biography

1 The Art of Biography
　Is different from Geography.
　Geography is about Maps,
　But Biography is about Chaps.
　　Edmund Clerihew Bentley 1875–1956: *Biography for
　　Beginners* (1905)

2 A well-written Life is almost as rare as a well-spent one.
　　Thomas Carlyle 1795–1881: *Critical and Miscellaneous
　　Essays* (1838)

3 An autobiography is an obituary in serial form with the last instalment missing.

    Quentin Crisp 1908–99: *The Naked Civil Servant* (1968)

4 It's an excellent life of somebody else. But I've really lived inside myself, and she can't get in there.

    Robertson Davies 1913–95: on a biography of himself; interview in *The Times* 4 April 1995

5 Read no history: nothing but biography, for that is life without theory.

    Benjamin Disraeli 1804–81: *Contarini Fleming* (1832)

6 But that perhaps is the point of any memoir—to walk with the dead and yet see them with our eyes, from our vantage point.

    Margaret Forster 1938– : *Hidden Lives: A Family Memoir* (1995)

7 Nobody can write the life of a man, but those who have eat and drunk and lived in social intercourse with him.

    Samuel Johnson 1709–84: James Boswell *Life of Johnson* (1791) 31 March 1772

8 Lives of great men all remind us
We can make our lives sublime,
And, departing, leave behind us
Footprints on the sands of time.

    Henry Wadsworth Longfellow 1807–82: 'A Psalm of Life' (1838)

9 To write one's memoirs is to speak ill of everybody except oneself.

    Marshal Pétain 1856–1951: in *Observer* 26 May 1946

10 Discretion is not the better part of biography.

    Lytton Strachey 1880–1932: M. Holroyd *Lytton Strachey* vol. 1 (1967)

11 Then there is my noble and biographical friend who has added a new terror to death.

    Charles Wetherell 1770–1846: on Lord Campbell's *Lives of the Lord Chancellors* being written without the consent of heirs or executors; also attributed to Lord Lyndhurst (1772–1863)

12 Every great man nowadays has his disciples, and it is
always Judas who writes the biography.
   Oscar Wilde 1854–1900: *Intentions* (1891) 'The Critic as
   Artist'

Birds

1 *Vox et praeterea nihil.*

A voice and nothing more.
   Anonymous: describing a nightingale. See Plutarch
   Moralia

2 That's the wise thrush; he sings each song twice over,
Lest you should think he never could recapture
The first fine careless rapture!
   Robert Browning 1812–89: 'Home-Thoughts, from
   Abroad' (1845)

3 The bisy larke, messager of day.
   Geoffrey Chaucer *c.*1343–1400: *The Canterbury Tales*
   'The Knight's Tale'

4 It was the Rainbow gave thee birth,
And left thee all her lovely hues.
   W. H. Davies 1871–1940: 'Kingfisher' (1910)

5 I caught this morning morning's minion, kingdom of
daylight's dauphin, dapple-dawn-drawn Falcon.
   Gerard Manley Hopkins 1844–89: 'The Windhover'
   (written 1877)

6 It took the whole of Creation
To produce my foot, my each feather:
Now I hold Creation in my foot.
   Ted Hughes 1930–98: 'Hawk Roosting' (1960)

7 Oh, a wondrous bird is the pelican!
His beak holds more than his belican.
He takes in his beak
Food enough for a week.
But I'll be darned if I know how the helican.
   Dixon Lanier Merritt 1879–1972: in *Nashville Banner*
   22 April 1913

8 Hail to thee, blithe Spirit!
Bird thou never wert,
That from Heaven, or near it,
Pourest thy full heart
In profuse strains of unpremeditated art.
   Percy Bysshe Shelley 1792–1822: 'To a Skylark' (1819)

9 Blackbirds are the cellos of the deep farms.
   Anne Stevenson 1933– : 'Green Mountain, Black
   Mountain' (1982)

10 He clasps the crag with crookèd hands;
Close to the sun in lonely lands,
Ringed with the azure world, he stands.
   Alfred, Lord Tennyson 1809–92: 'The Eagle' (1851)

11 Alone and warming his five wits,
The white owl in the belfry sits.
   Alfred, Lord Tennyson 1809–92: 'Song—The Owl' (1830)

12 O blithe new-comer! I have heard,
I hear thee and rejoice:
O Cuckoo! Shall I call thee bird,
Or but a wandering voice?
   William Wordsworth 1770–1850: 'To the Cuckoo' (1807)

Birth

1 In sorrow thou shalt bring forth children.
   Bible: Genesis

2 So for the mother's sake the child was dear,
And dearer was the mother for the child.
   Samuel Taylor Coleridge 1772–1834: 'Sonnet to a
   Friend Who Asked How I Felt When the Nurse First
   Presented My Infant to Me' (1797)

3 No phallic hero, no matter what he does to himself or to
another to prove his courage, ever matches the solitary,
existential courage of the woman who gives birth.
   Andrea Dworkin 1946– : *Our Blood* (1976)

4 The queen of Scots is this day leichter of a fair son, and I am but a barren stock.
Elizabeth I 1533–1603: to her ladies, 1566

5 I am not yet born; O fill me
With strength against those who would freeze my humanity.
Louis MacNeice 1907–63: 'Prayer Before Birth' (1944)

6 Death and taxes and childbirth! There's never any convenient time for any of them.
Margaret Mitchell 1900–49: *Gone with the Wind* (1936)

7 Men should be bewailed at their birth, and not at their death.
Montesquieu 1689–1755: *Lettres Persones* (1721), tr. J. Ozell, 1722

8 Good work, Mary. We all knew you had it in you.
Dorothy Parker 1893–1967: telegram to Mrs Sherwood on the arrival of her baby; A. Woollcott *While Rome Burns* (1934)

9 Love set you going like a fat gold watch.
The midwife slapped your footsoles, and your bald cry
Took its place among the elements.
Sylvia Plath 1932–63: 'Morning Song' (1965)

10 What you say of the pride of giving life to an immortal soul is very fine, dear, but I own I can not enter into that; I think much more of our being like a cow or a dog at such moments; when our poor nature becomes so very animal and unecstatic.
Queen Victoria 1819–1901: letter to the Princess Royal, 15 June 1858

11 Our birth is but a sleep and a forgetting . . .
Not in entire forgetfulness,
And not in utter nakedness,
But trailing clouds of glory do we come.
William Wordsworth 1770–1850: 'Ode. Intimations of Immortality' (1807)

The Body

1 Your cameraman might enjoy himself because my face
  looks like a wedding-cake left out in the rain.
  W. H. Auden 1907–73: H. Carpenter *W. H. Auden* (1963)

2 Entrails don't care for travel,
  Entrails don't care for stress:
  Entrails are better kept folded inside you
  For outside, they make a mess.
  Connie Bensley 1929– : 'Entrails' (1987)

3 I will give thanks unto thee, for I am fearfully and
  wonderfully made.
  Bible: Psalm 139

4 A woman watches her body uneasily, as though it were an
  unreliable ally in the battle for love.
  Leonard Cohen 1934– : *The Favourite Game* (1963)

5 i like my body when it is with your
  body. It is so quite new a thing.
  Muscles better and nerves more.
  e. e. cummings 1894–1962: 'Sonnets–Actualities' no. 8
  (1925)

6 Anatomy is destiny.
  Sigmund Freud 1856–1939: *Collected Writings* (1924)

7 Nudity is a deep worry if you have a body like a bin bag
  full of yoghurt, which I have.
  Stephen Fry 1957– : in *Observer* 12 March 2000

8 I am the family face;
  Flesh perishes, I live on.
  Thomas Hardy 1840–1928: 'Heredity' (1917)

9 Fain would I kiss my Julia's dainty leg,
  Which is as white and hairless as an egg.
  Robert Herrick 1591–1674: 'On Julia's Legs' (1648)

10 At 50, everyone has the face he deserves.
  George Orwell 1903–50: notebook, 17 April 1949

11 I'm fat, but I'm thin inside. Has it ever struck you that
there's a thin man inside every fat man, just as they say
there's a statue inside every block of stone?
   George Orwell 1903–50: *Coming up For Air* (1939)

12 Had Cleopatra's nose been shorter, the whole face of the
world would have changed.
   Blaise Pascal 1623–62: *Pensées* (1670)

13   There's no art
To find the mind's construction in the face.
   William Shakespeare 1564–1616: *Macbeth* (1606)

14 Our body is a machine for living. It is organized for that, it
is its nature. Let life go on in it unhindered and let it
defend itself.
   Leo Tolstoy 1828–1910: *War and Peace* (1865–9), tr. A. and
L. Maude

15 You can never be too rich or too thin.
   Duchess of Windsor 1896–1986: attributed

Books

See also **Libraries**, **Reading**, **Writing**

1 Some books are undeservedly forgotten; none are
undeservedly remembered.
   W. H. Auden 1907–73: *The Dyer's Hand* (1963) 'Reading'

2 Some books are to be tasted, others to be swallowed, and
some few to be chewed and digested.
   Francis Bacon 1561–1626: *Essays* (1625) 'Of Studies'

3 Books say: she did this because. Life says: she did this.
Books are where things are explained to you; life is where
things aren't.
   Julian Barnes 1946– : *Flaubert's Parrot* (1984)

4 Of making many books there is no end; and much study is
a weariness of the flesh.
   Bible: Ecclesiastes

5 What literature can and should do is change the people who teach the people who don't read the books.
A. S. Byatt 1936– : in *Newsweek* 5 June 1995

6 A great book is like great evil.
Callimachus *c*.305–*c*.240 BC: proverbially 'Great book, great evil'

7 Now Barabbas was a publisher.
Thomas Campbell 1777–1844: attributed, in Samuel Smiles *A Publisher and his Friends* (1891); also attributed, wrongly, to Byron

8 'What is the use of a book', thought Alice, 'without pictures or conversations?'
Lewis Carroll 1832–98: *Alice's Adventures in Wonderland* (1865)

9 The greatest masterpiece in literature is only a dictionary out of order.
Jean Cocteau 1889–1963: attributed

10 Dictionaries are like watches, the worst is better than none, and the best cannot be expected to go quite true.
Samuel Johnson 1709–84: letter to Francesco Sastres, 21 August 1784

11 Far too many relied on the classic formula of a beginning, a muddle, and an end.
Philip Larkin 1922–85: of the books entered for the 1977 Booker Prize; *New Fiction* January 1978

12 A good book is the precious life-blood of a master spirit.
John Milton 1608–74: *Areopagitica* (1644)

13 The principle of procrastinated rape is said to be the ruling one in all the great best-sellers.
V. S. Pritchett 1900–97: *The Living Novel* (1946)

14 A best-seller is the gilded tomb of a mediocre talent.
Logan Pearsall Smith 1865–1946: *Afterthoughts* (1931) 'Art and Letters'

15 No furniture so charming as books.
   Sydney Smith 1771–1845: Lady Holland *Memoir* (1855)

16 A good book is the best of friends, the same to-day and for ever.
   Martin Tupper 1810–89: *Proverbial Philosophy* Series I (1838) 'Of Reading'

17 '*Classic.*' A book which people praise and don't read.
   Mark Twain 1835–1910: *Following the Equator* (1897)

18 Publish and be damned.
   Duke of Wellington 1769–1852: replying to Harriette Wilson's blackmail threat, *c.*1825; attributed

19 There is no such thing as a moral or an immoral book. Books are well written, or badly written.
   Oscar Wilde 1854–1900: *The Picture of Dorian Gray* (1891)

20 This is an important book, the critic assumes, because it deals with war. This is an insignificant book because it deals with the feelings of women in a drawing-room.
   Virginia Woolf 1882–1941: *A Room of One's Own* (1929)

....

Bores and Boredom
....

1 Nothing happens, nobody comes, nobody goes, it's awful!
   Samuel Beckett 1906–89: *Waiting for Godot* (1955)

2 Life, friends, is boring. We must not say so . . .
   And moreover my mother taught me as a boy
   (repeatedly) 'Ever to confess you're bored
   means you have no
   Inner Resources.'
   John Berryman 1914–72: *77 Dream Songs* (1964)

3 Everyone is a bore to someone. That is unimportant. The thing to avoid is being a bore to oneself.
   Gerald Brenan 1894–1987: *Thoughts in a Dry Season* (1978)

4 What's wrong with being a boring kind of guy?
   George Bush 1924– : during the campaign for the
   Republican nomination, in *Daily Telegraph* 28 April 1988

5 Society is now one polished horde,
   Formed of two mighty tribes, the *Bores* and *Bored*.
   Lord Byron 1788–1824: *Don Juan* (1819–24)

6 Millions long for immortality who don't know what to do
   with themselves on a rainy Sunday afternoon.
   Susan Ertz 1894–1985: *Anger in the Sky* (1943)

7 He is not only dull in himself, but the cause of dullness in
   others.
   Samuel Foote 1720–77: of a dull law lord, in James
   Boswell *Life of Samuel Johnson* (1791)

8 Nothing, like something, happens anywhere.
   Philip Larkin 1922–85: 'I Remember, I Remember' (1955)

9 Boredom is . . . a vital problem for the moralist, since half
   the sins of mankind are caused by the fear of it.
   Bertrand Russell 1872–1970: *The Conquest of Happiness*
   (1930)

10 A healthy male adult bore consumes *each year* one and a
   half times his own weight in other people's patience.
   John Updike 1932– : *Assorted Prose* (1965)

11 The secret of being a bore . . . is to tell everything.
   Voltaire 1694–1778: *Discours en vers sur l'homme* (1737)

··

Britain
··

See also **England**

1 Great Britain has lost an empire and has not yet found a
   role.
   Dean Acheson 1893–1971: speech at the Military
   Academy, West Point, 5 December 1962

2 The land of embarrassment and breakfast.
   Julian Barnes 1946– : *Flaubert's Parrot* (1984)

3 The American dream is that any citizen can rise to the highest office in the land. The British dream is that the Queen drops in for tea.
   Michael Bywater: in *Independent* 20 October 1997

4 The British nation is unique in this respect. They are the only people who like to be told how bad things are, who like to be told the worst.
   Winston Churchill 1874–1965: speech, House of Commons, 10 June 1941

5 Britain will be honoured by historians more for the way she disposed of an empire than for the way in which she acquired it.
   Lord Harlech 1918–85: in *New York Times* 28 October 1962

6 Britain is no longer totally a white place where people ride horses, wear long frocks and drink tea. The national dish is no longer fish and chips, it's curry.
   Marianne Jean-Baptiste: in *Observer* 18 May 1997

7 What is our task? To make Britain a fit country for heroes to live in.
   David Lloyd George 1863–1945: speech at Wolverhampton, 23 November 1918

8 Fifty years on from now, Britain will still be the country of long shadows on county [cricket] grounds, warm beer, invincible green suburbs, dog lovers, and—as George Orwell said—old maids bicycling to Holy Communion through the morning mist.
   John Major 1943– : speech to the Conservative Group for Europe, 22 April 1993

9 What you have within the UK is three small nations who've been under the cosh of the English.
   Jack Straw 1946– : in *Sunday Times* 6 January 2000

10 Rule, Britannia, rule the waves;
   Britons never will be slaves.
   James Thomson 1700–48: *Alfred: a Masque* (1740)

11 Other nations use 'force'; we Britons alone use 'Might'.
   Evelyn Waugh 1903–66: *Scoop* (1938)

Broadcasting

1 Television . . . thrives on unreason, and unreason thrives on television . . . [It] strikes at the emotions rather than the intellect.
   Robin Day 1923–2000: *Grand Inquisitor* (1989)

2 Television has brought back murder into the home—where it belongs.
   Alfred Hitchcock 1899–1980: in *Observer* 19 December 1965

3 Television is simultaneously blamed, often by the same people, for worsening the world and for being powerless to change it.
   Clive James 1939– : *Glued to the Box* (1981)

4 Television brought the brutality of war into the comfort of the living room. Vietnam was lost in the living rooms of America—not the battlefields of Vietnam.
   Marshall McLuhan 1911–80: in *Montreal Gazette* 16 May 1975

5 When the politicians complain that TV turns their proceedings into a circus, it should be made plain that the circus was already there, and that TV has merely demonstrated that not all the performers are well trained.
   Ed Murrow 1908–65: attributed, 1959

6 Television is actually closer to reality than anything in books. The madness of TV is the madness of human life.
   Camille Paglia 1947– : in *Harper's Magazine* March 1991

7 Television has made dictatorship impossible, but democracy unbearable.
   Shimon Peres 1923– : at a Davos meeting, in *Financial Times* 31 January 1995

8 Nation shall speak peace unto nation.
   Montague John Rendall 1862–1950: motto of the BBC (1927)

9 A terminal blight has hit the TV industry nipping fun in
the bud and stunting our growth. This blight is
management—the dreaded Four M's: male, middle class,
middle-aged and mediocre.
   Janet Street-Porter 1946– : MacTaggart Lecture,
   Edinburgh Television Festival, 25 August 1995

10 Like having your own licence to print money.
   Roy Thomson 1894–1976: on the profitability of
   commercial television in Britain; in R. Braddon *Roy
   Thomson* (1965)

11 I hate television. I hate it as much as peanuts. But I can't
stop eating peanuts.
   Orson Welles 1915–85: in *New York Herald Tribune*
   12 October 1956

12 Television contracts the imagination and radio expands it.
   Terry Wogan 1938– : in *Observer* 30 December 1984

Bureaucracy

See also **Management**

1 A memorandum is written not to inform the reader but to
protect the writer.
   Dean Acheson 1893–1971: in *Wall Street Journal*
   8 September 1977

2 It is an inevitable defect, that bureaucrats will care more
for routine than for results.
   Walter Bagehot 1826–77: *The English Constitution* (1867)

3 Guidelines for bureaucrats: (1) When in charge, ponder. (2)
When in trouble, delegate. (3) When in doubt, mumble.
   James H. Boren 1925– : in *New York Times* 8 November
   1970

4 Give a civil servant a good case and he'll wreck it with
clichés, bad punctuation, double negatives and convoluted
apology.
   Alan Clark 1928–99: diary 22 July 1983

5 The Civil Service is profoundly deferential—'Yes, Minister!
No, Minister! If you wish it, Minister!'
   Richard Crossman 1907–74: diary, 22 October 1964

6 Whatever was required to be done, the Circumlocution
Office was beforehand with all the public departments in
the art of perceiving—HOW NOT TO DO IT.
   Charles Dickens 1812–70: *Little Dorrit* (1857)

7 The truth in these matters may be stated as a scientific
law: 'The persistence of public officials varies inversely
with the importance of the matter on which they are
persisting.'
   Bernard Levin 1928– : *In These Times* (1986)

8 The man who is denied the opportunity of taking decisions
of importance begins to regard as important the decisions
he is allowed to take.
   C. Northcote Parkinson 1909–93: *Parkinson's Law*
   (1958)

9 Back in the East you can't do much without the right
papers, but *with* the right papers you can do *anything*.
They *believe* in papers. Papers are power.
   Tom Stoppard 1937– : *Neutral Ground* (1983)

··

Business and Commerce
··

1 There is nothing more requisite in business than dispatch.
   Joseph Addison 1672–1719: *The Drummer* (1716)

2 A Company for carrying on an undertaking of Great
Advantage, but no one to know what it is.
   Anonymous: The South Sea Company Prospectus (1711)

3 A merchant shall hardly keep himself from doing wrong.
   Bible (Apocrypha): Ecclesiasticus

4 They [corporations] cannot commit treason, nor be
outlawed, nor excommunicate, for they have no souls.
   Edward Coke 1552–1634: *Reports of Sir Edward Coke*
   (1658) 'The case of Sutton's Hospital'

5 Here's the rule for bargains: 'Do other men, for they would
do you.' That's the true business precept.
  Charles Dickens 1812–70: *Martin Chuzzlewit* (1844)

6 If management are using a word you don't understand,
nine times out of ten they are making you redundant.
  John Edwards: on BBC Radio Four *Today*, 10 June 1996

7 Remember that time is money.
  Benjamin Franklin 1706–90: *Advice to a Young
Tradesman* (1748)

8 Necessity never made a good bargain.
  Benjamin Franklin 1706–90: *Poor Richard's Almanac*
(1735)

9 Only the paranoid survive.
  Andrew Grove 1936– : dictum on which he has long run
his company, the Intel Corporation; in *New York Times*
18 December 1994

10 Accountants are the witch-doctors of the modern world
and willing to turn their hands to any kind of magic.
  Lord Justice Harman 1894–1970: speech, February 1964,
in A. Sampson *The New Anatomy of Britain* (1971)

11 The best of all monopoly profits is a quiet life.
  J. R. Hicks 1904– : *Econometrica* (1935)

12 The green shoots of economic spring are appearing once
again.
  Norman Lamont 1942– : speech at Conservative Party
Conference, 9 October 1991; often quoted 'the green
shoots of recovery'

13 He's a man way out there in the blue, riding on a smile
and a shoeshine. And when they start not smiling back—
that's an earthquake . . . A salesman is got to dream, boy.
It comes with the territory.
  Arthur Miller 1915– : *Death of a Salesman* (1949)

14 Few have heard of Fra Luca Pacioli, the inventor of double-
entry book-keeping; but he has probably had much more
influence on human life than has Dante or Michelangelo.
  Herbert J. Muller 1905– : *Uses of the Past* (1957)

15 We even sell a pair of earrings for under £1, which is cheaper than a prawn sandwich from Marks & Spencers. But I have to say the earrings probably won't last as long.
  Gerald Ratner 1949– : speech to the Institute of Directors, Albert Hall, 23 April 1991

16 The customer is never wrong.
  César Ritz 1850–1918: R. Nevill and C. E. Jerningham *Piccadilly to Pall Mall* (1908)

17 I think that business practices would improve immeasurably if they were guided by 'feminine' principles—qualities like love and care and intuition.
  Anita Roddick 1942– : *Body and Soul* (1991)

18 Neither a borrower, nor a lender be.
  William Shakespeare 1564–1616: *Hamlet* (1601)

19 To found a great empire for the sole purpose of raising up a people of customers, may at first sight appear a project fit only for a nation of shopkeepers. It is, however, a project altogether unfit for a nation of shopkeepers; but extremely fit for a nation whose government is influenced by shopkeepers.
  Adam Smith 1723–90: *Wealth of Nations* (1776)

20 People of the same trade seldom meet together, even for merriment and diversion, but the conversation ends in a conspiracy against the public, or in some contrivance to raise prices.
  Adam Smith 1723–90: *Wealth of Nations* (1776)

21 Deals are my art form. Other people paint beautifully on canvas or write wonderful poetry. I like making deals, preferably big deals. That's how I get my kicks.
  Donald Trump 1946– : Donald Trump and Tony Schwartz *The Art of the Deal* (1987)

22 The public be damned! I'm working for my stockholders.
  William H. Vanderbilt 1821–85: comment to a news reporter, 2 October 1882

23 [Commercialism is] doing well that which should not be done at all.
  Gore Vidal 1925– : in *Listener* 7 August 1975

24 You cannot be a success in any business without believing
that it is the greatest business in the world . . . You have to
put your heart in the business and the business in your
heart.
   Thomas Watson Snr. 1874–1956: Robert Sobel *IBM:
   Colossus in Transition* (1981)

Canada

1 Dusty, cobweb-covered, maimed, and set at naught,
Beauty crieth in an attic, and no man regardeth.
O God! O Montreal!
   Samuel Butler 1835–1902: 'Psalm of Montreal' (1878)

2 I am rather inclined to believe that this is the land God
gave to Cain.
   Jacques Cartier 1491–1557: on discovering the northern
   shore of the Gulf of St Lawrence (now Labrador and
   Quebec) in 1534; *La Première Relation*

3 I see Canada as a country torn between a very northern,
rather extraordinary, mystical spirit which it fears and its
desire to present itself to the world as a Scotch banker.
   Robertson Davies 1913–95: *The Enthusiasms of
   Robertson Davies* (1990)

4 *Vive Le Québec Libre.*
Long Live Free Quebec.
   Charles de Gaulle 1890–1970: speech in Montreal,
   24 July 1967

5 If some countries have too much history, we have too much
geography.
   William Lyon Mackenzie King 1874–1950: speech,
   18 June 1936

6 The nineteenth century was the century of the United
States. I think we can claim that it is Canada that shall fill
the twentieth century.
   Wilfrid Laurier 1841–1919: speech in Ottawa, 18 January
   1904; usually quoted as 'The twentieth century belongs to
   Canada'

7 These two nations have been at war over a few acres of
snow near Canada, and . . . they are spending on this fine
struggle more than Canada itself is worth.
   Voltaire 1694–1778: of the struggle between the French
   and the British for the control of colonial north Canada;
   Candide (1759)

Careers

See also **Work**

1 I will undoubtedly have to seek what is happily known as
gainful employment, which I am glad to say does not
describe holding public office.
   Dean Acheson 1893–1971: in *Time* 22 December 1952

2 For promotion cometh neither from the east, nor from the
west: nor yet from the south.
   Bible: Psalm 75

3 McJob: A low-pay, low-prestige, low-dignity, low benefit,
no-future job in the service sector.
   Douglas Coupland 1961– : *Generation X* (1991)

4 To do nothing and get something, formed a boy's ideal of a
manly career.
   Benjamin Disraeli 1804–81: *Sybil* (1845)

5 It is wonderful, when a calculation is made, how little the
mind is actually employed in the discharge of any
profession.
   Samuel Johnson 1709–84: James Boswell *Life of
   Johnson* (1791) 6 April 1775

6 Professional men, they have no cares;
Whatever happens, they get theirs.
   Ogden Nash 1902–71: 'I Yield to My Learned Brother'
   (1935)

7 I have that normal male thing of valuing myself according
to the job I do. When I can't tell someone in one word what
I am, then something is missing. I don't represent
anything any more.
  Michael Portillo 1953– : in *Independent on Sunday*
  20 June 1999

8 Thou art not for the fashion of these times,
Where none will sweat but for promotion.
  William Shakespeare 1564–1616: *As You Like It* (1599)

9 The test of a vocation is the love of the drudgery it
involves.
  Logan Pearsall Smith 1865–1946: *Afterthoughts* (1931)

Cats

See also **Animals**

1 Macavity, Macavity, there's no one like Macavity,
There never was a Cat of such deceitfulness and suavity.
He always has an alibi, and one or two to spare:
At whatever time the deed took place—MACAVITY WASN'T
THERE!
  T. S. Eliot 1888–1965: 'Macavity: the Mystery Cat' (1939)

2 He walked by himself, and all places were alike to him.
  Rudyard Kipling 1865–1936: *Just So Stories* (1902) 'The
  Cat that Walked by Himself'

3 Cats seem to go on the principle that it never does any
harm to ask for what you want.
  Joseph Wood Krutch 1893–1970: *Twelve Seasons* (1949)

4 When I play with my cat, who knows whether she isn't
amusing herself with me more than I am with her?
  Montaigne 1533–92: *Essais* (1580)

5 The trouble with a kitten is
THAT
Eventually it becomes a
CAT.
  Ogden Nash 1902–71: 'The Kitten' (1940)

6 For I will consider my Cat Jeoffry . . .

For he counteracts the powers of darkness by his electrical
skin and glaring eyes.

For he counteracts the Devil, who is death, by brisking
about the life.

Christopher Smart 1722–71: *Jubilate Agno* (c.1758–63)

Censorship

1 The reading or non-reading a book—will never keep down
a single petticoat.

Lord Byron 1788–1824: letter to Richard Hoppner,
29 October 1819

2 One does not put Voltaire in the Bastille.

Charles de Gaulle 1890–1970: when asked to arrest
Sartre, in the 1960s; in *Encounter* June 1975

3 Is it a book you would even wish your wife or your
servants to read?

Mervyn Griffith-Jones 1909–79: of D. H. Lawrence's
Lady Chatterley's Lover, while appearing for the
prosecution at the Old Bailey; in *The Times* 21 October
1960

4 Wherever books will be burned, men also, in the end, are
burned.

Heinrich Heine 1797–1856: *Almansor* (1823)

5 One has to multiply thoughts to the point where there
aren't enough policemen to control them.

Stanislaw Lec 1909–66: *Unkempt Thoughts* (1962), tr. J.
Galazka

6 We have long passed the Victorian Era when asterisks
were followed after a certain interval by a baby.

W. Somerset Maugham 1874–1965: *The Constant Wife*
(1926)

7 The power of the press is very great, but not so great as
the power of suppress.

Lord Northcliffe 1865–1922: office message, *Daily Mail*
1918

8 If these writings of the Greeks agree with the book of God, they are useless and need not be preserved; if they disagree, they are pernicious and ought to be destroyed.

    Caliph Omar d. 644: on burning the library of Alexandria, AD c.641; Edward Gibbon *The Decline and Fall of the Roman Empire* (1776–88)

9 Don't you see that the whole aim of Newspeak is to narrow the range of thought? In the end we shall make thoughtcrime literally impossible, because there will be no words in which to express it.

    George Orwell 1903–50: *Nineteen Eighty-Four* (1949)

10 We all know that books burn—yet we have the greater knowledge that books can not be killed by fire. People die, but books never die. No man and no force can abolish memory. No man and no force can put thought in a concentration camp forever.

    Franklin D. Roosevelt 1882–1945: 'Message to the Booksellers of America' 6 May 1942

11 It is obvious that 'obscenity' is not a term capable of exact legal definition; in the practice of the Courts, it means 'anything that shocks the magistrate'.

    Bertrand Russell 1872–1970: *Sceptical Essays* (1928) 'The Recrudescence of Puritanism'

12 If decade after decade the truth cannot be told, each person's mind begins to roam irretrievably. One's fellow countrymen become harder to understand than Martians.

    Alexander Solzhenitsyn 1918– : *Cancer Ward* (1968)

13 Those who want the Government to regulate matters of the mind and spirit are like men who are so afraid of being murdered that they commit suicide to avoid assassination.

    Harry S. Truman 1884–1972: address at the National Archives, Washington, DC, 15 December 1952

14 I disapprove of what you say, but I will defend to the death your right to say it.

    Voltaire 1694–1778: attributed to Voltaire, but actually S. G. Tallentyre's summary of Voltaire's attitude towards Helvétius following the burning of the latter's *De l'esprit* in 1759; in *The Friends of Voltaire* (1907)

15 The Khomeini cry for the execution of Rushdie is an
infantile cry. From the beginning of time we have seen
that. To murder the thinker does not murder the thought.
Arnold Wesker 1932– : in *Weekend Guardian* 3 June
1989

Certainty and Doubt

1 My mind is not a bed to be made and re-made.
James Agate 1877–1947: diary, 9 June 1943

2 Probable impossibilities are to be preferred to improbable
possibilities.
Aristotle 384–322 BC: *Poetics*

3 If a man will begin with certainties, he shall end in
doubts; but if he will be content to begin with doubts, he
shall end in certainties.
Francis Bacon 1561–1626: *The Advancement of Learning*
(1605)

4 Oh! let us never, never doubt
What nobody is sure about!
Hilaire Belloc 1870–1953: 'The Microbe' (1897)

5 [The Government] go on in strange paradox, decided only
to be undecided, resolved to be irresolute, adamant for
drift, solid for fluidity.
Winston Churchill 1874–1965: speech, House of
Commons, 12 November 1936

6 The archbishop is usually to be found nailing his colours
to the fence.
Frank Field 1942– : of Archbishop Runcie; attributed in
Crockfords 1987/88 (1987)

7 I'll give you a definite maybe.
Sam Goldwyn 1882–1974: attributed

8 I am too much of a sceptic to deny the possibility of
anything.
T. H. Huxley 1825–95: letter to H. Spencer, 22 March 1886

9 I wish I was as cocksure of anything as Tom Macaulay is of everything.
  Lord Melbourne 1779–1848: in Lord Cowper's preface to *Lord Melbourne's Papers* (1889)

10 Ah, what a dusty answer gets the soul
  When hot for certainties in this our life!
  George Meredith 1828–1909: *Modern Love* (1862)

11 I respect faith but doubt is what gets you an education.
  Wilson Mizner 1876–1933: H. L. Mencken *A New Dictionary of Quotations* (1942)

12 Now, the melancholy god protect thee, and the tailor make thy doublet of changeable taffeta, for thy mind is a very opal.
  William Shakespeare 1564–1616: *Twelfth Night* (1601)

13 I must have a prodigious quantity of mind; it takes me as much as a week, sometimes, to make it up.
  Mark Twain 1835–1910: *The Innocents Abroad* (1869)

14 Life is doubt,
  And faith without doubt is nothing but death.
  Miguel de Unamuno 1864–1937: 'Salmo II' (1907)

15 Minds like beds always made up,
  (more stony than a shore)
  unwilling or unable.
  William Carlos Williams 1883–1963: *Paterson* (1946)

Chance

1 Cast thy bread upon the waters: for thou shalt find it after many days.
  Bible: Ecclesiastes

2 But for the grace of God there goes John Bradford.
  John Bradford c.1510–55: on seeing a group of criminals being led to their execution; in *Dictionary of National Biography* (1917–), usually quoted 'There but for the grace of God go I'

3 The best laid schemes o' mice an' men
Gang aft a-gley.
   Robert Burns 1759–96: 'To a Mouse' (1786)

4 The chapter of knowledge is a very short, but the chapter
of accidents is a very long one.
   Lord Chesterfield 1694–1773: letter to Solomon
   Dayrolles, 16 February 1753

5 At this moment he was unfortunately called out by a
person on business from Porlock.
   Samuel Taylor Coleridge 1772–1834: 'Kubla Khan'
   (1816) preliminary note, explaining why the poem
   remained unfinished

6 Accidents will occur in the best-regulated families.
   Charles Dickens 1812–70: *David Copperfield* (1850) Mr
   Micawber

7 If an army of monkeys were strumming on typewriters
they *might* write all the books in the British Museum.
   Arthur Eddington 1882–1944: *The Nature of the Physical
   World* (1928)

8 I am convinced that *He* [God] does not play dice.
   Albert Einstein 1879–1955: letter to Max Born,
   4 December 1926

9 Mr Bond, they have a saying in Chicago: 'Once is
happenstance. Twice is coincidence. The third time it's
enemy action.'
   Ian Fleming 1908–64: *Goldfinger* (1959)

10 All you know about it [luck] for certain is that it's bound
to change.
   Bret Harte 1836–1902: *The Outcasts of Poker Flat* (1871)

11 The chance of winning the lottery jackpot is less than that
of being struck by lightning. I have never bought a ticket
and plan to buy an insulating rubber helmet with the
money I save. It will increase my life expectancy by
precisely one fourteen-millionth.
   Steve Jones 1944– : in *Independent on Sunday*
   5 November 1995

12 Predictability: Does the flap of a butterfly's wings in Brazil
set off a tornado in Texas?
Edward N. Lorenz: title of paper given to the American
Association for the Advancement of Science,
Washington, 29 December 1979

13 O! many a shaft, at random sent,
Finds mark the archer little meant!
And many a word, at random spoken,
May soothe or wound a heart that's broken.
Sir Walter Scott 1771–1832: *The Lord of the Isles* (1813)

14 There is a tide in the affairs of men,
Which, taken at the flood, leads on to fortune;
Omitted, all the voyage of their life
Is bound in shallows and in miseries.
William Shakespeare 1564–1616: *Julius Caesar* (1599)

Change

See also **Beginnings and Endings**

1 Wandering between two worlds, one dead,
The other powerless to be born.
Matthew Arnold 1822–88: 'Stanzas from the Grande
Chartreuse' (1855)

2 He that will not apply new remedies must expect new
evils; for time is the greatest innovator.
Francis Bacon 1561–1626: *Essays* (1625) 'Of Innovations'

3 Can the Ethiopian change his skin, or the leopard his
spots?
Bible: Jeremiah

4 And now for something completely different.
Graham Chapman 1941–89 et al.: *Monty Python's Flying
Circus* (BBC TV programme, 1970)

5 Variety's the very spice of life,
That gives it all its flavour.
William Cowper 1731–1800: *The Task* (1785) 'The
Timepiece'

6 When it is not necessary to change, it is necessary not to change.
   Lucius Cary, Viscount Falkland 1610–43: 'A Speech concerning Episcopacy' (1641)

7 Most of the change we think we see in life
Is due to truths being in and out of favour.
   Robert Frost 1874–1963: 'The Black Cottage' (1914)

8 You can't step twice into the same river.
   Heraclitus c.540–c.480 BC: in Plato Cratylus

9 Consistency is contrary to nature, contrary to life. The only completely consistent people are the dead.
   Aldous Huxley 1894–1963: Do What You Will (1929)

10 There is a certain relief in change, even though it be from bad to worse . . . it is often a comfort to shift one's position and be bruised in a new place.
   Washington Irving 1783–1859: Tales of a Traveller (1824)

11 Change is not made without inconvenience, even from worse to better.
   Samuel Johnson 1709–84: Dictionary of the English Language (1755) preface

12 Plus ça change, plus c'est la même chose.
   The more things change, the more they are the same.
   Alphonse Karr 1808–90: Les Guêpes January 1849

13 It is best not to swap horses when crossing streams.
   Abraham Lincoln 1809–65: reply to National Union League, 9 June 1864

14 Change and decay in all around I see;
O Thou, who changest not, abide with me.
   Henry Francis Lyte 1793–1847: 'Abide with Me' (c.1847)

15 Tomorrow to fresh woods, and pastures new.
   John Milton 1608–74: 'Lycidas' (1638)

16 God, give us the serenity to accept what cannot be changed;
Give us the courage to change what should be changed;

Give us the wisdom to distinguish one from the other.
Reinhold Niebuhr 1892–1971: prayer said to have been first published in 1951; in R. W. Fox *Reinhold Niebuhr* (1985)

17 In olden days a glimpse of stocking
Was looked on as something shocking
Now, heaven knows,
Anything goes.
Cole Porter 1891–1964: 'Anything Goes' (1934 song)

18 The old order changeth, yielding place to new,
And God fulfils himself in many ways,
Lest one good custom should corrupt the world.
Alfred, Lord Tennyson 1809–92: *Idylls of the King* 'The Passing of Arthur' (1869)

19 If we do not find anything pleasant, at least we shall find something new.
Voltaire 1694–1778: *Candide* (1759)

20 All changed, changed utterly:
A terrible beauty is born.
W. B. Yeats 1865–1939: 'Easter, 1916' (1921)

Character

1 It is not in the still calm of life, or the repose of a pacific station, that great characters are formed . . . Great necessities call out great virtues.
Abigail Adams 1744–1818: letter to John Quincy Adams, 19 January 1780

2 A thick skin is a gift from God.
Konrad Adenauer 1876–1967: in *New York Times* 30 December 1959

3 It is the nature, and the advantage, of strong people that they can bring out the crucial questions and form a clear opinion about them. The weak always have to decide between alternatives that are not their own.
Dietrich Bonhoeffer 1906–45: *Widerstand und Ergebung* (1951), tr. R. Fuller

4 My parents were convinced that I would one day become
Mr Average, but almost 30 years on I am still an A1 freak.
> **Boy George** 1961– : in *Independent on Sunday* 28 March
> 1999

5 If you have bright plumage, people will take pot shots at
you.
> **Alan Clark** 1928–99: in *Independent* 25 June 1994

6 Claudia's the sort of person who goes through life holding
on to the sides.
> **Alice Thomas Ellis** 1932– : *The Other Side of the Fire*
> (1983)

7 Talent develops in quiet places, character in the full
current of human life.
> **Johann Wolfgang von Goethe** 1749–1832: *Torquato
> Tasso* (1790)

8 Those who stand for nothing fall for anything.
> **Alex Hamilton** 1936– : 'Born Old' (radio broadcast), in
> *Listener* 9 November 1978

9 A man's character is his fate.
> **Heraclitus** *c*.540–*c*.480 BC: *On the Universe*

10 If you can fill the unforgiving minute
With sixty seconds' worth of distance run,
Yours is the Earth and everything that's in it,
And—which is more—you'll be a Man, my son!
> **Rudyard Kipling** 1865–1936: 'If—' (1910)

11 I see the better things, and approve; I follow the worse.
> **Ovid** 43 BC–AD *c*.17: *Metamorphoses*

12 He's so wet you could shoot snipe off him.
> **Anthony Powell** 1905–2000: *A Question of Upbringing*
> (1951)

13 You can tell a lot about a fellow's character by his way of
eating jellybeans.
> **Ronald Reagan** 1911– : in *New York Times* 15 January
> 1981

14   My nature is subdued
To what it works in, like the dyer's hand.
> **William Shakespeare** 1564–1616: sonnet 111 (1609)

15 Fame vaporizes, money goes with the wind, and all that's left is character.

    O. J. Simpson 1947– : *Juice: O. J. Simpson's Life* (1977)

16 If you can't stand the heat, get out of the kitchen.

    Harry Vaughan: in *Time* 28 April 1952 (associated with Harry S. Truman, but attributed by him to Vaughan, his 'military jester')

Charm

1 Charm . . . it's a sort of bloom on a woman. If you have it, you don't need to have anything else; and if you don't have it, it doesn't much matter what else you have.

    J. M. Barrie 1860–1937: *What Every Woman Knows* (1908)

2 You know what charm is: a way of getting the answer yes without having asked any clear question.

    Albert Camus 1913–60: *The Fall* (1957)

3 All charming people have something to conceal, usually their total dependence on the appreciation of others.

    Cyril Connolly 1903–74: *Enemies of Promise* (1938)

4 Oozing charm from every pore,
He oiled his way around the floor.

    Alan Jay Lerner 1918–86: 'You Did It' (1956 song)

5 Charm is the great English blight. It does not exist outside these damp islands. It spots and kills anything it touches. It kills love, it kills art.

    Evelyn Waugh 1903–66: *Brideshead Revisited* (1945)

Children

See also **The Family**, **Parents**, **Youth**

1 Children sweeten labours, but they make misfortunes more bitter.

    Francis Bacon 1561–1626: *Essays* (1625) 'Of Parents and Children'

2 Suffer the little children to come unto me, and forbid them not: for of such is the kingdom of God.
Bible: St Mark

3 When I was a child, I spake as a child, I understood as a child, I thought as a child: but when I became a man, I put away childish things.
Bible: I Corinthians

4 There is no such thing as other people's children.
Hillary Rodham Clinton 1947– : in *Newsweek* 15 January 1996

5 There is no more sombre enemy of good art than the pram in the hall.
Cyril Connolly 1903–74: *Enemies of Promise* (1938)

6 There never was a child so lovely but his mother was glad to get asleep.
Ralph Waldo Emerson 1803–82: *Journal* 1836

7 Alas, regardless of their doom,
The little victims play!
No sense have they of ills to come,
Nor care beyond to-day.
Thomas Gray 1716–71: *Ode on a Distant Prospect of Eton College* (1747)

8 There is always one moment in childhood when the door opens and lets the future in.
Graham Greene 1904–91: *The Power and the Glory* (1940)

9 Oh, for an hour of Herod!
Anthony Hope 1863–1933: at the first night of *Peter Pan* (1904); D. Mackail *Story of JMB* (1941)

10 If there is anything that we wish to change in the child, we should first examine it and see whether it is not something that could better be changed in ourselves.
Carl Gustav Jung 1875–1961: 'Vom Werden der Persönlichkeit' (1932)

11 A child is owed the greatest respect; if you ever have
something disgraceful in mind, don't ignore your son's
tender years.
    Juvenal AD c.60–c.130: *Satires*

12 Literature is mostly about having sex and not much about
having children. Life is the other way round.
    David Lodge 1935– : *The British Museum is Falling
    Down* (1965)

13 It should be noted that children at play are not playing
about; their games should be seen as their most serious-
minded activity.
    Montaigne 1533–92: *Essais* (1580)

14 The affection you get back from children is sixpence given
as change for a sovereign.
    Edith Nesbit 1858–1924: J. Briggs *A Woman of Passion*
    (1987)

15 Men are generally more careful of the breed of their horses
and dogs than of their children.
    William Penn 1644–1718: *Some Fruits of Solitude* (1693)

16 Behold the child, by Nature's kindly law
Pleased with a rattle, tickled with a straw.
    Alexander Pope 1688–1744: *An Essay on Man* Epistle 2
    (1733)

17 A child is not a vase to be filled, but a fire to be lit.
    François Rabelais c.1494–c.1553: attributed

18 Any man who hates dogs and babies can't be all bad.
    Leo Rosten 1908–97: of W. C. Fields, and often attributed
    to him, in speech at Masquers' Club dinner, 16 February
    1939

19 Grown-ups never understand anything for themselves, and
it is tiresome for children to be always and forever
explaining things to them.
    Antoine de Saint-Exupéry 1900–44: *Le Petit Prince*
    (1943)

20   At first the infant,
Mewling and puking in the nurse's arms.
And then the whining schoolboy, with his satchel,
And shining morning face, creeping like snail

Unwillingly to school.
    William Shakespeare 1564–1616: *As You Like It* (1599)

21 The summer that I was ten—
Can it be there was only one
summer that I was ten? It must

have been a long one then.
    May Swenson 1919–89: 'The Centaur' (1958)

22 You will find as the children grow up that as a rule
children are a bitter disappointment—their greatest object
being to do precisely what their parents do not wish and
have anxiously tried to prevent.
    Queen Victoria 1819–1901: letter to the Crown Princess
of Prussia, 5 January 1876

23 The Child is father of the Man.
    William Wordsworth 1770–1850: 'My heart leaps up
when I behold' (1807)

Choice

1 White shall not neutralize the black, nor good
Compensate bad in man, absolve him so:
Life's business being just the terrible choice.
    Robert Browning 1812–89: *The Ring and the Book*
(1868–9)

2 The die is cast.
    Julius Caesar 100–44 BC: at the crossing of the Rubicon,
in Suetonius *Lives of the Caesars*

3 Any customer can have a car painted any colour that he
wants so long as it is black.
    Henry Ford 1863–1947: of the Model T Ford; Henry Ford
with Samuel Crowther *My Life and Work* (1922)

4 Two roads diverged in a wood, and I—
I took the one less travelled by,
And that has made all the difference.
    Robert Frost 1874–1963: 'The Road Not Taken' (1916)

5 How happy could I be with either,
   Were t'other dear charmer away!
      John Gay 1685–1732: *The Beggar's Opera* (1728)

6 Which do you want? A whipping and no turnips or turnips
   and no whipping?
      Toni Morrison 1931– : *The Bluest Eye* (1961)

7 You pays your money and you takes your choice.
      Punch: 1846

8 I'll make him an offer he can't refuse.
      Mario Puzo 1920– : *The Godfather* (1969)

9 To be, or not to be: that is the question.
      William Shakespeare 1564–1616: *Hamlet* (1601)

10 Take care to get what you like or you will be forced to like
   what you get.
      George Bernard Shaw 1856–1950: *Man and Superman*
   (1903)

11 There is no real alternative.
      Margaret Thatcher 1925– : speech at Conservative
   Women's Conference, 21 May 1980; popularly
   encapsulated in the acronym TINA

12 Between two evils, I always pick the one I never tried
   before.
      Mae West 1892–1980: *Klondike Annie* (1936)

··

Christmas

··

1 I'm dreaming of a white Christmas,
   Just like the ones I used to know.
      Irving Berlin 1888–1989: 'White Christmas' (1942 song)

2 And girls in slacks remember Dad,
   And oafish louts remember Mum,
   And sleepless children's hearts are glad,

And Christmas-morning bells say 'Come!'
John Betjeman 1906–84: 'Christmas' (1954)

3 She brought forth her firstborn son, and wrapped him in swaddling clothes, and laid him in a manger; because there was no room for them in the inn.
Bible: St Luke

4 Yes, Virginia, there is a Santa Claus.
Francis Pharcellus Church 1839–1906: editorial replying to a letter from eight-year-old Virginia O'Hanlon, in New York *Sun*, 21 September 1897

5 Christmas is the Disneyfication of Christianity.
Don Cupitt 1934– : in *Independent* 19 December 1996

6 'Bah,' said Scrooge. 'Humbug!'
Charles Dickens 1812–70: *A Christmas Carol* (1843)

7 Still xmas is a good time with all those presents and good food and i hope it will never die out or at any rate not until i am grown up and hav to pay for it all.
Geoffrey Willans 1911–58 and **Ronald Searle** 1920– : *How To Be Topp* (1954)

....

The Church

....

See also **Religion**

1 The nearer the Church the further from God.
Bishop Lancelot Andrewes 1555–1626: *Of the Nativity* (1622) Sermon 15

2 Railways and the Church have their critics, but both are the best ways of getting a man to his ultimate destination.
Revd W. Awdry 1911–97: in *Daily Telegraph* 22 March 1997; obituary

3 We must recall that the Church is always 'one generation away from extinction.'
George Carey 1935– : Working Party Report *Youth A Part: Young People and the Church* (1996) foreword

4 The two dangers which beset the Church of England are good music and bad preaching.
  Lord Hugh Cecil 1869–1956: in K. Rose *The Later Cecils* (1975)

5 He cannot have God for his father who has not the church for his mother.
  St Cyprian AD *c.*200–258: *De Ecclesiae Catholicae Unitate*

6 And of all plagues with which mankind are curst,
  Ecclesiastic tyranny's the worst.
  Daniel Defoe 1660–1731: *The True-Born Englishman* (1701)

7 Our cathedrals are like abandoned computers now, but they used to be prayer factories once.
  Lawrence Durrell 1912–90: in *Listener* 20 April 1978

8 In old time we had treen chalices and golden priests, but now we have treen priests and golden chalices.
  Bishop John Jewel 1522–71: *Certain Sermons Preached Before the Queen's Majesty* (1609)

9 I want to throw open the windows of the Church so that we can see out and the people can see in.
  Pope John XXIII 1881–1963: attributed

10 We are an Easter people and Alleluia is our song.
  Pope John Paul II 1920– : speech in Harlem, New York, 2 October 1979

11 'The Church is an anvil which has worn out many hammers', and the story of the first collision is, in essentials, the story of all.
  Alexander Maclaren 1826–1910: *Expositions of Holy Scripture: Acts of the Apostles* (1907)

12 The Church [of England] should go forward along the path of progress and be no longer satisfied only to represent the Conservative Party at prayer.
  Maude Royden 1876–1956: in *The Times* 17 July 1917

13 The Church can no longer contain the fizzy, explosive stuff that the true wine of the bottle ought to be.
  Donald Soper 1903–98: in *Methodist Recorder* 18 January 1968

14 I never saw, heard, nor read, that the clergy were beloved in any nation where Christianity was the religion of the country. Nothing can render them popular, but some degree of persecution.

Jonathan Swift 1667–1745: *Thoughts on Religion* (1765)

15 As often as we are mown down by you, the more we grow in numbers; the blood of Christians is the seed.

Tertullian AD c.160–c.225: *Apologeticus*, traditionally 'The blood of the martyrs is the seed of the Church'

16 I look upon all the world as my parish.

John Wesley 1703–91: diary, 11 June 1739

17 The Catholic Church has never really come to terms with women. What I object to is being treated either as Madonnas or Mary Magdalenes.

Shirley Williams 1930– : in *Observer* 22 March 1981

....

The Cinema

....

See also **Acting and the Theatre**

1 JOE GILLIS: You used to be in pictures. You used to be big.
NORMA DESMOND: I am big. It's the pictures that got small.

Charles Brackett 1892–1969 and **Billy Wilder** 1906– : *Sunset Boulevard* (1950 film, with D. M. Marshman Jr.)

2 There are no rules in film-making. Only sins. And the cardinal sin is dullness.

Frank Capra 1897–1991: in *People* 16 September 1991

3 All I need to make a comedy is a park, a policeman and a pretty girl.

Charlie Chaplin 1889–1977: *My Autobiography* (1964)

4 Bring on the empty horses!

Michael Curtiz 1888–1962: while directing *The Charge of the Light Brigade* (1936 film); in David Niven *Bring on the Empty Horses* (1975)

5 'Movies should have a beginning, a middle and an end,'
harrumphed French film maker Georges Franju . . .
'Certainly,' replied Jean-Luc Godard. 'But not necessarily
in that order.'
   Jean-Luc Godard 1930– : in *Time* 14 September 1981

6 Photography is truth. The cinema is truth 24 times per
second.
   Jean-Luc Godard 1930– : *Le Petit Soldat* (1960 film)

7 Pictures are for entertainment, messages should be
delivered by Western Union.
   Sam Goldwyn 1882–1974: A. Marx *Goldwyn* (1976)

8 Why should people go out and pay to see bad movies when
they can stay at home and see bad television for nothing?
   Sam Goldwyn 1882–1974: in *Observer* 9 September 1956

9 It would have been cheaper to lower the Atlantic!
   Lew Grade 1906–98: of the disaster movie *Raise the
Titanic*; *Still Dancing: My Story* (1987)

10 If I made Cinderella, the audience would immediately be
looking for a body in the coach.
   Alfred Hitchcock 1899–1980: in *Newsweek* 11 June 1956

11 If you gave him a good script, actors and technicians,
Mickey Mouse could direct a movie.
   Nicholas Hytner 1956– : in *Daily Telegraph* 24 February
1994

12 Hollywood money isn't money. It's congealed snow, melts
in your hand, and there you are.
   Dorothy Parker 1893–1967: Malcolm Cowley *Writers at
Work* 1st Series (1958)

13 The lunatics have taken charge of the asylum.
   Richard Rowland c.1881–1947: on the take-over of
United Artists by Charles Chaplin and others; T.
Ramsaye *A Million and One Nights* (1926)

14 The trouble, Mr Goldwyn, is that you are only interested
in art and I am only interested in money.
   George Bernard Shaw 1856–1950: telegraphed version
of the outcome of a conversation between Shaw and Sam
Goldwyn; A. Johnson *The Great Goldwyn* (1937)

15 This is the biggest electric train set any boy ever had!
  Orson Welles 1915–85: of the RKO studios; P. Noble *The Fabulous Orson Welles* (1956)

16 I wouldn't say when you've seen one Western you've seen the lot; but when you've seen the lot you get the feeling you've seen one.
  Katharine Whitehorn 1928– : *Sunday Best* (1976) 'Decoding the West'

17 It is like writing history with lightning. And my only regret is that it is all so terribly true.
  Woodrow Wilson 1856–1924: on seeing D. W. Griffith's film *The Birth of a Nation* at the White House, 18 February 1915

Civilization

1 The three great elements of modern civilization, Gunpowder, Printing, and the Protestant Religion.
  Thomas Carlyle 1795–1881: *Critical and Miscellaneous Essays* (1838)

2 Civilization and profits go hand in hand.
  Calvin Coolidge 1872–1933: speech in New York, 27 November 1920

3 JOURNALIST: Mr Gandhi, what do you think of modern civilization?
  GANDHI: That would be a good idea.
  Mahatma Gandhi 1869–1948: on arriving in England in 1930; E. F. Schumacher *Good Work* (1979)

4 The lamps are going out all over Europe; we shall not see them lit again in our lifetime.
  Lord Grey of Fallodon 1862–1933: on the eve of the First World War; *25 Years* (1925)

5 If a nation expects to be ignorant and free, in a state of civilization, it expects what never was and never will be.
  Thomas Jefferson 1743–1826: letter to Colonel Charles Yancey, 6 January 1816

6 Whenever I hear the word culture . . . I release the safety-catch of my Browning!

   Hanns Johst 1890–1978: *Schlageter* (1933) often attributed to Hermann Goering, and quoted 'Whenever I hear the word culture, I reach for my pistol!'

7 It is only in our advanced and synthetic civilization that mothers no longer sing to the babies they are carrying.

   Yehudi Menuhin 1916–99: in *Observer* 4 January 1987

8 If civilization had been left in female hands, we would still be living in grass huts.

   Camille Paglia 1947– : *Sexual Personae* (1990)

9 You can't say civilization don't advance, however, for in every war they kill you in a new way.

   Will Rogers 1879–1935: *New York Times* 23 December 1929

10 Civilization has made the peasantry its pack animal. The bourgeoisie in the long run only changed the form of the pack.

   Leon Trotsky 1879–1940: *History of the Russian Revolution* (1933)

11 'Sergeant Pepper'—a decisive moment in the history of Western Civilisation.

   Kenneth Tynan 1927–80: in 1967; Howard Elson *McCartney* (1986)

12 In Italy for thirty years under the Borgias they had warfare, terror, murder, bloodshed—they produced Michelangelo, Leonardo da Vinci and the Renaissance. In Switzerland they had brotherly love, five hundred years of democracy and peace and what did that produce . . . ? The cuckoo clock.

   Orson Welles 1915–85: *The Third Man* (1949 film); words added by Welles to Graham Greene's screenplay

13 Civilization advances by extending the number of important operations which we can perform without thinking about them.

   Alfred North Whitehead 1861–1947: *Introduction to Mathematics* (1911)

14 The soul of any civilization on earth has ever been and
still is Art and Religion, but neither has ever been found
in commerce, in government or the police.
   Frank Lloyd Wright 1867–1959: *A Testament* (1957)

Class

1 The rich man in his castle,
The poor man at his gate,
God made them, high or lowly,
And ordered their estate.
   Cecil Frances Alexander 1818–95: 'All Things Bright
   and Beautiful' (1848)

2 *Il faut épater le bourgeois.*

One must astonish the bourgeois.
   Charles Baudelaire 1821–67: attributed

3 Like many of the Upper Class
He liked the Sound of Broken Glass.
   Hilaire Belloc 1870–1953: 'About John' (1930)

4 Just because I have made a point of never losing my accent
it doesn't mean I am an eel-and-pie yob.
   Michael Caine 1933– : in *The Times* 15 April 2000

5 The Stately Homes of England,
How beautiful they stand,
To prove the upper classes
Have still the upper hand.
   Noël Coward 1899–1973: 'The Stately Homes of England'
   (1938 song).

6 O let us love our occupations,
Bless the squire and his relations,
Live upon our daily rations,
And always know our proper stations.
   Charles Dickens 1812–70: *The Chimes* (1844)

7 The bourgeois prefers comfort to pleasure, convenience to
liberty, and a pleasant temperature to the deathly inner
consuming fire.
   Hermann Hesse 1877–1962: *Der Steppenwolf* (1927)

8 The history of all hitherto existing society is the history of
class struggles.
   Karl Marx 1818–83 and **Friedrich Engels** 1820–95: *The
   Communist Manifesto* (1848)

9 The proletarians have nothing to lose but their chains.
They have a world to win. WORKING MEN OF ALL COUNTRIES,
UNITE!
   Karl Marx 1818–83 and **Friedrich Engels** 1820–95: *The
   Communist Manifesto* (1848); tr. S. Moore, 1888, commonly
   rendered 'Workers of the world, unite!'

10 We of the sinking middle class . . . may sink without
further struggles into the working class where we belong,
and probably when we get there it will not be so dreadful
as we feared, for, after all, we have nothing to lose but our
aitches.
   George Orwell 1903–50: *The Road to Wigan Pier* (1937)

11 First you take their faces from 'em by calling 'em the
masses and then you accuse 'em of not having any faces.
   J. B. Priestley 1894–1984: *Saturn Over the Water* (1961)

12 When Adam dalfe and Eve spane . . .
Where was than the pride of man?
   Richard Rolle de Hampole *c.*1290–1349: in G. G. Perry
   Religious Pieces (1914). Taken in the form 'When Adam
   delved and Eve span, who was then the gentleman?' by
   John Ball as the text of his revolutionary sermon on the
   outbreak of the Peasants' Revolt, 1381

13 The State is an instrument in the hands of the ruling class,
used to break the resistance of the adversaries of that
class.
   Joseph Stalin 1879–1953: *Foundations of Leninism* (1924)

14 Impotence and sodomy are socially O.K. but birth control is flagrantly middle-class.

Evelyn Waugh 1903–66: 'An Open Letter' in Nancy Mitford (ed.) *Noblesse Oblige* (1956)

Commerce

see **Business and Commerce**

Computers

1 To err is human but to really foul things up requires a computer.

Anonymous: *Farmers' Almanac for 1978* 'Capsules of Wisdom'

2 Computers are composed of nothing more than logic gates stretched out to the horizon in a vast numerical irrigation system.

Stan Augarten: *State of the Art: A Photographic History of the Integrated Circuit* (1983)

3 A modern computer hovers between the obsolescent and the nonexistent.

Sydney Brenner 1927– : attributed in *Science* 5 January 1990

4 The Internet is an elite organisation; most of the population of the world has never even made a phone call.

Noam Chomsky 1928– : in *Observer* 18 February 1996

5 Computers are anti-Faraday machines. He said he couldn't understand anything until he could count it, while computers count everything and understand nothing.

Ralph Cornes: in *Guardian* 28 March 1991

6 Silicon Valley is the Florence of the late 20th century.

Francis Fukuyama 1952– : in *Independent* 19 June 1999

7 The symbol of the atomic age, which tended to centralise power, was a nucleus with electrons held in tight orbit; the symbol of the digital age is the Web, with countless centres

of power all equally networked.
Walter Isaacson 1952– : in *Time* 29 December 1997

8 The PC is the LSD of the '90s.
Timothy Leary 1920–96: remark made in the early 1990s;
in *Guardian* 1 June 1996

9 The Analytical Engine weaves algebraic patterns just as
the Jacquard loom weaves flowers and leaves.
Ada Lovelace 1815–52: of Babbage's mechanical
computer; Luigi Menabrea *Sketch of the Analytical
Engine invented by Charles Babbage* (1843), translated
and annotated by Ada Lovelace, Note A

10 We used to have lots of questions to which there were no
answers. Now with the computer there are lots of answers
to which we haven't thought up the questions.
Peter Ustinov 1921– : in *Illustrated London News* 1 June
1968

11 We've all heard that a million monkeys banging on a
million typewriters will eventually reproduce the entire
works of Shakespeare. Now, thanks to the Internet, we
know this is not true.
Robert Wilensky 1951– : in *Mail on Sunday*
16 February 1997

Conscience

1 We have erred, and strayed from thy ways like lost sheep.
We have followed too much the devices and desires of our
own hearts.
Book of Common Prayer 1662: *Morning Prayer*

2 Conscience is thoroughly well-bred and soon leaves off
talking to those who do not wish to hear it.
Samuel Butler 1835–1902: *Further Extracts from
Notebooks* (1934)

3 *O dignitosa coscienza e netta,
Come t'è picciol fallo amaro morso!*

O pure and noble conscience, how bitter a sting to thee is a
little fault!

Dante Alighieri 1265–1321: *Divina Commedia*
'Purgatorio'

4 I cannot and will not cut my conscience to fit this year's
fashions.

Lillian Hellman 1905–84: letter to John S. Wood, 19 May
1952

5 Conscience: the inner voice which warns us that someone
may be looking.

H. L. Mencken 1880–1956: *A Little Book in C major* (1916)

6 Thus conscience doth make cowards of us all.

William Shakespeare 1564–1616: *Hamlet* (1601)

7 Corporations have neither bodies to be punished, nor souls
to be condemned, they therefore do as they like.

Edward, 1st Baron Thurlow 1731–1806: in J. Poynder
Literary Extracts (1844), usually quoted 'Did you ever
expect a corporation to have a conscience, when it has
no soul to be damned, and no body to be kicked?'

Conversation

See also **Speech and Speeches**

1 From politics, it was an easy step to silence.

Jane Austen 1775–1817: *Northanger Abbey* (1818)

2 Although there exist many thousand subjects for elegant
conversation, there are persons who cannot meet a cripple
without talking about feet.

Ernest Bramah 1868–1942: *The Wallet of Kai Lung* (1900)

3 'The time has come,' the Walrus said,
'To talk of many things:
Of shoes—and ships—and sealing wax—
Of cabbages—and kings.'

Lewis Carroll 1832–98: *Through the Looking-Glass* (1872)

4 Religion is by no means a proper subject of conversation in
a mixed company.
   Lord Chesterfield 1694–1773: *Letters . . . to his Godson
   and Successor* (1890)

5 Two may talk and one may hear, but three cannot take
part in a conversation of the most sincere and searching
sort.
   Ralph Waldo Emerson 1803–82: *Essays* (1841)
   'Friendship'

6 He talked on for ever; and you wished him to talk on for
ever.
   William Hazlitt 1778–1830: of Coleridge; *Lectures on the
   English Poets* (1818)

7 And, when you stick on conversation's burrs,
Don't strew your pathway with those dreadful *urs*.
   Oliver Wendell Holmes 1809–94: 'A Rhymed Lesson'
   (1848)

8 Questioning is not the mode of conversation among
gentlemen. It is assuming a superiority.
   Samuel Johnson 1709–84: James Boswell *Life of
   Johnson* (1791) 25 March 1776

9 The opposite of talking isn't listening. The opposite of
talking is waiting.
   Fran Lebowitz 1946– : *Social Studies* (1981)

10 He has occasional flashes of silence, that make his
conversation perfectly delightful.
   Sydney Smith 1771–1845: of Macaulay; Lady Holland
   Memoir (1855)

11 He speaks to Me as if I was a public meeting.
   Queen Victoria 1819–1901: of Gladstone; G. W. E. Russell
   Collections and Recollections (1898)

12 There is no such thing as conversation. It is an illusion.
There are intersecting monologues, that is all.
   Rebecca West 1892–1983: *There is No Conversation*
   (1935)

Cooperation

1 More than ever before in human history, we share a common destiny. We can master it only if we face it together. And that, my friends, is why we have the United Nations.
   Kofi Annan 1938– : in *Sunday Times* 2 January 2000

2 If a house be divided against itself, that house cannot stand.
   Bible: St Mark

3 When bad men combine, the good must associate; else they will fall, one by one, an unpitied sacrifice in a contemptible struggle.
   Edmund Burke 1729–97: *Thoughts on the Cause of the Present Discontents* (1770)

4 All for one, one for all.
   Alexandre Dumas 1802–70: *Les Trois Mousquetaires* (1844)

5 We must indeed all hang together, or, most assuredly, we shall all hang separately.
   Benjamin Franklin 1706–90: at the Signing of the Declaration of Independence, 4 July 1776 (possibly not original)

6 If someone claps his hand a sound arises. Listen to the sound of the single hand!
   Hakuin 1686–1769: attributed

7 If we cannot end now our differences, at least we can help make the world safe for diversity.
   John F. Kennedy 1917–63: address at American University, Washington, DC, 10 June 1963

8 We must learn to live together as brothers or perish together as fools.
   Martin Luther King 1929–68: speech at St Louis, 22 March 1964

9 When Hitler attacked the Jews I was not a Jew, therefore, I was not concerned. And when Hitler attacked the Catholics, I was not a Catholic, and therefore, I was not concerned. And when Hitler attacked the unions and the industrialists, I was not a member of the unions and I was not concerned. Then, Hitler attacked me and the Protestant church—and there was nobody left to be concerned.

Martin Niemöller 1892–1984: in *Congressional Record* 14 October 1968

10 Government and co-operation are in all things the laws of life; anarchy and competition the laws of death.

John Ruskin 1819–1900: *Unto this Last* (1862)

....

The Country and the Town
....

See also **Environment**

1 An industrial worker would sooner have a £5 note but a countryman must have praise.

Ronald Blythe 1922– : *Akenfield* (1969)

2 'Tis distance lends enchantment to the view,
And robes the mountain in its azure hue.

Thomas Campbell 1777–1844: *Pleasures of Hope* (1799)

3 If you would be known, and not know, vegetate in a village; if you would know, and not be known, live in a city.

Charles Caleb Colton c.1780–1832: *Lacon* (1820)

4 Slums may well be breeding-grounds of crime, but middle-class suburbs are incubators of apathy and delirium.

Cyril Connolly 1903–74: *The Unquiet Grave* (1944)

5 God made the country, and man made the town.

William Cowper 1731–1800: *The Task* (1785) 'The Sofa'

6 It is my belief, Watson, founded upon my experience, that the lowest and vilest alleys in London do not present a more dreadful record of sin than does the smiling and beautiful countryside.

Arthur Conan Doyle 1859–1930: *Adventures of Sherlock Holmes* (1892)

7 Green belts should be the start of the countryside, not a
ditch between Subtopias.
   Hugh Gaitskell 1906–63: in *Observer* 1 January 1961

8 There is nothing good to be had in the country, or if there
is, they will not let you have it.
   William Hazlitt 1778–1830: *The Round Table* (1817)

9 The Farmer will never be happy again;
   He carries his heart in his boots;
   For either the rain is destroying his grain
   Or the drought is destroying his roots.
   A. P. Herbert 1890–1971: 'The Farmer' (1922)

10 I have no relish for the country; it is a kind of healthy
grave.
   Sydney Smith 1771–1845: letter to Miss G. Harcourt,
   1838

....

Courage
....

1 No coward soul is mine,
   No trembler in the world's storm-troubled sphere:
   I see Heaven's glories shine,
   And faith shines equal, arming me from fear.
   Emily Brontë 1818–48: 'No coward soul is mine' (1846)

2 *De l'audace, et encore de l'audace, et toujours de l'audace!*

   Boldness, and again boldness, and always boldness!
   Georges Jacques Danton 1759–94: speech to the
   Legislative Committee of General Defence, 2 September
   1792

3 Grace under pressure.
   Ernest Hemingway 1899–1961: when asked what he
   meant by 'guts' in an interview with Dorothy Parker; in
   New Yorker 30 November 1929

4 There are those who never stretch out the hand for fear it will be bitten. But those who never stretch out the hand will never feel it clasped in friendship.

Michael Heseltine 1933– : *Where There's a Will* (1987)

5 Tender-handed stroke a nettle,
And it stings you for your pains;
Grasp it like a man of mettle,
And it soft as silk remains.

Aaron Hill 1685–1750: 'Verses Written on a Window in Scotland'

6 The brave man inattentive to his duty, is worth little more to his country, than the coward who deserts her in the hour of danger.

Andrew Jackson 1767–1845: to troops who had abandoned their lines during the battle of New Orleans, 8 January 1815; attributed

7 Courage is not simply *one* of the virtues but the form of every virtue at the testing point.

C. S. Lewis 1898–1963: Cyril Connolly *The Unquiet Grave* (1944)

8 As to moral courage, I have very rarely met with two o'clock in the morning courage: I mean instantaneous courage.

Napoleon I 1769–1821: E. A. de Las Cases *Mémorial de Ste-Hélène* (1823) 4–5 December 1815

9 All men would be cowards if they durst.

John Wilmot, Earl of Rochester 1647–80: 'A Satire against Mankind' (1679)

10 Cowards die many times before their deaths;
The valiant never taste of death but once.

William Shakespeare 1564–1616: *Julius Caesar* (1599)

11 *Audentis Fortuna iuvat.*

Fortune assists the bold.

Virgil 70–19 BC: *Aeneid*; often quoted 'Fortune favours the brave'

Crime and Punishment

See also **Justice**, **The Law and Lawyers**, **Murder**

1 As for rioting, the old Roman way of dealing with that is always the right one; flog the rank and file, and fling the ringleaders from the Tarpeian rock.
   Thomas Arnold 1795–1842: from a letter written before 1828

2 All punishment is mischief: all punishment in itself is evil.
   Jeremy Bentham 1748–1832: *Principles of Morals and Legislation* (1789)

3 My father hath chastised you with whips, but I will chastise you with scorpions.
   Bible: I Kings

4 He that spareth his rod hateth his son.
   Bible: Proverbs

5 Labour is the party of law and order in Britain today. Tough on crime and tough on the causes of crime.
   Tony Blair 1953– : speech at the Labour Party Conference, 30 September 1993

6 Once in the racket you're always in it.
   Al Capone 1899–1947: in *Philadelphia Public Ledger* 18 May 1929

7 Crime isn't a disease, it's a symptom. Cops are like a doctor that gives you aspirin for a brain tumour.
   Raymond Chandler 1888–1959: *The Long Good-Bye* (1953)

8 Thieves respect property. They merely wish the property to become their property that they may more perfectly respect it.
   G. K. Chesterton 1874–1936: *The Man who was Thursday* (1908)

9 Thou shalt not steal; an empty feat,
   When it's so lucrative to cheat.
   Arthur Hugh Clough 1819–61: 'The Latest Decalogue' (1862)

10 Excessive bail shall not be required, nor excessive fines
imposed, nor cruel and unusual punishment inflicted.
Constitution of the United States 1787: *Eighth
Amendment* (1791)

11 Singularity is almost invariably a clue. The more
featureless and commonplace a crime is, the more difficult
is it to bring it home.
Arthur Conan Doyle 1859–1930: *Adventures of Sherlock
Holmes* (1892)

12 Punishment is not for revenge, but to lessen crime and
reform the criminal.
Elizabeth Fry 1780–1845: Rachel E. Cresswell and
Katharine Fry *Memoir of the Life of Elizabeth Fry* (1848)

13 Whenever the offence inspires less horror than the
punishment, the rigour of penal law is obliged to give way
to the common feelings of mankind.
Edward Gibbon 1737–94: attributed

14 My object all sublime
I shall achieve in time—
To let the punishment fit the crime—
The punishment fit the crime.
W. S. Gilbert 1836–1911: *The Mikado* (1885)

15 Awaiting the sensation of a short, sharp shock,
From a cheap and chippy chopper on a big black block.
W. S. Gilbert 1836–1911: *The Mikado* (1885)

16 Men are not hanged for stealing horses, but that horses
may not be stolen.
George Savile, Marquess of Halifax 1633–95: *Political,
Moral, and Miscellaneous Thoughts* (1750)

17 This is the first of punishments, that no guilty man is
acquitted if judged by himself.
Juvenal AD *c.*60–*c.*130: *Satires*

18 In that case, if we are to abolish the death penalty, let the
murderers take the first step.
Alphonse Karr 1808–90: *Les Guêpes* January 1849

19 Society needs to condemn a little more and understand a little less.

> **John Major** 1943– : in *Mail on Sunday* 21 February 1993

20 For de little stealin' dey gits you in jail soon or late. For de big stealin' dey makes you Emperor and puts you in de Hall o' Fame when you croaks.

> **Eugene O'Neill** 1888–1953: *The Emperor Jones* (1921)

21 I went out to Charing Cross, to see Major-general Harrison hanged, drawn, and quartered; which was done there, he looking as cheerful as any man could do in that condition.

> **Samuel Pepys** 1633–1703: diary, 13 October 1660

22 A clever theft was praiseworthy amongst the Spartans; and it is equally so amongst Christians, provided it be on a sufficiently large scale.

> **Herbert Spencer** 1820–1903: *Social Statics* (1850)

23 A child, punished by selfish parents, does not feel anger. It goes to its little private corner to weep.

> **Rose Tremain** 1943– : *Restoration* (1989)

24 Any one who has been to an English public school will always feel comparatively at home in prison. It is the people brought up in the gay intimacy of the slums, Paul learned, who find prison so soul-destroying.

> **Evelyn Waugh** 1903–66: *Decline and Fall* (1928)

Crises

1 Comin' in on a wing and a pray'r.

> **Harold Adamson** 1906–80: title of song (1943)

2 Crisis? What Crisis?

> **Anonymous**: *Sun* headline, 11 January 1979, summarizing James Callaghan: 'I don't think other people in the world would share the view [that] there is mounting chaos'

3 We do not experience and thus we have no measure of the disasters we prevent.

> **J. K. Galbraith** 1908– : *A Life in our Times* (1981)

4 Swimming for his life, a man does not see much of the
country through which the river winds.
  W. E. Gladstone 1809–98: diary, 31 December 1868

5 The illustrious bishop of Cambrai was of more worth than
his chambermaid, and there are few of us that would
hesitate to pronounce, if his palace were in flames, and the
life of only one of them could be preserved, which of the
two ought to be preferred.
  William Godwin 1756–1836: *An Enquiry concerning the
  Principles of Political Justice* (1793)

6 For it is your business, when the wall next door catches
fire.
  Horace 65–8 BC: *Epistles*

7 If you can keep your head when all about you
Are losing theirs and blaming it on you.
  Rudyard Kipling 1865–1936: 'If—' (1910)

8 We're eyeball to eyeball, and I think the other fellow just
blinked.
  Dean Rusk 1909– : on the Cuban missile crisis, 24
  October 1962

9 I myself have always deprecated . . . in crisis after crisis,
appeals to the Dunkirk spirit as an answer to our
problems.
  Harold Wilson 1916–95: in the House of Commons, 26
  July 1961

10 I'm at my best in a messy, middle-of-the-road muddle.
  Harold Wilson 1916–95: remark in Cabinet, 21 January
  1975

Critics and Criticism

1 A man must serve his time to every trade
Save censure—critics all are ready made.
  Lord Byron 1788–1824: *English Bards and Scotch
  Reviewers* (1809)

2 Whom the gods wish to destroy they first call promising.
  Cyril Connolly 1903–74: *Enemies of Promise* (1938)

3 *Il n'y a pas de hors-texte.*

There is nothing outside of the text.
    Jacques Derrida 1930– : *Of Grammatology* (1967)

4 Everything must be like something, so what is this like?
    E. M. Forster 1879–1970: *Abinger Harvest* (1936)

5 Parodies and caricatures are the most penetrating of
criticisms.
    Aldous Huxley 1894–1963: *Point Counter Point* (1928)

6 I don't care anything about reasons, but I know what I
like.
    Henry James 1843–1916: *Portrait of a Lady* (1881)

7 This will never do.
    Francis, Lord Jeffrey 1773–1850: on Wordsworth's *The
Excursion* (1814) in *Edinburgh Review* November 1814

8 You *may* abuse a tragedy, though you cannot write one.
You may scold a carpenter who has made you a bad table,
though you cannot make a table. It is not your trade to
make tables.
    Samuel Johnson 1709–84: on literary criticism; James
Boswell *Life of Johnson* (1791) 25 June 1763

9 I cry all the way to the bank.
    Liberace 1919–87: on bad reviews, from the mid-1950s;
Autobiography (1973)

10 People who like this sort of thing will find this the sort of
thing they like.
    Abraham Lincoln 1809–65: judgement of a book, in G. W.
E. Russell *Collections and Recollections* (1898)

11 One should look long and carefully at oneself before one
considers judging others.
    Molière 1622–73: *Le Misanthrope* (1666)

12 I am sitting in the smallest room of my house. I have your
review before me. In a moment it will be behind me.
    Max Reger 1873–1916: responding to a savage review by
Rudolph Louis in *Münchener Neueste Nachrichten*, 7
February 1906

13 Remember, a statue has never been set up in honour of a critic!

    Jean Sibelius 1865–1957: B. de Törne *Sibelius: A Close-Up* (1937)

14 I never read a book before reviewing it; it prejudices a man so.

    Sydney Smith 1771–1845: H. Pearson *The Smith of Smiths* (1934)

15 Interpretation is the revenge of the intellect upon art.

    Susan Sontag 1933– : in *Evergreen Review* December 1964

16 As learned commentators view
In Homer more than Homer knew.

    Jonathan Swift 1667–1745: 'On Poetry' (1733)

17 A critic is a man who knows the way but can't drive the car.

    Kenneth Tynan 1927–80: in *New York Times Magazine* 9 January 1966

18 I maintain that two and two would continue to make four, in spite of the whine of the amateur for three, or the cry of the critic for five.

    James McNeill Whistler 1834–1903: *Whistler v. Ruskin. Art and Art Critics* (1878)

19 How science dwindles, and how volumes swell,
How commentators each dark passage shun,
And hold their farthing candle to the sun.

    Edward Young 1683–1765: *The Love of Fame* (1725–8)

....

Cruelty
....

1 Boys throw stones at frogs for fun, but the frogs don't die for 'fun', but in sober earnest.

    Bion *c.*325–*c.*255 BC: Plutarch *Moralia*

2 A robin red breast in a cage
Puts all Heaven in a rage.

    William Blake 1757–1827: 'Auguries of Innocence' (*c.*1803)

3 The wish to hurt, the momentary intoxication with pain, is the loophole through which the pervert climbs into the minds of ordinary men.
  Jacob Bronowski 1908–74: *The Face of Violence* (1954)

4 Man's inhumanity to man
Makes countless thousands mourn!
  Robert Burns 1759–96: 'Man was made to Mourn' (1786)

5 Our language lacks words to express this offence, the demolition of a man.
  Primo Levi 1919–87: of a year spent in Auschwitz; *If This is a Man* (1958)

6 Death may be inevitable but cruelty is not. If we must eat meat, then we must ensure that the animals we kill for our food live the best possible lives before they die.
  Desmond Morris 1928– : *The Animal Contract* (1990)

7 The infliction of cruelty with a good conscience is a delight to moralists. That is why they invented Hell.
  Bertrand Russell 1872–1970: *Sceptical Essays* (1928)

8 I must be cruel only to be kind.
  William Shakespeare 1564–1616: *Hamlet* (1601)

9 This was the most unkindest cut of all.
  William Shakespeare 1564–1616: *Julius Caesar* (1599)

Custom and Habit

1 One can't carry one's father's corpse about everywhere.
  Guillaume Apollinaire 1880–1918: on tradition, in *Les peintres cubistes* (1965)

2 Habit is a great deadener.
  Samuel Beckett 1906–89: *Waiting for Godot* (1955)

3 Custom reconciles us to everything.
  Edmund Burke 1729–97: *On the Sublime and Beautiful* (1757)

4 Tradition means giving votes to the most obscure of all classes, our ancestors. It is the democracy of the dead.
  G. K. Chesterton 1874–1936: *Orthodoxy* (1908)

5 Habit with him was all the test of truth,
  'It must be right: I've done it from my youth.'
  George Crabbe 1754–1832: *The Borough* (1810)

6 Actions receive their tincture from the times,
  And as they change are virtues made or crimes.
  Daniel Defoe 1660–1731: *A Hymn to the Pillory* (1703)

7 Custom, then, is the great guide of human life.
  David Hume 1711–76: *An Enquiry Concerning Human Understanding* (1748)

8 The tradition of all the dead generations weighs like a nightmare on the brain of the living.
  Karl Marx 1818–83: *The Eighteenth Brumaire of Louis Bonaparte* (1852)

9 Sow an act, and you reap a habit. Sow a habit and you reap a character. Sow a character, and you reap a destiny.
  Charles Reade 1814–84: attributed

10 But to my mind,—though I am native here,
   And to the manner born,—it is a custom
   More honoured in the breach than the observance.
   William Shakespeare 1564–1616: *Hamlet* (1601)

Cynicism

1 Kill them all; God will recognize his own.
  Arnald-Amaury d. 1225: when asked how the true Catholics could be distinguished from the heretics at the massacre of Béziers, 1209; Jonathan Sumption *The Albigensian Crusade* (1978)

2 Never glad confident morning again!
  Robert Browning 1812–89: 'The Lost Leader' (1845)

3 What makes all doctrines plain and clear?
  About two hundred pounds a year.
  And that which was proved true before,
  Prove false again? Two hundred more.
  Samuel Butler 1612–80: *Hudibras* pt. 3 (1680)

4 To get practice in being refused.
   Diogenes 404–323 BC: reply when asked why he was
   begging for alms from a statue; Diogenes Laertius *Lives
   of the Philosophers*

5 Pathos, piety, courage—they exist, but are identical, and so
   is filth. Everything exists, nothing has value.
   E. M. Forster 1879–1970: *A Passage to India* (1924)

6 Cynicism is an unpleasant way of saying the truth.
   Lillian Hellman 1905–84: *The Little Foxes* (1939)

7 Paris is well worth a mass.
   Henri IV 1553–1610: attributed to Henri IV; alternatively
   to his minister Sully, in conversation with him

8 A man who knows the price of everything and the value of
   nothing.
   Oscar Wilde 1854–1900: definition of a cynic; *Lady
   Windermere's Fan* (1892)

Dance

1 A dance is a measured pace, as a verse is a measured
   speech.
   Francis Bacon 1561–1626: *The Advancement of Learning*
   (1605)

2 There may be trouble ahead,
   But while there's moonlight and music and love and
      romance,
   Let's face the music and dance.
   Irving Berlin 1888–1989: 'Let's Face the Music and
   Dance' (1936 song)

3 On with the dance! let joy be unconfined;
   No sleep till morn, when Youth and Pleasure meet
   To chase the glowing Hours with flying feet.
   Lord Byron 1788–1824: *Childe Harold's Pilgrimage*
   (1812–18)

4 This wondrous miracle did Love devise,
For dancing is love's proper exercise.
Sir John Davies 1569–1626: 'Orchestra, or a Poem of
Dancing' (1596)

5 The truest expression of a people is in its dances and its
music. Bodies never lie.
Agnes de Mille 1908– : in *New York Times Magazine*
11 May 1975

6 Dance is the hidden language of the soul.
Martha Graham 1894–1991: *Blood Memory* (1991)

7 Sport that wrinkled Care derides,
And Laughter holding both his sides.
Come, and trip it as ye go
On the light fantastic toe.
John Milton 1608–74: 'L'Allegro' (1645)

8 [Dancing is] a perpendicular expression of a horizontal
desire.
George Bernard Shaw 1856–1950: in *New Statesman*
23 March 1962 (attributed)

9 Everyone knows that the real business of a ball is either to
look out for a wife, to look after a wife, or to look after
somebody else's wife.
R. S. Surtees 1805–64: *Mr Facey Romford's Hounds*
(1865)

Day and Night

1 Lighten our darkness, we beseech thee, O Lord; and by thy
great mercy defend us from all perils and dangers of this
night.
Book of Common Prayer 1662: *Evening Prayer*

2 The Sun's rim dips; the stars rush out;
At one stride comes the dark.
Samuel Taylor Coleridge 1772–1834: 'The Rime of the
Ancient Mariner' (1798)

3 Let us go then, you and I,
When the evening is spread out against the sky

Like a patient etherized upon a table.
   T. S. Eliot 1888–1965: 'Love Song of J. Alfred Prufrock'
   (1917)

4 The curfew tolls the knell of parting day,
The lowing herd wind slowly o'er the lea,
The ploughman homeward plods his weary way,
And leaves the world to darkness and to me.
   Thomas Gray 1716–71: *Elegy Written in a Country
   Churchyard* (1751)

5 Summer afternoon—summer afternoon . . . the two most
beautiful words in the English language.
   Henry James 1843–1916: Edith Wharton *A Backward
   Glance* (1934)

6 What are days for?
Days are where we live.
   Philip Larkin 1922–85: 'Days' (1964)

7 The cares that infest the day
Shall fold their tents, like the Arabs,
And as silently steal away.
   Henry Wadsworth Longfellow 1807–82: 'The Day is
   Done' (1844)

8 I have a horror of sunsets, they're so romantic, so operatic.
   Marcel Proust 1871–1922: *Cities of the Plain* (1922)

9 Night's candles are burnt out, and jocund day
Stands tiptoe on the misty mountain tops.
   William Shakespeare 1564–1616: *Romeo and Juliet*
   (1595)

10 The splendour falls on castle walls
And snowy summits old in story:
The long light shakes across the lakes,
And the wild cataract leaps in glory.
   Alfred, Lord Tennyson 1809–92: *The Princess* (1847)
   song (added 1850)

11 There midnight's all a glimmer, and noon a purple glow,
And evening full of the linnet's wings.
   W. B. Yeats 1865–1939: 'The Lake Isle of Innisfree' (1892)

Death

See also **Epitaphs**, **Last Words**, **Murder**

1 It's not that I'm afraid to die. I just don't want to be there when it happens.
  Woody Allen 1935– : *Death* (1975)

2 Death has got something to be said for it:
There's no need to get out of bed for it.
  Kingsley Amis 1922–95: 'Delivery Guaranteed' (1979)

3 Do not stand at my grave and weep:
I am not there. I do not sleep.
I am a thousand winds that blow.
I am the diamond glints on snow . . .
Do not stand at my grave and cry;
I am not there, I did not die.
  Anonymous: quoted in letter left by British soldier Stephen Cummins when killed by the IRA, March 1989; origin uncertain, attributed to various authors

4 He was my North, my South, my East and West,
My working week and my Sunday rest,
My noon, my midnight, my talk, my song;
I thought that love would last for ever: I was wrong.
  W. H. Auden 1907–73: 'Funeral Blues' (1936)

5 Revenge triumphs over death; love slights it; honour aspireth to it; grief flieth to it.
  Francis Bacon 1561–1626: *Essays* (1625) 'Of Death'

6 To die will be an awfully big adventure.
  J. M. Barrie 1860–1937: *Peter Pan* (1928)

7 Even death is unreliable: instead of zero it may be some ghastly hallucination, such as the square root of minus one.
  Samuel Beckett 1906–89: attributed

8 For dust thou art, and unto dust shalt thou return.
  Bible: Genesis

9 O death, where is thy sting? O grave, where is thy victory?
Bible: I Corinthians

10 In the midst of life we are in death.
Book of Common Prayer 1662: *The Burial of the Dead*

11 Forasmuch as it hath pleased Almighty God of his great
mercy to take unto himself the soul of our dear brother
here departed, we therefore commit his body to the
ground; earth to earth, ashes to ashes, dust to dust; in sure
and certain hope of the Resurrection to eternal life.
Book of Common Prayer 1662: *The Burial of the Dead*

12 If I should die, think only this of me:
That there's some corner of a foreign field
That is for ever England.
Rupert Brooke 1887–1915: 'The Soldier' (1914)

13 He shouts play death more sweetly this Death is a master
from Deutschland.
Paul Celan 1920–70: 'Deathfugue' (written 1944)

14 This parrot is no more! It has ceased to be! It's expired and
gone to meet its maker! This is a late parrot! It's a stiff!
Bereft of life it rests in peace—if you hadn't nailed it to the
perch it would be pushing up the daisies! It's rung down
the curtain and joined the choir invisible! THIS IS AN
EX–PARROT!
Graham Chapman 1941–89 et al.: *Monty Python's Flying
Circus* (BBC TV programme, 1969)

15 However many ways there may be of being alive, it is
certain that there are vastly more ways of being dead.
Richard Dawkins 1941– : *The Blind Watchmaker* (1986)

16 Any man's death diminishes me, because I am involved in
Mankind; And therefore never send to know for whom the
bell tolls; it tolls for thee.
John Donne 1572–1631: *Devotions upon Emergent
Occasions* (1624)

17 Death be not proud, though some have called thee
Mighty and dreadful, for thou art not so.
John Donne 1572–1631: 'Death, be not proud' (1609)

18 The bodies of those that made such a noise and tumult
when alive, when dead, lie as quietly among the graves of
their neighbours as any others.
  Jonathan Edwards 1703–58: *Miscellaneous Discourses*

19 Webster was much possessed by death
And saw the skull beneath the skin.
  T. S. Eliot 1888–1965: 'Whispers of Immortality' (1919)

20 Death, therefore, the most awful of evils, is nothing to us,
seeing that, when we are death is not come, and when
death is come, we are not.
  Epicurus 341–271 BC: Diogenes Laertius *Lives of Eminent
  Philosophers*

21 Death is nothing if one can approach it as such. I was just
a tiny night-light, suffocated in its own wax, and on the
point of expiring.
  E. M. Forster 1879–1970: Philip Gardner (ed.) *E. M.
  Forster: Commonplace Book* (1985)

22 Death is nothing at all; it does not count. I have only
slipped away into the next room.
  Henry Scott Holland 1847–1918: sermon preached on
  Whitsunday, 1910

23 I would rather be tied to the soil as another man's serf,
even a poor man's, who hadn't much to live on himself,
than be King of all these the dead and destroyed.
  Homer 8th century BC: *The Odyssey*

24 *Non omnis moriar.*
  I shall not altogether die.
  Horace 65–8 BC: *Odes*

25 Depend upon it, Sir, when a man knows he is to be hanged
in a fortnight, it concentrates his mind wonderfully.
  Samuel Johnson 1709–84: James Boswell *Life of
  Johnson* (1791) 19 September 1777

26 Now more than ever seems it rich to die,
To cease upon the midnight with no pain.
  John Keats 1795–1821: 'Ode to a Nightingale' (1820)

27 A man's dying is more the survivors' affair than his own.
   Thomas Mann 1875–1955: *The Magic Mountain* (1924), tr.
   H. T. Lowe-Porter

28 Let me die a youngman's death
   Not a clean & in-between-
   The-sheets, holy-water death.
   Roger McGough 1937– : 'Let Me Die a Youngman's
   Death' (1967)

29 A suicide kills two people, Maggie, that's what it's for!
   Arthur Miller 1915– : *After the Fall* (1964)

30 And all our calm is in that balm—
   Not lost but gone before.
   Caroline Norton 1808–77: 'Not Lost but Gone Before'.

31 Guns aren't lawful;
   Nooses give;
   Gas smells awful;
   You might as well live.
   Dorothy Parker 1893–1967: 'Résumé' (1937)

32 We shall die alone.
   Blaise Pascal 1623–62: *Pensées* (1670)

33 *Abiit ad plures.*
   He's gone to join the majority [the dead].
   Petronius d. AD 65: *Satyricon*

34 'Tis a sharp remedy, but a sure one for all ills.
   Walter Ralegh c.1552–1618: on feeling the edge of the
   axe prior to his execution

35 Anyone can stop a man's life, but no one his death; a
   thousand doors open on to it.
   Seneca ('the Younger') c.4 BC–AD 65: *Phoenissae*

36   Nothing in his life
   Became him like the leaving it.
   William Shakespeare 1564–1616: *Macbeth* (1606)

37 I care not; a man can die but once; we owe God a death.
   William Shakespeare 1564–1616: *Henry IV, Part 2* (1597)

38   To die, to sleep;
To sleep: perchance to dream: ay, there's the rub;
For in that sleep of death what dreams may come
When we have shuffled off this mortal coil,
Must give us pause.
      William Shakespeare 1564–1616: *Hamlet* (1601)

39 Death must be distinguished from dying, with which it is
often confused.
      Sydney Smith 1771–1845: H. Pearson *The Smith of
      Smiths* (1934)

40 If there wasn't death, I think you couldn't go on.
      Stevie Smith 1902–71: in *Observer* 9 November 1969

41 One death is a tragedy, a million deaths a statistic.
      Joseph Stalin 1879–1953: attributed

42 For though from out our bourne of time and place
The flood may bear me far,
I hope to see my pilot face to face
When I have crossed the bar.
      Alfred, Lord Tennyson 1809–92: 'Crossing the Bar'
      (1889)

43 Though lovers be lost love shall not;
And death shall have no dominion.
      Dylan Thomas 1914–53: 'And death shall have no
      dominion' (1936)

44 I know death hath ten thousand several doors
For men to take their exits.
      John Webster *c.*1580–*c.*1625: *The Duchess of Malfi* (1623)

45   The good die first,
And they whose hearts are dry as summer dust
Burn to the socket.
      William Wordsworth 1770–1850: *The Excursion* (1814)

46 Nor dread nor hope attend
A dying animal;
A man awaits his end

Dreading and hoping all.
W. B. Yeats 1865–1939: 'Death' (1933)

....

Democracy
....

See also **Minorities and Majorities**, **Politics**,
Voting

1 After each war there is a little less democracy to save.
Brooks Atkinson 1894–1984: *Once Around the Sun* (1951)

2 Democracy means government by discussion, but it is only
effective if you can stop people talking.
Clement Attlee 1883–1967: speech at Oxford, 14 June
1957

3 One man shall have one vote.
John Cartwright 1740–1824: *The People's Barrier
Against Undue Influence* (1780)

4 Democracy is the worst form of Government except all
those other forms that have been tried from time to time.
Winston Churchill 1874–1965: speech, House of
Commons, 11 November 1947

5 So Two cheers for Democracy: one because it admits
variety and two because it permits criticism. Two cheers
are quite enough: there is no occasion to give three. Only
Love the Beloved Republic deserves that.
E. M. Forster 1879–1970: *Two Cheers for Democracy*
(1951) 'Love, the beloved republic' borrowed from
Swinburne's poem 'Hertha'

6 All the world over, I will back the masses against the
classes.
W. E. Gladstone 1809–98: speech in Liverpool, 28 June
1886

7 No, Democracy is *not* identical with majority rule.
Democracy is a *State* which recognizes the subjection of
the minority to the majority, that is, an organization for
the systematic use of *force* by one class against the other,

by one part of the population against another.
Lenin 1870–1924: *State and Revolution* (1919)

8 We here highly resolve that the dead shall not have died in
vain, that this nation, under God, shall have a new birth of
freedom; and that government of the people, by the people,
and for the people, shall not perish from the earth.
Abraham Lincoln 1809–65: address at the Dedication of
the National Cemetery at Gettysburg, 19 November 1863;
the Lincoln Memorial inscription reads 'by the people,
for the people'

9 Man's capacity for justice makes democracy possible, but
man's inclination to injustice makes democracy necessary.
Reinhold Niebuhr 1892–1971: *Children of Light and
Children of Darkness* (1944)

10 I never could believe that Providence had sent a few men
into the world, ready booted and spurred to ride, and
millions ready saddled and bridled to be ridden.
Richard Rumbold *c.*1622–85: on the scaffold, in T. B.
Macaulay *History of England* vol. 1 (1849)

11 Democracy substitutes election by the incompetent many
for appointment by the corrupt few.
George Bernard Shaw 1856–1950: *Man and Superman*
(1903)

12 If one must serve, I hold it better to serve a well-bred lion,
who is naturally stronger than I am, than two hundred
rats of my own breed.
Voltaire 1694–1778: letter to a friend; Alexis de
Tocqueville *The Ancien Régime* (1856)

13 The world must be made safe for democracy.
Woodrow Wilson 1856–1924: speech to Congress, 2 April
1917

Despair

see **Hope and Despair**

Determination

1 Thought shall be the harder, heart the keener, courage the greater, as our might lessens.

Anonymous: *The Battle of Maldon* (c.1000), tr. R. K. Gordon

2 *Nil carborundum illegitimi.*

Anonymous: cod Latin for 'Don't let the bastards grind you down', in circulation during the Second World War, though possibly of earlier origin

3 I was ever a fighter, so—one fight more,
The best and the last!
I would hate that death bandaged my eyes, and forbore,
And bade me creep past.

Robert Browning 1812–89: 'Prospice' (1864)

4 Obstinacy, Sir, is certainly a great vice . . . It happens, however, very unfortunately, that almost the whole line of the great and masculine virtues, constancy, gravity, magnanimity, fortitude, fidelity, and firmness are closely allied to this disagreeable quality.

Edmund Burke 1729–97: *On American Taxation* (1775)

5 I will fight for what I believe in until I drop dead. And that's what keeps you alive.

Barbara Castle 1910– : in *Guardian* 14 January 1998

6 Say not the struggle naught availeth,
The labour and the wounds are vain,
The enemy faints not, nor faileth,
And as things have been, things remain.

Arthur Hugh Clough 1819–61: 'Say not the struggle naught availeth' (1855)

7 Nothing in the world can take the place of persistence. Talent will not; nothing is more common than unsuccessful men with talent. Genius will not; unrewarded genius is almost a proverb. Education will not; the world is full of educated derelicts. Persistence and determination are omnipotent. The slogan 'press on' has solved and

always will solve the problems of the human race.
Calvin Coolidge 1872–1933: attributed, 1933

8 Pick yourself up,
Dust yourself off,
Start all over again.
Dorothy Fields 1905–74: 'Pick Yourself Up' (1936 song)

9 The best way out is always through.
Robert Frost 1874–1963: 'A Servant to Servants' (1914)

10 Under the bludgeonings of chance
My head is bloody, but unbowed.
W. E. Henley 1849–1903: 'Invictus. In Memoriam
R.T.H.B.' (1888)

11 When the going gets tough, the tough get going.
Joseph P. Kennedy 1888–1969: J. H. Cutler *Honey Fitz*
(1962); also attributed to Knute Rockne

12 The drop of rain maketh a hole in the stone, not by
violence, but by oft falling.
Hugh Latimer c.1485–1555: *Second Sermon preached
before the King's Majesty* (19 April 1549)

13 Perseverance, dear my lord,
Keeps honour bright.
William Shakespeare 1564–1616: *Troilus and Cressida*
(1602)

14 One man that has a mind and knows it can always beat ten
men who haven't and don't.
George Bernard Shaw 1856–1950: *The Apple Cart* (1930)

15 'Tis known by the name of perseverance in a good cause,—
and of obstinacy in a bad one.
Laurence Sterne 1713–68: *Tristram Shandy* (1759–67)

16 That which we are, we are;
One equal temper of heroic hearts,
Made weak by time and fate, but strong in will
To strive, to seek, to find, and not to yield.
Alfred, Lord Tennyson 1809–92: 'Ulysses' (1842)

17 What is the victory of a cat on a hot tin roof?—I wish I knew . . . Just staying on it, I guess, as long as she can.
   Tennessee Williams 1911–83: *Cat on a Hot Tin Roof* (1955)

Diaries

1 What is more dull than a discreet diary? One might just as well have a discreet soul.
   Henry 'Chips' Channon 1897–1958: diary, 26 July 1935

2 I want to go on living even after death!
   Anne Frank 1929–45: diary, 4 April 1944

3 To be a good diarist one must have a little snouty, sneaky mind.
   Harold Nicolson 1886–1968: diary, 9 November 1947

4 One need not write in a diary what one is to remember for ever.
   Sylvia Townsend Warner 1893–1978: diary, 22 October 1930

5 I always say, keep a diary and some day it'll keep you.
   Mae West 1892–1980: *Every Day's a Holiday* (1937 film)

6 I never travel without my diary. One should always have something sensational to read in the train.
   Oscar Wilde 1854–1900: *The Importance of Being Earnest* (1895)

Diplomacy

1 In things that are tender and unpleasing, it is good to break the ice by some whose words are of less weight, and to reserve the more weighty voice to come in as by chance.
   Francis Bacon 1561–1626: *Essays* (1625) 'Of Cunning'

2 To jaw-jaw is always better than to war-war.
   Winston Churchill 1874–1965: speech at White House, 26 June 1954

3 Treaties, you see, are like girls and roses: they last while
they last.
  Charles de Gaulle 1890–1970: speech at Elysée Palace,
  2 July 1963

4 I feel happier now that we have no allies to be polite to and
to pamper.
  George VI 1895–1952: to Queen Mary, 27 June 1940

5 Let us never negotiate out of fear. But let us never fear to
negotiate.
  John F. Kennedy 1917–63: inaugural address, 20
  January 1961

6 Negotiating with de Valera . . . is like trying to pick up
mercury with a fork.
  David Lloyd George 1863–1945: to which de Valera
  replied, 'Why doesn't he use a spoon?'; in M. J.
  MacManus *Eamon de Valera* (1944)

7 One of the things I learnt when I was negotiating was that
until I changed myself I could not change others.
  Nelson Mandela 1918– : in *Sunday Times* 16 April 2000

8 We are prepared to go to the gates of Hell—but no further.
  Pope Pius VII 1742–1823: attempting to reach an
  agreement with Napoleon, *c.*1800–1

9 I'm afraid you've got a bad egg, Mr Jones.
Oh no, my Lord, I assure you! Parts of it are excellent!
  Punch: 1895

10 Speak softly and carry a big stick; you will go far.
  Theodore Roosevelt 1858–1919: speech, 3 April 1903
  (quoting an 'old adage')

11 By indirections find directions out.
  William Shakespeare 1564–1616: *Hamlet* (1601)

12 An ambassador is an honest man sent to lie abroad for the
good of his country.
  Henry Wotton 1568–1639: written in the album of
  Christopher Fleckmore in 1604

Discontent

see **Satisfaction and Discontent**

Discoveries

see **Inventions and Discoveries**

Dogs

See also **Animals**

1 The great pleasure of a dog is that you may make a fool of yourself with him and not only will he not scold you, but he will make a fool of himself too.
   Samuel Butler 1835–1902: *Notebooks* (1912)

2 Near this spot are deposited the remains of one who possessed beauty without vanity, strength without insolence, courage without ferocity, and all the virtues of Man, without his vices.
   Lord Byron 1788–1824: 'Inscription on the Monument of a Newfoundland Dog' (1808)

3 A door is what a dog is perpetually on the wrong side of.
   Ogden Nash 1902–71: 'A Dog's Best Friend is his Illiteracy' (1953)

4 I am his Highness' dog at Kew;
   Pray, tell me sir, whose dog are you?
   Alexander Pope 1688–1744: 'Epigram Engraved on the Collar of a Dog which I gave to his Royal Highness' (1738)

5 That indefatigable and unsavoury engine of pollution, the dog.
   John Sparrow 1906–92: letter to *The Times* 30 September 1975

6 The more one gets to know of men, the more one values dogs.
  A. Toussenel 1803–85: *L'Esprit des bêtes* (1847), attributed to Mme Roland in the form 'The more I see of men, the more I like dogs'

Doubt

see **Certainty and Doubt**

Drawing

see **Painting and Drawing**

Dreams

see **Sleep and Dreams**

Dress

1 It is totally impossible to be well dressed in cheap shoes.
  Hardy Amies 1909– : *The Englishman's Suit* (1994)

2 From the cradle to the grave, underwear first, last and all the time.
  Bertolt Brecht 1898–1956: *The Threepenny Opera* (1928)

3 No perfumes, but very fine linen, plenty of it, and country washing.
  Beau Brummell 1778–1840: *Memoirs of Harriette Wilson* (1825)

4 The sense of being well-dressed gives a feeling of inward tranquillity which religion is powerless to bestow.
  Miss C. F. Forbes 1817–1911: R. W. Emerson *Letters and Social Aims* (1876)

5 A sweet disorder in the dress
Kindles in clothes a wantonness.
Robert Herrick 1591–1674: 'Delight in Disorder' (1648)

6 You should never have your best trousers on when you go
out to fight for freedom and truth.
Henrik Ibsen 1828–1906: *An Enemy of the People* (1882)

7 Haute Couture should be fun, foolish and almost
unwearable.
Christian Lacroix 1951– : in *Observer* 27 December 1987

8 Men seldom make passes
At girls who wear glasses.
Dorothy Parker 1893–1967: 'News Item' (1937)

9 His socks compelled one's attention without losing one's
respect.
Saki (H. H. Munro) 1870–1916: *Chronicles of Clovis* (1911)

10 The apparel oft proclaims the man.
William Shakespeare 1564–1616: *Hamlet* (1601)

11 Beware of all enterprises that require new clothes.
Henry David Thoreau 1817–62: *Walden* (1854) 'Economy'

Drink

see **Food and Drink**

Drugs

1 Death is the final penalty, but the life of a sportsman on
drugs is a perpetual living penalty because he is offending
against himself.
Christopher Brasher : in *Observer* 11 June 1978

2 I'll die young, but it's like kissing God.
Lenny Bruce 1925–66: on his drug addiction; attributed

3 Junk is the ideal product . . . the ultimate merchandise. No
  sales talk necessary. The client will crawl through a sewer
  and beg to buy.
  William S. Burroughs 1914–97: *The Naked Lunch* (1959)

4 I experimented with marijuana a time or two. And I didn't
  like it, and I didn't inhale.
  Bill Clinton 1946– : in *Washington Post* 30 March 1992

5 Thou hast the keys of Paradise, oh just, subtle, and mighty
  opium!
  Thomas De Quincey 1785–1859: *Confessions of an
  English Opium Eater* (1822)

6 Drugs is like getting up and having a cup of tea in the
  morning.
  Noel Gallagher 1967– : radio interview, 28 January 1997

7 In this country, don't forget, a habit is no damn private
  hell. There's no solitary confinement outside of jail. A
  habit is hell for those you love.
  Billie Holiday 1915–59: *Lady Sings the Blues* (1956, with
  William F. Duffy)

8 Every form of addiction is bad, no matter whether the
  narcotic be alcohol or morphine or idealism.
  Carl Gustav Jung 1875–1961: *Erinnerungen, Träume,
  Gedanken* (1962)

9 Sure thing, man. I used to be a laboratory myself once.
  Keith Richards 1943– : on being asked to autograph a
  fan's school chemistry book; in *Independent on Sunday*
  7 August 1994

Economics

1 There's no such thing as a free lunch.
  Anonymous: colloquial axiom in US economics from the
  1960s, much associated with Milton Friedman; first found
  in printed form in Robert Heinlein *The Moon is a Harsh
  Mistress* (1966)

2 There is enough in the world for everyone's need, but not enough for everyone's greed.
   Frank Buchman 1878–1961: *Remaking the World* (1947)

3 Capitalism is using its money; we socialists throw it away.
   Fidel Castro 1927– : in *Observer* 8 November 1964

4 Inflation is the one form of taxation that can be imposed without legislation.
   Milton Friedman 1912– : in *Observer* 22 September 1974

5 Trickle-down theory—the less than elegant metaphor that if one feeds the horse enough oats, some will pass through to the road for the sparrows.
   J. K. Galbraith 1908– : *The Culture of Contentment* (1992)

6 Finance is, as it were, the stomach of the country, from which all the other organs take their tone.
   W. E. Gladstone 1809–98: article on finance, 1858

7 Rising unemployment and the recession have been the price that we've had to pay to get inflation down. [Labour shouts] That is a price well worth paying.
   Norman Lamont 1942– : speech in House of Commons, 16 May 1991

8 Every year the international finance system kills more people than the second world war. But at least Hitler was mad, you know.
   Ken Livingstone 1945– : in *Sunday Times* 16 April 2000

9 If the policy isn't hurting, it isn't working.
   John Major 1943– : on controlling inflation; speech in Northampton, 27 October 1989

10 Call a thing immoral or ugly, soul-destroying or a degradation of man, a peril to the peace of the world or to the well-being of future generations: as long as you have not shown it to be 'uneconomic' you have not really questioned its right to exist, grow, and prosper.
   E. F. Schumacher 1911–77: *Small is Beautiful* (1973)

11 It's a recession when your neighbour loses his job; it's a depression when you lose yours.
Harry S. Truman 1884–1972: in *Observer* 13 April 1958

12 What a country calls its vital economic interests are not the things which enable its citizens to live, but the things which enable it to make war.
Simone Weil 1909–43: W. H. Auden *A Certain World* (1971)

13 Greed—for lack of a better word—is good. Greed is right. Greed works.
Stanley Weiser and **Oliver Stone** 1946– : *Wall Street* (1987 film)

14 It is not that pearls fetch a high price *because* men have dived for them; but on the contrary, men dive for them because they fetch a high price.
Richard Whately 1787–1863: *Introductory Lectures on Political Economy* (1832)

··

Education

··

See also **Teaching**

1 What one knows is, in youth, of little moment; they know enough who know how to learn.
Henry Brooks Adams 1838–1918: *The Education of Henry Adams* (1907)

2 Give me a child for the first seven years, and you may do what you like with him afterwards.
Anonymous: attributed as a Jesuit maxim, in *Lean's Collectanea* (1903)

3 I said . . . how, and why, young children, were sooner allured by love, than driven by beating, to attain good learning.
Roger Ascham 1515–68: *The Schoolmaster* (1570)

4 Histories make men wise; poets, witty; the mathematics,
subtle; natural philosophy, deep; moral, grave; logic and
rhetoric, able to contend.
Francis Bacon 1561–1626: *Essays* (1625) 'Of Studies'

5 The dread of beatings! Dread of being late!
And, greatest dread of all, the dread of games!
John Betjeman 1906–84: *Summoned by Bells* (1960)

6 Ask me my three main priorities for Government, and I
tell you: education, education and education.
Tony Blair 1953– : speech at the Labour Party
Conference, 1 October 1996

7 'That's the reason they're called lessons,' the Gryphon
remarked: 'because they lessen from day to day.'
Lewis Carroll 1832–98: *Alice's Adventures in Wonderland*
(1865)

8 And gladly wolde he lerne and gladly teche.
Geoffrey Chaucer *c.*1343–1400: *The Canterbury Tales*
'General Prologue'

9 That lyf so short, the craft so long to lerne.
Geoffrey Chaucer *c.*1343–1400: *The Parliament of Fowls*

10 Examinations are formidable even to the best prepared, for
the greatest fool may ask more than the wisest man can
answer.
Charles Caleb Colton *c.*1780–1832: *Lacon* (1820)

11 In education there should be no class distinction.
Confucius 551–479 BC: *Analects*

12 C-l-e-a-n, clean, verb active, to make bright, to scour. W-i-n,
win, d-e-r, der, winder, a casement. When the boy knows
this out of the book, he goes and does it.
Charles Dickens 1812–70: *Nicholas Nickleby* (1839) Mr
Squeers

13 You send your child to the schoolmaster, but 'tis the
schoolboys who educate him.
Ralph Waldo Emerson 1803–82: *Conduct of Life* (1860)

14 The proper study of mankind is books.
Aldous Huxley 1894–1963: *Crome Yellow* (1921)

15 My spelling is Wobbly. It's good spelling but it Wobbles,
and the letters get in the wrong places.
A. A. Milne 1882–1956: *Winnie-the-Pooh* (1926)

16 Know then thyself, presume not God to scan;
The proper study of mankind is man.
Alexander Pope 1688–1744: *An Essay on Man* Epistle 2
(1733)

17 I would I had bestowed that time in the tongues that I have
in fencing, dancing, and bear-baiting. O! had I but followed
the arts!
William Shakespeare 1564–1616: *Twelfth Night* (1601)

18 Education is what survives when what has been learned
has been forgotten.
B. F. Skinner 1904–90: in *New Scientist* 21 May 1964

19 The best thing for being sad . . . is to learn something.
T. H. White 1906–64: *The Sword in the Stone* (1938)

Endeavour

see **Achievement and Endeavour**

Endings

see **Beginnings and Endings**

Enemies

1 He who has a thousand friends has not a friend to spare,
And he who has one enemy will meet him everywhere.
Ali ibn-Abi-Talib *c.*602–661: *A Hundred Sayings*

2 Not while I'm alive 'e ain't!
   Ernest Bevin 1881–1951: reply to the observation that
   Nye Bevan was sometimes his own worst enemy; in R.
   Barclay *Ernest Bevin and the Foreign Office* (1975)

3 Love your enemies, do good to them which hate you.
   Bible: St Luke

4 Fidel Castro is right. You do not quieten your enemy by
   talking with him like a priest, but by burning him.
   Nicolae Ceauşescu 1918–89: at a Communist Party
   meeting, 17 December 1989

5 An injury is much sooner forgotten than an insult.
   Lord Chesterfield 1694–1773: *Letters to his Son* (1774)
   9 October 1746

6 You can calculate the worth of a man by the number of his
   enemies, and the importance of a work of art by the harm
   that is spoken of it.
   Gustave Flaubert 1821–80: letter to Louise Colet,
   14 June 1853

7 An open foe may prove a curse,
   But a pretended friend is worse.
   John Gay 1685–1732: *Fables* (1727) 'The Shepherd's Dog
   and the Wolf'

8 Better to have him inside the tent pissing out, than outside
   pissing in.
   Lyndon Baines Johnson 1908–73: of J. Edgar Hoover, in
   D. Halberstam *The Best and the Brightest* (1972)

9 People wish their enemies dead—but I do not; I say give
   them the gout, give them the stone!
   Lady Mary Wortley Montagu 1689–1762: quoted in
   letter from Horace Walpole to Earl of Harcourt,
   17 September 1778

10 There is nothing in the whole world so painful as feeling
   that one is not liked. It always seems to me that people
   who hate me must be suffering from some strange form of
   lunacy.
   Sei Shōnagon c.966–c.1013: *The Pillow Book of Sei
   Shōnagon*

England and the English

See also **Britain**, **London**, **Places**

1 And did those feet in ancient time
Walk upon England's mountains green?
And was the holy Lamb of God
On England's pleasant pastures seen? . . .
I will not cease from mental fight,
Nor shall my sword sleep in my hand,
Till we have built Jerusalem,
In England's green and pleasant land.
   William Blake 1757–1827: *Milton* (1804–10)

2 Oh, to be in England
Now that April's there.
   Robert Browning 1812–89: 'Home-Thoughts, from
   Abroad' (1845)

3 The Thames is liquid history.
   John Burns 1858–1943: to an American, who had
   compared the Thames disparagingly with the
   Mississippi; in *Daily Mail* 25 January 1943

4 In England there are sixty different religions, and only one
sauce.
   Francesco Caracciolo 1752–99: attributed

5   An Englishman,
Being flattered, is a lamb; threatened, a lion.
   George Chapman *c.*1559–1634: *Alphonsus, Emperor of
   Germany* (1654)

6 Mad dogs and Englishmen
Go out in the midday sun.
   Noël Coward 1899–1973: 'Mad Dogs and Englishmen'
   (1931 song)

7 England's not a bad country . . . It's just a mean, cold, ugly,
divided, tired, clapped-out, post-imperial, post-industrial
slag-heap covered in polystyrene hamburger cartons.
   Margaret Drabble 1939– : *A Natural Curiosity* (1989)

8 What should they know of England who only England
know?
Rudyard Kipling 1865–1936: 'The English Flag' (1892)

9 Let not England forget her precedence of teaching nations
how to live.
John Milton 1608–74: *The Doctrine and Discipline of
Divorce* (1643) 'To the Parliament of England'

10 England is a nation of shopkeepers.
Napoleon I 1769–1821: in B. O'Meara *Napoleon in Exile*
(1822)

11 England expects that every man will do his duty.
Horatio, Lord Nelson 1758–1805: at the battle of
Trafalgar, in R. Southey *Life of Nelson* (1813)

12 It resembles a family, a rather stuffy Victorian family, with
not many black sheep in it but with all its cupboards
bursting with skeletons . . . A family with the wrong
members in control—that, perhaps, is as near as one can
come to describing England in a phrase.
George Orwell 1903–50: *The Lion and the Unicorn* (1941)

13 Ask any man what nationality he would prefer to be, and
ninety-nine out of a hundred will tell you that they would
prefer to be Englishmen.
Cecil Rhodes 1853–1902: G. Le Sueur *Cecil Rhodes* (1913)

14 This royal throne of kings, this sceptred isle,
This earth of majesty, this seat of Mars . . .
This blessèd plot, this earth, this realm, this England.
William Shakespeare 1564–1616: *Richard II* (1595)

15 Englishmen never will be slaves: they are free to do
whatever the Government and public opinion allow them
to do.
George Bernard Shaw 1856–1950: *Man and Superman*
(1903)

16 This Englishwoman is so refined
She has no bosom and no behind.
Stevie Smith 1902–71: 'This Englishwoman' (1937)

17 The English take their pleasures sadly after the fashion of
their country.
> **Maximilien de Béthune, Duc de Sully** 1559–1641:
> attributed

18 The French want no-one to be their *superior*. The English
want *inferiors*. The Frenchman constantly raises his eyes
above him with anxiety. The Englishman lowers his
beneath him with satisfaction.
> **Alexis de Tocqueville** 1805–59: *Voyage en Angleterre et
> en Irlande de 1835* 8 May 1835

19 A soggy little island huffing and puffing to keep up with
Western Europe.
> **John Updike** 1932– : *Picked Up Pieces* (1976) 'London
> Life' (written 1969)

20 You never find an Englishman among the under-dogs—
except in England, of course.
> **Evelyn Waugh** 1903–66: *The Loved One* (1948)

21 The English country gentleman galloping after a fox—the
unspeakable in full pursuit of the uneatable.
> **Oscar Wilde** 1854–1900: *A Woman of No Importance*
> (1893)

....

Environment
....

See also **The Country and the Town,
Pollution**

1 Come, friendly bombs, and fall on Slough!
It isn't fit for humans now,
There isn't grass to graze a cow.
Swarm over, Death!
> **John Betjeman** 1906–84: 'Slough' (1937)

2 Woe unto them that join house to house, that lay field to
field, till there be no place.
> **Bible**: Isaiah

3 And was Jerusalem builded here
Among these dark Satanic mills?
   William Blake 1757–1827: *Milton* (1804–10)

4 O all ye Green Things upon the Earth, bless ye the Lord.
   Book of Common Prayer 1662: *Morning Prayer*

5 I do not know of any environmental group in any country
that does not view its government as an adversary.
   Gro Harlem Brundtland 1939– : in *Time* 25 September
   1989

6 Praise the green earth. Chance has appointed her
home, workshop, larder, middenpit.
Her lousy skin scabbed here and there by
cities provides us with name and nation.
   Basil Bunting 1900–85: 'Attis: or, Something Missing'
   (1931)

7 O leave this barren spot to me!
Spare, woodman, spare the beechen tree.
   Thomas Campbell 1777–1844: 'The Beech-Tree's
   Petition' (1800)

8 Over increasingly large areas of the United States, spring
now comes unheralded by the return of the birds, and the
early mornings are strangely silent where once they were
filled with the beauty of bird song.
   Rachel Carson 1907–64: *The Silent Spring* (1962)

9 How inappropriate to call this planet Earth when it is
clearly Ocean.
   Arthur C. Clarke 1917– : attributed in *Nature* 1990

10 Make it a *green* peace.
   Bill Darnell: at a meeting of the Don't Make a Wave
   Committee, which preceded the formation of Greenpeace,
   in Vancouver, 1970; Robert Hunter *The Greenpeace
   Chronicle* (1979)

11 Now there is one outstandingly important fact regarding
Spaceship Earth, and that is that no instruction book came
with it.
   R. Buckminster Fuller 1895–1983: *Operating Manual for
   Spaceship Earth* (1969)

12 What would the world be, once bereft
Of wet and wildness? Let them be left,
O let them be left, wildness and wet;
Long live the weeds and the wilderness yet.
   Gerard Manley Hopkins 1844–89: 'Inversnaid' (written
   1881)

13 I am I plus my surroundings and if I do not preserve the
latter, I do not preserve myself.
   José Ortega y Gasset 1883–1955: *Meditaciones del
   Quijote* (1914)

14 The parks are the lungs of London.
   William Pitt 1708–78: quoted by William Windham in the
   House of Commons, 30 June 1808

15 Consult the genius of the place in all.
   Alexander Pope 1688–1744: *Epistles to Several Persons*
   'To Lord Burlington' (1731)

16 Little boxes on the hillside . . .
And they're all made out of ticky-tacky
And they all look just the same.
   Malvina Reynolds 1900–78: 'Little Boxes' (1962 song); on
   the tract houses in the hills to the south of San
   Francisco

17 Small is beautiful.
   E. F. Schumacher 1911–77: title of book (1973)

18 If I were a Brazilian without land or money or the means
to feed my children, I would be burning the rain forest too.
   Sting 1951– : in *International Herald Tribune* 14 April
   1989

Envy and Jealousy

1 Thou shalt not covet thy neighbour's house, thou shalt not
covet thy neighbour's wife.
   Bible: Exodus

2 Jealousy is no more than feeling alone against smiling enemies.
    Elizabeth Bowen 1899–1973: *The House in Paris* (1935)

3 Thou shalt not covet; but tradition
Approves all forms of competition.
    Arthur Hugh Clough 1819–61: 'The Latest Decalogue' (1862)

4 Some folks rail against other folks, because other folks have what some folks would be glad of.
    Henry Fielding 1707–54: *Joseph Andrews* (1742)

5 To jealousy, nothing is more frightful than laughter.
    Françoise Sagan 1935– : *La Chamade* (1965)

6   O! beware, my lord, of jealousy;
It is the green-eyed monster which doth mock
The meat it feeds on.
    William Shakespeare 1564–1616: *Othello* (1602–4)

Epitaphs

See also **Death**

1 *Si monumentum requiris, circumspice.*
    If you seek a monument, gaze around.
    Anonymous: inscription in St Paul's Cathedral, London, attributed to the son of Sir Christopher Wren 1632–1723, its architect

2 *Et in Arcadia ego.*
    And I too in Arcadia.
    Anonymous: tomb inscription, of disputed meaning, often depicted in classical paintings

3 Free at last, free at last
Thank God almighty
We are free at last.
    Anonymous: epitaph of Martin Luther King (1929–68), Atlanta, Georgia, quoting a spiritual, with which he ended his 'I have a dream' speech

4 A soldier of the Great War known unto God.
   Anonymous: adopted by the War Graves Commission as the standard epitaph for the unidentified dead of World War One

5 Saul and Jonathan were lovely and pleasant in their lives, and in their death they were not divided.
   Bible: II Samuel

6 They shall grow not old, as we that are left grow old.
   Age shall not weary them, nor the years condemn.
   At the going down of the sun and in the morning
   We will remember them.
   Laurence Binyon 1869–1943: 'For the Fallen' (1914)

7 When you go home, tell them of us and say,
   'For your tomorrows these gave their today.'
   John Maxwell Edmonds 1875–1958: *Inscriptions Suggested for War Memorials* (1919). Particularly associated with the Burma campaign of the Second World War, in the form 'For your tomorrow, we gave our today'

8 Under this stone, Reader, survey
   Dead Sir John Vanbrugh's house of clay.
   Lie heavy on him, Earth! for he
   Laid many heavy loads on thee!
   Abel Evans 1679–1737: 'Epitaph on Sir John Vanbrugh, Architect of Blenheim Palace'

9 Here lies W. C. Fields. I would rather be living in Philadelphia.
   W. C. Fields 1880–1946: suggested epitaph for himself, in *Vanity Fair* June 1925

10 Life is a jest; and all things show it.
   I thought so once; but now I know it.
   John Gay 1685–1732: 'My Own Epitaph' (1720)

11 His foe was folly and his weapon wit.
   Anthony Hope 1863–1933: inscription for W. S. Gilbert's memorial on the Victoria Embankment, London (1915)

12 Rest in soft peace, and, asked, say here doth lie
Ben Jonson his best piece of poetry.
   Ben Jonson c.1573–1637: 'On My First Son' (1616)

13 Here lies one whose name was writ in water.
   John Keats 1795–1821: epitaph for himself, in R.
   Monckton Milnes *Life, Letters and Literary Remains of
   John Keats* (1848)

14 Here lies a great and mighty king
Whose promise none relies on;
He never said a foolish thing,
Nor ever did a wise one.
   John Wilmot, Earl of Rochester 1647–80: 'The King's
   Epitaph' (alternatively 'Here lies our sovereign lord the
   King'), to which Charles II replied 'This is very true: for
   my words are my own, and my actions are my
   ministers"; in C. E. Doble et al. *Thomas Hearne: Remarks
   and Collections* (1885–1921) 17 November 1706

15 Good friend, for Jesu's sake forbear
To dig the dust enclosed here.
Blest be the man that spares these stones,
And curst be he that moves my bones.
   William Shakespeare 1564–1616: epitaph on his tomb,
   probably composed by himself

16 Go, tell the Spartans, thou who passest by,
That here obedient to their laws we lie.
   Simonides c.556–468 BC: in Herodotus *Histories*
   (attributed)

17 Here he lies where he longed to be;
Home is the sailor, home from sea,
And the hunter home from the hill.
   Robert Louis Stevenson 1850–94: 'Requiem' (1887)

18 Where fierce indignation can no longer tear his heart.
   Jonathan Swift 1667–1745: Swift's epitaph. See S. Leslie
   The Skull of Swift (1928)

19 God damn you all: I told you so.
   H. G. Wells 1866–1946: suggestion for his own epitaph,
   1939; Ernest Barker *Age and Youth* (1953)

Equality

See also **Human Rights**

1 He maketh his sun to rise on the evil and on the good, and sendeth rain on the just and on the unjust.
   Bible: St Matthew

2 A man's a man for a' that.
   Robert Burns 1759–96: 'For a' that and a' that' (1790)

3 Maybe people in America think being a sir is a big deal, but I think we should all be misters together.
   Albert Finney 1936– : in *Sunday Times* 30 April 2000

4 When every one is somebodee,
   Then no one's anybody.
   W. S. Gilbert 1836–1911: *The Gondoliers* (1889)

5 Your levellers wish to level *down* as far as themselves; but they cannot bear levelling *up* to themselves.
   Samuel Johnson 1709–84: James Boswell *Life of Johnson* (1791) 21 July 1763

6 I have a dream that one day on the red hills of Georgia the sons of former slaves and the sons of former slave owners will be able to sit down together at the table of brotherhood.
   Martin Luther King 1929–68: speech at Civil Rights March in Washington, 28 August 1963

7 All animals are equal but some animals are more equal than others.
   George Orwell 1903–50: *Animal Farm* (1945)

8 Hath not a Jew eyes? hath not a Jew hands, organs, dimensions, senses, affections, passions? . . . If you prick us, do we not bleed? if you tickle us, do we not laugh? if you poison us, do we not die? and if you wrong us, shall we not revenge?
   William Shakespeare 1564–1616: *The Merchant of Venice* (1596–8)

9 Make all men equal today, and God has so created them that they shall all be unequal tomorrow.
   Anthony Trollope 1815–82: *Autobiography* (1883)

Europe and Europeans

See also **Places**

1 *Qui parle Europe a tort, notion géographique.*
Whoever speaks of Europe is wrong, [it is] a geographical concept.
    Otto von Bismarck 1815–98: marginal note on a letter from the Russian Chancellor Gorchakov, November 1876

2 Fog in Channel—Continent isolated.
    Russell Brockbank 1913– : newspaper placard in cartoon, *Round the Bend with Brockbank* (1948)

3 The age of chivalry is gone.—That of sophisters, economists, and calculators, has succeeded; and the glory of Europe is extinguished for ever.
    Edmund Burke 1729–97: *Reflections on the Revolution in France* (1790)

4 You ask if they were happy. This is not a characteristic of a European. To be contented—that's for the cows.
    Coco Chanel 1883–1971: A. Madsen *Coco Chanel* (1990)

5 From Stettin in the Baltic to Trieste in the Adriatic an iron curtain has descended across the Continent.
    Winston Churchill 1874–1965: speech at Westminster College, Fulton, Missouri, 5 March 1946. 'Iron curtain' previously had been applied by others to the Soviet Union or her sphere of influence

6 Without Britain Europe would remain only a torso.
    Ludwig Erhard 1897–1977: remark on West German television, 27 May 1962

7 It means the end of a thousand years of history.
    Hugh Gaitskell 1906–63: on a European federation; speech at Labour Party Conference, 3 October 1962

8 The policy of European integration is in reality a question of war and peace in the 21st century.
    Helmut Kohl 1930– : speech at Louvain University, 2 February 1996

9 I want the whole of Europe to have one currency; it will make trading much easier.
   Napoleon I 1769–1821: letter to his brother Louis, 6 May 1807

10 Roll up that map; it will not be wanted these ten years.
   William Pitt 1759–1806: of a map of Europe, on hearing of Napoleon's victory at Austerlitz, December 1805

11 *Je regrette l'Europe aux anciens parapets!*
   I pine for Europe of the ancient parapets!
   Arthur Rimbaud 1854–91: 'Le Bâteau ivre' (1883)

12 Better fifty years of Europe than a cycle of Cathay.
   Alfred, Lord Tennyson 1809–92: 'Locksley Hall' (1842)

13 We have not successfully rolled back the frontiers of the State in Britain only to see them reimposed at European level, with a European super-State exercising a new dominance from Brussels.
   Margaret Thatcher 1925– : speech in Bruges, 20 September 1988

....

Evil

....

see **Good and Evil**

....

Experience

....

1 All experience is an arch to build upon.
   Henry Brooks Adams 1838–1918: *The Education of Henry Adams* (1907)

2 You should make a point of trying every experience once, excepting incest and folk-dancing.
   Anonymous: Arnold Bax (1883–1953), quoting 'a sympathetic Scot' in *Farewell My Youth* (1943)

3 Experience isn't interesting till it begins to repeat itself—in fact, till it does that, it hardly *is* experience.
   Elizabeth Bowen 1899–1973: *Death of the Heart* (1938)

4 Experience is the child of Thought, and Thought is the child of Action. We cannot learn men from books.
Benjamin Disraeli 1804–81: *Vivian Grey* (1826)

5 We had the experience but missed the meaning.
T. S. Eliot 1888–1965: *Four Quartets* 'The Dry Salvages' (1941)

6 Experience is not what happens to a man; it is what a man does with what happens to him.
Aldous Huxley 1894–1963: *Texts and Pretexts* (1932)

7 We took risks, we knew we took them; things have come out against us, and therefore we have no cause for complaint.
Robert Falcon Scott 1868–1912: 'The Last Message' in *Scott's Last Expedition* (1913)

8 Education is when you read the fine print; experience is what you get when you don't.
Pete Seeger 1919– : L. Botts *Loose Talk* (1980)

9 *Experto credite.*
Trust one who has gone through it.
Virgil 70–19 BC: *Aeneid*

10 Experience is the name everyone gives to their mistakes.
Oscar Wilde 1854–1900: *Lady Windermere's Fan* (1892)

Failure

see **Success and Failure**

Fame

1 Seven wealthy towns contend for HOMER dead
Through which the living HOMER begged his bread.
Anonymous: epilogue to *Aesop at Tunbridge* By No Person of Quality (1698)

2 Fame is like a river, that beareth up things light and swollen, and drowns things weighty and solid.
Francis Bacon 1561–1626: *Essays* (1625) 'Of Praise'

3 There's no such thing as bad publicity except your own obituary.
   Brendan Behan 1923–64: in Dominic Behan *My Brother Brendan* (1965)

4 He's always backing into the limelight.
   Lord Berners 1883–1950: of T. E. Lawrence; oral tradition

5 A prophet is not without honour, save in his own country, and in his own house.
   Bible: St Matthew

6 I awoke one morning and found myself famous.
   Lord Byron 1788–1824: on the instantaneous success of *Childe Harold*, in Thomas Moore *Letters and Journals of Lord Byron* (1830)

7 The deed is all, the glory nothing.
   Johann Wolfgang von Goethe 1749–1832: *Faust* pt. 2 (1832)

8 Far from the madding crowd's ignoble strife,
   Their sober wishes never learned to stray;
   Along the cool sequestered vale of life
   They kept the noiseless tenor of their way.
   Thomas Gray 1716–71: *Elegy Written in a Country Churchyard* (1751)

9 *Exegi monumentum aere perennius.*
   I have erected a monument more lasting than bronze.
   Horace 65–8 BC: *Odes*

10 The best fame is a writer's fame: it's enough to get a table at a good restaurant, but not enough that you get interrupted when you eat.
   Fran Lebowitz 1946– : in *Observer* 30 May 1993

11 We're more popular than Jesus now; I don't know which will go first—rock 'n' roll or Christianity.
   John Lennon 1940–80: of The Beatles; interview in *Evening Standard* 4 March 1966

12 Fame is the spur that the clear spirit doth raise
   (That last infirmity of noble mind)

To scorn delights, and live laborious days.
John Milton 1608–74: 'Lycidas' (1638)

13 Famous men have the whole earth as their memorial.
Pericles c.495–429 BC: in Thucydides *History of the Peloponnesian War* (tr. R. Warner)

14 So long as men can breathe, or eyes can see,
So long lives this, and this gives life to thee.
William Shakespeare 1564–1616: sonnet 18

15 Celebrity is a mask that eats into the face.
John Updike 1932– : *Self-Consciousness: Memoirs* (1989)

16 In the future everybody will be world famous for fifteen minutes.
Andy Warhol 1927–87: in *Andy Warhol* (1968)

The Family

See also **Children**, **Parents**

1 He that hath wife and children hath given hostages to fortune; for they are impediments to great enterprises, either of virtue or mischief.
Francis Bacon 1561–1626: *Essays* (1625) 'Of Marriage and the Single Life'

2 I have never understood this liking for war. It panders to instincts already catered for within the scope of any respectable domestic establishment.
Alan Bennett 1934– : *Forty Years On* (1969)

3 Thy wife shall be as the fruitful vine: upon the walls of thine house.
Thy children like the olive-branches: round about thy table.
Bible: Psalm 128

4 We begin our public affections in our families. No cold relation is a zealous citizen.
Edmund Burke 1729–97: *Reflections on the Revolution in France* (1790)

5 The truth is that it is not the sins of the fathers that
   descend unto the third generation, but the sorrows of the
   mothers.
   Marilyn French 1929– : *Her Mother's Daughter* (1987)

6 Far from being the basis of the good society, the family,
   with its narrow privacy and tawdry secrets, is the source
   of all our discontents.
   Edmund Leach 1910– : BBC Reith Lectures, 1967

7 One would be in less danger
   From the wiles of the stranger
   If one's own kin and kith
   Were more fun to be with.
   Ogden Nash 1902–71: 'Family Court' (1931)

8 I want to spend more time with my family, but I'm not
   sure they want to spend more time with me.
   Esther Rantzen 1940– : in *Independent* 29 April 2000

9 A little more than kin, and less than kind.
   William Shakespeare 1564–1616: *Hamlet* (1601)

10 Family! . . . the home of all social evil, a charitable
    institution for comfortable women, an anchorage for
    house-fathers, and a hell for children.
    August Strindberg 1849–1912: *The Son of a Servant*
    (1886)

11 If a man's character is to be abused, say what you will,
    there's nobody like a relation to do the business.
    William Makepeace Thackeray 1811–63: *Vanity Fair*
    (1847–8)

12 All happy families resemble one another, but each
    unhappy family is unhappy in its own way.
    Leo Tolstoy 1828–1910: *Anna Karenina* (1875–7), tr. A.
    and L. Maude

13 It is no use telling me that there are bad aunts and good
    aunts. At the core, they are all alike. Sooner or later, out
    pops the cloven hoof.
    P. G. Wodehouse 1881–1975: *The Code of the Woosters*
    (1938)

Fate

1 The spring is wound up tight. It will uncoil of itself. That is what is so convenient in tragedy. The least little turn of the wrist will do the job. Anything will set it going.
   Jean Anouilh 1910–87: *Antigone* (1944), tr. L. Galantiere

2 Must it be? It must be.
   Ludwig van Beethoven 1770–1827: *String Quartet in F Major* (1827) epigraph

3 Canst thou bind the sweet influences of Pleiades, or loose the bands of Orion?
   Bible: Job

4 Fate is not an eagle, it creeps like a rat.
   Elizabeth Bowen 1899–1973: *The House in Paris* (1935)

5 Nothing have I found stronger than Necessity.
   Euripides *c.*485–*c.*406 BC: *Alcestis*

6 There once was an old man who said, 'Damn!
   It is borne in upon me I am
   An engine that moves
   In determinate grooves,
   I'm not even a bus, I'm a tram.'
   Maurice Evan Hare 1886–1967: 'Limerick' (1905)

7 I [Death] was astonished to see him in Baghdad, for I had an appointment with him tonight in Samarra.
   W. Somerset Maugham 1874–1965: *Sheppey* (1933)

8 Not a whit, we defy augury; there's a special providence in the fall of a sparrow. If it be now, 'tis not to come; if it be not to come, it will be now; if it be not now, yet it will come: the readiness is all.
   William Shakespeare 1564–1616: *Hamlet* (1601)

9 Out flew the web and floated wide;
   The mirror cracked from side to side;
   'The curse is come upon me,' cried
   The Lady of Shalott.
   Alfred, Lord Tennyson 1809–92: 'The Lady of Shalott' (1832)

10 We are merely the stars' tennis-balls, struck and bandied
Which way please them.
    John Webster c.1580–c.1625: *The Duchess of Malfi* (1623)

11 Every bullet has its billet.
    William III 1650–1702: in John Wesley's diary, 6 June 1765

Fear

1 Now a man talks frankly only with his wife, at night, with
the blanket over his head.
    Isaac Babel 1894–1940: remark c.1937, of the Stalinist
purges; Solomon Volkov *St Petersburg* (1996)

2 We must travel in the direction of our fear.
    John Berryman 1914–72: 'A Point of Age' (1942)

3 No passion so effectually robs the mind of all its powers of
acting and reasoning as fear.
    Edmund Burke 1729–97: *On the Sublime and Beautiful*
(1757)

4 If hopes were dupes, fears may be liars.
    Arthur Hugh Clough 1819–61: 'Say not the struggle
naught availeth' (1855)

5 I will show you fear in a handful of dust.
    T. S. Eliot 1888–1965: *The Waste Land* (1922)

6 There is no terror in a bang, only in the anticipation of it.
    Alfred Hitchcock 1899–1980: attributed

7 Terror . . . often arises from a pervasive sense of
disestablishment; that things are in the unmaking.
    Stephen King 1947– : *Danse Macabre* (1981)

8 The only thing we have to fear is fear itself.
    Franklin D. Roosevelt 1882–1945: inaugural address, 4
March 1933

9   Present fears
Are less than horrible imaginings.
    William Shakespeare 1564–1616: *Macbeth* (1606)

10 In time we hate that which we often fear.
  William Shakespeare 1564–1616: *Antony and Cleopatra*
  (1606–7)

11 Our deepest fear is not that we are inadequate. Our
  deepest fear is that we are powerful beyond measure. It is
  our light, not our darkness, that most frightens us.
  Marianne Williamson 1953– : *A Return to Love* (1992)

Fitness

see **Health and Fitness**

Flowers

1 Unkempt about those hedges blows
  An English unofficial rose.
  Rupert Brooke 1887–1915: 'The Old Vicarage,
  Grantchester' (1915)

2 That wel by reson men it calle may
  The 'dayesye,' or elles the 'ye of day,'
  The emperice and flour of floures alle.
  Geoffrey Chaucer *c.*1343–1400: *The Legend of Good
  Women*

3 Oh, no man knows
  Through what wild centuries
  Roves back the rose.
  Walter de la Mare 1873–1956: 'All That's Past' (1912)

4 I sometimes think that never blows so red
  The rose as where some buried Caesar bled.
  Edward Fitzgerald 1809–83: *The Rubáiyát of Omar
  Khayyám* (1859)

5 The rose of all the world is not for me.
  I want for my part
  Only the little white rose of Scotland

That smells sharp and sweet—and breaks the heart.
   Hugh MacDiarmid 1892–1978: 'The Little White Rose'
   (1934)

6 People from a planet without flowers would think we must
be mad with joy the whole time to have such things about
us.
   Iris Murdoch 1919–99: *A Fairly Honourable Defeat* (1970)

7 I know a bank whereon the wild thyme blows,
Where oxlips and the nodding violet grows
Quite over-canopied with luscious woodbine,
With sweet musk-roses, and with eglantine.
   William Shakespeare 1564–1616: *A Midsummer Night's
   Dream* (1595–6)

8   Daffodils,
That come before the swallow dares, and take
The winds of March with beauty.
   William Shakespeare 1564–1616: *The Winter's Tale*
   (1610–11)

9 I wandered lonely as a cloud
That floats on high o'er vales and hills,
When all at once I saw a crowd,
A host, of golden daffodils;
Beside the lake, beneath the trees,
Fluttering and dancing in the breeze.
   William Wordsworth 1770–1850: 'I wandered lonely as a
   cloud' (1815 ed.)

Food and Drink

See also **Alcohol**

1 She brought forth butter in a lordly dish.
   Bible: Judges

2 Tell me what you eat and I will tell you what you are.
   Anthelme Brillat-Savarin 1755–1826: *Physiologie du
   Goût* (1825)

3 Cooking is the most ancient of the arts, for Adam was
born hungry.
  Anthelme Brillat-Savarin 1755–1826: *Physiologie du
  Goût* (1825)

4 Some have meat and cannot eat,
Some cannot eat that want it:
But we have meat and we can eat,
Sae let the Lord be thankit.
  Robert Burns 1759–96: 'The Kirkudbright Grace' (1790),
  also known as 'The Selkirk Grace'

5 That all-softening, overpowering knell,
The tocsin of the soul—the dinner bell.
  Lord Byron 1788–1824: *Don Juan* (1819–24)

6 Hunger is the best sauce in the world.
  Cervantes 1547–1616: *Don Quixote* (1605)

7 Take away that pudding—it has no theme.
  Winston Churchill 1874–1965: Lord Home *The Way the
  Wind Blows* (1976)

8 It [bingeing] gives you a feeling of comfort. It's like having
a pair of arms around you, but it's temporary. Then you're
disgusted at the bloatedness of your stomach, and then you
bring it all up again.
  Diana, Princess of Wales 1961–97: interview on
  Panorama, BBC1 TV, 20 November 1995

9 Please, sir, I want some more.
  Charles Dickens 1812–70: *Oliver Twist* (1838)

10 Milk's leap toward immortality.
  Clifton Fadiman 1904– : of cheese; *Any Number Can
  Play* (1957)

11 Heaven sends us good meat, but the Devil sends cooks.
  David Garrick 1717–79: 'On Doctor Goldsmith's
  Characteristical Cookery' (1777)

12 Take your hare when it is cased.
  Hannah Glasse fl. 1747: *The Art of Cookery Made Plain
  and Easy* (1747) (*cased* skinned); the proverbial 'First
  catch your hare' dates from *c*.1300

13 I do wish we could chat longer, but I'm having an old friend for dinner.
Thomas Harris 1940– and **Ted Tally** 1952– : *The Silence of the Lambs* (1991 film)

14 A cucumber should be well sliced, and dressed with pepper and vinegar, and then thrown out, as good for nothing.
Samuel Johnson 1709–84: James Boswell *Journal of a Tour to the Hebrides* (1785) 5 October 1773

15 Kissing don't last: cookery do!
George Meredith 1828–1909: *The Ordeal of Richard Feverel* (1859)

16 Time for a little something.
A. A. Milne 1882–1956: *Winnie-the-Pooh* (1926)

17 One should eat to live, and not live to eat.
Molière 1622–73: *L'Avare* (1669)

18 I never see any home cooking. All I get is fancy stuff.
Prince Philip, Duke of Edinburgh 1921– : in *Observer* 28 October 1962

19 Coffee, (which makes the politician wise,
And see thro' all things with his half-shut eyes).
Alexander Pope 1688–1744: *The Rape of the Lock* (1714)

20 The appetite grows by eating.
François Rabelais *c*.1494–*c*.1553: *Gargantua* (1534)

21 The cook was a good cook, as cooks go; and as cooks go, she went.
Saki (H. H. Munro) 1870–1916: *Reginald* (1904)

22 I am a great eater of beef, and I believe that does harm to my wit.
William Shakespeare 1564–1616: *Twelfth Night* (1601)

23 We each day dig our graves with our teeth.
Samuel Smiles 1812–1904: *Duty* (1880)

24 A hen's egg is, quite simply, a work of art, a masterpiece of design and construction with, it has to be said, brilliant packaging.
Delia Smith: *How To Cook* (1998)

25 Serenely full, the epicure would say,
Fate cannot harm me, I have dined to-day.
   Sydney Smith 1771–1845: Lady Holland *Memoir* (1855)

26 A good, honest, wholesome, hungry breakfast.
   Izaak Walton 1593–1683: *The Compleat Angler* (1653)

27 I discovered that dinners follow the order of creation—fish
first, then entrées, then joints, lastly the apple as dessert.
The soup is chaos.
   Sylvia Townsend Warner 1893–1978: diary, 26 May 1929

Fools and Foolishness

1 The world is full of fools, and he who would not see it
should live alone and smash his mirror.
   Anonymous: adaptation of an original form attributed
   to Claude Le Petit (1640–65) in *Discours satiriques* (1686)

2 There's a sucker born every minute.
   Phineas T. Barnum 1810–91: attributed

3 Answer not a fool according to his folly, lest thou also be
like unto him.
Answer a fool according to his folly, lest he be wise in his
own conceit.
   Bible: Proverbs

4 For ye suffer fools gladly, seeing ye yourselves are wise.
   Bible: II Corinthians

5 If the fool would persist in his folly he would become wise.
   William Blake 1757–1827: *The Marriage of Heaven and
   Hell* (1790–3) 'Proverbs of Hell'

6 The picture, placed the busts between,
Adds to the thought much strength:
Wisdom and Wit are little seen,
But Folly's at full length.
   Jane Brereton 1685–1740: 'On Mr Nash's Picture at Full
   Length, between the Busts of Sir Isaac Newton and Mr
   Pope' (1744)

7 I am two fools, I know,
For loving, and for saying so

In whining poetry.
   John Donne 1572–1631: 'The Triple Fool'

8 Never give a sucker an even break.
   W. C. Fields 1880–1946: title of a W. C. Fields film (1941);
   the catch-phrase is said to have originated in the musical
   comedy *Poppy* (1923)

9 *Misce stultitiam consiliis brevem:*
   Dulce est desipere in loco.

   Mix a little foolishness with your prudence: it's good to be
   silly at the right moment.
   Horace 65–8 BC: *Odes*

10 You may fool all the people some of the time; you can even
   fool some of the people all the time; but you can't fool all of
   the people all the time.
   Abraham Lincoln 1809–65: A. McClure *Lincoln's Yarns
   and Stories* (1904); also attributed to Phineas Barnum

11 A knowledgeable fool is a greater fool than an ignorant
   fool.
   Molière 1622–73: *Les Femmes savantes* (1672)

12 Fools rush in where angels fear to tread.
   Alexander Pope 1688–1744: *An Essay on Criticism* (1711)

13 The follies which a man regrets most, in his life, are those
   which he didn't commit when he had the opportunity.
   Helen Rowland 1875–1950: *A Guide to Men* (1922)

14 The ultimate result of shielding men from the effects of
   folly, is to fill the world with fools.
   Herbert Spencer 1820–1903: *Essays* (1891) vol. 3 'State
   Tamperings with Money and Banks'

15 Let us be thankful for the fools. But for them the rest of us
   could not succeed.
   Mark Twain 1835–1910: *Following the Equator* (1897)

16   Be wise with speed;
   A fool at forty is a fool indeed.
   Edward Young 1683–1765: *The Love of Fame* (1725–8)

Forgiveness

1 Her sins, which are many, are forgiven; for she loved much.
Bible: St Luke

2 I shall be an autocrat: that's my trade. And the good Lord will forgive me: that's his.
Empress Catherine the Great 1729–96: attributed

3 After such knowledge, what forgiveness?
T. S. Eliot 1888–1965: 'Gerontion' (1920)

4 God may pardon you, but I never can.
Elizabeth I 1533–1603: to the dying Countess of Nottingham

5 True reconciliation does not consist in merely forgetting the past.
Nelson Mandela 1918– : speech, 7 January 1996

6 We read that we ought to forgive our enemies; but we do not read that we ought to forgive our friends.
Cosimo de' Medici 1389–1464: Francis Bacon *Apophthegms* (1625)

7 To err is human; to forgive, divine.
Alexander Pope 1688–1744: *An Essay on Criticism* (1711)

8 Youth, which is forgiven everything, forgives itself nothing: age, which forgives itself everything, is forgiven nothing.
George Bernard Shaw 1856–1950: *Man and Superman* (1903)

9 The stupid neither forgive nor forget; the naïve forgive and forget; the wise forgive but do not forget.
Thomas Szasz 1920– : *The Second Sin* (1973)

10 God of forgiveness, do not forgive those murderers of Jewish children here.
Elie Wiesel 1928– : at an unofficial ceremony at Auschwitz, 26 January 1995

France and the French

See also **Places**

1 France was long a despotism tempered by epigrams.
   Thomas Carlyle 1795–1881: *History of the French Revolution* (1837)

2 How can you govern a country which has 246 varieties of cheese?
   Charles de Gaulle 1890–1970: E. Mignon *Les Mots du Général* (1962)

3 *France, mère des arts, des armes et des lois.*
   France, mother of arts, of warfare, and of laws.
   Joachim Du Bellay 1522–60: *Les Regrets* (1558)

4 The best thing I know between France and England is—the sea.
   Douglas Jerrold 1803–57: *Wit and Opinions* (1859) 'The Anglo-French Alliance'

5 *Ce qui n'est pas clair n'est pas français.*
   What is not clear is not French.
   Antoine de Rivarol 1753–1801: *Discours sur l'Universalité de la Langue Française* (1784)

6 That sweet enemy, France.
   Philip Sidney 1554–86: *Astrophil and Stella* (1591)

7 They order, said I, this matter better in France.
   Laurence Sterne 1713–68: *A Sentimental Journey* (1768)

8 Tilling and grazing are the two breasts by which France is fed.
   Maximilien de Béthune, Duc de Sully 1559–1641: *Mémoires* (1638)

9 The French want no-one to be their *superior.* The English want *inferiors.* The Frenchman constantly raises his eyes above him with anxiety. The Englishman lowers his

beneath him with satisfaction.
    Alexis de Tocqueville 1805–59: *Voyage en Angleterre et en Irlande de 1835* 8 May 1835

10 If the French noblesse had been capable of playing cricket with their peasants, their chateaux would never have been burnt.
    G. M. Trevelyan 1876–1962: *English Social History* (1942)

....

Friendship

....

1 Oh, the comfort—the inexpressible comfort of feeling safe with a person, having neither to weigh thoughts, nor measure words, but pouring them all out, just as they are, chaff and grain together; knowing that a faithful hand will take and sift them—keep what is worth keeping—and with the breath of kindness blow the rest away.
    Anonymous: 'Friendship'; often attributed to George Eliot or Dinah Mulock Craik (1826–87)

2 One soul inhabiting two bodies.
    Aristotle 384–322 BC: definition of a friend, in Diogenes Laertius *Lives of Philosophers*

3 A crowd is not company, and faces are but a gallery of pictures, and talk but a tinkling cymbal, where there is no love.
    Francis Bacon 1561–1626: *Essays* (1625) 'Of Friendship'

4 Intreat me not to leave thee, or to return from following after thee: for whither thou goest, I will go; and where thou lodgest, I will lodge: thy people shall be my people, and thy God my God:
    Bible: Ruth

5 There is no man so friendless but what he can find a friend sincere enough to tell him disagreeable truths.
    Edward Bulwer-Lytton 1803–73: *What will he do with it?* (1857)

6 Should auld acquaintance be forgot
   And never brought to mind?
   Robert Burns 1759–96: 'Auld Lang Syne' (1796)

7 Give me the avowed, erect and manly foe;
   Firm I can meet, perhaps return the blow;
   But of all plagues, good Heaven, thy wrath can send,
   Save me, oh, save me, from the candid friend.
   George Canning 1770–1827: 'New Morality' (1821)

8 A woman can become a man's friend only in the following
   stages—first an acquaintance, next a mistress, and only
   then a friend.
   Anton Chekhov 1860–1904: *Uncle Vanya* (1897)

9 The only reward of virtue is virtue; the only way to have a
   friend is to be one.
   Ralph Waldo Emerson 1803–82: *Essays* (1841)
   'Friendship'

10 If a man does not make new acquaintance as he advances
   through life, he will soon find himself left alone. A man,
   Sir, should keep his friendship in constant repair.
   Samuel Johnson 1709–84: James Boswell *Life of
   Johnson* (1791) 1755

11 Oh I get by with a little help from my friends,
   Mm, I get high with a little help from my friends.
   John Lennon 1940–80 and **Paul McCartney** 1942– :
   'With a Little Help From My Friends' (1967 song)

12 After first confidences between people moving towards
   friendship, a rest between exchanges of information
   somehow hastens, not impedes, the growing trust.
   Candia McWilliam 1955– : *Debatable Land* (1994)

13 Friendship is constant in all other things
   Save in the office and affairs of love.
   William Shakespeare 1564–1616: *Much Ado About
   Nothing* (1598–9)

14 I do not believe that friends are necessarily the people you
   like best, they are merely the people who got there first.
   Peter Ustinov 1921– : *Dear Me* (1977)

The Future

1 'We are always doing', says he, 'something for Posterity, but I would fain see Posterity do something for us.'
   Joseph Addison 1672–1719: in *Spectator* 20 August 1714

2 Some of the jam we thought was for tomorrow, we've already eaten.
   Tony Benn 1925– : attributed, 1969

3 The future ain't what it used to be.
   Yogi Berra 1925– : attributed

4 You can never plan the future by the past.
   Edmund Burke 1729–97: *Letter to a Member of the National Assembly* (1791)

5 The empires of the future are the empires of the mind.
   Winston Churchill 1874–1965: speech at Harvard, 6 September 1943

6 I never think of the future. It comes soon enough.
   Albert Einstein 1879–1955: in an interview given on the *Belgeniand*, December 1930

7 High on the agenda for the 21st century will be the need to restore some kind of tragic consciousness.
   Carlos Fuentes 1928– : Rushworth M. Kidder *An Agenda for the 21st Century* (1987)

8 You cannot fight against the future. Time is on our side.
   W. E. Gladstone 1809–98: speech on the Reform Bill, House of Commons, 27 April 1866

9 We have trained them [men] to think of the Future as a promised land which favoured heroes attain—not as something which everyone reaches at the rate of sixty minutes an hour, whatever he does, whoever he is.
   C. S. Lewis 1898–1963: *The Screwtape Letters* (1942)

10 If you want a picture of the future, imagine a boot stamping on a human face—for ever.
   George Orwell 1903–50: *Nineteen Eighty-Four* (1949)

11 Lord! we know what we are, but know not what we may be.
   William Shakespeare 1564–1616: *Hamlet* (1601)

Gardens

1 I value my garden more for being full of blackbirds than of cherries, and very frankly give them fruit for their songs.
Joseph Addison 1672–1719: in *Spectator* 6 September 1712

2 Nothing is more pleasant to the eye than green grass kept finely shorn.
Francis Bacon 1561–1626: *Essays* (1625) 'Of Gardens'

3 And the Lord God planted a garden eastward in Eden.
Bible: Genesis

4 A garden is a lovesome thing, God wot!
T. E. Brown 1830–97: 'My Garden' (1893)

5 What is a weed? A plant whose virtues have not been discovered.
Ralph Waldo Emerson 1803–82: *Fortune of the Republic* (1878)

6 He that plants trees loves others beside himself.
Thomas Fuller 1654–1734: *Gnomologia* (1732)

7 Sowe Carrets in your Gardens, and humbly praise God for them, as for a singular and great blessing.
Richard Gardiner b. *c*.1533: *Profitable Instructions for the Manuring, Sowing and Planting of Kitchen Gardens* (1599)

8 The kiss of the sun for pardon,
The song of the birds for mirth,
One is nearer God's Heart in a garden
Than anywhere else on earth.
Dorothy Frances Gurney 1858–1932: 'God's Garden' (1913)

9 But though an old man, I am but a young gardener.
Thomas Jefferson 1743–1826: letter to Charles Willson Peale, 20 August 1811

10 Our England is a garden, and such gardens are not made
By singing:—'Oh, how beautiful!' and sitting in the shade,

While better men than we go out and start their working
lives
At grubbing weeds from gravel paths with broken dinner-
knives.
   Rudyard Kipling 1865–1936: 'The Glory of the Garden'
   (1911)

11 A garden was the primitive prison till man with
Promethean felicity and boldness luckily sinned himself
out of it.
   Charles Lamb 1775–1834: letter to William Wordsworth,
   22 January 1830

12 Annihilating all that's made
To a green thought in a green shade.
   Andrew Marvell 1621–78: 'The Garden' (1681)

13 There can be no other occupation like gardening in which,
if you were to creep behind someone at their work, you
would find them smiling.
   Mirabel Osler: *A Gentle Plea for Chaos* (1989)

14 Come into the garden, Maud,
For the black bat, night, has flown,
Come into the garden, Maud,
I am here at the gate alone;
And the woodbine spices are wafted abroad,
And the musk of the rose is blown.
   Alfred, Lord Tennyson 1809–92: *Maud* (1855)

The Generation Gap

See also **Youth**

1 Each year brings new problems of Form and Content,
new foes to tug with: at Twenty I tried to
vex my elders, past Sixty it's the young whom
I hope to bother.
   W. H. Auden 1907–73: 'Shorts I' (1969)

2 Come mothers and fathers,
   Throughout the land
   And don't criticize
   What you can't understand.
      Bob Dylan 1941– : 'The Times They Are A-Changing'
      (1964 song)

3 *Si jeunesse savait; si vieillesse pouvait.*
   If youth knew; if age could.
      Henri Estienne 1531–98: *Les Prémices* (1594)

4 Every generation revolts against its fathers and makes
   friends with its grandfathers.
      Lewis Mumford 1895–1982: *The Brown Decades* (1931)

5 Crabbed age and youth cannot live together:
   Youth is full of pleasance, age is full of care.
      William Shakespeare 1564–1616: *The Passionate
      Pilgrim* (1599)

6 It's all that the young can do for the old, to shock them
   and keep them up to date.
      George Bernard Shaw 1856–1950: *Fanny's First Play*
      (1914)

7 Hope I die before I get old.
      Pete Townshend 1945– : 'My Generation' (1965 song)

8 When I was a boy of 14, my father was so ignorant I could
   hardly stand to have the old man around. But when I got
   to be 21, I was astonished at how much the old man had
   learned in seven years.
      Mark Twain 1835–1910: attributed in *Reader's Digest*
      September 1939, but not traced in his works

9 Where, where but here have Pride and Truth,
   That long to give themselves for wage,
   To shake their wicked sides at youth
   Restraining reckless middle age?
      W. B. Yeats 1865–1939: 'On hearing that the Students of
      our New University have joined the Agitation against
      Immoral Literature' (1912)

Genius

1 Genius is only a greater aptitude for patience.
   Comte de Buffon 1707–88: H. de Séchelles *Voyage à Montbar* (1803)

2 Mediocrity knows nothing higher than itself, but talent instantly recognizes genius.
   Arthur Conan Doyle 1859–1930: *The Valley of Fear* (1915)

3 Great wits are sure to madness near allied,
   And thin partitions do their bounds divide.
   John Dryden 1631–1700: *Absalom and Achitophel* (1681)

4 Genius is one per cent inspiration, ninety-nine per cent perspiration.
   Thomas Alva Edison 1847–1931: said *c*.1903, in *Harper's Monthly Magazine* September 1932

5 Little minds are interested in the extraordinary; great minds in the commonplace.
   Elbert Hubbard 1859–1915: *Thousand and One Epigrams* (1911)

6 The true genius is a mind of large general powers, accidentally determined to some particular direction.
   Samuel Johnson 1709–84: *Lives of the English Poets* (1779–81)

7 Genius does what it must, and Talent does what it can.
   Owen Meredith 1831–91: 'Last Words of a Sensitive Second-Rate Poet' (1868)

8 Every positive value has its price in negative terms . . . The genius of Einstein leads to Hiroshima.
   Pablo Picasso 1881–1973: F. Gilot and C. Lake *Life With Picasso* (1964)

9 When a true genius appears in the world, you may know him by this sign, that the dunces are all in confederacy against him.
   Jonathan Swift 1667–1745: *Thoughts on Various Subjects* (1711)

10 I have nothing to declare except my genius.
   Oscar Wilde 1854–1900: at the New York Custom House;
   in Frank Harris *Oscar Wilde* (1918)

....

Gifts and Giving

....

1 Surprises are foolish things. The pleasure is not enhanced,
   and the inconvenience is often considerable.
   Jane Austen 1775–1817: *Emma* (1816)

2 Give, and it shall be given unto you; good measure, pressed
   down, and shaken together, and running over.
   Bible: St Luke

3 It is more blessed to give than to receive.
   Bible: Acts of the Apostles

4 God loveth a cheerful giver.
   Bible: II Corinthians

5 They gave it me,—for an un-birthday present.
   Lewis Carroll 1832–98: *Through the Looking-Glass* (1872)

6 CHAIRMAN: What is service?
   CANDIDATE: The rent we pay for our room on earth.
   Tubby Clayton 1885–1972: admission ceremony of Toc H;
   Tresham Lever *Clayton of Toc H* (1971)

7 Why is it no one ever sent me yet
   One perfect limousine, do you suppose?
   Ah no, it's always just my luck to get
   One perfect rose.
   Dorothy Parker 1893–1967: 'One Perfect Rose' (1937)

8 *Inopi beneficium bis dat qui dat celeriter.*

   He gives the poor man twice as much good who gives
   quickly.
   Publilius Syrus 1st century BC: *Sententiae* (proverbially
   '*Bis dat qui cito dat* [He gives twice who gives soon]')

9 The Christian usually tries to give away his own money, whilst the philosopher usually tries to give away the money of someone else.

   Lord Salisbury 1830–1903: C. S. Kenny *Property for Charitable Uses* (1880)

10 When they will not give a doit to relieve a lame beggar, they will lay out ten to see a dead Indian.

   William Shakespeare 1564–1616: *The Tempest* (1611)

11 Thy necessity is yet greater than mine.

   Philip Sidney 1554–86: on giving his water-bottle to a dying soldier on the battle-field of Zutphen, 1586; in Fulke Greville *Life of Sir Philip Sidney* (1652). Commonly quoted 'thy need is greater than mine'

12 [Gratitude] is a sickness suffered by dogs.

   Joseph Stalin 1879–1953: Nikolai Tolstoy *Stalin's Secret War* (1981)

13 No one would remember the Good Samaritan if he'd only had good intentions. He had money as well.

   Margaret Thatcher 1925– : television interview, 6 January 1980

14 Behold, I do not give lectures or a little charity,
When I give I give myself.

   Walt Whitman 1819–92: 'Song of Myself' (written 1855)

....

God

....

See also **The Bible**, **Religion**

1 The nature of God is a circle of which the centre is everywhere and the circumference is nowhere.

   Anonymous: said to have been traced to a lost treatise of Empedocles; quoted in the *Roman de la Rose*, and by St Bonaventura

2 In the beginning was the Word, and the Word was with God, and the Word was God.

   Bible: St John

3 He that loveth not knoweth not God; for God is love.
   Bible: I John

4 All service ranks the same with God—
   With God, whose puppets, best and worst,
   Are we: there is no last nor first.
   Robert Browning 1812–89: *Pippa Passes* (1841)

5 When men stop believing in God they don't believe in
   nothing; they believe in anything.
   G. K. Chesterton 1874–1936: widely attributed, although
   not traced in his works

6 God moves in a mysterious way
   His wonders to perform;
   He plants his footsteps in the sea,
   And rides upon the storm.
   William Cowper 1731–1800: 'Light Shining out of
   Darkness' (1779)

7 God is subtle but he is not malicious.
   Albert Einstein 1879–1955: remark made at Princeton
   University, May 1921

8 The word is the Verb, and the Verb is God.
   Victor Hugo 1802–85: *Contemplations* (1856)

9 Operationally, God is beginning to resemble not a ruler but
   the last fading smile of a cosmic Cheshire cat.
   Julian Huxley 1887–1975: *Religion without Revelation*
   (1957 ed.)

10 An honest God is the noblest work of man.
   Robert G. Ingersoll 1833–99: *The Gods* (1876)

11 I am not clear that God manoeuvres physical things . . .
   After all, a conjuring trick with bones only proves that it
   is as clever as a conjuring trick with bones.
   David Jenkins, Bishop of Durham 1925– : on the
   Resurrection; radio interview, 4 October 1984

12 God seems to have left the receiver off the hook, and time
   is running out.
   Arthur Koestler 1905–83: *The Ghost in the Machine*
   (1967)

13 Though the mills of God grind slowly, yet they grind
exceeding small;
Though with patience He stands waiting, with exactness
grinds He all.
Henry Wadsworth Longfellow 1807–82: 'Retribution'
(1870); translation of Friedrich von Logau *Sinnegedichte*
(1654), being itself a translation of an anonymous line in
Sextus Empiricus *Adversus Mathematicos*

14 Whatever your heart clings to and confides in, that is
really your God.
Martin Luther 1483–1546: *Large Catechism* (1529) 'The
First Commandment'

15 If the triangles were to make a God they would give him
three sides.
Montesquieu 1689–1755: *Lettres Persones* (1721), tr. J.
Ozell, 1722

16 'God is or he is not.' But to which side shall we incline?
. . . Let us weigh the gain and the loss in wagering that
God is. Let us estimate the two chances. If you gain, you
gain all; if you lose, you lose nothing. Wager then without
hesitation that he is.
Blaise Pascal 1623–62: *Pensées* (1670); known as Pascal's
wager

17 God is really only another artist. He invented the giraffe,
the elephant, and the cat. He has no real style. He just goes
on trying other things.
Pablo Picasso 1881–1973: F. Gilot and C. Lake *Life With
Picasso* (1964)

18 The Buddha, the Godhead, resides quite as comfortably in
the circuits of a digital computer or the gears of a cycle
transmission as he does at the top of a mountain or in the
petals of a flower.
Robert M. Pirsig 1928– : *Zen and the Art of Motorcycle
Maintenance* (1974)

19 O Lord, to what a state dost Thou bring those who love
Thee!
St Teresa of Ávila 1512–82: *Interior Castle* (tr.
Benedictines of Stanbrook, 1921)

20 For man proposes, but God disposes.
    Thomas à Kempis *c.*1380–1471: *De Imitatione Christi*

21 God is on the side not of the heavy battalions, but of the best shots.
    Voltaire 1694–1778: 'The Piccini Notebooks' (*c.*1735–50)

22 If God did not exist, it would be necessary to invent him.
    Voltaire 1694–1778: *Épîtres* (1769)

23 Our God, our help in ages past
Our hope for years to come,
Our shelter from the stormy blast,
And our eternal home.
    Isaac Watts 1674–1748: *Psalms of David Imitated* (1719)
    'Our God' altered to 'O God' by John Wesley, 1738

Good and Evil

See also **Virtue and Vice**

1 The fearsome, word-and-thought-defying *banality of evil*.
    Hannah Arendt 1906–75: *Eichmann in Jerusalem* (1963)

2 Every art and every investigation, and likewise every practical pursuit or undertaking, seems to aim at some good: hence it has been well said that the Good is That at which all things aim.
    Aristotle 384–322 BC: *Nicomachean Ethics*

3 I and the public know
What all schoolchildren learn,
Those to whom evil is done
Do evil in return.
    W. H. Auden 1907–73: 'September 1, 1939' (1940)

4 With love for mankind and hatred of sins.
    St Augustine of Hippo AD 354–430: letter 211 in J.-P. Migne (ed.) *Patrologiae Latinae* (1845), often quoted 'Love the sinner but hate the sin'

5 There is no peace, saith the Lord, unto the wicked.
    Bible: Isaiah

6 For the good that I would I do not: but the evil which I would not, that I do.
   Bible: Romans

7 He who would do good to another, must do it in minute particulars.
   William Blake 1757–1827: *Jerusalem* (1815)

8 It is necessary only for the good man to do nothing for evil to triumph.
   Edmund Burke 1729–97: attributed (in a number of forms) to Burke, but not found in his writings

9 The face of 'evil' is always the face of total need.
   William S. Burroughs 1914–97: *The Naked Lunch* (1959)

10 No people do so much harm as those who go about doing good.
   Bishop Mandell Creighton 1843–1901: in *Life and Letters of Mandell Creighton* by his wife (1904)

11 As soon as men decide that all means are permitted to fight an evil, then their good becomes indistinguishable from the evil that they set out to destroy.
   Christopher Dawson 1889–1970: *The Judgement of the Nations* (1942)

12 What we call evil is simply ignorance bumping its head in the dark.
   Henry Ford 1863–1947: in *Observer* 16 March 1930

13 Innocence always calls mutely for protection, when we would be so much wiser to guard ourselves against it: innocence is like a dumb leper who has lost his bell, wandering the world meaning no harm.
   Graham Greene 1904–91: *The Quiet American* (1955)

14 I expect to pass through this world but once; any good thing therefore that I can do, or any kindness that I can show to any fellow-creature, let me do it now; let me not defer or neglect it, for I shall not pass this way again.
   Stephen Grellet 1773–1855: attributed. See John o' London *Treasure Trove* (1925) for some of the many other claimants to authorship

15 For, where God built a church, there the devil would also
build a chapel . . . In such sort is the devil always God's
ape.
Martin Luther 1483–1546: *Colloquia Mensalia* (1566) tr. H.
Bell, 1652

16 Farewell remorse! All good to me is lost;
Evil, be thou my good.
John Milton 1608–74: *Paradise Lost* (1667)

17 Let humble Allen, with an awkward shame,
Do good by stealth, and blush to find it fame.
Alexander Pope 1688–1744: *Imitations of Horace* (1738)

18 There is nothing either good or bad, but thinking makes it
so.
William Shakespeare 1564–1616: *Hamlet* (1601)

19 I come to bury Caesar, not to praise him.
The evil that men do lives after them,
The good is oft interrèd with their bones.
William Shakespeare 1564–1616: *Julius Caesar* (1599)

20 By the pricking of my thumbs,
Something wicked this way comes.
William Shakespeare 1564–1616: *Macbeth* (1606)

21 'Goodness, what beautiful diamonds!'
'Goodness had nothing to do with it.'
Mae West 1892–1980: *Night After Night* (1932 film)

22 That best portion of a good man's life,
His little, nameless, unremembered, acts
Of kindness and of love.
William Wordsworth 1770–1850: 'Lines composed a few
miles above Tintern Abbey' (1798)

Gossip

1 There is so much good in the worst of us,
And so much bad in the best of us,
That it hardly becomes any of us

To talk about the rest of us.
Anonymous: attributed, among others, to E. W. Hoch
(1849–1945), but disclaimed by him

2 Careless talk costs lives.
Anonymous: Second World War security slogan

3 How these curiosities would be quite forgot, did not such
idle fellows as I am put them down.
John Aubrey 1626–97: *Brief Lives*

4 Every man is surrounded by a neighbourhood of voluntary
spies.
Jane Austen 1775–1817: *Northanger Abbey* (1818)

5 They come together like the Coroner's Inquest, to sit upon
the murdered reputations of the week.
William Congreve 1670–1729: *The Way of the World*
(1700)

6 *Che ti fa ciò che quivi pispiglia?*
Vien dietro a me, e lascia dir le genti.

What is it to thee what they whisper there? Come after me
and let the people talk.
Dante Alighieri 1265–1321: *Divina Commedia*
'Purgatorio'

7 Gossip is a sort of smoke that comes from the dirty
tobacco-pipes of those who diffuse it: it proves nothing but
the bad taste of the smoker.
George Eliot 1819–80: *Daniel Deronda* (1876)

8 Love and scandal are the best sweeteners of tea.
Henry Fielding 1707–54: *Love in Several Masques* (1728)

9 Like all gossip—it's merely one of those half-alive things
that try to crowd out real life.
E. M. Forster 1879–1970: *A Passage to India* (1924)

10 It takes your enemy and your friend, working together, to
hurt you to the heart: the one to slander you and the other
to get the news to you.
Mark Twain 1835–1910: *Following the Equator* (1897)

11 There is only one thing in the world worse than being
talked about, and that is not being talked about.
   Oscar Wilde 1854–1900: *The Picture of Dorian Gray*
   (1891)

....

Government
....

See also **Politics**

1 Let them hate, so long as they fear.
   Accius 170–*c*.86 BC: from *Atreus*

2 The happiness of society is the end of government.
   John Adams 1735–1826: *Thoughts on Government* (1776)

3 A monarchy is a merchantman which sails well, but will
sometimes strike on a rock, and go to the bottom; whilst a
republic is a raft which would never sink, but then your
feet are always in the water.
   Fisher Ames 1758–1808: speech in the House of
   Representatives, 1795; attributed by R. W. Emerson in
   Essays (1844)

4 Every country has its own constitution; ours is absolutism
moderated by assassination.
   Anonymous: 'An intelligent Russian', in *Political
   Sketches of the State of Europe, 1814–1867* (1868)

5 England is the mother of Parliaments.
   John Bright 1811–89: speech at Birmingham, 18 January
   1865

6 The use of force alone is but *temporary.* It may subdue for
a moment; but it does not remove the necessity of
subduing again; and a nation is not governed, which is
perpetually to be conquered.
   Edmund Burke 1729–97: *On Conciliation with America*
   (1775)

7 Democracy means government by the uneducated, while
aristocracy means government by the badly educated.
   G. K. Chesterton 1874–1936: in *New York Times* 1
   February 1931

8 No Government can be long secure without a formidable Opposition.
  Benjamin Disraeli 1804–81: *Coningsby* (1844)

9 All empire is no more than power in trust.
  John Dryden 1631–1700: *Absalom and Achitophel* (1681)

10 Though God hath raised me high, yet this I count the glory of my crown: that I have reigned with your loves.
  Elizabeth I 1533–1603: The Golden Speech, 1601

11 If the Government is big enough to give you everything you want, it is big enough to take away everything you have.
  Gerald Ford 1909– : J. F. Parker *If Elected* (1960)

12 The state is like the human body. Not all of its functions are dignified.
  Anatole France 1844–1924: *Les Opinions de M. Jerome Coignard* (1893)

13 My people and I have come to an agreement which satisfies us both. They are to say what they please, and I am to do what I please.
  Frederick the Great 1712–86: his interpretation of benevolent despotism (attributed)

14 Your business is not to govern the country but it is, if you think fit, to call to account those who do govern it.
  W. E. Gladstone 1809–98: speech to the House of Commons, 29 January 1855

15 Many journalists have fallen for the conspiracy theory of government. I do assure you that they would produce more accurate work if they adhered to the cock-up theory.
  Bernard Ingham 1932– : in *Observer* 17 March 1985

16 The important thing for Government is not to do things which individuals are doing already, and to do them a little better or a little worse; but to do those things which at present are not done at all.
  John Maynard Keynes 1883–1946: *End of Laissez-Faire* (1926)

17 *Gouverner, c'est choisir.*

To govern is to choose.
> **Duc de Lévis** 1764–1830: *Maximes et Réflexions* (1812 ed.)

18 We give the impression of being in office but not in power.
> **Norman Lamont** 1942– : speech, House of Commons, 9 June 1993

19 It is much safer for a prince to be feared than loved, if he is to fail in one of the two.
> **Niccolò Machiavelli** 1469–1527: *The Prince* (1513) tr. A. Gilbert

20 Now, is it to lower the price of corn, or isn't it? It is not much matter which we say, but mind, we must all say *the same.*
> **Lord Melbourne** 1779–1848: on cabinet government; attributed, in Walter Bagehot *The English Constitution* (1867)

21 The best government is that which governs least.
> **John L. O'Sullivan** 1813–95: *United States Magazine and Democratic Review* (1837)

22 BIG BROTHER IS WATCHING YOU.
> **George Orwell** 1903–50: *Nineteen Eighty-Four* (1949)

23 Dost thou not know, my son, with how little wisdom the world is governed?
> **Count Oxenstierna** 1583–1654: letter to his son, 1648. In *Table Talk* (1689), John Selden quotes 'a certain Pope': 'Thou little thinkest what *a little foolery governs the whole world!*'

24 Government, even in its best state, is but a necessary evil; in its worst state, an intolerable one. Government, like dress, is the badge of lost innocence; the palaces of kings are built upon the ruins of the bowers of paradise.
> **Thomas Paine** 1737–1809: *Common Sense* (1776)

25 A parliament can do any thing but make a man a woman, and a woman a man.
> **2nd Earl of Pembroke** c.1534–1601: quoted by his son, the 4th Earl

26 For forms of government let fools contest;
Whate'er is best administered is best.
   Alexander Pope 1688–1744: *An Essay on Man* Epistle 3
   (1733)

27 Wherever you have an efficient government you have a
dictatorship.
   Harry S. Truman 1884–1972: lecture at Columbia
   University, 28 April 1959

28 Governments need both shepherds and butchers.
   Voltaire 1694–1778: 'The Piccini Notebooks' (*c*.1735–50)

Greatness

1 The beauty of Israel is slain upon thy high places: how are
the mighty fallen!
   Bible: II Samuel

2 To be great is to be misunderstood.
   Ralph Waldo Emerson 1803–82: *Essays* (1841) 'Self-
   Reliance'

3 A man does not attain the status of Galileo merely because
he is persecuted; he must also be right.
   Stephen Jay Gould 1941– : *Ever since Darwin* (1977)

4   Rightly to be great
Is not to stir without great argument,
But greatly to find quarrel in a straw
When honour's at the stake.
   William Shakespeare 1564–1616: *Hamlet* (1601)

5 But be not afraid of greatness: some men are born great,
some achieve greatness, and some have greatness thrust
upon them.
   William Shakespeare 1564–1616: *Twelfth Night* (1601)

6 All the world's great have been little boys who wanted the
moon.
   John Steinbeck 1902–68: *Cup of Gold* (1953)

Habit

see **Custom and Habit**

Happiness

1 Mirth is like a flash of lightning that breaks through a
gloom of clouds, and glitters for a moment: cheerfulness
keeps up a kind of day-light in the mind.
   Joseph Addison 1672–1719: *The Spectator* 17 May 1712

2 A large income is the best recipe for happiness I ever
heard of. It certainly may secure all the myrtle and turkey
part of it.
   Jane Austen 1775–1817: *Mansfield Park* (1814)

3 For all the happiness mankind can gain
Is not in pleasure, but in rest from pain.
   John Dryden 1631–1700: *The Indian Emperor* (1665)

4 Happiness makes up in height for what it lacks in length.
   Robert Frost 1874–1963: title of poem (1942)

5 Point me out the happy man and I will point you out
either egotism, selfishness, evil—or else an absolute
ignorance.
   Graham Greene 1904–91: *The Heart of the Matter* (1948)

6 *Nil admirari prope res est una, Numici,*
Solaque quae possit facere et servare beatum.
To marvel at nothing is just about the one and only thing,
Numicius, that can make a man happy and keep him that
way.
   Horace 65–8 BC: *Epistles*

7 I can sympathize with people's pains, but not with their
pleasures. There is something curiously boring about
somebody else's happiness.
   Aldous Huxley 1894–1963: *Limbo* (1920)

8 Happiness is not an ideal of reason but of imagination.
   Immanuel Kant 1724–1804: *Fundamental Principles of
the Metaphysics of Ethics* (1785), tr. T. K. Abbott

9 Happiness is a state of which you are unconscious, of which you are not aware. The moment you are aware that you are happy, you cease to be happy . . . You want to be consciously happy; the moment you are consciously happy, happiness is gone.

    Jiddu Krishnamurti 1895–1986: *Penguin Krishnamurti Reader* (1970)

10 Happiness is a warm gun.

    John Lennon 1940–80: title of song (1968)

11 Ask yourself whether you are happy, and you cease to be so.

    John Stuart Mill 1806–73: *Autobiography* (1873)

12 Not to admire, is all the art I know,
To make men happy, and to keep them so.

    Alexander Pope 1688–1744: *Imitations of Horace* (1738)

13 I always say I don't think everyone has the right to happiness or to be loved. Even the Americans have written into their constitution that you have the right to the 'pursuit of happiness'. You have the right to try but that is all.

    Claire Rayner 1931– : G. Kinnock and F. Miller *By Faith and Daring* (1993)

14 *Freude, schöner Götterfunken,
Tochter aus Elysium.*

Joy, beautiful radiance of the gods, daughter of Elysium.

    Friedrich von Schiller 1759–1805: 'An die Freude' (1785)

15 But a lifetime of happiness! No man alive could bear it: it would be hell on earth.

    George Bernard Shaw 1856–1950: *Man and Superman* (1903)

16 Call no man happy before he dies, he is at best but fortunate.

    Solon *c.*640–after 556 BC: Herodotus *Histories*

17 Happiness is an imaginary condition, formerly often attributed by the living to the dead, now usually attributed by adults to children, and by children to adults.

    Thomas Szasz 1920– : *The Second Sin* (1973) 'Emotions'

Hatred

1 Better is a dinner of herbs where love is, than a stalled ox and hatred therewith.

Bible: Proverbs

2 I do not love thee, Dr Fell.
The reason why I cannot tell;
But this I know, and know full well,
I do not love thee, Dr Fell.

Thomas Brown 1663–1704: written while an undergraduate at Christ Church, Oxford, of which Dr Fell was Dean

3 Now hatred is by far the longest pleasure;
Men love in haste, but they detest at leisure.

Lord Byron 1788–1824: *Don Juan* (1819–24)

4 Love, friendship, respect do not unite people as much as common hatred for something.

Anton Chekhov 1860–1904: *Notebooks* (1921)

5 I never hated a man enough to give him diamonds back.

Zsa Zsa Gabor 1919– : in *Observer* 25 August 1957

6 What we need is hatred. From it our ideas are born.

Jean Genet 1910–86: *The Blacks* (1959); epigraph

7 We can scarcely hate any one that we know.

William Hazlitt 1778–1830: *Table Talk* (1822)

8 If you hate a person, you hate something in him that is part of yourself. What isn't part of ourselves doesn't disturb us.

Hermann Hesse 1877–1962: *Demian* (1919)

9 No one is born hating another person because of the colour of his skin, or his background, or his religion. People must learn to hate, and if they can learn to hate, they can be taught to love, for love comes more naturally to the human heart than its opposite.

Nelson Mandela 1918– : *Long Walk to Freedom* (1994)

10 *Non amo te, Sabidi, nec possum dicere quare:*
Hoc tantum possum dicere, non amo te.
I don't love you, Sabidius, and I can't tell you why; all I

can tell you is this, that I don't love you.
Martial AD c.40–c.104: *Epigrammata*

11 Always remember, others may hate you. Those who hate
you don't win unless you hate them. And then you destroy
yourself.
Richard Nixon 1913–94: address to staff, 9 August 1974

12 One cannot overestimate the power of a good rancorous
hatred on the part of the *stupid*. The stupid have so much
more industry and energy to expend on hating. They build
it up like coral insects.
Sylvia Townsend Warner 1893–1978: diary 26
September 1954

Health and Fitness

1 The first law of dietetics seems to be: if it tastes good, it's
bad for you.
Isaac Asimov 1920–92: attributed

2 Therapy has become what I think of as the tenth American
muse.
Jacob Bronowski 1908–74: attributed

3 In the face of such overwhelming statistical possibilities,
hypochondria has always seemed to me to be the only
rational position to take on life.
John Diamond: *C: Because Cowards Get Cancer Too*
(1998)

4 Exercise is the yuppie version of bulimia.
Barbara Ehrenreich 1941– : *The Worst Years of Our
Lives* (1991) 'Food Worship'

5 Exercise is bunk. If you are healthy, you don't need it: if
you are sick you shouldn't take it.
Henry Ford 1863–1947: attributed

6 The sovereign invigorator of the body is exercise, and of
all the exercises, walking is best.
Thomas Jefferson 1743–1826: letter to Thomas Mann
Randolph Jr., 27 August 1786

7 *Mens sana in corpore sano.*

A sound mind in a sound body.
   Juvenal AD c.60–c.130: *Satires*

8 Life's not just being alive, but being well.
   Martial AD c.40–c.104: *Epigrammata*

9 The only exercise I take is walking behind the coffins of friends who took exercise.
   Peter O'Toole 1932– : in *Mail on Sunday* 27 December 1998

10 Early to rise and early to bed makes a male healthy and wealthy and dead.
   James Thurber 1894–1961: 'The Shrike and the Chipmunks' in *New Yorker* 18 February 1939

11 Look to your health; and if you have it, praise God, and value it next to a good conscience; for health is the second blessing that we mortals are capable of; a blessing that money cannot buy.
   Izaak Walton 1593–1683: *The Compleat Angler* (1653)

The Heart

1 The desires of the heart are as crooked as corkscrews
   Not to be born is the best for man.
   W. H. Auden 1907–73: 'Death's Echo' (1937)

2 The human heart likes a little disorder in its geometry.
   Louis de Bernières 1954– : *Captain Corelli's Mandolin* (1994)

3 A man who has not passed through the inferno of his passions has never overcome them.
   Carl Gustav Jung 1875–1961: *Memories, Dreams, Reflections* (1962)

4 Calm of mind, all passion spent.
   John Milton 1608–74: *Samson Agonistes* (1671)

5 The heart is an organ of fire.
   Michael Ondaatje 1943– : *The English Patient* (1992)

6 The heart has its reasons which reason knows nothing of.
Blaise Pascal 1623–62: *Pensées* (1670)

7 Unlearn'd, he knew no schoolman's subtle art,
No language, but the language of the heart.
Alexander Pope 1688–1744: 'An Epistle to Dr Arbuthnot' (1735)

8   A man whose blood
Is very snow-broth; one who never feels
The wanton stings and motions of the sense.
William Shakespeare 1564–1616: *Measure for Measure* (1604)

9 Now that my ladder's gone
I must lie down where all ladders start
In the foul rag and bone shop of the heart.
W. B. Yeats 1865–1939: 'The Circus Animals' Desertion' (1939)

Heaven and Hell

1 Hell, madam, is to love no more.
Georges Bernanos 1888–1948: *Journal d'un curé de campagne* (1936)

2 And I saw a new heaven and a new earth: for the first heaven and the first earth were passed away; and there was no more sea.
Bible: Revelation

3 LASCIATE OGNI SPERANZA VOI CH'ENTRATE!
Abandon all hope, you who enter!
Dante Alighieri 1265–1321: inscription at the entrance to Hell; *Divina Commedia* 'Inferno'

4 What is hell?
Hell is oneself,
Hell is alone, the other figures in it
Merely projections.
T. S. Eliot 1888–1965: *The Cocktail Party* (1950)

5 Better to reign in hell, than serve in heaven.
John Milton 1608–74: *Paradise Lost* (1667)

6 The true paradises are the paradises that we have lost.
   Marcel Proust 1871–1922: *Time Regained* (1926)

7 Hell is other people.
   Jean-Paul Sartre 1905–80: *Huis Clos* (1944)

8 A perpetual holiday is a good working definition of hell.
   George Bernard Shaw 1856–1950: *Parents and Children*
   (1914)

9 Hell is a city much like London.
   Percy Bysshe Shelley 1792–1822: 'Peter Bell the Third'
   (1819)

10 My idea of heaven is, eating *pâté de foie gras* to the sound
   of trumpets.
   Sydney Smith 1771–1845: in H. Pearson *The Smith of*
   Smiths (1934)

11 I will spend my heaven doing good on earth.
   St Teresa of Lisieux 1873–97: T. N. Taylor (ed.) *Soeur*
   Thérèse of Lisieux (1912)

Heroes

1 Faster than a speeding bullet! . . . Look! Up in the sky! It's
   a bird! It's a plane! It's Superman! Yes, it's Superman! . . .
   who—disguised as Clark Kent, mild-mannered reporter for
   a great metropolitan newspaper—fights a never ending
   battle for truth, justice and the American way!
   Anonymous: *Superman* (US radio show, 1940 onwards)
   preamble

2 ANDREA: Unhappy the land that has no heroes! . . .
   GALILEO: No. Unhappy the land that needs heroes.
   Bertolt Brecht 1898–1956: *Life of Galileo* (1939)

3 Down these mean streets a man must go who is not
   himself mean, who is neither tarnished nor afraid.
   Raymond Chandler 1888–1959: in *Atlantic Monthly*
   December 1944 'The Simple Art of Murder'

4 No man is a hero to his valet.
   Mme Cornuel 1605–94: in *Lettres de Mlle Aïssé à Madame C* (1787) Letter 13 'De Paris, 1728'

5 I think that's just another word for a washed-up has-been.
   Bob Dylan 1941– : on being an 'icon'; in *Mail on Sunday* 18 January 1998

6 Every hero becomes a bore at last.
   Ralph Waldo Emerson 1803–82: *Representative Men* (1850)

7 If the myth gets bigger than the man, print the myth.
   Dorothy Johnson 1905–84: *Indian Country* (1953) 'The Man Who Shot Liberty Valance'

8 Ultimately a hero is a man who would argue with the Gods, and so awakens devils to contest his vision.
   Norman Mailer 1923– : *The Presidential Papers* (1976)

9 Heroing is one of the shortest-lived professions there is.
   Will Rogers 1879–1935: newspaper article, 15 February 1925

10 In this world I would rather live two days like a tiger, than two hundred years like a sheep.
   Tipu Sultan *c.*1750–99: Alexander Beatson *A View of the Origin and Conduct of the War with Tippoo Sultaun* (1800)

History

1 Does history repeat itself, the first time as tragedy, the second time as farce? No, that's too grand, too considered a process. History just burps, and we taste again that raw-onion sandwich it swallowed centuries ago.
   Julian Barnes 1946– : *A History of the World in 10½ Chapters* (1989)

2 That great dust-heap called 'history'.
   Augustine Birrell 1850–1933: *Obiter Dicta* (1884)

3 History is the essence of innumerable biographies.
   Thomas Carlyle 1795–1881: *Critical and Miscellaneous Essays* (1838) 'On History'

4 History is philosophy from examples.
   Dionysius of Halicarnassus fl. 30–7 BC: *Ars Rhetorica*

5 History is more or less bunk.
   Henry Ford 1863–1947: in *Chicago Tribune* 25 May 1916

6 History is past politics, and politics is present history.
   E. A. Freeman 1823–92: *Methods of Historical Study* (1886)

7 History . . . is, indeed, little more than the register of the crimes, follies, and misfortunes of mankind.
   Edward Gibbon 1737–94: *Decline and Fall of the Roman Empire* (1776–88)

8 War makes rattling good history; but Peace is poor reading.
   Thomas Hardy 1840–1928: *The Dynasts* (1904)

9 What experience and history teach is this—that nations and governments have never learned anything from history, or acted upon any lessons they might have drawn from it.
   G. W. F. Hegel 1770–1831: *Lectures on the Philosophy of World History: Introduction* (1830), tr. H. B. Nisbet

10 Hegel says somewhere that all great events and personalities in world history reappear in one fashion or another. He forgot to add: the first time as tragedy, the second as farce.
   Karl Marx 1818–83: *Eighteenth Brumaire of Louis Bonaparte* (1852)

11 Happy the people whose annals are blank in history-books!
   Montesquieu 1689–1755: attributed by Thomas Carlyle

12 History is not what you thought. *It is what you can remember.*
   W. C. Sellar 1898–1951 and **R. J. Yeatman** 1898–1968: *1066 and All That* (1930) 'Compulsory Preface'

13 History gets thicker as it approaches recent times.
   A. J. P. Taylor 1906–90: *English History 1914–45* (1965)
   bibliography

14 History is a gallery of pictures in which there are few
   originals and many copies.
   Alexis de Tocqueville 1805–59: *L'Ancien régime* (1856),
   tr. M. W. Patterson

15 Human history becomes more and more a race between
   education and catastrophe.
   H. G. Wells 1866–1946: *The Outline of History* (1920)

The Home and Housework

1 Home is home, though it be never so homely.
   John Clarke d. 1658: *Paraemiologia Anglo-Latina* (1639)

2 For a man's house is his castle, *et domus sua cuique est
   tutissimum refugium* [and each man's home is his safest
   refuge].
   Edward Coke 1552–1634: *Third Part of the Institutes of
   the Laws of England* (1628)

3 Conran's Law of Housework—it expands to fill the time
   available plus half an hour.
   Shirley Conran 1932– : *Superwoman 2* (1977)

4 There was no need to do any housework at all. After the
   first four years the dirt doesn't get any worse.
   Quentin Crisp 1908–99: *The Naked Civil Servant* (1968)

5 'Home is the place where, when you have to go there,
   They have to take you in.'
   'I should have called it
   Something you somehow haven't to deserve.'
   Robert Frost 1874–1963: 'The Death of the Hired Man'
   (1914)

6   The best
Thing we can do is to make wherever we're lost in
Look as much like home as we can.
> **Christopher Fry** 1907– : *The Lady's not for Burning*
> (1949)

7 Dirt is only matter out of place.
> **John Chipman Gray** 1839–1915: *Restraints on the
> Alienation of Property* (2nd ed., 1895)

8 What's the good of a home if you are never in it?
> **George Grossmith** 1847–1912 and **Weedon Grossmith**
> 1854–1919: *Diary of a Nobody* (1894)

9 There is scarcely any less bother in the running of a
family than in that of an entire state. And domestic
business is no less importunate for being less important.
> **Montaigne** 1533–92: *Essais* (1580)

10 Have nothing in your houses that you do not know to be
useful, or believe to be beautiful.
> **William Morris** 1834–96: *Hopes and Fears for Art* (1882)

11 Mid pleasures and palaces though we may roam,
Be it ever so humble, there's no place like home.
> **J. H. Payne** 1791–1852: 'Home, Sweet Home' (1823)

12 Home is the girl's prison and the woman's workhouse.
> **George Bernard Shaw** 1856–1950: *Man and Superman*
> (1903)

13 Home is where you come to when you have nothing better
to do.
> **Margaret Thatcher** 1925– : in *Vanity Fair* May 1991

14 MR PRITCHARD: I must dust the blinds and then I must
raise them.
MRS OGMORE-PRITCHARD: And before you let the sun in,
mind it wipes its shoes.
> **Dylan Thomas** 1914–53: *Under Milk Wood* (1954)

15 Hatred of domestic work is a natural and admirable result
of civilization.
> **Rebecca West** 1892–1983: in *The Freewoman* 6 June
> 1912

Honour

1 The louder he talked of his honour, the faster we counted our spoons.
  Ralph Waldo Emerson 1803–82: *The Conduct of Life* (1860)

2 Remember, you're fighting for this woman's honour . . . which is probably more than she ever did.
  Bert Kalmar 1884–1947 et al.: *Duck Soup* (1933 film); spoken by Groucho Marx

3 I could not love thee, Dear, so much,
  Loved I not honour more.
  Richard Lovelace 1618–58: 'To Lucasta, Going to the Wars' (1649)

4 Who steals my purse steals trash; 'tis something, nothing;
  'Twas mine, 'tis his, and has been slave to thousands;
  But he that filches from me my good name
  Robs me of that which not enriches him,
  And makes me poor indeed.
  William Shakespeare 1564–1616: *Othello* (1602–4)

5 O! I have lost my reputation. I have lost the immortal part of myself, and what remains is bestial.
  William Shakespeare 1564–1616: *Othello* (1602–4)

6 His honour rooted in dishonour stood,
  And faith unfaithful kept him falsely true.
  Alfred, Lord Tennyson 1809–92: *Idylls of the King* 'Lancelot and Elaine' (1859)

Hope and Despair

See also **Optimism and Pessimism**

1 Hope deferred maketh the heart sick: but when the desire cometh, it is a tree of life.
  Bible: Proverbs

2 What is hope? nothing but the paint on the face of
Existence; the least touch of truth rubs it off, and then we
see what a hollow-cheeked harlot we have got hold of.
  Lord Byron 1788–1824: letter to Thomas Moore, 28
  October 1815

3 Work without hope draws nectar in a sieve,
And hope without an object cannot live.
  Samuel Taylor Coleridge 1772–1834: 'Work without
  Hope' (1828)

4 There is no despair so absolute as that which comes with
the first moments of our first great sorrow, when we have
not yet known what it is to have suffered and be healed, to
have despaired and have recovered hope.
  George Eliot 1819–80: *Adam Bede* (1859)

5 In a real dark night of the soul it is always three o'clock in
the morning.
  F. Scott Fitzgerald 1896–1940: 'Handle with Care' in
  Esquire March 1936

6 He that lives upon hope will die fasting.
  Benjamin Franklin 1706–90: *Poor Richard's Almanac*
  (1758)

7 Walk on, walk on, with hope in your heart,
And you'll never walk alone.
  Oscar Hammerstein II 1895–1960: 'You'll never walk
  alone' (1945 song)

8 If way to the Better there be, it exacts a full look at the
worst.
  Thomas Hardy 1840–1928: 'De Profundis' (1902)

9 Hope is definitely not the same thing as optimism. It is not
the conviction that something will turn out well, but the
certainty that something makes sense, regardless of how it
turns out.
  Václav Havel 1936– : *Disturbing the Peace* (1986)

10 He that lives in hope danceth without music.
  George Herbert 1593–1633: *Outlandish Proverbs* (1640)

11 Not, I'll not, carrion comfort, Despair, not feast on thee;
Not untwist—slack they may be—these last strands of man
In me or, most weary, cry *I can no more*. I can;

Can something, hope, wish day come, not choose not to be.
  Gerard Manley Hopkins 1844–89: 'Carrion Comfort'
  (written 1885)

12 *Nil desperandum.*

Never despair.
  Horace 65–8 BC: *Odes*

13 After all, tomorrow is another day.
  Margaret Mitchell 1900–49: *Gone with the Wind* (1936)

14 Anything that consoles is fake.
  Iris Murdoch 1919–99: R. Harries *Prayer and the Pursuit
  of Happiness* (1985)

15 Hope springs eternal in the human breast:
Man never Is, but always To be blest.
  Alexander Pope 1688–1744: *An Essay on Man* Epistle 1
  (1733)

16 Human life begins on the far side of despair.
  Jean-Paul Sartre 1905–80: *Les Mouches* (1943)

17 He who has never hoped can never despair.
  George Bernard Shaw 1856–1950: *Caesar and Cleopatra*
  (1901)

18   O, Wind,
If Winter comes, can Spring be far behind?
  Percy Bysshe Shelley 1792–1822: 'Ode to the West
  Wind' (1819)

··

The Human Race
··

1 Drinking when we are not thirsty and making love all year
round, madam; that is all there is to distinguish us from
other animals.
  Pierre-Augustin Caron de Beaumarchais 1732–99:
  The Marriage of Figaro (1785)

2 There's a man all over for you, blaming on his boots the
faults of his feet.
   Samuel Beckett 1906–89: *Waiting for Godot* (1955)

3 For Mercy has a human heart
Pity a human face:
And Love, the human form divine,
And Peace, the human dress.
   William Blake 1757–1827: *Songs of Innocence* (1789) 'The
   Divine Image'

4 Cruelty has a human heart,
And Jealousy a human face;
Terror the human form divine,
And Secrecy the human dress.
   William Blake 1757–1827: 'A Divine Image'; etched but
   not included in *Songs of Experience* (1794)

5 We carry within us the wonders we seek without us: there
is all Africa and her prodigies in us.
   Sir Thomas Browne 1605–82: *Religio Medici* (1643)

6 I hate 'Humanity' and all such abstracts: but I love *people*.
Lovers of 'Humanity' generally hate *people and children*,
and keep parrots or puppy dogs.
   Roy Campbell 1901–57: *Light on a Dark Horse* (1951)

7 By nature men are alike. Through practice they have
become far apart.
   Confucius 551–479 BC: *Analects*

8 What is man, when you come to think upon him, but a
minutely set, ingenious machine for turning, with infinite
artfulness, the red wine of Shiraz into urine?
   Isak Dinesen 1885–1962: *Seven Gothic Tales* (1934)

9 Is man an ape or an angel? Now I am on the side of the
angels.
   Benjamin Disraeli 1804–81: speech at Oxford, 25
   November 1864

10 Man is a tool-making animal.
   Benjamin Franklin 1706–90: James Boswell *Life of
   Samuel Johnson* (1791) 7 April 1778

11 Out of the crooked timber of humanity no straight thing can ever be made.

 Immanuel Kant 1724–1804: *Idee zu einer allgemeinen Geschichte in weltbürgerlicher Absicht* (1784)

12 To say, for example, that a man is made up of certain chemical elements is a satisfactory description only for those who intend to use him as a fertilizer.

 H. J. Muller 1890–1967: *Science and Criticism* (1943)

13 I teach you the superman. Man is something to be surpassed.

 Friedrich Nietzsche 1844–1900: *Also Sprach Zarathustra* (1883)

14 What is man in nature? A nothing in respect of that which is infinite, an all in respect of nothing, a middle betwixt nothing and all.

 Blaise Pascal 1623–62: *Pensées* (1670)

15 Man is only a reed, the weakest thing in nature; but he is a thinking reed.

 Blaise Pascal 1623–62: *Pensées* (1670)

16 An honest man's the noblest work of God.

 Alexander Pope 1688–1744: *An Essay on Man* Epistle 4 (1734)

17 Man is the measure of all things.

 Protagoras b. *c.*485 BC: in Plato *Theaetetus*

18 How beauteous mankind is! O brave new world,
That has such people in't.

 William Shakespeare 1564–1616: *The Tempest* (1611)

19   We are such stuff
As dreams are made on, and our little life
Is rounded with a sleep.

 William Shakespeare 1564–1616: *The Tempest* (1611)

20 What a piece of work is a man! How noble in reason! how infinite in faculty! in form, in moving, how express and admirable! in action how like an angel! in apprehension how like a god! the beauty of the world! the paragon of animals!

 William Shakespeare 1564–1616: *Hamlet* (1601)

21 There are many wonderful things, and nothing is more
wonderful than man.
Sophocles c.496–406 BC: *Antigone*

22 Man, unlike any other thing organic or inorganic in the
universe, grows beyond his work, walks up the stairs of
his concepts, emerges ahead of his accomplishments.
John Steinbeck 1902–68: *Grapes of Wrath* (1939)

23 I am a man, I count nothing human foreign to me.
Terence c.190–159 BC: *Heauton Timorumenos*

24 Man is the Only Animal that Blushes. Or needs to.
Mark Twain 1835–1910: *Following the Equator* (1897)

25 We're all of us guinea pigs in the laboratory of God.
Humanity is just a work in progress.
Tennessee Williams 1911–83: *Camino Real* (1953)

Human Rights

1 We hold these truths to be self-evident, that all men are
created equal, that they are endowed by their Creator with
certain unalienable rights, that among these are life,
liberty and the pursuit of happiness.
American Declaration of Independence 1776: from a
draft by Thomas Jefferson (1743–1826)

2 *Liberté! Égalité! Fraternité!*

Freedom! Equality! Brotherhood!
Anonymous: motto of the French Revolution, but of
earlier origin

3 Natural rights is simple nonsense: natural and
imprescriptible rights, rhetorical nonsense—nonsense
upon stilts.
Jeremy Bentham 1748–1832: *Anarchical Fallacies*

4 Whatever each man can separately do, without trespassing
upon others, he has a right to do for himself; and he has a
right to a fair portion of all which society, with all its

combinations of skill and force, can do in his favour.
>   **Edmund Burke** 1729–97: *Reflections on the Revolution in France* (1790)

5 No man can put a chain about the ankle of his fellow man without at last finding the other end fastened about his own neck.
>   **Frederick Douglass** c.1818–95: speech at Civil Rights Mass Meeting, Washington, DC, 22 October 1883

6 To no man will we sell, or deny, or delay, right or justice.
>   **Magna Carta** 1215: clause 40

7 The poorest he that is in England hath a life to live as the greatest he.
>   **Thomas Rainborowe** d. 1648: during the Army debates at Putney, 29 October 1647

8 Any law which violates the inalienable rights of man is essentially unjust and tyrannical; it is not a law at all.
>   **Maximilien Robespierre** 1758–94: *Déclaration des droits de l'homme* 24 April 1793

9 We look forward to a world founded upon four essential human freedoms. The first is freedom of speech and expression—everywhere in the world. The second is freedom of every person to worship God in his own way—everywhere in the world. The third is freedom from want . . . The fourth is freedom from fear.
>   **Franklin D. Roosevelt** 1882–1945: message to Congress, 6 January 1941

10 That little man . . . he says women can't have as much rights as men, cause Christ wasn't a woman. Where did your Christ come from? From God and a woman. Man had nothing to do with Him.
>   **Sojourner Truth** c.1797–1883: speech at Women's Rights Convention, Akron, Ohio, 1851

11 All human beings are born free and equal in dignity and rights.
>   **Universal Declaration of Human Rights** 1948: article 1

Humour

1 If we may believe our logicians, man is distinguished from
  all other creatures by the faculty of laughter.
  Joseph Addison 1672–1719: *The Spectator* 26 September
  1712

2 Among those whom I like or admire, I can find no common
  denominator, but among those whom I love, I can: all of
  them make me laugh.
  W. H. Auden 1907–73: *The Dyer's Hand* (1963) 'Notes on
  the Comic'

3 For what do we live, but to make sport for our neighbours,
  and laugh at them in our turn?
  Jane Austen 1775–1817: *Pride and Prejudice* (1813)

4 I make myself laugh at everything, for fear of having to
  weep at it.
  Pierre-Augustin Caron de Beaumarchais 1732–99: *Le
  Barbier de Séville* (1755)

5 What is an Epigram? a dwarfish whole,
  Its body brevity, and wit its soul.
  Samuel Taylor Coleridge 1772–1834: 'Epigram' (1809)

6 The trouble with Freud is that he never had to play the old
  Glasgow Empire on a Saturday night after Rangers and
  Celtic had both lost.
  Ken Dodd 1931– : in *Guardian* 30 April 1991; quoted in
  many forms since the mid-1960s

7 A thing well said will be wit in all languages.
  John Dryden 1631–1700: *Essay of Dramatic Poesy* (1668)

8 A difference of taste in jokes is a great strain on the
  affections.
  George Eliot 1819–80: *Daniel Deronda* (1876)

9 The funniest thing about comedy is that you never know
  why people laugh. I know *what* makes them laugh but
  trying to get your hands on the *why* of it is like trying to
  pick an eel out of a tub of water.
  W. C. Fields 1880–1946: R. J. Anobile *A Flask of Fields*
  (1972)

10 Nothing is so impenetrable as laughter in a language you don't understand.

> **William Golding** 1911–93: *An Egyptian Journal* (1985)

11 What do you mean, funny? Funny-peculiar or funny ha-ha?

> **Ian Hay** 1876–1952: *The Housemaster* (1938)

12 People must not do things for fun. We are not here for fun. There is no reference to fun in any Act of Parliament.

> **A. P. Herbert** 1890–1971: *Uncommon Law* (1935)

13 [A pun] is a pistol let off at the ear; not a feather to tickle the intellect.

> **Charles Lamb** 1775–1834: *Last Essays of Elia* (1833) 'Popular Fallacies'

14 Wit is the epitaph of an emotion.

> **Friedrich Nietzsche** 1844–1900: *Menschliches, Allzumenschliches* (1867–80)

15 Laughter is pleasant, but the exertion is too much for me.

> **Thomas Love Peacock** 1785–1866: *Nightmare Abbey* (1818)

16 Everything is funny as long as it is happening to Somebody Else.

> **Will Rogers** 1879–1935: *The Illiterate Digest* (1924)

17 I am not only witty in myself, but the cause that wit is in other men.

> **William Shakespeare** 1564–1616: *Henry IV, Part 2* (1597)

18 Brevity is the soul of wit.

> **William Shakespeare** 1564–1616: *Hamlet* (1601)

19 Delight hath a joy in it either permanent or present. Laughter hath only a scornful tickling.

> **Philip Sidney** 1554–86: *The Defence of Poetry* (1595)

20 Humour is emotional chaos remembered in tranquillity.

> **James Thurber** 1894–1961: in *New York Post* 29 February 1960

21 We are not amused.

> **Queen Victoria** 1819–1901: attributed, in Caroline Holland *Notebooks of a Spinster Lady* (1919) 2 January 1900

Hypocrisy

1 Ye are like unto whited sepulchres.
   Bible: St Matthew

2 Compound for sins, they are inclined to,
   By damning those they have no mind to.
   Samuel Butler 1612–80: *Hudibras* pt. 1 (1663)

3 The smylere with the knyf under the cloke.
   Geoffrey Chaucer c.1343–1400: *The Canterbury Tales*
   'The Knight's Tale'

4 Keep up appearances; there lies the test;
   The world will give thee credit for the rest.
   Outward be fair, however foul within;
   Sin if thou wilt, but then in secret sin.
   Charles Churchill 1731–64: *Night* (1761)

5 My tongue swore, but my mind's unsworn.
   Euripides c.485–c.406 BC: *Hippolytus* (lamenting the
   breaking of an oath)

6 Hypocrisy is a tribute which vice pays to virtue.
   Duc de la Rochefoucauld 1613–80: *Maximes* (1678)

7 Hypocrisy, the only evil that walks
   Invisible, except to God alone.
   John Milton 1608–74: *Paradise Lost* (1667)

8 Do not, as some ungracious pastors do,
   Show me the steep and thorny way to heaven,
   Whiles, like a puffed and reckless libertine,
   Himself the primrose path of dalliance treads,
   And recks not his own rede.
   William Shakespeare 1564–1616: *Hamlet* (1601)

9   I want that glib and oily art
   To speak and purpose not.
   William Shakespeare 1564–1616: *King Lear* (1605–6)

10 All Reformers, however strict their social conscience, live
   in houses just as big as they can pay for.
   Logan Pearsall Smith 1865–1946: *Afterthoughts* (1931)

11 I sit on a man's back, choking him and making him carry me, and yet assure myself and others that I am very sorry for him and wish to ease his lot by all possible means—except by getting off his back.

Leo Tolstoy 1828–1910: *What Then Must We Do?* (1886), tr. A. Maude

Idealism

1 A cause may be inconvenient, but it's magnificent. It's like champagne or high heels, and one must be prepared to suffer for it.

Arnold Bennett 1867–1931: *The Title* (1918)

2 Where there is no vision, the people perish.

Bible: Proverbs

3 Oh, the vision thing.

George Bush 1924– : responding to the suggestion that he turn his attention from short-term campaign objectives and look to the longer term; in *Time* 26 January 1987

4 If a man hasn't discovered something he will die for, he isn't fit to live.

Martin Luther King 1929–68: speech in Detroit, 23 June 1963

5 I have dedicated my life to this struggle of the African people. I have fought against white domination, and I have fought against black domination. I have cherished the ideal of a democratic and free society in which all persons live together in harmony with equal opportunities. It is an ideal which I hope to live for, and to achieve. But my lord, if needs be, it is an ideal for which I am prepared to die.

Nelson Mandela 1918– : speech at his trial in Pretoria, 20 April 1964, which he quoted on his release in Cape Town, 11 February 1990

6 We are all in the gutter, but some of us are looking at the stars.

Oscar Wilde 1854–1900: *Lady Windermere's Fan* (1892)

7 I have spread my dreams under your feet;
   Tread softly because you tread on my dreams.
   W. B. Yeats 1865–1939: 'He Wishes for the Cloths of
   Heaven' (1899)

Ideas

See also **Thinking**

1 Nothing is more dangerous than an idea, when you have
  only one idea.
  Alain 1868–1951: *Propos sur la religion* (1938)

2 There is one thing stronger than all the armies in the
  world; and that is an idea whose time has come.
  Anonymous: in *Nation* 15 April 1943

3 It isn't that they can't see the solution. It is that they can't
  see the problem.
  G. K. Chesterton 1874–1936: *The Scandal of Father
  Brown* (1935)

4 A stand can be made against invasion by an army; no
  stand can be made against invasion by an idea.
  Victor Hugo 1802–85: *Histoire d'un Crime* (written
  1851–2, published 1877)

5 It is better to entertain an idea than to take it home to live
  with you for the rest of your life.
  Randall Jarrell 1914–65: *Pictures from an Institution*
  (1954)

6 When you are a Bear of Very Little Brain, and you Think
  of Things, you find sometimes that a Thing which seemed
  very Thingish inside you is quite different when it gets out
  into the open and has other people looking at it.
  A. A. Milne 1882–1956: *The House at Pooh Corner* (1928)

7 It could be said of me that in this book I have only made
  up a bunch of other men's flowers, providing of my own
  only the string that ties them together.
  Montaigne 1533–92: *Essais* (1580)

8 You see things; and you say 'Why?' But I dream things that never were; and I say 'Why not?'
   George Bernard Shaw 1856–1950: *Back to Methuselah* (1921)

9 It is the nature of an hypothesis, when once a man has conceived it, that it assimilates every thing to itself, as proper nourishment; and, from the first moment of your begetting it, it generally grows the stronger by every thing you see, hear, read, or understand.
   Laurence Sterne 1713–68: *Tristram Shandy* (1759–67)

10 How seldom is it that theories stand the wear and tear of practice!
   Anthony Trollope 1815–82: *Thackeray* (1879)

11 *Ideas won't keep.* Something must be done about them.
   Alfred North Whitehead 1861–1947: *Dialogues* (1954) 28 April 1938

Idleness

1 A man who has nothing to do with his own time has no conscience in his intrusion on that of others.
   Jane Austen 1775–1817: *Sense and Sensibility* (1811)

2 Go to the ant thou sluggard; consider her ways, and be wise.
   Bible: Proverbs

3 The foul sluggard's comfort: 'It will last my time.'
   Thomas Carlyle 1795–1881: *Critical and Miscellaneous Essays* (1838)

4 Idleness is only the refuge of weak minds.
   Lord Chesterfield 1694–1773: *Letters to his Son* (1774) 20 July 1749

5 I do nothing, granted. But I see the hours pass—which is better than trying to fill them.
   E. M. Cioran 1911–95: in *Guardian* 11 May 1993

6 It is better to wear out than to rust out.
   Bishop Richard Cumberland 1631–1718: in G. Horne
   The Duty of Contending for the Faith (1786)

7 Bankrupt of life, yet prodigal of ease.
   John Dryden 1631–1700: *Absalom and Achitophel* (1681)

8 It is impossible to enjoy idling thoroughly unless one has
   plenty of work to do.
   Jerome K. Jerome 1859–1927: *Idle Thoughts of an Idle
   Fellow* (1886)

9 I was raised to feel that doing nothing was a sin. I had to
   learn to do nothing.
   Jenny Joseph 1932– : in *Observer* 19 April 1998

10 procrastination is the
   art of keeping
   up with yesterday.
   Don Marquis 1878–1937: *archy and mehitabel* (1927)

11 Some people are born slack—others have slacking thrust
   upon them.
   Will Self 1961– : in *Observer* 2 January 1994

12 The worst crime is to leave a man's hands empty.
   Men are born makers, with that primal simplicity
   In every maker since Adam.
   Derek Walcott 1930– : *Omeros* (1990)

13 For Satan finds some mischief still
   For idle hands to do.
   Isaac Watts 1674–1748: *Divine Songs for Children* (1715)
   'Against Idleness and Mischief'

14 Procrastination is the thief of time.
   Edward Young 1683–1765: *Night Thoughts* (1742–5)

....

Ignorance
....

1 Where people wish to attach, they should always be
   ignorant. To come with a well-informed mind, is to come
   with an inability of administering to the vanity of others,

which a sensible person would always wish to avoid. A woman especially, if she have the misfortune of knowing any thing, should conceal it as well as she can.

> **Jane Austen** 1775–1817: *Northanger Abbey* (1818)

2 Ignorance is not innocence but sin.

> **Robert Browning** 1812–89: *The Inn Album* (1875)

3 Whatever Nature has in store for mankind, unpleasant as it may be, men must accept, for ignorance is never better than knowledge.

> **Enrico Fermi** 1901–54: Laura Fermi *Atoms in the Family* (1955)

4   Where ignorance is bliss,
'Tis folly to be wise.

> **Thomas Gray** 1716–71: *Ode on a Distant Prospect of Eton College* (1747)

5 Ignorance, madam, pure ignorance.

> **Samuel Johnson** 1709–84: on being asked why he had defined *pastern* as the 'knee' of a horse, 1755; in James Boswell *Life of Johnson* (1791)

6 You know everybody is ignorant, only on different subjects.

> **Will Rogers** 1879–1935: in *New York Times* 31 August 1924

7 For most men, an ignorant enjoyment is better than an informed one; it is better to conceive the sky as a blue dome than a dark cavity; and the cloud as a golden throne than a sleety mist.

> **John Ruskin** 1819–1900: *Modern Painters* (1856)

8 If one does not know to which port one is sailing, no wind is favourable.

> **Seneca ('the Younger')** c.4 BC–AD 65: *Epistulae Morales*

9 As any fule kno.

> **Geoffrey Willans** 1911–58 and **Ronald Searle** 1920– : *Down with Skool!* (1953)

Imagination

1 All fantasy should have a solid base in reality.
   Max Beerbohm 1872–1956: *Zuleika Dobson* (1946 ed.)
   note

2 To see a world in a grain of sand
   And a heaven in a wild flower
   Hold infinity in the palm of your hand
   And eternity in an hour.
   William Blake 1757–1827: 'Auguries of Innocence'
   (*c*.1803)

3 When the imagination sleeps, words are emptied of their
   meaning.
   Albert Camus 1913–60: *Resistance, Rebellion and Death*
   (1961)

4 Go, and catch a falling star,
   Get with child a mandrake root,
   Tell me, where all past years are,
   Or who cleft the Devil's foot.
   John Donne 1572–1631: 'Song: Go and catch a falling
   star'

5 Where there is no imagination there is no horror.
   Arthur Conan Doyle 1859–1930: *A Study in Scarlet* (1888)

6 Were it not for imagination, Sir, a man would be as happy
   in the arms of a chambermaid as of a Duchess.
   Samuel Johnson 1709–84: in James Boswell *Life of
   Johnson* (1791) 9 May 1778

7 Heard melodies are sweet, but those unheard
   Are sweeter.
   John Keats 1795–1821: 'Ode on a Grecian Urn' (1820)

8 His imagination resembled the wings of an ostrich. It
   enabled him to run, though not to soar.
   Lord Macaulay 1800–59: 'John Dryden' (1828)

9 I'm up to my neck in the real world, every day. Just you try
   doing your VAT return with a head full of goblins.
   Terry Pratchett 1948– : in *Sunday Times* 27 February
   2000

10 The lunatic, the lover, and the poet,
Are of imagination all compact.
> **William Shakespeare** 1564–1616: *A Midsummer Night's Dream* (1595–6)

11 Must then a Christ perish in torment in every age to save those that have no imagination?
> **George Bernard Shaw** 1856–1950: *Saint Joan* (1924) epilogue

12 Whither is fled the visionary gleam?
Where is it now, the glory and the dream?
> **William Wordsworth** 1770–1850: 'Ode. Intimations of Immortality' (1807)

··

Indifference
··

1 All colours will agree in the dark.
> **Francis Bacon** 1561–1626: *Essays* (1625) 'Of Unity in Religion'

2 Oasis are still the best band as far as I'm concerned. But I'm not bothered about that kind of stuff anymore. When you've got four houses and nine cars it doesn't really matter.
> **Noel Gallagher** 1967– : in *Sunday Times* 23 January 2000

3 Catholics and Communists have committed great crimes, but at least they have not stood aside, like an established society, and been indifferent. I would rather have blood on my hands than water like Pilate.
> **Graham Greene** 1904–91: *The Comedians* (1966)

4 *Qu'ils mangent de la brioche.*
Let them eat cake.
> **Marie-Antoinette** 1755–93: on being told that her people had no bread. In *Confessions* (1740) Rousseau refers to a similar remark being a well-known saying; in *Relation d'un Voyage à Bruxelles à Coblentz en 1791* (1823), Louis XVIII attributes 'Why don't they eat pastry?' to Marie-Thérèse (1638–83), wife of Louis XIV

5 I wish I could care what you do or where you go but I can't
. . . My dear, I don't give a damn.
   Margaret Mitchell 1900–49: *Gone with the Wind* (1936).
   'Frankly, my dear, I don't give a damn!' in Sidney
   Howard's 1939 screenplay

6 Vacant heart and hand, and eye,—
Easy live and quiet die.
   Sir Walter Scott 1771–1832: *The Bride of Lammermoor*
   (1819)

7 It is the disease of not listening, the malady of not
marking, that I am troubled withal.
   William Shakespeare 1564–1616: *Henry IV, Part 2* (1597)

8 The worst sin towards our fellow creatures is not to hate
them, but to be indifferent to them: that's the essence of
inhumanity.
   George Bernard Shaw 1856–1950: *The Devil's Disciple*
   (1901)

9 I was much further out than you thought
And not waving but drowning.
   Stevie Smith 1902–71: 'Not Waving but Drowning' (1957)

10 The opposite of love is not hate, it's indifference. The
opposite of art is not ugliness, it's indifference. The
opposite of faith is not heresy, it's indifference. And the
opposite of life is not death, it's indifference.
   Elie Wiesel 1928– : in *U.S. News and World Report*
   27 October 1986

11 Cast a cold eye
On life, on death.
Horseman pass by!
   W. B. Yeats 1865–1939: 'Under Ben Bulben' (1939)

Intelligence and Intellectuals

1 See the happy moron,
He doesn't give a damn,
I wish I were a moron,

My God! perhaps I am!
Anonymous: *Eugenics Review* July 1929

2 To the man-in-the-street, who, I'm sorry to say,
Is a keen observer of life,
The word 'Intellectual' suggests straight away
A man who's untrue to his wife.
W. H. Auden 1907–73: *New Year Letter* (1941)

3 An intellectual is someone whose mind watches itself.
Albert Camus 1913–60: *Notebooks 1935–42* (1963)

4 'Excellent,' I cried. 'Elementary,' said he.
Arthur Conan Doyle 1859–1930: *Memoirs of Sherlock Holmes* (1894). 'Elementary, my dear Watson' is not found in any book by Conan Doyle, but is first found in P. G. Wodehouse *Psmith Journalist* (1915)

5 As a human being, one has been endowed with just enough intelligence to be able to see clearly how utterly inadequate that intelligence is when confronted with what exists.
Albert Einstein 1879–1955: letter to Queen Elizabeth of Belgium, 19 September 1932

6 The test of a first-rate intelligence is the ability to hold two opposed ideas in the mind at the same time, and still retain the ability to function.
F. Scott Fitzgerald 1896–1940: in *Esquire* February 1936

7 Sir, I have found you an argument; but I am not obliged to find you an understanding.
Samuel Johnson 1709–84: in James Boswell *Life of Johnson* (1791) June 1784

8 So dumb he can't fart and chew gum at the same time.
Lyndon Baines Johnson 1908–73: of Gerald Ford, in R. Reeves *A Ford, not a Lincoln* (1975)

9 *I think, therefore I am* is the statement of an intellectual who underrates toothaches.
Milan Kundera 1929– : *Immortality* (1991)

10 No one in this world, so far as I know—and I have
searched the records for years, and employed agents to
help me—has ever lost money by underestimating the
intelligence of the great masses of the plain people.
   H. L. Mencken 1880–1956: *Chicago Tribune* 19 September
   1926

11 You beat your pate, and fancy wit will come:
Knock as you please, there's nobody at home.
   Alexander Pope 1688–1744: 'Epigram: You beat your
   pate' (1732)

12 With stupidity the gods themselves struggle in vain.
   Friedrich von Schiller 1759–1805: *Die Jungfrau von
   Orleans* (1801)

13 Not body enough to cover his mind decently with; his
intellect is improperly exposed.
   Sydney Smith 1771–1845: in Lady Holland *Memoir* (1855)

14 Intelligence is quickness to apprehend as distinct from
ability, which is capacity to act wisely on the thing
apprehended.
   Alfred North Whitehead 1861–1947: *Dialogues* (1954)
   15 December 1939

Inventions and Discoveries

See also **Science**

1 When man wanted to make a machine that would walk he
created the wheel, which does not resemble a leg.
   Guillaume Apollinaire 1880–1918: *Les Mamelles de
   Tirésias* (1918)

2 *Eureka!*

I've got it!
   Archimedes *c.*287–212 BC: Vitruvius Pollio *De
   Architectura*

3 Printing, gunpowder, and the mariner's needle [compass]
. . . these three have changed the whole face and state of
things throughout the world.
    Francis Bacon 1561–1626: *Novum Organum* (1620)

4 *Au fond de l'Inconnu pour trouver du nouveau!*
Through the unknown, we'll find the new.
    Charles Baudelaire 1821–67: *Les fleurs du mal* (1857), tr.
Robert Lowell

5 Now who is responsible for this work of development on
which so much depends? To whom must the praise be
given? To the boys in the back rooms. They do not sit in
the limelight. But they are the men who do the work.
    Lord Beaverbrook 1879–1964: in *Listener* 27 March 1941

6 Thus were they stained with their own works: and went a
whoring with their own inventions.
    Bible: Psalm 106

7 The discovery of a new dish does more for human
happiness than the discovery of a star.
    Anthelme Brillat-Savarin 1755–1826: *Physiologie du
Goût* (1826)

8 LORD CARNARVON: Can you see anything?
CARTER: Yes, wonderful things.
    Howard Carter 1874–1939: on first looking into the tomb
of Tutankhamun, 26 November 1922; *The Tomb of Tut-
ankh-Amen* (1923)

9 Why sir, there is every possibility that you will soon be
able to tax it!
    Michael Faraday 1791–1867: to Gladstone, when asked
about the usefulness of electricity; in W. E. H. Lecky
Democracy and Liberty (1899 ed.)

10 What is the use of a new-born child?
    Benjamin Franklin 1706–90: when asked what was the
use of a new invention

11 Then felt I like some watcher of the skies
When a new planet swims into his ken;
Or like stout Cortez when with eagle eyes
He stared at the Pacific—and all his men

Looked at each other with a wild surmise—
Silent, upon a peak in Darien.
   John Keats 1795–1821: 'On First Looking into
   Chapman's Homer' (1817)

12 praise without end the go-ahead zeal
of whoever it was invented the wheel;
but never a word for the poor soul's sake
that thought ahead, and invented the brake.
   Howard Nemerov 1920–91: 'To the Congress of the
   United States, Entering Its Third Century' 26 February
   1989

13 I don't know what I may seem to the world, but as to
myself, I seem to have been only like a boy playing on the
sea-shore and diverting myself in now and then finding a
smoother pebble or a prettier shell than ordinary, whilst
the great ocean of truth lay all undiscovered before me.
   Isaac Newton 1642–1727: Joseph Spence *Anecdotes* (ed.
   J. Osborn, 1966)

14 I remembered the line from the Hindu scripture, the
Bhagavad Gita . . . 'I am become death, the destroyer of
worlds.'
   J. Robert Oppenheimer 1904–67: on the explosion of
   the first atomic bomb near Alamogordo, New Mexico, 16
   July 1945; Len Giovannitti and Fred Freed *The Decision
   to Drop the Bomb* (1965)

15 *Semper aliquid novi Africam adferre.*

Africa always brings [us] something new.
   Pliny the Elder AD 23–79: *Historia Naturalis* (often
   quoted '*Ex Africa semper aliquid novi* [Always something
   new out of Africa]')

16 Discovery consists of seeing what everybody has seen and
thinking what nobody has thought.
   Albert von Szent-Györgyi 1893–1986: I. Good (ed.) *The
   Scientist Speculates* (1962)

17 Name the greatest of all the inventors. Accident.
   Mark Twain 1835–1910: *Notebook* (1935)

Ireland and the Irish

1 I met wid Napper Tandy, and he took me by the hand,
And he said, 'How's poor ould Ireland, and how does she
stand?'
She's the most disthressful country that iver yet was seen,
For they're hangin' men an' women for the wearin' o' the
Green.
  Anonymous: 'The Wearin' o' the Green' (*c.*1795 ballad)

2 I could wish that the English kept history in mind more,
that the Irish kept it in mind less.
  Elizabeth Bowen 1899–1973: 'Notes on Eire' 9 November
1949

3 For the great Gaels of Ireland
Are the men that God made mad,
For all their wars are merry,
And all their songs are sad.
  G. K. Chesterton 1874–1936: *The Ballad of the White
Horse* (1911)

4 Ulster will fight; Ulster will be right.
  Lord Randolph Churchill 1849–94: public letter, 7 May
1886

5 Thus you have a starving population, an absentee
aristocracy, and an alien Church, and in addition the
weakest executive in the world. That is the Irish Question.
  Benjamin Disraeli 1804–81: speech, House of Commons,
16 February 1844

6   The famous
Northern reticence, the tight gag of place
And times.
  Seamus Heaney 1939– : 'Whatever You Say Say
Nothing' (1975)

7 Ireland is the old sow that eats her farrow.
  James Joyce 1882–1941: *A Portrait of the Artist as a
Young Man* (1916)

8 In Ireland the inevitable never happens and the
unexpected constantly occurs.

> **John Pentland Mahaffy** 1839–1919: in W. B. Stanford
> and R. B. McDowell *Mahaffy* (1971)

9 The moment the very name of Ireland is mentioned, the
English seem to bid adieu to common feeling, common
prudence, and common sense, and to act with the
barbarity of tyrants, and the fatuity of idiots.

> **Sydney Smith** 1771–1845: *Letters of Peter Plymley* (1807)

10 Romantic Ireland's dead and gone,
It's with O'Leary in the grave.

> **W. B. Yeats** 1865–1939: 'September, 1913' (1914)

....

Jealousy
....

see **Envy and Jealousy**

....

Journalism
....

see **News and Journalism**

....

Justice
....

See also **The Law and Lawyers**

1 If it falls to me to start a fight to cut out the cancer of bent
and twisted journalism in our country with the simple
sword of truth and the trusty shield of British fair play, so
be it.

> **Jonathan Aitken** 1942– : statement, London, 10 April
> 1995

2 I'm armed with more than complete steel—The justice of
my quarrel.

> **Anonymous**: *Lust's Dominion* (1657) attributed to
> Marlowe, though of doubtful authorship

3 *Jedem das Seine.*

To each his own.

Anonymous: inscription on the gate of Buchenwald concentration camp, *c.*1937; often quoted as 'Everyone gets what he deserves'

4 *Audi partem alteram.*

Hear the other side.

St Augustine of Hippo AD 354–430: *De Duabus Animabus contra Manicheos*

5 The price of justice is eternal publicity.

Arnold Bennett 1867–1931: *Things that have Interested Me* (1923) 'Secret Trials'

6 Life for life,

Eye for eye, tooth for tooth.

Bible: Exodus

7 They have sown the wind, and they shall reap the whirlwind.

Bible: Hosea

8 It is better that ten guilty persons escape than one innocent suffer.

William Blackstone 1723–80: *Commentaries on the Laws of England* (1765)

9 When I hear of an 'equity' in a case like this, I am reminded of a blind man in a dark room—looking for a black hat—which isn't there.

Lord Bowen 1835–94: J. A. Foote *Pie-Powder* (1911)

10 No! No! Sentence first—verdict afterwards.

Lewis Carroll 1832–98: *Alice's Adventures in Wonderland* (1865)

11 The life sentence goes on. It's like a runaway train that you can't just get off.

Gerry Conlon 1954– : of life after his conviction was quashed by the Court of Appeal; in *Irish Post* 13 September 1997

12 Justice is truth in action.

Benjamin Disraeli 1804–81: speech, House of Commons, 11 February 1851

13 All sensible people are selfish, and nature is tugging at
every contract to make the terms of it fair.
   Ralph Waldo Emerson 1803–82: *The Conduct of Life*
   (1860)

14 *Fiat justitia et pereat mundus.*
   Let justice be done, though the world perish.
   Emperor Ferdinand I 1503–64: motto

15 Justice should not only be done, but should manifestly and
undoubtedly be seen to be done.
   Lord Hewart 1870–1943: Rex v Sussex Justices,
   9 November 1923

16 A lawyer has no business with the justice or injustice of
the cause which he undertakes, unless his client asks his
opinion, and then he is bound to give it honestly. The
justice or injustice of the cause is to be decided by the
judge.
   Samuel Johnson 1709–84: James Boswell *Journal of a
   Tour to the Hebrides* (1785) 15 August 1773

17 Injustice anywhere is a threat to justice everywhere.
   Martin Luther King 1929–68: letter from Birmingham
   Jail, Alabama, 16 April 1963

18 In England, justice is open to all—like the Ritz Hotel.
   James Mathew 1830–1908: R. E. Megarry *Miscellany-
   at-Law* (1955).

19 Here they hang a man first, and try him afterwards.
   Molière 1622–73: *Monsieur de Pourceaugnac* (1670)

20 What I say is that 'just' or 'right' means nothing but what
is in the interest of the stronger party.
   Plato 429–347 BC: spoken by Thrasymachus in *The
   Republic* (tr. F. M. Cornford)

21 The quality of mercy is not strained,
   It droppeth as the gentle rain from heaven
   Upon the place beneath: it is twice blessed;
   It blesseth him that gives and him that takes.
   William Shakespeare 1564–1616: *The Merchant of
   Venice* (1596–8)

22 Thrice is he armed that hath his quarrel just.
   William Shakespeare 1564–1616: *Henry VI, Part 2* (1592)

23 Two wrongs don't make a right, but they make a good excuse.
   Thomas Szasz 1920– : *The Second Sin* (1973)

Knowledge

1 Everyman, I will go with thee, and be thy guide,
   In thy most need to go by thy side.
   Anonymous: *Everyman* (c.1509–19) spoken by Knowledge

2 The fox knows many things—the hedgehog one *big* one.
   Archilochus 7th century BC: fragment

3 For also knowledge itself is power.
   Francis Bacon 1561–1626: *Meditationes Sacrae* (1597)

4 We have first raised a dust and then complain we cannot see.
   Bishop George Berkeley 1685–1753: *A Treatise Concerning the Principles of Human Knowledge* (1710)

5 The price of wisdom is above rubies.
   Bible: Job

6 For now we see through a glass, darkly; but then face to face: now I know in part; but then shall I know even as also I am known.
   Bible: I Corinthians

7 It is better to know nothing than to know what ain't so.
   Josh Billings 1818–85: *Proverb* (1874)

8 If the doors of perception were cleansed everything would appear to man as it is, infinite.
   William Blake 1757–1827: *The Marriage of Heaven and Hell* (1790–3)

9 An expert is one who knows more and more about less and less.
   Nicholas Murray Butler 1862–1947: Commencement address at Columbia University (attributed)

10 Knowledge may give weight, but accomplishments give lustre, and many more people see than weigh.
Lord Chesterfield 1694–1773: *Maxims* (1774)

11 There is no such thing on earth as an uninteresting subject; the only thing that can exist is an uninterested person.
G. K. Chesterton 1874–1936: *Heretics* (1905)

12 Now, what I want is, Facts . . . Facts alone are wanted in life.
Charles Dickens 1812–70: *Hard Times* (1854) Mr Gradgrind

13 Where is the wisdom we have lost in knowledge?
Where is the knowledge we have lost in information?
T. S. Eliot 1888–1965: *The Rock* (1934)

14 For lust of knowing what should not be known,
We take the Golden Road to Samarkand.
James Elroy Flecker 1884–1915: *The Golden Journey to Samarkand* (1913)

15 And still they gazed, and still the wonder grew,
That one small head could carry all he knew.
Oliver Goldsmith 1728–74: *The Deserted Village* (1770)

16 If a little knowledge is dangerous, where is the man who has so much as to be out of danger?
T. H. Huxley 1825–95: 'On Elementary Instruction in Physiology' (written 1877)

17 Knowledge is of two kinds. We know a subject ourselves, or we know where we can find information upon it.
Samuel Johnson 1709–84: in James Boswell *Life of Johnson* (1791) 18 April 1775

18 The motto of all the mongoose family is, 'Run and find out.'
Rudyard Kipling 1865–1936: *The Jungle Book* (1897)

19 A little learning is a dangerous thing;
Drink deep, or taste not the Pierian spring.
Alexander Pope 1688–1744: *An Essay on Criticism* (1711)

20 I know nothing except the fact of my ignorance.
Socrates 469–399 BC: in Diogenes Laertius *Lives of the Philosophers*

21 Knowledge is good. It does not have to look good or sound good or even do good. It is good just by being knowledge. And the only thing that makes it knowledge is that it is true. You can't have too much of it and there is no little too little to be worth having.
Tom Stoppard 1937– : *The Invention of Love* (1997)

22 Our meddling intellect
Mis-shapes the beauteous forms of things:—
We murder to dissect.
William Wordsworth 1770–1850: 'The Tables Turned' (1798)

Language

See also **Meaning**, **Words**

1 One picture is worth ten thousand words.
Frederick R. Barnard: *Printers' Ink* 10 March 1927

2 A word fitly spoken is like apples of gold in pictures of silver.
Bible: Proverbs

3 A definition is the enclosing a wilderness of idea within a wall of words.
Samuel Butler 1835–1902: *Notebooks* (1912)

4 Take care of the sense, and the sounds will take care of themselves.
Lewis Carroll 1832–98: *Alice's Adventures in Wonderland* (1865)

5 When I split an infinitive, God damn it, I split it so it will stay split.
Raymond Chandler 1888–1959: on a proof-reader's corrections to his work; letter to Edward Weeks, 18 January 1947

6 Colourless green ideas sleep furiously.
   Noam Chomsky 1928– : *Syntactic Structures* (1957)
   illustrating that grammatical structure is independent of
   meaning

7 This is the sort of English up with which I will not put.
   Winston Churchill 1874–1965: Ernest Gowers *Plain
   Words* (1948) 'Troubles with Prepositions'

8 The man who first abused his fellows with swear-words
   instead of bashing their brains out with a club should be
   counted among those who laid the foundations of
   civilization.
   John Cohen 1911– : in *Observer* 21 November 1965

9 He who understands baboon would do more towards
   metaphysics than Locke.
   Charles Darwin 1809–82: Notebook M (16 August 1838)

10 Language is fossil poetry.
   Ralph Waldo Emerson 1803–82: *Essays* (1844) 'The Poet'

11 Where in this small-talking world can I find
   A longitude with no platitude?
   Christopher Fry 1907– : *The Lady's not for Burning*
   (1949)

12 Merely corroborative detail, intended to give artistic
   verisimilitude to an otherwise bald and unconvincing
   narrative.
   W. S. Gilbert 1836–1911: *The Mikado* (1885)

13 When they call you articulate, that's another way of saying
   'He talks good for a black guy'.
   Ice-T 1958– : in *Independent* 30 December 1995

14 Language is the dress of thought.
   Samuel Johnson 1709–84: *Lives of the English Poets*
   (1779–81)

15 The mystery of language was revealed to me. I knew then
   that 'w-a-t-e-r' meant the wonderful cool something that
   was flowing over my hand. That living word awakened my
   soul, gave it light, joy, set it free!
   Helen Keller 1880–1968: *The Story of My Life* (1902)

16 Language tethers us to the world; without it we spin like atoms.
   Penelope Lively 1933– : *Moon Tiger* (1987)

17 All that is not prose is verse; and all that is not verse is prose.
   Molière 1622–73: *Le Bourgeois Gentilhomme* (1671)

18 Good heavens! For more than forty years I have been speaking prose without knowing it.
   Molière 1622–73: *Le Bourgeois Gentilhomme* (1671)

19 Slang is a language that rolls up its sleeves, spits on its hands and goes to work.
   Carl Sandburg 1878–1967: in *New York Times* 13 February 1959

20 You taught me language; and my profit on't
   Is, I know how to curse.
   William Shakespeare 1564–1616: *The Tempest* (1611)

21 A language is a dialect with an army and a navy.
   Max Weinreich 1894–1969: Steven Pinker *The Language Instinct* (1994)

22 The limits of my language mean the limits of my world.
   Ludwig Wittgenstein 1889–1951: *Tractatus Logico-Philosophicus* (1922)

Languages

1 The great breeding people had gone out and multiplied; colonies in every clime attest our success; French is the *patois* of Europe; English is the language of the world.
   Walter Bagehot 1826–77: in *National Review* January 1856 'Edward Gibbon'

2 It is a thing plainly repugnant to the Word of God, and the custom of the Primitive Church, to have publick Prayer in the Church, or to minister the Sacraments in a tongue not understood of the people.
   Book of Common Prayer 1662: *Articles of Religion* (1562)

3 The original is unfaithful to the translation.
   Jorge Luis Borges 1899–1986: of Henley's translation, in
   Sobre el 'Vathek' de William Beckford (1943)

4 To God I speak Spanish, to women Italian, to men French,
   and to my horse—German.
   Emperor Charles V 1500–58: attributed

5 My English text is chaste, and all licentious passages are
   left in the obscurity of a learned language.
   Edward Gibbon 1737–94: *Memoirs of My Life* (1796)
   parodied as 'decent obscurity' in the *Anti-Jacobin*, 1797–8

6 I am always sorry when any language is lost, because
   languages are the pedigree of nations.
   Samuel Johnson 1709–84: James Boswell *Journal of a
   tour to the Hebrides* (1785)

7 We are walking lexicons. In a single sentence of idle
   chatter we preserve Latin, Anglo-Saxon, Norse; we carry a
   museum inside our heads, each day we commemorate
   peoples of whom we have never heard.
   Penelope Lively 1933– : *Moon Tiger* (1987)

8 England and America are two countries divided by a
   common language.
   George Bernard Shaw 1856–1950: attributed in this and
   other forms, but not found in Shaw's published writings

9 So now they have made our English tongue a gallimaufry
   or hodgepodge of all other speeches.
   Edmund Spenser c.1552–99: *The Shepherd's Calendar*
   (1579)

Last Words

1 He had been, he said, an unconscionable time dying; but
   he hoped that they would excuse it.
   Charles II 1630–85: Lord Macaulay *History of England*
   (1849)

2 My design is to make what haste I can to be gone.
   Oliver Cromwell 1599–1658: J. Morley *Oliver Cromwell*
   (1900)

3 It is a far, far better thing that I do, than I have ever done; it is a far, far better rest that I go to, than I have ever known.

> **Charles Dickens** 1812–70: *A Tale of Two Cities* (1859)
> Sydney Carton

4 All my possessions for a moment of time.

> **Elizabeth I** 1533–1603: attributed, probably apocryphal

5 Why fear death? It is the most beautiful adventure in life.

> **Charles Frohman** 1860–1915: before drowning in the *Lusitania*, 7 May 1915

6 We are all going to Heaven, and Vandyke is of the company.

> **Thomas Gainsborough** 1727–88: attributed in W. B. Boulton *Thomas Gainsborough*

7 Bugger Bognor.

> **George V** 1865–1936: attributed; possibly on his deathbed. See K. Rose *King George V* (1983)

8 More light!

> **Johann Wolfgang von Goethe** 1749–1832: attributed; actually 'Open the second shutter, so that more light can come in'

9 *Dieu me pardonnera, c'est son métier.*
God will pardon me, it is His trade.

> **Heinrich Heine** 1797–1856: on his deathbed; A. Meissner *Heinrich Heine. Erinnerungen* (1856)

10 I am about to take my last voyage, a great leap in the dark.

> **Thomas Hobbes** 1588–1679: last words

11 I pray you, master Lieutenant, see me safe up, and my coming down let me shift for my self.

> **Sir Thomas More** 1478–1535: on mounting the scaffold; William Roper *Life of Sir Thomas More*

12 Kiss me, Hardy.

> **Horatio, Lord Nelson** 1758–1805: at the battle of Trafalgar; R. Southey *Life of Nelson* (1813)

13 I am just going outside and may be some time.

> **Captain Lawrence Oates** 1880–1912: Robert Falcon Scott's diary, 16–17 March 1912

14 Die, my dear Doctor, that's the last thing I shall do!
Lord Palmerston 1784–1865: E. Latham *Famous Sayings
and their Authors* (1904)

15 Oh, my country! how I leave my country!
William Pitt 1759–1806: Earl Stanhope *Life of the Rt. Hon.
William Pitt* vol. 3 (1879). Also variously reported as
'How I love my country'; 'My country! oh, my country!';
'I think I could eat one of Bellamy's veal pies'

16 I am going to seek a great perhaps . . . Bring down the
curtain, the farce is played out.
François Rabelais *c*.1494–*c*.1553: attributed

17 So the heart be right, it is no matter which way the head
lies.
Walter Ralegh *c*.1552–1618: at his execution, on being
asked which way he preferred to lay his head

18 So little done, so much to do.
Cecil Rhodes 1853–1902: on the day of his death; L.
Michell *Life of Rhodes* (1910).

19 For God's sake look after our people.
Robert Falcon Scott 1868–1912: last diary entry, 29
March 1912

20 Crito, we owe a cock to Aesculapius; please pay it and
don't forget it.
Socrates 469–399 BC: Plato *Phaedo*

21 If this is dying, then I don't think much of it.
Lytton Strachey 1880–1932: on his deathbed; M. Holroyd
Lytton Strachey vol. 2 (1968)

22 This is no time for making new enemies.
Voltaire 1694–1778: on being asked to renounce the
Devil, on his deathbed (attributed)

23 Had I but served God as diligently as I have served the
King, he would not have given me over in my grey hairs.
Cardinal Wolsey *c*.1475–1530: George Cavendish
Negotiations of Thomas Wolsey (1641)

The Law and Lawyers

See also **Crime and Punishment**, **Justice**

1 Written laws are like spider's webs; they will catch, it is true, the weak and poor, but would be torn in pieces by the rich and powerful.
Anacharsis 6th century BC: Plutarch *Parallel Lives*

2 Law is a bottomless pit.
Dr Arbuthnot 1667–1735: *The History of John Bull* (1712)

3 The sabbath was made for man, and not man for the sabbath.
Bible: St Mark

4 Bad laws are the worst sort of tyranny.
Edmund Burke 1729–97: *Speech at Bristol, previous to the Late Election* (1780)

5 *Salus populi suprema est lex.*

The good of the people is the chief law.
Cicero 106–43 BC: *De Legibus*

6 *Cui bono?*

To whose profit?
Cicero 106–43 BC: *Pro Roscio Amerino* and *Pro Milone* (quoting L. Cassius Longinus Ravilla)

7 If the law supposes that . . . the law is a ass—a idiot.
Charles Dickens 1812–70: *Oliver Twist* (1838) Bumble

8 'You must not tell us what the soldier, or any other man, said, sir,' interposed the judge; 'it's not evidence.'
Charles Dickens 1812–70: *Pickwick Papers* (1837)

9 The Law is the true embodiment
Of everything that's excellent.
It has no kind of fault or flaw,
And I, my Lords, embody the Law.
W. S. Gilbert 1836–1911: *Iolanthe* (1882)

10 No poet ever interpreted nature as freely as a lawyer
interprets the truth.
   Jean Giraudoux 1882–1944: *La Guerre de Troie n'aura
   pas lieu* (1935) tr. Christopher Fry as *Tiger at the Gates*,
   1955

11 Laws grind the poor, and rich men rule the law.
   Oliver Goldsmith 1728–74: *The Traveller* (1764)

12 A verbal contract isn't worth the paper it is written on.
   Sam Goldwyn 1882–1974: A. Johnston *The Great
   Goldwyn* (1937)

13 I know no method to secure the repeal of bad or obnoxious
laws so effective as their stringent execution.
   Ulysses S. Grant 1822–85: inaugural address, 4 March
   1869

14 You may object that it is not a trial at all; you are quite
right, for it is only a trial if I recognize it as such.
   Franz Kafka 1883–1924: *The Trial* (1925)

15 Loopholes are not always of a fixed dimension. They tend
to enlarge as the numbers that pass through wear them
away.
   Harold Lever 1914–95: speech to Finance Bill
   Committee, 22 May 1968

16 I don't know as I want a lawyer to tell me what I cannot
do. I hire him to tell me how to do what I want to do.
   John Pierpont Morgan 1837–1913: Ida M. Tarbell *The
   Life of Elbert H. Gary* (1925)

17 No brilliance is needed in the law. Nothing but common
sense, and relatively clean finger nails.
   John Mortimer 1923– : *A Voyage Round My Father*
   (1971)

18 Laws were made to be broken.
   Christopher North 1785–1854: *Blackwood's Magazine*
   May 1830

19 The hungry judges soon the sentence sign,
And wretches hang that jury-men may dine.
   Alexander Pope 1688–1744: *The Rape of the Lock* (1714)

20 A lawyer with his briefcase can steal more than a hundred men with guns.
   Mario Puzo 1920– : *The Godfather* (1969)

21 Ignorance of the law excuses no man; not that all men know the law, but because 'tis an excuse every man will plead, and no man can tell how to confute him.
   John Selden 1584–1654: *Table Talk* (1689) 'Law'

22 The first thing we do, let's kill all the lawyers.
   William Shakespeare 1564–1616: *Henry VI, Part 2* (1592)

23 A precedent embalms a principle.
   Lord Stowell 1745–1836: an opinion, while Advocate-General, 1788, quoted by Disraeli in House of Commons, 22 February 1848

24 Everything not forbidden is compulsory.
   T. H. White 1906–64: *The Sword in the Stone* (1938)

25 Asking the ignorant to use the incomprehensible to decide the unknowable.
   Hiller B. Zobel 1932– : on the jury system; 'The Jury on Trial' in *American Heritage* July–August 1995

Leadership

1 Be neither saint nor sophist-led, but be a man.
   Matthew Arnold 1822–88: *Empedocles on Etna* (1852)

2 By the structure of the world we often want, at the sudden occurrence of a grave tempest, to change the helmsman—to replace the pilot of the calm by the pilot of the storm.
   Walter Bagehot 1826–77: *The English Constitution* (1867) 'The Cabinet'

3 If the blind lead the blind, both shall fall into the ditch.
   Bible: St Matthew

4 The art of leadership is saying no, not yes. It is very easy to say yes.
   Tony Blair 1953– : in *Mail on Sunday* 2 October 1994

5 Leaders should never, ever try to look cool—that's for dictators.
   Ben Elton 1959– : in *Radio Times* 18 April 1998

6 The art of leadership . . . consists in consolidating the attention of the people against a single adversary and taking care that nothing will split up that attention.
   Adolf Hitler 1889–1945: *Mein Kampf* (1925)

7 The final test of a leader is that he leaves behind him in other men the conviction and the will to carry on.
   Walter Lippmann 1889–1974: in *New York Herald Tribune* 14 April 1945

8 To grasp and hold a vision, that is the very essence of successful leadership—not only on the movie set where I learned it, but everywhere.
   Ronald Reagan 1911– : in *Wilson Quarterly* Winter 1994; attributed

9 I don't mind how much my Ministers talk, so long as they do what I say.
   Margaret Thatcher 1925– : in *Observer* 27 January 1980

10 The buck stops here.
   Harry S. Truman 1884–1972: unattributed motto on Truman's desk, when President

Leisure

1 We are closer to the ants than to the butterflies. Very few people can endure much leisure.
   Gerald Brenan 1894–1987: *Thoughts in a Dry Season* (1978)

2 What is this life if, full of care,
   We have no time to stand and stare.
   W. H. Davies 1871–1940: 'Leisure' (1911)

3 To be able to fill leisure intelligently is the last product of civilization.
   Bertrand Russell 1872–1970: *The Conquest of Happiness* (1930)

4 If all the year were playing holidays,
To sport would be as tedious as to work;
But when they seldom come, they wished for come.
   William Shakespeare 1564–1616: *Henry IV, Part 1* (1597)

5 Conspicuous leisure and consumption . . . In the one case
it is a waste of time and effort, in the other it is a waste of
goods.
   Thorstein Veblen 1857–1929: *Theory of the Leisure Class*
   (1899)

6 The world is too much with us; late and soon,
Getting and spending, we lay waste our powers.
   William Wordsworth 1770–1850: 'The world is too much
   with us' (1807)

Letters and Letter-writing

1 You bid me burn your letters. But I must forget you first.
   John Adams 1735–1826: letter to Abigail Adams, 28
   April 1776

2 Letters of thanks, letters from banks,
Letters of joy from girl and boy,
Receipted bills and invitations
To inspect new stock or to visit relations,
And applications for situations,
And timid lovers' declarations,
And gossip, gossip from all the nations.
   W. H. Auden 1907–73: *Night Mail* (1936)

3 She'll vish there wos more, and that's the great art o' letter
writin'.
   Charles Dickens 1812–70: *Pickwick Papers* (1837-8)

4 Sir, more than kisses, letters mingle souls.
   John Donne 1572–1631: 'To Sir Henry Wotton' (1597-8)

5 It's very dangerous if you keep love letters from someone
who is not now your husband.
   Diana Dors 1931–84: in *Observer* 28 December 1980

6 It is wonderful how much news there is when people write every other day; if they wait for a month, there is nothing that seems worth telling.
  O. Douglas 1877–1948: *Penny Plain* (1920)

7 All letters, methinks, should be free and easy as one's discourse, not studied as an oration, nor made up of hard words like a charm.
  Dorothy Osborne 1627–95: letter to William Temple, September 1653

8 I have made this [letter] longer than usual, only because I have not had the time to make it shorter.
  Blaise Pascal 1623–62: *Lettres Provinciales* (1657)

9 Don't think that this is a letter. It is only a small eruption of a disease called friendship.
  Jean Renoir 1894–1979: letter to Janine Bazin, 12 June 1974

10 Correspondences are like small-clothes before the invention of suspenders; it is impossible to keep them up.
  Sydney Smith 1771–1845: Peter Virgin *Sydney Smith* (1994)

11 A woman seldom writes her mind but in her postscript.
  Richard Steele 1672–1729: in *Spectator* 31 May 1711

Liberty

1 Liberty is always unfinished business.
  Anonymous: title of Annual Report of the American Civil Liberties Union (1956)

2 Liberty is liberty, not equality or fairness or justice or human happiness or a quiet conscience.
  Isaiah Berlin 1909–97: *Two Concepts of Liberty* (1958)

3 The people never give up their liberties except under some delusion.
  Edmund Burke 1729–97: speech at County Meeting of Buckinghamshire, 1784; attributed

4 The condition upon which God hath given liberty to man is eternal vigilance.
   John Philpot Curran 1750–1817: speech, 10 July 1790

5 I know not what course others may take; but as for me, give me liberty, or give me death!
   Patrick Henry 1736–99: speech, 23 March 1775

6 It is better to die on your feet than to live on your knees.
   Dolores Ibarruri 1895–1989: speech in Paris,
   3 September 1936; also attributed to Emiliano Zapata

7 The enemies of Freedom do not argue; they shout and they shoot.
   Dean Inge 1860–1954: *End of an Age* (1948)

8 The tree of liberty must be refreshed from time to time with the blood of patriots and tyrants. It is its natural manure.
   Thomas Jefferson 1743–1826: letter to W. S. Smith, 13 November 1787

9 They took away my liberty, not my freedom.
   Brian Keenan 1950– : of his captivity in Lebanon; news conference, Dublin, 30 August 1990

10 We shall pay any price, bear any burden, meet any hardship, support any friend, oppose any foe to assure the survival and the success of liberty.
   John F. Kennedy 1917–63: inaugural address, 20 January 1961

11 Liberty is precious—so precious that it must be rationed.
   Lenin 1870–1924: Sidney and Beatrice Webb *Soviet Communism* (1936)

12 Stone walls do not a prison make,
   Nor iron bars a cage.
   Richard Lovelace 1618–58: 'To Althea, From Prison' (1649)

13 Freedom is always and exclusively freedom for the one who thinks differently.
   Rosa Luxemburg 1871–1919: *Die Russische Revolution* (1918)

14 If men are to wait for liberty till they become wise and good in slavery, they may indeed wait for ever.
  Lord Macaulay 1800–59: *Essays* (1843) 'Milton'

15 The liberty of the individual must be thus far limited; he must not make himself a nuisance to other people.
  John Stuart Mill 1806–73: *On Liberty* (1859)

16 Ask the first man you meet what he means by defending freedom, and he'll tell you privately he means defending the standard of living.
  Martin Niemöller 1892–1984: address at Augsburg, January 1958

17 Freedom is the freedom to say that two plus two make four. If that is granted, all else follows.
  George Orwell 1903–50: *Nineteen Eighty-Four* (1949)

18 Tyranny is always better organised than freedom.
  Charles Péguy 1873–1914: *Basic Verities* (1943)

19 O liberty! what crimes are committed in thy name!
  Mme Roland 1754–93: A. de Lamartine *Histoire des Girondins* (1847)

20 Man was born free, and everywhere he is in chains.
  Jean-Jacques Rousseau 1712–78: *Du Contrat social* (1762)

21 What is freedom of expression? Without the freedom to offend, it ceases to exist.
  Salman Rushdie 1947– : in *Weekend Guardian* 10 February 1990

22 I am condemned to be free.
  Jean-Paul Sartre 1905–80: *L'Être et le néant* (1943)

23 Of course liberty is not licence. Liberty in my view is conforming to majority opinion.
  Hugh Scanlon 1913– : television interview, 9 August 1977

24 Liberty means responsibility. That is why most men dread it.
> **George Bernard Shaw** 1856–1950: *Man and Superman* (1903)

25 A free society is a society where it is safe to be unpopular.
> **Adlai Stevenson** 1900–65: speech in Detroit, 7 October 1952

Libraries

See also **Books**, **Reading**

1 The true University of these days is a collection of books.
> **Thomas Carlyle** 1795–1881: *On Heroes, Hero-Worship, and the Heroic* (1841)

2 A man should keep his little brain attic stocked with all the furniture that he is likely to use, and the rest he can put away in the lumber room of his library, where he can get it if he wants it.
> **Arthur Conan Doyle** 1859–1930: *Adventures of Sherlock Holmes* (1892)

3 No place affords a more striking conviction of the vanity of human hopes, than a public library.
> **Samuel Johnson** 1709–84: in *The Rambler* 23 March 1751

4 Your *borrowers of books*—those mutilators of collections, spoilers of the symmetry of shelves, and creators of odd volumes.
> **Charles Lamb** 1775–1834: *Essays of Elia* (1823) 'The Two Races of Men'

5 A library is thought in cold storage.
> **Lord Samuel** 1870–1963: *A Book of Quotations* (1947)

6 Come, and take choice of all my library,
And so beguile thy sorrow.
> **William Shakespeare** 1564–1616: *Titus Andronicus* (1590)

Lies and Lying

See also **Truth**

1 An abomination unto the Lord, but a very present help in
time of trouble.
Anonymous: definition of a lie, an amalgamation of
Proverbs 12.22 and Psalms 46.1, often attributed to Adlai
Stevenson

2 And, after all, what is a lie? 'Tis but
The truth in masquerade.
Lord Byron 1788–1824: *Don Juan* (1819–24)

3 One sometimes sees more clearly in the man who lies than
in the man who tells the truth. Truth, like the light, blinds.
Lying, on the other hand, is a beautiful twilight, which
gives to each object its value.
Albert Camus 1913–60: attributed; Lord Trevelyan
Diplomatic Channels (1973)

4 That branch of the art of lying which consists in very
nearly deceiving your friends without quite deceiving your
enemies.
Francis M. Cornford 1874–1943: on propaganda;
Microcosmographia Academica (1922 ed.)

5 There are three kinds of lies: lies, damned lies and
statistics.
Benjamin Disraeli 1804–81: attributed to Disraeli in
Mark Twain *Autobiography* (1924)

6 Without lies humanity would perish of despair and
boredom.
Anatole France 1844–1924: *La Vie en fleur* (1922)

7 Whoever would lie usefully should lie seldom.
Lord Hervey 1696–1743: *Memoirs of the Reign of George
II*

8 The broad mass of a nation . . . will more easily fall victim
to a big lie than to a small one.
Adolf Hitler 1889–1945: *Mein Kampf* (1925)

9 There is no worse lie than a truth misunderstood by those
who hear it.
William James 1842–1910: *Varieties of Religious
Experience* (1902)

10 Calumnies are answered best with silence.
Ben Jonson c.1573–1637: *Volpone* (1605)

11 The lie in the soul is a true lie.
Benjamin Jowett 1817–93: introduction to his
translation (1871) of Plato's *Republic*

12 He would, wouldn't he?
Mandy Rice-Davies 1944– : at the trial of Stephen
Ward, 29 June 1963, on hearing that Lord Astor denied
her allegations

13 O what a tangled web we weave,
When first we practise to deceive!
Sir Walter Scott 1771–1832: *Marmion* (1808)

14 The retort courteous . . . the quip modest . . . the reply
churlish . . . the reproof valiant . . . the countercheck
quarrelsome . . . the lie circumstantial . . . the lie direct.
William Shakespeare 1564–1616: *As You Like It* (1599),
of the degrees of a lie

15 It is well said in the old proverb, 'a lie will go round the
world while truth is pulling its boots on'.
C. H. Spurgeon 1834–92: *Gems from Spurgeon* (1859)

16 The cruellest lies are often told in silence.
Robert Louis Stevenson 1850–94: *Virginibus Puerisque*
(1881)

17 He replied that I must needs be mistaken, or that I *said the
thing which was not*. (For they have no word in their
language to express lying or falsehood.)
Jonathan Swift 1667–1745: *Gulliver's Travels* (1726)

18 One of the most striking differences between a cat and a
lie is that a cat has only nine lives.
Mark Twain 1835–1910: *Pudd'nhead Wilson* (1894)

19 He will lie even when it is inconvenient: the sign of the
true artist.
Gore Vidal 1925– : attributed

Life

See also **Life Sciences**, **Living**

1 The Answer to the Great Question Of . . . Life, the Universe and Everything . . . [is] Forty-two.
   Douglas Adams 1952– : *The Hitch Hiker's Guide to the Galaxy* (1979)

2 It is in life as it is in ways, the shortest way is commonly the foulest, and surely the fairer way is not much about.
   Francis Bacon 1561–1626: *The Advancement of Learning* (1605)

3 The life of every man is a diary in which he means to write one story, and writes another; and his humblest hour is when he compares the volume as it is with what he vowed to make it.
   J. M. Barrie 1860–1937: *The Little Minister* (1891)

4 If it were possible to talk to the unborn, one could never explain to them how it feels to be alive, for life is washed in the speechless real.
   Jacques Barzun 1907– : *The House of Intellect* (1959)

5 I couldn't have done it otherwise, gone on I mean. I could not have gone on through the awful wretched mess of life without having left a stain upon the silence.
   Samuel Beckett 1906–89: Deirdre Bair *Samuel Beckett* (1978)

6 'Such,' he said, 'O King, seems to me the present life of men on earth, in comparison with that time which to us is uncertain, as if when on a winter's night you sit feasting with your ealdormen and thegns,—a single sparrow should fly swiftly into the hall, and coming in at one door, instantly fly out through another'.
   The Venerable Bede AD 673–735: *Ecclesiastical History of the English People*

7 Man that is born of a woman is of few days, and full of trouble.
   Bible: Job

8 All that a man hath will he give for his life.
Bible: Job

9 Life is just a bowl of cherries.
Lew Brown 1893–1958: title of song (1931)

10 To live is like to love—all reason is against it, and all
healthy instinct for it.
Samuel Butler 1835–1902: *Notebooks* (1912)

11 Life is a horizontal fall.
Jean Cocteau 1889–1963: *Opium* (1930)

12 Life is an incurable disease.
Abraham Cowley 1618–67: 'To Dr Scarborough' (1656)

13 It's a funny old world—a man's lucky if he gets out of it
alive.
Walter de Leon and **Paul M. Jones**: *You're Telling Me*
(1934 film); spoken by W. C. Fields

14 Youth is a blunder; Manhood a struggle; Old Age a regret.
Benjamin Disraeli 1804–81: *Coningsby* (1844)

15 Yet we have gone on living,
Living and partly living.
T. S. Eliot 1888–1965: *Murder in the Cathedral* (1935)

16 All that matters is love and work.
Sigmund Freud 1856–1939: attributed

17 Man wants but little here below,
Nor wants that little long.
Oliver Goldsmith 1728–74: 'Edwin and Angelina, or the
Hermit' (1766)

18 No arts; no letters; no society; and which is worst of all,
continual fear and danger of violent death; and the life of
man, solitary, poor, nasty, brutish, and short.
Thomas Hobbes 1588–1679: *Leviathan* (1651)

19 Life is just one damned thing after another.
Elbert Hubbard 1859–1915: in *Philistine* December 1909,
often attributed to Frank Ward O'Malley

20 Cats and monkeys—monkeys and cats—all human life is there!

  Henry James 1843–1916: *The Madonna of the Future* (1879) 'All human life is there' became the slogan of the *News of the World* from the late 1950s

21 Human life is everywhere a state in which much is to be endured, and little to be enjoyed.

  Samuel Johnson 1709–84: *Rasselas* (1759)

22 As far as we can discern, the sole purpose of human existence is to kindle a light in the darkness of mere being.

  Carl Gustav Jung 1875–1961: *Memories, Dreams, Reflections* (1962)

23 Life must be understood backwards; but . . . it must be lived forwards.

  Sören Kierkegaard 1813–1855: *Journals and Papers* (1843)

24 Man has but three events in his life: to be born, to live, and to die. He is not conscious of his birth, he suffers at his death and he forgets to live.

  Jean de la Bruyère 1645–96: *The Characters, or The Manners of the Age* (1688)

25 *Ah! que la vie est quotidienne.*

  Oh, what a day-to-day business life is.

  Jules Laforgue 1860–87: *Complainte sur certains ennuis* (1885)

26 Life is first boredom, then fear.

  Philip Larkin 1922–85: 'Dockery & Son' (1964)

27 Many men would take the death-sentence without a whimper to escape the life-sentence which fate carries in her other hand.

  T. E. Lawrence 1888–1935: *The Mint* (1955)

28 Life is like a sewer. What you get out of it depends on what you put into it.

  Tom Lehrer 1928– : 'We Will All Go Together When We Go' (1953 song), preamble

29 Life well spent is long.

> **Leonardo da Vinci** 1452–1519: E. McCurdy (ed. and trans.) *Leonardo da Vinci's Notebooks* (1906)

30 Life is real! Life is earnest!
And the grave is not its goal;
Dust thou art, to dust returnest,
Was not spoken of the soul.

> **Henry Wadsworth Longfellow** 1807–82: 'A Psalm of Life' (1838)

31 And life is given to none freehold, but it is leasehold for all.

> **Lucretius** c.94–55 BC: *De Rerum Natura*

32 What, knocked a tooth out? Never mind, dear, laugh it off, laugh it off; it's all part of life's rich pageant.

> **Arthur Marshall** 1910–89: *The Games Mistress* (recorded monologue, 1937)

33 We live, not as we wish to, but as we can.

> **Menander** 342–c.292 BC: *Dis Exapaton*

34 I've looked at life from both sides now,
From win and lose and still somehow
It's life's illusions I recall;
I really don't know life at all.

> **Joni Mitchell** 1945– : 'Both Sides Now' (1967 song)

35 The ceaseless labour of your life is to build the house of death.

> **Montaigne** 1533–92: *Essais* (1580)

36 Man is born to live, not to prepare for life.

> **Boris Pasternak** 1890–1960: *Doctor Zhivago* (1958)

37 My momma always said life was like a box of chocolates . . . you never know what you're gonna get.

> **Eric Ross**: *Forrest Gump* (1994 film), based on the novel (1986) by Winston Groom; spoken by Tom Hanks

38 All the world's a stage,
And all the men and women merely players:
They have their exits and their entrances;

And one man in his time plays many parts,
His acts being seven ages.
    William Shakespeare 1564–1616: *As You Like It* (1599)

39 Life's but a walking shadow, a poor player,
That struts and frets his hour upon the stage,
And then is heard no more; it is a tale
Told by an idiot, full of sound and fury,
Signifying nothing.
    William Shakespeare 1564–1616: *Macbeth* (1606)

40 Not to be born is, past all prizing, best.
    Sophocles c.496–406 BC: *Oedipus Coloneus* (tr. R. C. Jebb)

41 One's prime is elusive. You little girls, when you grow up,
must be on the alert to recognise your prime at whatever
time of your life it may occur.
    Muriel Spark 1918– : *The Prime of Miss Jean Brodie*
(1961)

42 Life is a gamble at terrible odds—if it was a bet, you
wouldn't take it.
    Tom Stoppard 1937– : *Rosencrantz and Guildenstern are
Dead* (1967)

43 Oh, isn't life a terrible thing, thank God?
    Dylan Thomas 1914–53: *Under Milk Wood* (1954)

44 Our life is frittered away by detail . . . Simplify, simplify.
    Henry David Thoreau 1817–62: *Walden* (1854)

45 The mass of men lead lives of quiet desperation.
    Henry David Thoreau 1817–62: *Walden* (1854)

46 Expect nothing. Live frugally
on surprise.
    Alice Walker 1944– : 'Expect nothing' (1973)

47 This world is a comedy to those that think, a tragedy to
those that feel.
    Horace Walpole 1717–97: letter to Anne, Countess of
Upper Ossory, 16 August 1776

48 All the business of war, and indeed all the business of life,
is to endeavour to find out what you don't know by what
you do; that's what I called 'guessing what was at the other
side of the hill'.
  Duke of Wellington 1769–1852: *The Croker Papers* (1885)

49 I enjoy almost everything. Yet I have some restless
searcher in me. Why is there not a discovery in life?
Something one can lay one's hands on and say "This is
it"?
  Virginia Woolf 1882–1941: diary, 27 February 1926

50 Never to have lived is best, ancient writers say;
  Never to have drawn the breath of life, never to have
    looked into the eye of day;
  The second best's a gay goodnight and quickly turn away.
  W. B. Yeats 1865–1939: 'From *Oedipus at Colonus*' (1928)

Life Sciences

See also **Science**

1 The Microbe is so very small
  You cannot make him out at all.
  Hilaire Belloc 1870–1953: 'The Microbe' (1897)

2 Men will not be content to manufacture life: they will want
to improve on it.
  J. D. Bernal 1901–71: *The World, the Flesh and the Devil*
  (1929)

3 [The science of life] is a superb and dazzlingly lighted hall
which may be reached only by passing through a long and
ghastly kitchen.
  Claude Bernard 1813–78: *An Introduction to the Study of
  Experimental Medicine* (1865)

4 It has, I believe, been often remarked that a hen is only an
egg's way of making another egg.
  Samuel Butler 1835–1902: *Life and Habit* (1877)

5 Today we are learning the language in which God created life.
   Bill Clinton 1946– : announcing the deciphering of 90% of the human genome; in *Independent* 27 June 2000

6 Almost all aspects of life are engineered at the molecular level, and without understanding molecules we can only have a very sketchy understanding of life itself.
   Francis Crick 1916– : *What Mad Pursuit* (1988)

7 I have called this principle, by which each slight variation, if useful, is preserved, by the term of Natural Selection.
   Charles Darwin 1809–82: *On the Origin of Species* (1859)

8 The essence of life is statistical improbability on a colossal scale.
   Richard Dawkins 1941– : *The Blind Watchmaker* (1986)

9 That which *is* grows, while that which *is not* becomes.
   Galen AD 129–199: *On the Natural Faculties*

10 I'd lay down my life for two brothers or eight cousins.
   J. B. S. Haldane 1892–1964: attributed; in *New Scientist* 8 August 1974

11 Life exists in the universe only because the carbon atom possesses certain exceptional properties.
   James Jeans 1877–1946: *The Mysterious Universe* (1930)

12 The biologist passes, the frog remains.
   Jean Rostand 1894–1977: *Inquiétudes d'un biologiste* (1967); sometimes quoted as 'Theories pass. The frog remains'

13 Survival of the fittest implies multiplication of the fittest.
   Herbert Spencer 1820–1903: *Principles of Biology* (1865)

14 Genes are not like engineering blueprints; they are more like recipes in a cookbook. They tell us what ingredients to use, in what quantities, and in what order—but they do not provide a complete, accurate plan of the final result.
   Ian Stewart 1945– : *Life's Other Secret* (1998) preface

15 So, naturalists observe, a flea
   Hath smaller fleas that on him prey;
   And these have smaller fleas to bite 'em,

And so proceed *ad infinitum*.
Jonathan Swift 1667–1745: 'On Poetry' (1733)

16 Water is life's *mater* and *matrix*, mother and medium.
There is no life without water.
Albert von Szent-Györgyi 1893–1986: *Perspectives in Biology and Medicine* Winter 1971

17 Was it through his grandfather or his grandmother that he claimed his descent from a monkey?
Bishop Samuel Wilberforce 1805–73: addressed to T. H. Huxley in a debate on Darwin's theory of evolution at Oxford, June 1860

18 Biology is the search for the chemistry that works.
R. J. P. Williams 1926– : lecture in Oxford, June 1996

Literature

See also **Writing**

1 'Oh! it is only a novel! . . . only Cecilia, or Camilla, or Belinda:' or, in short, only some work in which the most thorough knowledge of human nature, the happiest delineation of its varieties, the liveliest effusions of wit and humour are conveyed to the world in the best chosen language.
Jane Austen 1775–1817: *Northanger Abbey* (1818)

2 A losing trade, I assure you, sir: literature is a drug.
George Borrow 1803–81: *Lavengro* (1851)

3 There is no other antidote to the vulgarity of the human heart than doubt and good taste, which one finds fused in works of great literature.
Joseph Brodsky 1940–96: 'Letter to a President [Václav Havel]' (1993), in *On Grief and Reason* (1996)

4 All tragedies are finished by a death,
All comedies are ended by a marriage;

The future states of both are left to faith.
Lord Byron 1788–1824: *Don Juan* (1819–24)

5 Literature is a luxury; fiction is a necessity.
G. K. Chesterton 1874–1936: *The Defendant* (1901) 'A Defence of Penny Dreadfuls'

6 The central function of imaginative literature is to make you realize that other people act on moral convictions different from your own.
William Empson 1906–84: *Milton's God* (1981)

7 Yes—oh dear yes—the novel tells a story.
E. M. Forster 1879–1970: *Aspects of the Novel* (1927)

8 Works of serious purpose and grand promises often have a purple patch or two stitched on, to shine far and wide.
Horace 65–8 BC: *Ars Poetica*

9 It takes a great deal of history to produce a little literature.
Henry James 1843–1916: *Hawthorne* (1879)

10 Never trust the artist. Trust the tale.
D. H. Lawrence 1885–1930: *Studies in Classic American Literature* (1923)

11 Our American professors like their literature clear and cold and pure and very dead.
Sinclair Lewis 1885–1951: *The American Fear of Literature* (Nobel Prize Address, 12 December 1930)

12 Literature is news that STAYS news.
Ezra Pound 1885–1972: *The ABC of Reading* (1934)

13 A novel is a mirror which passes over a highway. Sometimes it reflects to your eyes the blue of the skies, at others the churned-up mud of the road.
Stendhal 1783–1842: *Le Rouge et le noir* (1830)

14 The good ended happily, and the bad unhappily. That is what fiction means.
Oscar Wilde 1854–1900: *The Importance of Being Earnest* (1895)

Living

See also **Life**

1 I've lived a life that's full, I've travelled each and ev'ry
highway
And more, much more than this. I did it my way.
Paul Anka 1941– : *My Way* (1969 song)

2 *Quidquid agis, prudenter agas, et respice finem.*
Whatever you do, do cautiously, and look to the end.
Anonymous: *Gesta Romanorum*

3 Love and do what you will.
St Augustine of Hippo AD 354–430: *In Epistolam
Joannis ad Parthos* (AD 413)

4 A man hath no better thing under the sun, than to eat, and
to drink, and to be merry.
Bible: Ecclesiastes

5 Thou shalt love thy neighbour as thyself.
Bible: Leviticus. See also St Matthew

6 Do what thou wilt shall be the whole of the Law.
Aleister Crowley 1875–1947: *Book of the Law* (1909)

7 Live all you can; it's a mistake not to. It doesn't so much
matter what you do in particular, so long as you have your
life. If you haven't had that, what *have* you had?
Henry James 1843–1916: *Ambassadors* (1903)

8 If I had no duties, and no reference to futurity, I would
spend my life in driving briskly in a post-chaise with a
pretty woman.
Samuel Johnson 1709–84: James Boswell *Life of
Johnson* (1791) 19 September 1777

9 Turn on, tune in and drop out.
Timothy Leary 1920–96: lecture, June 1966; *The Politics
of Ecstasy* (1968)

10 *Mon métier et mon art c'est vivre.*
Living is my job and my art.
Montaigne 1533–92: *Essais* (1580)

11 Believe me! The secret of reaping the greatest fruitfulness
and the greatest enjoyment from life is *to live dangerously*!
  Friedrich Nietzsche 1844–1900: *Die fröhliche
  Wissenschaft* (1882)

12 To live at all is miracle enough.
  Mervyn Peake 1911–68: *The Glassblower* (1950)

13 *Fais ce que voudras.*
  Do what you like.
  François Rabelais *c.*1494–*c.*1553: *Gargantua* (1534)

14 You only live once, and the way I live, once is enough.
  Frank Sinatra 1915–98: attributed, in *The Times* 16 May
  1998

15 Take short views, hope for the best, and trust in God.
  Sydney Smith 1771–1845: in Lady Holland *Memoir* (1855)

16 I'm not living with you. We occupy the same cage.
  Tennessee Williams 1911–83: *Cat on a Hot Tin Roof*
  (1955)

17 It's better to burn out
  Than to fade away.
  Neil Young 1945– : 'My My, Hey Hey (Out of the Blue)'
  (1978 song, with Jeff Blackburn); quoted by Kurt Cobain
  in his suicide note, 8 April 1994

London

1 *Was für Plunder!*
  What rubbish!
  Gebhard Lebrecht Blücher 1742–1819: of London as
  seen from the Monument in June 1814, often misquoted
  '*Was für plündern* [What a place to plunder]!'

2 The great wen of all.
  William Cobbett 1762–1835: *Rural Rides* 5 January 1822

3 London Pride has been handed down to us.
  London Pride is a flower that's free.
  London Pride means our own dear town to us,

And our pride it for ever will be.
Noël Coward 1899–1973: 'London Pride' (1941 song)

4 Crowds without company, and dissipation without pleasure.
Edward Gibbon 1737–94: *Memoirs of My Life* (1796)

5 When a man is tired of London, he is tired of life.
Samuel Johnson 1709–84: James Boswell *Life of Johnson* (1791) 20 September 1777

6 I thought of London spread out in the sun,
Its postal districts packed like squares of wheat.
Philip Larkin 1922–85: *The Whitsun Weddings* (1964)

7 Earth has not anything to show more fair:
Dull would he be of soul who could pass by
A sight so touching in its majesty.
William Wordsworth 1770–1850: 'Composed upon Westminster Bridge' (1807)

Love

See also **Marriage**, **Sex**

1 You know very well that love is, above all, the gift of oneself!
Jean Anouilh 1910–87: *Ardèle* (1949)

2 Many waters cannot quench love, neither can the floods drown it.
Bible: Song of Solomon

3 Greater love hath no man than this, that a man lay down his life for his friends.
Bible: St John

4 Though I speak with the tongues of men and of angels, and have not charity, I am become as sounding brass, or a tinkling cymbal.
And though I have the gift of prophecy, and understand all mysteries, and all knowledge; and though I have all faith;

so that I could remove mountains; and have not charity, I am nothing.

Bible: I Corinthians

5 And now abideth faith, hope, charity, these three; but the greatest of these is charity.

Bible: I Corinthians

6 There is no fear in love; but perfect love casteth out fear.

Bible: I John

7 Love seeketh not itself to please,
Nor for itself hath any care;
But for another gives its ease,
And builds a Heaven in Hell's despair.

William Blake 1757–1827: 'The Clod and the Pebble' (1794)

8 O, my Luve's like a red, red rose
That's newly sprung in June;
O my Luve's like the melodie
That's sweetly play'd in tune.

Robert Burns 1759–96: 'A Red Red Rose' (1796); derived from various folk-songs

9 To enlarge or illustrate this power and effect of love is to set a candle in the sun.

Robert Burton 1577–1640: *Anatomy of Melancholy* (1621–51)

10 Love wol nat been constreyned by maistrye.
When maistrie comth, the God of Love anon
Beteth his wynges, and farewel, he is gon!

Geoffrey Chaucer c.1343–1400: *The Canterbury Tales* 'The Franklin's Tale'

11 Love and a cottage! Eh, Fanny! Ah, give me indifference and a coach and six!

George Colman, the Elder 1732–94 and **David Garrick** 1717–79: *The Clandestine Marriage* (1766)

12 Say what you will, 'tis better to be left than never to have been loved.

William Congreve 1670–1729: *The Way of the World* (1700)

13 *L'amor che muove il sole e l'altre stelle.*

The love that moves the sun and the other stars.
   Dante Alighieri 1265–1321: *Divina Commedia* 'Paradiso'

14 Love itself is what is left over when being in love has
burned away.
   Louis de Bernières 1954– : *Captain Corelli's Mandolin*
   (1994)

15 If you could see my legs when I take my boots off, you'd
form some idea of what unrequited affection is.
   Charles Dickens 1812–70: *Dombey and Son* (1848) Mr
   Toots

16 Love is a growing or full constant light;
And his first minute, after noon, is night.
   John Donne 1572–1631: 'A Lecture in the Shadow'

17 Love built on beauty, soon as beauty, dies.
   John Donne 1572–1631: 'The Anagram' (*c.*1595)

18 I am the Love that dare not speak its name.
   Lord Alfred Douglas 1870–1945: 'Two Loves' (1896)

19 And love's the noblest frailty of the mind.
   John Dryden 1631–1700: *The Indian Emperor* (1665)

20 Love's pleasure lasts but a moment; love's sorrow lasts all
through life.
   Jean-Pierre Claris de Florian 1755–94: *Célestine* (1784)

21 If I love you, what does that matter to you!
   Johann Wolfgang von Goethe 1749–1832: *Wilhelm
   Meister's Apprenticeship* (1795-6)

22 Love is a universal migraine.
A bright stain on the vision
Blotting out reason.
   Robert Graves 1895–1985: 'Symptoms of Love'

23 Love in a hut, with water and a crust,
Is—Love, forgive us!—cinders, ashes, dust.
   John Keats 1795–1821: 'Lamia' (1820)

24 How alike are the groans of love to those of the dying.
   Malcolm Lowry 1909–57: *Under the Volcano* (1947)

25 Where both deliberate, the love is slight;
  Who ever loved that loved not at first sight?
  Christopher Marlowe 1564–93: *Hero and Leander* (1598)

26 Difficult or easy, pleasant or bitter, you are the same you: I
  cannot live with you—or without you.
  Martial AD *c.*40–*c.*104: *Epigrammata*

27 Had we but world enough, and time,
  This coyness, lady, were no crime.
  Andrew Marvell 1621–78: 'To His coy Mistress' (1681)

28 The love that lasts longest is the love that is never
  returned.
  W. Somerset Maugham 1874–1965: *A Writer's Notebook*
  (1949) written in 1894

29 If I am pressed to say why I loved him, I feel it can only be
  explained by replying: 'Because it was he; because it was
  me.'
  Montaigne 1533–92: *Essais* (1580)

30 No, there's nothing half so sweet in life
  As love's young dream.
  Thomas Moore 1779–1852: 'Love's Young Dream' (1807)

31 If I can't love Hitler, I can't love at all.
  Rev. A. J. Muste 1885–1967: at a Quaker meeting 1940; in
  New York Times 12 February 1967

32 Birds do it, bees do it,
  Even educated fleas do it.
  Let's do it, let's fall in love.
  Cole Porter 1891–1964: 'Let's Do It' (1954 song; words
  added to the 1928 original)

33 Life has taught us that love does not consist in gazing at
  each other but in looking together in the same direction.
  Antoine de Saint-Exupéry 1900–44: *Terre des Hommes*
  (translated as 'Wind, Sand and Stars', 1939)

34 Love means not ever having to say you're sorry.
  Erich Segal 1937– : *Love Story* (1970)

35 ANTONY: There's beggary in the love that can be reckoned.
  CLEOPATRA: I'll set a bourn how far to be beloved.

ANTONY: Then must thou needs find out new heaven, new earth.
William Shakespeare 1564–1616: *Antony and Cleopatra* (1606–7)

36 The course of true love never did run smooth.
William Shakespeare 1564–1616: *A Midsummer Night's Dream* (1595–6)

37   Then, must you speak
Of one that loved not wisely but too well.
William Shakespeare 1564–1616: *Othello* (1602–4)

38 For stony limits cannot hold love out,
And what love can do that dares love attempt.
William Shakespeare 1564–1616: *Romeo and Juliet* (1595)

39   To be wise, and love,
Exceeds man's might.
William Shakespeare 1564–1616: *Troilus and Cressida* (1602)

40 Let me not to the marriage of true minds
Admit impediments. Love is not love
Which alters when it alteration finds.
William Shakespeare 1564–1616: sonnet 116 (1609)

41 The fickleness of the women I love is only equalled by the infernal constancy of the women who love me.
George Bernard Shaw 1856–1950: *The Philanderer* (1898)

42 Why so pale and wan, fond lover?
Prithee, why so pale?
Will, when looking well can't move her,
Looking ill prevail?
John Suckling 1609–42: *Aglaura* (1637)

43 'Tis better to have loved and lost
Than never to have loved at all.
Alfred, Lord Tennyson 1809–92: *In Memoriam A. H. H.* (1850)

44 *Omnia vincit Amor: et nos cedamus Amori.*

Love conquers all things: let us too give in to Love.
> **Virgil** 70–19 BC: *Eclogues*

45 Yet each man kills the thing he loves,
By each let this be heard,
Some do it with a bitter look,
Some with a flattering word.
The coward does it with a kiss,
The brave man with a sword!
> **Oscar Wilde** 1854–1900: *The Ballad of Reading Gaol*
> (1898)

46 A pity beyond all telling,
Is hid in the heart of love.
> **W. B. Yeats** 1865–1939: 'The Pity of Love' (1893)

Madness

1 Whenever God prepares evil for a man, He first damages his mind, with which he deliberates.
> **Anonymous**: scholiastic annotation to Sophocles's
> *Antigone*

2 Babylon in all its desolation is a sight not so awful as that of the human mind in ruins.
> **Scrope Davies** c.1783–1852: letter to Thomas Raikes,
> May 1835

3 *Quem Jupiter vult perdere, dementat prius.*

Whom God would destroy He first sends mad.
> **James Duport** 1606–79: *Homeri Gnomologia* (1660)

4 Mad, is he? Then I hope he will *bite* some of my other generals.
> **George II** 1683–1760: replying to the Duke of Newcastle,
> who had complained that General Wolfe was a madman

5 There was only one catch and that was Catch-22 . . . Orr would be crazy to fly more missions and sane if he didn't, but if he was sane he had to fly them. If he flew them he

was crazy and didn't have to; but if he didn't want to he
was sane and had to.
   Joseph Heller 1923–99: *Catch-22* (1961)

6 Every one is more or less mad on one point.
   Rudyard Kipling 1865–1936: *Plain Tales from the Hills*
   (1888)

7 Madness need not be all breakdown. It may also be breakthrough.
   R. D. Laing 1927–89: *The Politics of Experience* (1967)

8 They called me mad, and I called them mad, and damn
them, they outvoted me.
   Nathaniel Lee c.1653–92: R. Porter *A Social History of
   Madness* (1987)

9 Is there no way out of the mind?
   Sylvia Plath 1932–63: 'Apprehensions' (1971)

10 The psychopath is the furnace that gives no heat.
   Derek Raymond 1931–94: *The Hidden Files* (1992)

11 Though this be madness, yet there is method in't.
   William Shakespeare 1564–1616: *Hamlet* (1601)

12 O! let me not be mad, not mad, sweet heaven;
Keep me in temper; I would not be mad!
   William Shakespeare 1564–1616: *King Lear* (1605–6)

....

Majorities
....
see **Minorities and Majorities**

....

Management
....
See also **Bureaucracy**, **Careers**

1 Committee—a group of men who individually can do
nothing but as a group decide that nothing can be done.
   Fred Allen 1894–1956: attributed

2 A place for everything and everything in its place.
   Mrs Beeton 1836–65: *Book of Household Management*
   (1861), often attributed to Samuel Smiles

3 This island is made mainly of coal and surrounded by fish.
   Only an organizing genius could produce a shortage of
   coal and fish at the same time.
   Aneurin Bevan 1897–1960: speech at Blackpool, 24 May
   1945

4 Oh, the Germans classify, but the French arrange!
   Willa Cather 1873–1947: *Death Comes For the Archbishop*
   (1927))

5 You're either part of the solution or you're part of the
   problem.
   Eldridge Cleaver 1935–98: speech in San Francisco, 1968

6 A camel is a horse designed by a committee.
   Alec Issigonis 1906–88: on his dislike of working in
   teams

7 There cannot be a crisis next week. My schedule is already
   full.
   Henry Kissinger 1923– : in *New York Times Magazine*
   1 June 1969

8 If it ain't broke, don't fix it.
   Bert Lance 1931– : in *Nation's Business* May 1977

9 Every time I create an appointment, I create a hundred
   malcontents and one ingrate.
   Louis XIV 1638–1715: Voltaire *Siècle de Louis XIV* (1768
   ed.)

10 Time spent on any item of the agenda will be in inverse
   proportion to the sum involved.
   C. Northcote Parkinson 1909–93: *Parkinson's Law*
   (1958)

11 In a hierarchy every employee tends to rise to his level of
   incompetence.
   Laurence Peter 1919– : *The Peter Principle* (1969)

12 A problem left to itself dries up or goes rotten. But fertilize
a problem with a solution—you'll hatch out dozens.
N. F. Simpson 1919– : *A Resounding Tinkle* (1958)

13 The shortest way to do many things is to do only one thing
at once.
Samuel Smiles 1812–1904: *Self-Help* (1859)

14 Management that wants to change an institution must first
show it loves that institution.
John Tusa 1936– : in *Observer* 27 February 1994

15 *Dans ce pays-ci il est bon de tuer de temps en temps un
amiral pour encourager les autres.*

In this country [England] it is thought well to kill an
admiral from time to time to encourage the others.
Voltaire 1694–1778: *Candide* (1759)

....

Manners
....

See also **Behaviour**

1 Evil communications corrupt good manners.
Bible: I Corinthians

2 Most vices may be committed very genteelly: a man may
debauch his friend's wife genteelly: he may cheat at cards
genteelly.
James Boswell 1740–95: *Life of Samuel Johnson* (1791)

3 The tribute which intelligence pays to humbug.
St John Brodrick 1856–1942: definition of tact; Lady
Ribblesdale to Lord Curzon 3 April 1891; Kenneth Rose
Superior Person (1969)

4 Curtsey while you're thinking what to say. It saves time.
Lewis Carroll 1832–98: *Through the Looking-Glass* (1872)

5 Take the tone of the company that you are in.
Lord Chesterfield 1694–1773: *Letters to his Son* (1774) 16
October 1747

6 Very notable was his distinction between coarseness and
   vulgarity (coarseness, revealing something; vulgarity,
   concealing something).
   E. M. Forster 1879–1970: *The Longest Journey* (1907)

7 The art of pleasing consists in being pleased.
   William Hazlitt 1778–1830: *The Round Table* (1817) 'On
   Manner'

8 There are few who would not rather be taken in adultery
   than in provincialism.
   Aldous Huxley 1894–1963: *Antic Hay* (1923)

9 To Americans, English manners are far more frightening
   than none at all.
   Randall Jarrell 1914–65: *Pictures from an Institution*
   (1954)

10 Punctuality is the politeness of kings.
   Louis XVIII 1755–1824: attributed

11 Stand not upon the order of your going.
   William Shakespeare 1564–1616: *Macbeth* (1606)

12 He is the very pineapple of politeness!
   Richard Brinsley Sheridan 1751–1816: *The Rivals* (1775)

13 JUDGE: You are extremely offensive, young man.
   SMITH: As a matter of fact, we both are, and the only
   difference between us is that I am trying to be, and you
   can't help it.
   F. E. Smith 1872–1930: 2nd Earl of Birkenhead *Earl of
   Birkenhead* (1933)

14 The Japanese have perfected good manners and made
   them indistinguishable from rudeness.
   Paul Theroux 1941– : *The Great Railway Bazaar* (1975)

15 This is the only country in the world where you step on
   somebody's foot and he apologises.
   Keith Waterhouse 1929– : in *Independent* 1 April 2000

16 Manners are especially the need of the plain. The pretty
   can get away with anything.
   Evelyn Waugh 1903–66: in *Observer* 15 April 1962

Marriage

See also **Love**, **Sex**

1 If it were not for the presents, an elopement would be preferable.
   George Ade 1866–1944: *Forty Modern Fables* (1901)

2 It is a truth universally acknowledged, that a single man in possession of a good fortune, must be in want of a wife.
   Jane Austen 1775–1817: *Pride and Prejudice* (1813)

3 Wives are young men's mistresses, companions for middle age, and old men's nurses.
   Francis Bacon 1561–1626: *Essays* (1625) 'Of Marriage and the Single Life'

4 A man's mother is his misfortune, but his wife is his fault.
   Walter Bagehot 1826–77: on being urged to marry by his mother; Norman St John Stevas *Works of Walter Bagehot* (1986) vol. 15

5 Being a husband is a whole-time job. That is why so many husbands fail. They cannot give their entire attention to it.
   Arnold Bennett 1867–1931: *The Title* (1918)

6 Never marry a man who hates his mother, because he'll end up hating you.
   Jill Bennett 1931–90: in *Observer* 12 September 1982

7 What therefore God hath joined together, let not man put asunder.
   Bible: St Matthew

8 Wilt thou love her, comfort her, honour, and keep her in sickness and in health; and, forsaking all other, keep thee only unto her, so long as ye both shall live?
   Book of Common Prayer 1662: *Solemnization of Matrimony*

9 To have and to hold from this day forward, for better for worse, for richer for poorer, in sickness and in health, to love, cherish, and to obey, till death us do part.
   Book of Common Prayer 1662: *Solemnization of Matrimony*

10 Think you, if Laura had been Petrarch's wife,
He would have written sonnets all his life?
   Lord Byron 1788–1824: *Don Juan* (1819–24)

11 Still I can't contradict, what so oft has been said,
'Though women are angels, yet wedlock's the devil.'
   Lord Byron 1788–1824: 'To Eliza' (1806)

12 The deep, deep peace of the double-bed after the hurly-
burly of the chaise-longue.
   Mrs Patrick Campbell 1865–1940: on her recent
   marriage; A. Woollcott *While Rome Burns* (1934)

13 Oh! how many torments lie in the small circle of a
wedding-ring!
   Colley Cibber 1671–1757: *The Double Gallant* (1707)

14 Courtship to marriage, as a very witty prologue to a very
dull play.
   William Congreve 1670–1729: *The Old Bachelor* (1693)

15 SHARPER: Thus grief still treads upon the heels of pleasure:
Married in haste, we may repent at leisure.
SETTER: Some by experience find those words mis-placed:
At leisure married, they repent in haste.
   William Congreve 1670–1729: *The Old Bachelor* (1693)

16 Marriage is a wonderful invention; but, then again, so is a
bicycle repair kit.
   Billy Connolly 1942– : Duncan Campbell *Billy Connolly*
   (1976)

17 I would be married, but I'd have no wife,
I would be married to a single life.
   Richard Crashaw *c.*1612–49: 'On Marriage' (1646)

18 There were three of us in this marriage, so it was a bit
crowded.
   Diana, Princess of Wales 1961–97: interview on
   Panorama, BBC1 TV, 20 November 1995

19 The chains of marriage are so heavy that it takes two to
bear them, and sometimes three.
   Alexandre Dumas 1824–95: Léon Treich *L'Esprit
   d'Alexandre Dumas*

20 A woman dictates before marriage in order that she may
   have an appetite for submission afterwards.
   George Eliot 1819–80: *Middlemarch* (1871–2)

21 Do you think your mother and I should have lived
   comfortably so long together, if ever we had been married?
   John Gay 1685–1732: *The Beggar's Opera* (1728)

22 You shall be together when the white wings of death
      scatter your days.
   Ay, you shall be together even in the silent memory of God.
   But let there be spaces in your togetherness,
   And let the winds of the heavens dance between you.
   Kahlil Gibran 1883–1931: *The Prophet* (1923)

23 I . . . chose my wife, as she did her wedding gown, not for
   a fine glossy surface, but such qualities as would wear
   well.
   Oliver Goldsmith 1728–74: *The Vicar of Wakefield* (1766)

24 The critical period in matrimony is breakfast-time.
   A. P. Herbert 1890–1971: *Uncommon Law* (1935)

25 Then be not coy, but use your time;
   And while ye may, go marry:
   For having lost but once your prime,
   You may for ever tarry.
   Robert Herrick 1591–1674: 'To the Virgins, to Make
   Much of Time' (1648)

26 The triumph of hope over experience.
   Samuel Johnson 1709–84: of a man who remarried
   immediately after the death of a wife with whom he had
   been unhappy, 1770; James Boswell *Life of Johnson* (1791)

27 So they were married—to be the more together—
   And found they were never again so much together,
   Divided by the morning tea,
   By the evening paper,
   By children and tradesmen's bills.
   Louis MacNeice 1907–63: *Plant and Phantom* (1941)

28 One doesn't have to get anywhere in a marriage. It's not a
   public conveyance.
   Iris Murdoch 1919–99: *A Severed Head* (1961)

29 Marriage may often be a stormy lake, but celibacy is
almost always a muddy horsepond.
Thomas Love Peacock 1785–1866: *Melincourt* (1817)

30 Strange to say what delight we married people have to see
these poor fools decoyed into our condition.
Samuel Pepys 1633–1703: diary, 25 December 1665

31 It doesn't much signify whom one marries, for one is sure
to find next morning that it was someone else.
Samuel Rogers 1763–1855: A. Dyce (ed.) *Table Talk of
Samuel Rogers* (1860)

32 A young man married is a man that's marred.
William Shakespeare 1564–1616: *All's Well that Ends
Well* (1603–4)

33 Men are April when they woo, December when they wed:
maids are May when they are maids, but the sky changes
when they are wives.
William Shakespeare 1564–1616: *As You Like It* (1599)

34 Marriage is popular because it combines the maximum of
temptation with the maximum of opportunity.
George Bernard Shaw 1856–1950: *Man and Superman*
(1903)

35 Chains do not hold a marriage together. It is threads,
hundreds of tiny threads which sew people together
through the years. That is what makes a marriage last—
more than passion or even sex!
Simone Signoret 1921–85: in *Daily Mail* 4 July 1978

36 My definition of marriage . . . it resembles a pair of shears,
so joined that they cannot be separated; often moving in
opposite directions, yet always punishing anyone who
comes between them.
Sydney Smith 1771–1845: Lady Holland *Memoir* (1855)

37 Marriage is like life in this—that it is a field of battle, and
not a bed of roses.
Robert Louis Stevenson 1850–94: *Virginibus Puerisque*
(1881)

38 Marriage isn't a word . . . it's a *sentence*!
King Vidor 1895–1982: *The Crowd* (1928 film)

39 Marriage is the waste-paper basket of the emotions.
    Sidney Webb 1859–1947: Bertrand Russell *Autobiography* (1967)

40 In married life three is company and two none.
    Oscar Wilde 1854–1900: *The Importance of Being Earnest* (1895)

41 Chumps always make the best husbands ... All the unhappy marriages come from the husbands having brains.
    P. G. Wodehouse 1881–1975: *The Adventures of Sally* (1920)

Mathematics

1 Let no one enter who does not know geometry [mathematics].
    Anonymous: inscription on Plato's door, probably at the Academy at Athens

2 Multiplication is vexation,
Division is as bad;
The Rule of Three doth puzzle me,
And Practice drives me mad.
    Anonymous: *Lean's Collectanea* (1904), possibly 16th-century

3 If in other sciences we should arrive at certainty without doubt and truth without error, it behoves us to place the foundations of knowledge in mathematics.
    Roger Bacon c.1220–c.1292: *Opus Majus*

4 They are neither finite quantities, or quantities infinitely small, nor yet nothing. May we not call them the ghosts of departed quantities?
    Bishop George Berkeley 1685–1753: *The Analyst* (1734), on Newton's infinitesimals

5 I have often admired the mystical way of Pythagoras, and the secret magic of numbers.
    Sir Thomas Browne 1605–82: *Religio Medici* (1643)

6 I never could make out what those damned dots meant.
Lord Randolph Churchill 1849–94: on decimal points; W.
S. Churchill *Lord Randolph Churchill* (1906)

7 Equations are more important to me, because politics is
for the present, but an equation is something for eternity.
Albert Einstein 1879–1955: Stephen Hawking *A Brief
History of Time* (1988)

8 There is no 'royal road' to geometry.
Euclid fl. *c.*300 BC: addressed to Ptolemy I, in Proclus
Commentary on the First Book of Euclid's Elementa

9 This book is written in mathematical language and its
characters are triangles, circles and other geometrical
figures, without whose help . . . one wanders in vain
through a dark labyrinth.
Galileo Galilei 1564–1642: *The Assayer* (1623); often
quoted as 'The book of nature is written . . . '

10 Mathematics are a species of Frenchman; if you say
something to them, they translate it into their own
language and presto! it is something entirely different.
Johann Wolfgang von Goethe 1749–1832: attributed; R.
L. Weber *A Random Walk in Science* (1973)

11 Beauty is the first test: there is no permanent place in the
world for ugly mathematics.
Godfrey Harold Hardy 1877–1947: *A Mathematician's
Apology* (1940)

12 Someone told me that each equation I included in the book
would halve the sales.
Stephen Hawking 1942– : *A Brief History of Time* (1988)

13 God made the integers, all the rest is the work of man.
Leopold Kronecker 1823–91: *Jahrsberichte der
Deutschen Mathematiker Vereinigung* bk. 2

14 In mathematics you don't understand things. You just get
used to them.
John von Neumann 1903–57: Gary Zukav *The Dancing
Wu Li Masters* (1979)

15 Mathematics may be defined as the subject in which we
never know what we are talking about, nor whether what
we are saying is true.
  Bertrand Russell 1872–1970: *Mysticism and Logic* (1918)

16 Mathematics, rightly viewed, possesses not only truth, but
supreme beauty—a beauty cold and austere, like that of
sculpture.
  Bertrand Russell 1872–1970: *Philosophical Essays* (1910)

17 What would life be like without arithmetic, but a scene of
horrors?
  Sydney Smith 1771–1845: letter to Miss [Lucie Austen],
  22 July 1835

Meaning

See also **Words**

1 No one means all he says, and yet very few say all they
mean, for words are slippery and thought is viscous.
  Henry Brooks Adams 1838–1918: *The Education of
  Henry Adams* (1907)

2 'Then you should say what you mean,' the March Hare
went on. 'I do,' Alice hastily replied; 'at least—at least I
mean what I say—that's the same thing, you know.' 'Not
the same thing a bit!' said the Hatter. 'Why, you might just
as well say that "I see what I eat" is the same thing as "I
eat what I see!" '
  Lewis Carroll 1832–98: *Alice's Adventures in Wonderland*
  (1865)

3 It depends on what the meaning of 'is' is.
  Bill Clinton 1946– : videotaped evidence to the grand
  jury; tapes broadcast 21 September 1998

4 The meaning doesn't matter if it's only idle chatter of a
transcendental kind.
  W. S. Gilbert 1836–1911: *Patience* (1881)

5 It all depends what you mean by . . .
   C. E. M. Joad 1891–1953: replying to questions on 'The
   Brains Trust' (formerly 'Any Questions'), BBC radio
   (1941–8)

6 God and I both knew what it meant once; now God alone
   knows.
   Friedrich Klopstock 1724–1803: C. Lombroso *The Man
   of Genius* (1891); also attributed to Browning, apropos
   Sordello, in the form 'When it was written, God and
   Robert Browning knew what it meant; now only God
   knows'

7 I pray thee, understand a plain man in his plain meaning.
   William Shakespeare 1564–1616: *The Merchant of
   Venice* (1596–8)

8 The little girl had the making of a poet in her who, being
   told to be sure of her meaning before she spoke, said, 'How
   can I know what I think till I see what I say?'
   Graham Wallas 1858–1932: *The Art of Thought* (1926)

....

Medicine
....

See also **Sickness and Health**

1 Medicinal discovery,
   It moves in mighty leaps,
   It leapt straight past the common cold
   And gave it us for keeps.
   Pam Ayres 1947– : 'Oh no, I got a cold' (1976)

2 Cure the disease and kill the patient.
   Francis Bacon 1561–1626: *Essays* (1625) 'Of Friendship'

3 The remedy is worse than the disease.
   Francis Bacon 1561–1626: *Essays* (1625) 'Of Seditions
   and Troubles'

4 Physicians of the Utmost Fame
   Were called at once; but when they came

They answered, as they took their Fees,
'There is no Cure for this Disease.'
   Hilaire Belloc 1870–1953: 'Henry King' (1907)

5 Physician, heal thyself.
   Bible: St Luke

6 He that sinneth before his Maker, let him fall into the hand
of the physician.
   Bible (Apocrypha): Ecclesiasticus

7 We all labour against our own cure, for death is the cure of
all diseases.
   Sir Thomas Browne 1605–82: *Religio Medici* (1643)

8 Every day, in every way, I am getting better and better.
   Émile Coué 1857–1926: to be said 15 to 20 times, morning
and evening; *De la suggestion et de ses applications* (1915)

9 The wounded surgeon plies the steel
That questions the distempered part;
Beneath the bleeding hands we feel
The sharp compassion of the healer's art
Resolving the enigma of the fever chart.
   T. S. Eliot 1888–1965: *Four Quartets* 'East Coker' (1940)

10 Life is short, the art long.
   Hippocrates *c*.460–357 BC: *Aphorisms*; often quoted '*Ars
longa, vita brevis*', after Seneca *De Brevitate Vitae*

11 It is a most extraordinary thing, but I never read a patent
medicine advertisement without being impelled to the
conclusion that I am suffering from the particular disease
therein dealt with in its most virulent form.
   Jerome K. Jerome 1859–1927: *Three Men in a Boat*
(1889)

12 GÉRONTE: It seems to me you are locating them wrongly:
the heart is on the left and the liver is on the right.
SGANARELLE: Yes, in the old days that was so, but we have
changed all that.
   Molière 1622–73: *Le Médecin malgré lui* (1667)

13 It may seem a strange principle to enunciate as the very
first requirement in a Hospital that it should do the sick
no harm.
> **Florence Nightingale** 1820–1910: *Notes on Hospitals*
> (1863 ed.) preface

14 One finger in the throat and one in the rectum makes a
good diagnostician.
> **William Osler** 1849–1919: *Aphorisms from his Bedside
> Teachings* (1961)

15 Throw physic to the dogs; I'll none of it.
> **William Shakespeare** 1564–1616: *Macbeth* (1606)

16 There is at bottom only one genuinely scientific treatment
for all diseases, and that is to stimulate the phagocytes.
> **George Bernard Shaw** 1856–1950: *The Doctor's
> Dilemma* (1911)

17 Formerly, when religion was strong and science weak, men
mistook magic for medicine; now, when science is strong
and religion weak, men mistake medicine for magic.
> **Thomas Szasz** 1920– : *The Second Sin* (1973) 'Science
> and Scientism'

Meeting and Parting

1 Yet meet we shall, and part, and meet again
Where dead men meet, on lips of living men.
> **Samuel Butler** 1835–1902: 'Not on sad Stygian shore'
> (1904)

2 *Atque in perpetuum, frater, ave atque vale.*
And so, my brother, hail, and farewell evermore!
> **Catullus** *c.*84–*c.*54 BC: *Carmina*

3 You have sat too long here for any good you have been
doing. Depart, I say, and let us have done with you. In the
name of God, go!
> **Oliver Cromwell** 1599–1658: addressing the Rump
> Parliament, 20 April 1653 (oral tradition; quoted by Leo
> Amery, House of Commons, 7 May 1940)

4 Parting is all we know of heaven,
   And all we need of hell.
   Emily Dickinson 1830–86: 'My life closed twice before its
   close'

5 Since there's no help, come let us kiss and part,
   Nay, I have done: you get no more of me.
   Michael Drayton 1563–1631: sonnet (1619)

6 If you can't leave in a taxi you can leave in a huff. If that's
   too soon, you can leave in a minute and a huff.
   Bert Kalmar 1884–1947 et al.: *Duck Soup* (1933 film);
   spoken by Groucho Marx

7 Fare well my dear child and pray for me, and I shall for
   you and all your friends that we may merrily meet in
   heaven.
   Sir Thomas More 1478–1535: letter to his daughter
   Margaret, 5 July 1535, on the eve of his execution

8 How d'ye do, and how is the old complaint?
   Lord Palmerston 1784–1865: reputed to be his greeting
   to all those he did not know; A. West *Recollections* (1899)

9 We'll meet again, don't know where,
   Don't know when,
   But I know we'll meet again some sunny day.
   Ross Parker 1914–74 and **Hugh Charles** 1907– : 'We'll
   Meet Again' (1939 song)

10 For I, who hold sage Homer's rule the best,
   Welcome the coming, speed the going guest.
   Alexander Pope 1688–1744: *Imitations of Horace* (1734);
   'speed the parting guest' in Pope's translation of *The
   Odyssey* (1725–6)

11 When shall we three meet again
   In thunder, lightning, or in rain?
   William Shakespeare 1564–1616: *Macbeth* (1606)

12 Ill met by moonlight, proud Titania.
   William Shakespeare 1564–1616: *A Midsummer Night's
   Dream* (1595–6)

13 Good-night, good-night! parting is such sweet sorrow
That I shall say good-night till it be morrow.
  William Shakespeare 1564–1616: *Romeo and Juliet*
  (1595)

14 Dr Livingstone, I presume?
  Henry Morton Stanley 1841–1904: *How I found Livingstone* (1872)

15 Their meetings made December June,
Their every parting was to die.
  Alfred, Lord Tennyson 1809–92: *In Memoriam A. H. H.*
  (1850)

16 Why don't you come up sometime, and see me?
  Mae West 1892–1980: *She Done Him Wrong* (1933 film);
  usually quoted 'Why don't you come up and see me sometime?'

Memory

1 Memories are hunting horns
Whose sound dies on the wind.
  Guillaume Apollinaire 1880–1918: 'Cors de Chasse'
  (1912)

2 And we forget because we must
And not because we will.
  Matthew Arnold 1822–88: 'Absence' (1852)

3 Someone said that God gave us memory so that we might have roses in December.
  J. M. Barrie 1860–1937: Rectorial Address at St Andrew's, 3 May 1922

4 Nobody can remember more than seven of anything.
  Cardinal Robert Bellarmine 1542–1621: reason for omitting the eight beatitudes from his catechism; John Bossy *Christianity in the West 1400-1700* (1985)

5 Memories are not shackles, Franklin, they are garlands.
  Alan Bennett 1934– : *Forty Years On* (1969)

6 Am in Market Harborough. Where ought I to be?
    G. K. Chesterton 1874–1936: telegram said to have been
    sent to his wife; *Autobiography* (1936)

7 Our memories are card-indexes consulted, and then put
back in disorder by authorities whom we do not control.
    Cyril Connolly 1903–74: *The Unquiet Grave* (1944)

8 I have forgot much, Cynara! gone with the wind,
Flung roses, roses, riotously, with the throng,
Dancing, to put thy pale, lost lilies out of mind.
    Ernest Dowson 1867–1900: 'Non Sum Qualis Eram'
    (1896)

9 Footfalls echo in the memory
Down the passage which we did not take
Towards the door we never opened
Into the rose-garden.
    T. S. Eliot 1888–1965: *Four Quartets* 'Burnt Norton' (1936)

10 Everyone seems to remember with great clarity what they
were doing on November 22nd, 1963, at the precise moment
they heard President Kennedy was dead.
    Frederick Forsyth 1938– : *The Odessa File* (1972)

11 Your memory is a monster; *you* forget—*it* doesn't. It simply
files things away. It keeps things for you, or hides things
from you—and summons them to your recall with a will of
its own. You think you have a memory; but it has you!
    John Irving 1942– : *A Prayer for Owen Meany* (1989)

12 A cigarette that bears a lipstick's traces,
An airline ticket to romantic places.
    Holt Marvell 1901–69: 'These Foolish Things Remind Me
    of You' (1935 song)

13 You may break, you may shatter the vase, if you will,
But the scent of the roses will hang round it still.
    Thomas Moore 1779–1852: 'Farewell!—but whenever'
    (1807)

14 And suddenly the memory revealed itself. The taste was
that of the little piece of madeleine which . . . my aunt
Léonie used to give me, dipping it first in her own cup of
tea or tisane.
    Marcel Proust 1871–1922: *Swann's Way* (1913)

245

15 Better by far you should forget and smile
Than that you should remember and be sad.
   Christina Rossetti 1830–94: 'Remember' (1862)

16 When to the sessions of sweet silent thought
I summon up remembrance of things past.
   William Shakespeare 1564–1616: sonnet 30 (1609)

17 There's rosemary, that's for remembrance; pray, love,
remember.
   William Shakespeare 1564–1616: *Hamlet* (1601)

18 Music, when soft voices die,
Vibrates in the memory—
Odours, when sweet violets sicken,
Live within the sense they quicken.
   Percy Bysshe Shelley 1792–1822: 'To—: Music, when
soft voices die' (1824)

19 For oft, when on my couch I lie
In vacant or in pensive mood,
They flash upon that inward eye
Which is the bliss of solitude;
And then my heart with pleasure fills,
And dances with the daffodils.
   William Wordsworth 1770–1850: 'I wandered lonely as a
cloud' (1815 ed.)

Men

1 Are all men in disguise except those crying?
   Dannie Abse 1923– : 'Encounter at a greyhound bus
station' (1986)

2 Men have had every advantage of us in telling their own
story. Education has been theirs in so much higher a
degree; the pen has been in their hands.
   Jane Austen 1775–1817: *Persuasion* (1818)

3 Every modern male has, lying at the bottom of his psyche,
a large, primitive being covered with hair down to his feet.
Making contact with this Wild Man is the step the Eighties

male or the Nineties male has yet to take.
Robert Bly 1926– : *Iron John* (1990)

4 The three most important things a man has are, briefly, his
private parts, his money, and his religious opinions.
Samuel Butler 1835–1902: *Further Extracts from
Notebooks* (1934)

5 Why would I talk about the men in my life? For me, life is
not about men.
Catherine Deneuve 1943– : on writing her
autobiography; in *Independent* 26 April 1997

6 Men are but children of a larger growth;
Our appetites as apt to change as theirs,
And full as craving too, and full as vain.
John Dryden 1631–1700: *All for Love* (1678)

7 Whatever they may be in public life, whatever their
relations with men, in their relations with women, all men
are rapists, and that's all they are. They rape us with their
eyes, their laws, and their codes.
Marilyn French 1929– : *The Women's Room* (1977)

8 We are lads. We have burgled houses and nicked car
stereos, and we like girls and swear and go to the football
and take the piss.
Noel Gallagher 1967– : in *Melody Maker* 30 March 1996

9 A man . . . is *so* in the way in the house!
Elizabeth Gaskell 1810–65: *Cranford* (1853)

10 Man is Nature's sole mistake!
W. S. Gilbert 1836–1911: *Princess Ida* (1884)

11 Years ago, manhood was an opportunity for achievement,
and now it is a problem to be overcome.
Garrison Keillor 1942– : *The Book of Guys* (1994)

12 Why can't a woman be more like a man?
Men are so honest, so thoroughly square;
Eternally noble, historically fair.
Alan Jay Lerner 1918–86: 'A Hymn to Him' (1956 song)

13 Somehow a bachelor never quite gets over the idea that he
is a thing of beauty and a boy forever.
Helen Rowland 1875–1950: *A Guide to Men* (1922)

14 Sigh no more, ladies, sigh no more,
Men were deceivers ever.
   William Shakespeare 1564–1616: *Much Ado About Nothing* (1598–9)

15 It's not the men in my life that counts—it's the life in my men.
   Mae West 1892–1980: *I'm No Angel* (1933 film)

....

Men and Women
....

See also **Woman's Role**

1 Women are really much nicer than men:
No wonder we like them.
   Kingsley Amis 1922–95: 'A Bookshop Idyll' (1956)

2 In societies where men are truly confident of their own worth, women are not merely tolerated but valued.
   Aung San Suu Kyi 1945– : videotape speech at NGO Forum on Women, China, September 1995

3 What is it men in women do require
The lineaments of gratified desire
What is it women do in men require
The lineaments of gratified desire.
   William Blake 1757–1827: *MS Note-Book*

4 Man's love is of man's life a thing apart,
'Tis woman's whole existence.
   Lord Byron 1788–1824: *Don Juan* (1819–24)

5 Women deprived of the company of men pine, men deprived of the company of women become stupid.
   Anton Chekhov 1860–1904: *Notebooks* (1921)

6 The man's desire is for the woman; but the woman's desire is rarely other than for the desire of the man.
   Samuel Taylor Coleridge 1772–1834: *Table Talk* (1835) 23 July 1827

7 There is more difference within the sexes than between them.
   Ivy Compton-Burnett 1884–1969: *Mother and Son* (1955)

8 In the sex-war thoughtlessness is the weapon of the male, vindictiveness of the female.
   Cyril Connolly 1903–74: *Unquiet Grave* (1944)

9   Just such disparity
   As is 'twixt air and angels' purity,
   'Twixt women's love, and men's will ever be.
   John Donne 1572–1631: 'Air and Angels'

10 Women have very little idea of how much men hate them.
   Germaine Greer 1939– : *The Female Eunuch* (1971)

11 So court a mistress, she denies you;
   Let her alone, she will court you.
   Say, are not women truly then
   Styled but the shadows of us men?
   Ben Jonson *c.*1573–1637: 'That Women are but Men's Shadows' (1616)

12 The female of the species is more deadly than the male.
   Rudyard Kipling 1865–1936: 'The Female of the Species' (1919)

13 A woman can forgive a man for the harm he does her, but she can never forgive him for the sacrifices he makes on her account.
   W. Somerset Maugham 1874–1965: *The Moon and Sixpence* (1919)

14 Men have a much better time of it than women. For one thing, they marry later. For another thing, they die earlier.
   H. L. Mencken 1880–1956: *Chrestomathy* (1949)

15 He for God only, she for God in him.
   John Milton 1608–74: *Paradise Lost* (1667)

16 I admit it is better fun to punt than to be punted, and that a desire to have all the fun is nine-tenths of the law of chivalry.
   Dorothy L. Sayers 1893–1957: *Gaudy Night* (1935)

17 Of all human struggles there is none so treacherous and remorseless as the struggle between the artist man and the mother woman.
   George Bernard Shaw 1856–1950: *Man and Superman* (1903)

18 A woman without a man is like a fish without a bicycle.
   Gloria Steinem 1934– : attributed

19 Whereas nature turns girls into women, society has to
   make boys into men.
   Anthony Stevens: *Archetype* (1982)

20 'Tis strange what a man may do, and a woman yet think
   him an angel.
   William Makepeace Thackeray 1811–63: *The History of
   Henry Esmond* (1852)

21 Me Tarzan, you Jane.
   Johnny Weissmuller 1904–84: summing up his role in
   Tarzan, the Ape Man (1932 film); in *Photoplay Magazine*
   June 1932. The words occur neither in the film nor the
   original, by Edgar Rice Burroughs

22 Whatever women do they must do twice as well as men to
   be thought half as good.
   Charlotte Whitton 1896–1975: in *Canada Month* June
   1963

23 All women become like their mothers. That is their
   tragedy. No man does. That's his.
   Oscar Wilde 1854–1900: *The Importance of Being Earnest*
   (1895)

24 Women have served all these centuries as looking-glasses
   possessing the magic and delicious power of reflecting the
   figure of a man at twice its natural size.
   Virginia Woolf 1882–1941: *A Room of One's Own* (1929)

Middle Age

1 Years ago we discovered the exact point, the dead centre of
   middle age. It occurs when you are too young to take up
   golf and too old to rush up to the net.
   Franklin P. Adams 1881–1960: *Nods and Becks* (1944)

Middle Age

2 You are living in a land you no longer recognize. You don't know the language.
   Martin Amis 1949– : on his 'cataclysmic mid-life crisis'; in *Times* 21 August 1997

3 I am past thirty, and three parts iced over.
   Matthew Arnold 1822–88: letter to Arthur Hugh Clough, 12 February 1853

4 Mr Salteena was an elderly man of 42.
   Daisy Ashford 1881–1972: *The Young Visiters* (1919)

5 At eighteen our convictions are hills from which we look; at forty-five they are caves in which we hide.
   F. Scott Fitzgerald 1896–1940: 'Bernice Bobs her Hair' (1920)

6 The afternoon of human life must also have a significance of its own and cannot be merely a pitiful appendage to life's morning.
   Carl Gustav Jung 1875–1961: *The Stages of Life* (1930)

7 Men at forty
Learn to close softly
The doors to rooms they will not be
Coming back to.
   Donald Justice 1925– : 'Men at Forty' (1967)

8 At forty-five,
What next, what next?
At every corner,
I meet my Father,
my age, still alive.
   Robert Lowell 1917–77: 'Middle Age' (1964)

9 Do you think my mind is maturing late,
Or simply rotted early?
   Ogden Nash 1902–71: 'Lines on Facing Forty' (1942)

10 One of the pleasures of middle age is to *find out* that one WAS right, and that one was much righter than one knew at say 17 or 23.
   Ezra Pound 1885–1972: *ABC of Reading* (1934)

The Mind

1 On earth there is nothing great but man; in man there is
nothing great but mind.
   William Hamilton 1788–1856: *Lectures on Metaphysics
   and Logic* (1859), attributed in a Latin form to Favorinus
   (2nd century AD)

2 O the mind, mind has mountains; cliffs of fall
Frightful, sheer, no-man-fathomed.
   Gerard Manley Hopkins 1844–89: 'No worst, there is
   none' (written 1885)

3 The mind is its own place, and in itself
Can make a heaven of hell, a hell of heaven.
   John Milton 1608–74: *Paradise Lost* (1667)

4 Consciousness . . . is the phenomenon whereby the
universe's very existence is made known.
   Roger Penrose 1931– : *The Emperor's New Mind* (1989)

5 That's the classical mind at work, runs fine inside but
looks dingy on the surface.
   Robert M. Pirsig 1928– : *Zen and the Art of Motorcycle
   Maintenance* (1974)

6 Why waste money on psychotherapy when you can listen
to the B Minor Mass?
   Michael Torke 1961– : in *Observer* 23 September 1990

7 We are not interested in the fact that the brain has the
consistency of cold porridge.
   Alan Turing 1912–54: A. P. Hodges *Alan Turing: the
   Enigma* (1983)

8 Mind in its purest play is like some bat
That beats about in caverns all alone,
Contriving by a kind of senseless wit
Not to conclude against a wall of stone.
   Richard Wilbur 1921– : 'Mind' (1956)

9 Every human brain is born not as a blank tablet (a *tabula rasa*) waiting to be filled in by experience but as 'an exposed negative waiting to be slipped into developer fluid'.

    Edward O. Wilson 1929– : on the nature v. nurture debate; attributed

10 To give a sex to mind was not very consistent with the principles of a man [Rousseau] who argued so warmly, and so well, for the immortality of the soul.

    Mary Wollstonecraft 1759–97: *A Vindication of the Rights of Woman* (1792), often quoted 'Mind has no sex'

Minorities and Majorities

See also **Democracy**

1 *Nec audiendi qui solent dicere, Vox populi, vox Dei, quum tumultuositas vulgi semper insaniae proxima sit.*

  And those people should not be listened to who keep saying the voice of the people is the voice of God, since the riotousness of the crowd is always very close to madness.

    Alcuin *c.*735–804: *Works* (1863) letter 164

2 'It's always best on these occasions to do what the mob do.' 'But suppose there are two mobs?' suggested Mr Snodgrass. 'Shout with the largest,' replied Mr Pickwick.

    Charles Dickens 1812–70: *Pickwick Papers* (1837)

3 As for our majority . . . one is enough.

    Benjamin Disraeli 1804–81: *Endymion* (1880); now often associated with Churchill

4 Nor is the people's judgement always true:
  The most may err as grossly as the few.

    John Dryden 1631–1700: *Absalom and Achitophel* (1681)

5 The majority never has right on its side. Never I say! That is one of the social lies that a free, thinking man is bound to rebel against. Who makes up the majority in any given country? Is it the wise men or the fools? I think we must agree that the fools are in a terrible overwhelming

majority, all the wide world over.
   Henrik Ibsen 1828–1906: *The Master Builder* (1892)

6 Never forget that only dead fish swim with the stream.
   Malcolm Muggeridge 1903–90: quoting a supporter, in
   Radio Times 9 July 1964

7 The fact that an opinion has been widely held is no
   evidence whatever that it is not utterly absurd; indeed in
   view of the silliness of the majority of mankind, a
   widespread belief is more likely to be foolish than sensible.
   Bertrand Russell 1872–1970: *Marriage and Morals* (1929)

8 Minorities . . . are almost always in the right.
   Sydney Smith 1771–1845: H. Pearson *The Smith of
   Smiths* (1934)

Misfortune

1 Prosperity doth best discover vice, but adversity doth best
   discover virtue.
   Francis Bacon 1561–1626: *Essays* (1625) 'Of Adversity'

2 And always keep a-hold of Nurse
   For fear of finding something worse.
   Hilaire Belloc 1870–1953: 'Jim' (1907)

3 Man is born unto trouble, as the sparks fly upward.
   Bible: Job

4 For in every ill-turn of fortune the most unhappy sort of
   unfortunate man is the one who has been happy.
   Boethius AD c.476–524: *De Consolatione Philosophiae*

5 . . . *Nessun maggior dolore,*
   Che ricordarsi del tempo felice
   Nella miseria.

   There is no greater pain than to remember a happy time
   when one is in misery.
   Dante Alighieri 1265–1321: *Divina Commedia* 'Inferno'

6 And all my endeavours are unlucky explorers
come back, abandoning the expedition.
> **Keith Douglas** 1920–44: 'On Return from Egypt, 1943–4'
> (1946)

7 In the words of one of my more sympathetic
correspondents, it has turned out to be an 'annus
horribilis'.
> **Elizabeth II** 1926– : speech at Guildhall, London, 24
> November 1992

8 I left the room with silent dignity, but caught my foot in
the mat.
> **George Grossmith** 1847–1912 and **Weedon Grossmith**
> 1854–1919: *Diary of a Nobody* (1894)

9 In the misfortune of our best friends, we always find
something which is not displeasing to us.
> **Duc de la Rochefoucauld** 1613–80: *Réflexions ou*
> *Maximes Morales* (1665)

10 now and then
there is a person born
who is so unlucky
that he runs into accidents
which started to happen
to somebody else.
> **Don Marquis** 1878–1937: *archys life of mehitabel* (1933)

11 I had never had a piece of toast
Particularly long and wide,
But fell upon the sanded floor,
And always on the buttered side.
> **James Payn** 1830–98: in *Chambers's Journal* 2 February
> 1884

12 Sweet are the uses of adversity,
Which like the toad, ugly and venomous,
Wears yet a precious jewel in his head.
> **William Shakespeare** 1564–1616: *As You Like It* (1599)

13 The fatal law of gravity: when you are down everything
falls on you.
> **Sylvia Townsend Warner** 1893–1978: attributed

14 One likes people much better when they're battered down
by a prodigious siege of misfortune than when they
triumph.
  Virginia Woolf 1882–1941: diary 13 August 1921

Mistakes

1 The weak have one weapon: the errors of those who think
they are strong.
  Georges Bidault 1899–1983: in *Observer* 15 July 1962

2 Truth lies within a little and certain compass, but error is
immense.
  Henry St John, 1st Viscount Bolingbroke 1678–1751:
  Reflections upon Exile (1716)

3 It is worse than a crime, it is a blunder.
  Antoine Boulay de la Meurthe 1761–1840: on hearing
  of the execution of the Duc d'Enghien, 1804

4 I would rather be wrong, by God, with Plato . . . than be
correct with those men.
  Cicero 106–43 BC: *Tusculanae Disputationes* (of
  Pythagoreans)

5 I beseech you, in the bowels of Christ, think it possible you
may be mistaken.
  Oliver Cromwell 1599–1658: letter to the General
  Assembly of the Kirk of Scotland, 3 August 1650

6 Errors, like straws, upon the surface flow;
He who would search for pearls must dive below.
  John Dryden 1631–1700: *All for Love* (1678)

7 If all else fails, immortality can always be assured by a
spectacular error.
  J. K. Galbraith 1908– : attributed

8 Mistakes are a fact of life
It is the response to error that counts.
  Nikki Giovanni 1943– : 'Of Liberation' (1970)

9 An expert is someone who knows some of the worst mistakes that can be made in his subject and who manages to avoid them.

Werner Heisenberg 1901–76: *Der Teil und das Ganze* (1969) tr. A. J. Pomerans as *Physics and Beyond* (1971)

10 I'm aggrieved when sometimes even excellent Homer nods.

Horace 65–8 BC: *Ars Poetica*

11 Crooked things may be as stiff and unflexible as straight: and men may be as positive in error as in truth.

John Locke 1632–1704: *Essay concerning Human Understanding* (1690)

12 The man who makes no mistakes does not usually make anything.

Edward John Phelps 1822–1900: speech, 24 January 1889

13 One Galileo in two thousand years is enough.

Pope Pius XII 1876–1958: on being asked to proscribe the works of Teilhard de Chardin; attributed; Stafford Beer *Platform for Change* (1975)

14 A man should never be ashamed to own he has been in the wrong, which is but saying, in other words, that he is wiser to-day than he was yesterday.

Alexander Pope 1688–1744: *Miscellanies* (1727) 'Thoughts on Various Subjects'

15 Like most of those who study history, he [Napoleon III] learned from the mistakes of the past how to make new ones.

A. J. P. Taylor 1906–90: in *Listener* 6 June 1963

16 'Forward, the Light Brigade!'
Was there a man dismayed?
Not though the soldier knew
Some one had blundered.

Alfred, Lord Tennyson 1809–92: 'The Charge of the Light Brigade' (1854)

17 To lose one parent, Mr Worthing, may be regarded as a misfortune; to lose both looks like carelessness.

Oscar Wilde 1854–1900: *The Importance of Being Earnest* (1895)

Moderation

1 Nothing in excess.
   Anonymous: inscribed on the temple of Apollo at
   Delphi, and variously ascribed to the Seven Wise Men

2 To many, total abstinence is easier than perfect
   moderation.
   St Augustine of Hippo AD 354–430: *On the Good of
   Marriage* (AD 401)

3 We know what happens to people who stay in the middle of
   the road. They get run down.
   Aneurin Bevan 1897–1960: in *Observer* 6 December 1953

4 Because thou art lukewarm, and neither cold nor hot, I
   will spew thee out of my mouth.
   Bible: Revelation

5 I would remind you that extremism in the defence of
   liberty is no vice! And let me remind you also that
   moderation in the pursuit of justice is no virtue!
   Barry Goldwater 1909–98: accepting the presidential
   nomination, 16 July 1964

6 There's nothing in the middle of the road but yellow
   stripes and dead armadillos.
   Jim Hightower: attributed, 1984

7 There is moderation in everything.
   Horace 65–8 BC: *Satires*

8 You will go most safely by the middle way.
   Ovid 43 BC–AD c.17: *Metamorphoses*

9 To gild refinèd gold, to paint the lily . . .
   Is wasteful and ridiculous excess.
   William Shakespeare 1564–1616: *King John* (1591–8)

10 Above all, gentlemen, not the slightest zeal.
   Charles-Maurice de Talleyrand 1754–1838: P. Chasles
   Voyages d'un critique à travers la vie et les livres (1868)

Money

See also **Poverty**, **Wealth**

1 The almighty dollar is the only object of worship.
Anonymous: *Philadelphia Public Ledger* 2 December 1836

2 Nothing that costs only a dollar is worth having.
Elizabeth Arden 1876–1966: attributed; in *Fortune* October 1973

3 An annuity is a very serious business.
Jane Austen 1775–1817: *Sense and Sensibility* (1811)

4 Money is like muck, not good except it be spread.
Francis Bacon 1561–1626: *Essays* (1625) 'Of Seditions and Troubles'

5 Money, it turned out, was exactly like sex, you thought of nothing else if you didn't have it and thought of other things if you did.
James Baldwin 1924–87: in *Esquire* May 1961

6 Money speaks sense in a language all nations understand.
Aphra Behn 1640–89: *The Rover* pt. 2 (1681)

7 The love of money is the root of all evil.
Bible: I Timothy

8 Nothing to be done without a bribe I find, in love as well as law.
Susannah Centlivre c.1669–1723: *The Perjured Husband* (1700)

9 The sinews of war, unlimited money.
Cicero 106–43 BC: *Fifth Philippic*

10 Annual income twenty pounds, annual expenditure nineteen nineteen six, result happiness. Annual income twenty pounds, annual expenditure twenty pounds ought and six, result misery.
Charles Dickens 1812–70: *David Copperfield* (1850) Mr Micawber

11 Money doesn't talk, it swears.
   Bob Dylan 1941– : 'It's Alright, Ma (I'm Only Bleeding)'
   (1965 song)

12 A bank is a place that will lend you money if you can
   prove that you don't need it.
   Bob Hope 1903– : A. Harrington *Life in the Crystal
   Palace* (1959)

13 If possible honestly, if not, somehow, make money.
   Horace 65–8 BC: *Epistles*

14 Money . . . is none of the wheels of trade: it is the oil
   which renders the motion of the wheels more smooth and
   easy.
   David Hume 1711–76: *Essays: Moral and Political*
   (1741–2) 'Of Money'

15 For I don't care too much for money,
   For money can't buy me love.
   John Lennon 1940–80 and **Paul McCartney** 1942– :
   'Can't Buy Me Love' (1964 song)

16 Take care of the pence, and the pounds will take care of
   themselves.
   William Lowndes 1652–1724: Lord Chesterfield *Letters to
   his Son* (1774) 5 February 1750

17 Money is like a sixth sense without which you cannot
   make a complete use of the other five.
   W. Somerset Maugham 1874–1965: *Of Human Bondage*
   (1915)

18 Money couldn't buy friends but you got a better class of
   enemy.
   Spike Milligan 1918– : *Puckoon* (1963)

19 I want to spend, and spend, and spend.
   Vivian Nicholson 1936– : said to reporters on arriving
   to collect football pools winnings of £152,000, 27
   September 1961

20 Expenditure rises to meet income.
   C. Northcote Parkinson 1909–93: *The Law and the
   Profits* (1960)

21 But it is pretty to see what money will do.
Samuel Pepys 1633–1703: diary, 21 March 1667

22 'My boy,' he says, 'always try to rub up against money, for if you rub up against money long enough, some of it may rub off on you.'
Damon Runyon 1884–1946: in *Cosmopolitan* August 1929

23 I can get no remedy against this consumption of the purse: borrowing only lingers and lingers it out, but the disease is incurable.
William Shakespeare 1564–1616: *Henry IV, Part 2* (1597)

24 Pennies don't fall from heaven. They have to be earned on earth.
Margaret Thatcher 1925– : in *Observer* 18 November 1979

25   *Quid non mortalia pectora cogis,*
Auri sacra fames!

To what do you not drive human hearts, cursed craving for gold!
Virgil 70–19 BC: *Aeneid*

26 From now the pound abroad is worth 14 per cent or so less in terms of other currencies. It does not mean, of course, that the pound here in Britain, in your pocket or purse or in your bank, has been devalued.
Harold Wilson 1916–95: ministerial broadcast, 19 November 1967

Morality

1 Morality is a private and costly luxury.
Henry Brooks Adams 1838–1918: *The Education of Henry Adams* (1907)

2 We do not look in great cities for our best morality.
Jane Austen 1775–1817: *Mansfield Park* (1814)

3 Standards are always out of date. That is what makes them standards.
Alan Bennett 1934– : *Forty Years On* (1969)

4 Food comes first, then morals.
Bertolt Brecht 1898–1956: *The Threepenny Opera* (1928)

5 *Cum finis est licitus, etiam media sunt licita.*
The end justifies the means.
Hermann Busenbaum 1600–68: *Medulla Theologiae Moralis* (1650); literally 'When the end is allowed, the means also are allowed'

6 What I know most surely about morality and the duty of man I owe to sport.
Albert Camus 1913–60: Herbert R. Lottman *Albert Camus* (1979); often quoted as, ' . . . I owe to football'

7 The last temptation is the greatest treason:
To do the right deed for the wrong reason.
T. S. Eliot 1888–1965: *Murder in the Cathedral* (1935)

8 State a moral case to a ploughman and a professor. The former will decide it as well, and often better than the latter, because he has not been led astray by artificial rules.
Thomas Jefferson 1743–1826: letter to Peter Carr, 10 August 1787

9 Two things fill the mind with ever new and increasing wonder and awe, the more often and the more seriously reflection concentrates upon them: the starry heaven above me and the moral law within me.
Immanuel Kant 1724–1804: *Critique of Practical Reason* (1788)

10 We know no spectacle so ridiculous as the British public in one of its periodical fits of morality.
Lord Macaulay 1800–59: *Essays* (1843) 'Moore's *Life of Lord Byron*'

11 If people want a sense of purpose, they should get it from their archbishops. They should not hope to receive it from their politicians.
Harold Macmillan 1894–1986: to Henry Fairlie, 1963; H. Fairlie *The Life of Politics* (1968)

12 The most useful thing about a principle is that it can always be sacrificed to expediency.
W. Somerset Maugham 1874–1965: *The Circle* (1921)

13 Morality is the herd-instinct in the individual.
   Friedrich Nietzsche 1844–1900: *Die fröhliche Wissenschaft* (1882)

14 We know that a man can read Goethe or Rilke in the evening, that he can play Bach and Schubert, and go to his day's work at Auschwitz in the morning.
   George Steiner 1926– : *Language and Silence* (1967)

15 Moral indignation is jealousy with a halo.
   H. G. Wells 1866–1946: *The Wife of Sir Isaac Harman* (1914)

Murder

1 Thou shalt not kill.
   Bible: Exodus

2 Mordre wol out; that se we day by day.
   Geoffrey Chaucer c.1343–1400: *The Canterbury Tales* 'The Nun's Priest's Tale'

3 Thou shalt not kill; but need'st not strive
   Officiously to keep alive.
   Arthur Hugh Clough 1819–61: 'The Latest Decalogue' (1862)

4 Murder considered as one of the fine arts.
   Thomas De Quincey 1785–1859: in *Blackwood's Magazine* February 1827 (essay title)

5 It's not the guns that kill, it's the maladjusted kids.
   Charlton Heston 1924– : in *Independent* 22 April 2000

6 Kill a man, and you are an assassin. Kill millions of men, and you are a conqueror. Kill everyone, and you are a god.
   Jean Rostand 1894–1977: *Pensées d'un biologiste* (1939)

7 Killing no murder briefly discourst in three questions.
   Edward Sexby d. 1658: title of pamphlet (an apology for tyrannicide, 1657)

8 Murder most foul, as in the best it is;
   But this most foul, strange, and unnatural.
   William Shakespeare 1564–1616: *Hamlet* (1601)

9 I don't think a man who has watched the sun going down
could walk away and commit a murder.
   Laurens van der Post 1906–96: in *Daily Telegraph* 17
   December 1996; obituary

....

Music

....

See also **Singing**

1 Please do not shoot the pianist. He is doing his best.
   Anonymous: printed notice in a dancing saloon; Oscar
   Wilde *Impressions of America* (*c*.1882–3)

2 If you still have to ask . . . shame on you.
   Louis Armstrong 1901–71: when asked what jazz is, in
   Max Jones et al. *Salute to Satchmo* (1970); sometimes
   quoted 'Man, if you gotta ask you'll never know'

3 All music is folk music, I ain't never heard no horse sing a
song.
   Louis Armstrong 1901–71: in *New York Times* 7 July
   1971

4 There are two golden rules for an orchestra: start together
and finish together. The public doesn't give a damn what
goes on in between.
   Thomas Beecham 1879–1961: H. Atkins and A.
   Newman *Beecham Stories* (1978)

5 Icelandic peoples were the ones who memorized sagas . . .
We were the first rappers of Europe.
   Björk 1965– : attributed, January 1996

6 Music has charms to sooth a savage breast.
   William Congreve 1670–1729: *The Mourning Bride* (1697)

7 The whole problem can be stated quite simply by asking,
'Is there a meaning to music?' My answer to that would be,
'Yes.' And 'Can you state in so many words what the
meaning is?' My answer to that would be, 'No.'
   Aaron Copland 1900–90: *What to Listen for in Music*
   (1939)

8 Extraordinary how potent cheap music is.
Noël Coward 1899–1973: *Private Lives* (1930)

9 It is only that which cannot be expressed otherwise that is
worth expressing in music.
Frederick Delius 1862–1934: in *Sackbut* September 1920
'At the Crossroads'

10 There is music in the air.
Edward Elgar 1857–1934: R. J. Buckley *Sir Edward
Elgar* (1905)

11 It will be generally admitted that Beethoven's Fifth
Symphony is the most sublime noise that has ever
penetrated into the ear of man.
E. M. Forster 1879–1970: *Howards End* (1910)

12 The hills are alive with the sound of music,
With songs they have sung for a thousand years.
Oscar Hammerstein II 1895–1960: 'The Sound of Music'
(1959 song)

13 He [Hill] did not see any reason why the devil should have
all the good tunes.
Rowland Hill 1744–1833: E. W. Broome *Rowland Hill*
(1881)

14 Difficult do you call it, Sir? I wish it were impossible.
Samuel Johnson 1709–84: on the performance of a
celebrated violinist; W. Seward *Supplement to the
Anecdotes of Distinguished Persons* (1797)

15 Perhaps the self-same song that found a path
Through the sad heart of Ruth, when, sick for home,
She stood in tears amid the alien corn;
The same that oft-times hath
Charmed magic casements, opening on the foam
Of perilous seas, in faery lands forlorn.
John Keats 1795–1821: 'Ode to a Nightingale' (1820)

16 Down the road someone is practising scales,
The notes like little fishes vanish with a wink of tails.
Louis MacNeice 1907–63: 'Sunday Morning' (1935)

17 Fortissimo at last!
   Gustav Mahler 1860–1911: on seeing Niagara Falls; K.
   Blaukopf *Gustav Mahler* (1973)

18 The symphony must be like the world. It must embrace
   everything.
   Gustav Mahler 1860–1911: remark to Sibelius, Helsinki,
   1907

19 Such sweet compulsion doth in music lie.
   John Milton 1608–74: 'Arcades' (1645)

20 Music is spiritual. The music business is not.
   Van Morrison 1945– : in *The Times* 6 July 1990

21 Melody is the essence of music. I compare a good melodist
   to a fine racer, and counterpoints to hack post-horses.
   Wolfgang Amadeus Mozart 1756–91: remark to Michael
   Kelly, 1786; Michael Kelly *Reminiscences* (1826)

22 Music is your own experience, your thoughts, your
   wisdom. If you don't live it, it won't come out of your horn.
   Charlie Parker 1920–55: Nat Shapiro and Nat Hentoff
   Hear Me Talkin' to Ya (1955)

23 Music begins to atrophy when it departs too far from the
   dance . . . poetry begins to atrophy when it gets too far
   from music.
   Ezra Pound 1885–1972: *The ABC of Reading* (1934)

24 Applause is a receipt, not a note of demand.
   Artur Schnabel 1882–1951: in *Saturday Review of
   Literature* 29 September 1951

25 If music be the food of love, play on;
   Give me excess of it, that, surfeiting,
   The appetite may sicken, and so die.
   William Shakespeare 1564–1616: *Twelfth Night* (1601)

26 Hell is full of musical amateurs: music is the brandy of the
   damned.
   George Bernard Shaw 1856–1950: *Man and Superman*
   (1903)

27 Improvisation is too good to leave to chance.
   Paul Simon 1942– : in *International Herald Tribune* 12
   October 1990

28 Music is feeling, then, not sound.
> **Wallace Stevens** 1879–1955: 'Peter Quince at the Clavier' (1923)

29 A good composer does not imitate; he steals.
> **Igor Stravinsky** 1882–1971: P. Yates *Twentieth Century Music* (1967)

30 You just pick a chord, go twang, and you've got music.
> **Sid Vicious** 1957–79: attributed

Musicians

1 Everything will pass, and the world will perish but the Ninth Symphony will remain.
> **Michael Bakunin** 1814–76: Edmund Wilson *To The Finland Station* (1940)

2 Whether the angels play only Bach in praising God I am not quite sure; I am sure, however, that en famille they play Mozart.
> **Karl Barth** 1886–1968: in *New York Times* 11 December 1968

3 Too much counterpoint; what is worse, Protestant counterpoint.
> **Thomas Beecham** 1879–1961: of J. S. Bach; in *Guardian* 8 March 1971

4 The immortal god of harmony.
> **Ludwig van Beethoven** 1770–1827: of J. S. Bach; letter to Breitkopf und Härtel, 22 April 1801

5 Most people get into bands for three very simple rock and roll reasons: to get laid, to get fame, and to get rich.
> **Bob Geldof** 1954– : in *Melody Maker* 27 August 1977

6 Too beautiful for our ears, and much too many notes, dear Mozart.
> **Joseph II** 1741–90: of *The Abduction from the Seraglio* (1782); F. X. Niemetschek *Life of Mozart* (1798)

7 If I play Tchaikovsky I play his melodies and skip his spiritual struggles . . . If there's any time left over I fill in with a lot of runs up and down the keyboard.
   Liberace 1919–87: Stuart Hall and Paddy Whannel (eds.) *The Popular Arts* (1964)

8 Ballads and babies. That's what happened to me.
   Paul McCartney 1942– : on reaching the age of fifty; in *Time* 8 June 1992

9 I have been told that Wagner's music is better than it sounds.
   Bill Nye: Mark Twain *Autobiography* (1924)

10 Wagner has lovely moments but awful quarters of an hour.
   Gioacchino Rossini 1792–1868: E. Naumann *Italienische Tondichter* (1883), April 1867

11 The notes I handle no better than many pianists. But the pauses between the notes—ah, that is where the art resides!
   Artur Schnabel 1882–1951: in *Chicago Daily News* 11 June 1958

12 Hats off, gentlemen—a genius!
   Robert Schumann 1810–56: on Chopin; 'An Opus 2' (1831); H. Pleasants (ed.) *Schumann on Music* (1965)

13 My music is best understood by children and animals.
   Igor Stravinsky 1882–1971: in *Observer* 8 October 1961

14 I don't know whether I like it, but it's what I meant.
   Ralph Vaughan Williams 1872–1958: on his 4th symphony; C. Headington *Bodley Head History of Western Music* (1974)

Nature

1 Nature, Mr Allnutt, is what we are put into this world to rise above.
   James Agee 1909–55: *The African Queen* (1951 film); not in the novel by C. S. Forester

2 Nature does nothing without purpose or uselessly.
  Aristotle 384–322 BC: *Politics*

3 All things are artificial, for nature is the art of God.
  Sir Thomas Browne 1605–82: *Religio Medici* (1643)

4 There is a pleasure in the pathless woods,
There is a rapture on the lonely shore,
There is society, where none intrudes,
By the deep sea, and music in its roar:
I love not man the less, but nature more.
  Lord Byron 1788–1824: *Childe Harold's Pilgrimage*
  (1812–18)

5 What a book a devil's chaplain might write on the clumsy,
wasteful, blundering, low, and horridly cruel works of
nature!
  Charles Darwin 1809–82: letter to J. D. Hooker, 13 July
  1856

6 People thought they could explain and conquer nature—
yet the outcome is that they destroyed it and disinherited
themselves from it.
  Václav Havel 1936– : Lewis Wolpert *The Unnatural
  Nature of Science* (1993)

7 You may drive out nature with a pitchfork, yet she'll be
constantly running back.
  Horace 65–8 BC: *Epistles*

8 For nature, heartless, witless nature,
Will neither care nor know
What stranger's feet may find the meadow
And trespass there and go.
  A. E. Housman 1859–1936: *Last Poems* (1922) no. 40

9 The roaring of the wind is my wife and the stars through
the window pane are my children.
  John Keats 1795–1821: letter to George and Georgiana
  Keats, 24 October 1818

10 In her [Nature's] inventions nothing is lacking, and
nothing is superfluous.
  Leonardo da Vinci 1452–1519: E. McCurdy (ed. and
  trans.) *Leonardo da Vinci's Notebooks* (1906)

11 And this our life, exempt from public haunt,
Finds tongues in trees, books in the running brooks,
Sermons in stones, and good in everything.
   William Shakespeare 1564–1616: *As You Like It* (1599)

12 Nature, red in tooth and claw.
   Alfred, Lord Tennyson 1809–92: *In Memoriam A. H. H.*
   (1850)

13 Nature is not a temple, but a workshop, and man's the
workman in it.
   Ivan Turgenev 1818–83: *Fathers and Sons* (1862), tr. R.
   Edmonds

14 To me the meanest flower that blows can give
Thoughts that do often lie too deep for tears.
   William Wordsworth 1770–1850: 'Ode. Intimations of
   Immortality' (1807)

15 There was a time when meadow, grove, and stream,
The earth, and every common sight,
To me did seem
Apparelled in celestial light,
The glory and the freshness of a dream.
   William Wordsworth 1770–1850: 'Ode. Intimations of
   Immortality' (1807)

News and Journalism

1 Anyone here been raped and speaks English?
   Anonymous: shouted by a British TV reporter in a
   crowd of Belgian civilians waiting to be airlifted out of
   the Belgian Congo, *c.*1960; Edward Behr *Anyone Here
   been Raped and Speaks English?* (1981)

2 *The Times* has made many ministries.
   Walter Bagehot 1826–77: *The English Constitution* (1867)

3 Journalists say a thing that they know isn't true, in the
hope that if they keep on saying it long enough it *will* be
true.
   Arnold Bennett 1867–1931: *The Title* (1918)

4 I read the newspapers avidly. It is my one form of
continuous fiction.
 Aneurin Bevan 1897–1960: in *The Times* 29 March 1960

5 Tell it not in Gath, publish it not in the streets of Askelon.
 Bible: II Samuel

6 As cold waters to a thirsty soul, so is good news from a far
country.
 Bible: Proverbs

7 When a dog bites a man, that is not news, because it
happens so often. But if a man bites a dog, that is news.
 John B. Bogart 1848–1921: F. M. O'Brien *Story of the*
 [New York] *Sun* (1918), often attributed to Charles A.
 Dana

8 When seagulls follow a trawler, it is because they think
sardines will be thrown into the sea.
 Eric Cantona 1966– : at a press conference, 31 March
 1995

9 Small earthquake in Chile. Not many dead.
 Claud Cockburn 1904–81: winning entry for a dullest
 headline competition at *The Times*; *In Time of Trouble*
 (1956)

10 Ill news hath wings, and with the wind doth go,
Comfort's a cripple and comes ever slow.
 Michael Drayton 1563–1631: *The Barons' Wars* (1603)

11 Go to where the silence is and say something.
 Amy Goodman 1957– : accepting an award for her
 coverage of the 1991 massacre in East Timor by
 Indonesian troops; in *Columbia Journalism Review*
 March/April 1994

12 You furnish the pictures and I'll furnish the war.
 William Randolph Hearst 1863–1951: message to the
 artist Frederic Remington in Havana, Cuba, during the
 Spanish-American War of 1898; attributed

13 Editor: a person employed by a newspaper, whose business
it is to separate the wheat from the chaff, and to see that
the chaff is printed.
 Elbert Hubbard 1859–1915: *The Roycroft Dictionary*
 (1914)

14 Blood sport is brought to its ultimate refinement in the gossip columns.

> **Bernard Ingham** 1932– : speech, 5 February 1986

15 Power without responsibility: the prerogative of the harlot throughout the ages.

> **Rudyard Kipling** 1865–1936: summing up Lord Beaverbrook's political standpoint *vis-à-vis* the *Daily Express*; quoted by Stanley Baldwin, 18 March 1931

16 The journalists have constructed for themselves a little wooden chapel, which they also call the Temple of Fame, in which they put up and take down portraits all day long and make such a hammering you can't hear yourself speak.

> **Georg Christoph Lichtenberg** 1742–99: A. Leitzmann *Georg Christoph Lichtenberg Aphorismen* (1904)

17 An odious exhibition of journalists dabbling their fingers in the stuff of other people's souls.

> **Lord McGregor** 1921– : on press coverage of the marriage of the Prince and Princess of Wales; in *The Times* 9 June 1992

18 A good newspaper, I suppose, is a nation talking to itself.

> **Arthur Miller** 1915– : in *Observer* 26 November 1961

19 All the news that's fit to print.

> **Adolph S. Ochs** 1858–1935: motto of the *New York Times*, from 1896

20 A cynical, mercenary, demagogic, corrupt press will produce in time a people as base as itself.

> **Joseph Pulitzer** 1847–1911: inscribed on the gateway to the Columbia School of Journalism in New York

21 The men with the muck-rakes are often indispensable to the well-being of society; but only if they know when to stop raking the muck.

> **Theodore Roosevelt** 1858–1919: speech, 14 April 1906

22 Comment is free, but facts are sacred.

> **C. P. Scott** 1846–1932: in *Manchester Guardian* 5 May 1921

23 The nature of bad news infects the teller.
  William Shakespeare 1564–1616: *Antony and Cleopatra*
  (1606–7)

24 Comment is free but facts are on expenses.
  Tom Stoppard 1937– : *Night and Day* (1978)

25 We must try to find ways to starve the terrorist and the
  hijacker of the oxygen of publicity on which they depend.
  Margaret Thatcher 1925– : speech to American Bar
  Association in London, 15 July 1985

26 The report of my death was an exaggeration.
  Mark Twain 1835–1910: *New York Journal* 2 June 1897,
  usually quoted 'Reports of my death have been greatly
  exaggerated'

27 News is what a chap who doesn't care much about
  anything wants to read. And it's only news until he's read
  it. After that it's dead.
  Evelyn Waugh 1903–66: *Scoop* (1938)

28 Rock journalism is people who can't write interviewing
  people who can't talk for people who can't read.
  Frank Zappa 1940–93: L. Botts *Loose Talk* (1980)

Night

see **Day and Night**

Old Age

1 Age will not be defied.
  Francis Bacon 1561–1626: *Essays* (1625) 'Of Regimen of
  Health'

2 To me old age is always fifteen years older than I am.
  Bernard Baruch 1870–1965: in *Newsweek* 29 August 1955

3 The days of our age are threescore years and ten; and
  though men be so strong that they come to fourscore

years: yet is their strength then but labour and sorrow; so
soon passeth it away, and we are gone.
   Bible: Psalm 90

4 If I'd known I was gonna live this long, I'd have taken
better care of myself.
   Eubie Blake 1883–1983: on reaching the age of 100; in
   Observer 13 February 1983

5 What is called the serenity of age is only perhaps a
euphemism for the fading power to feel the sudden shock
of joy or sorrow.
   Arthur Bliss 1891–1975: *As I Remember* (1970)

6 The man who works and is not bored is never old.
   Pablo Casals 1876–1973: J. Lloyd Webber (ed.) *Song of
   the Birds* (1985)

7 Considering the alternative, it's not too bad at all.
   Maurice Chevalier 1888–1972: when asked what he felt
   about the advancing years on his 72nd birthday; M.
   Freedland *Maurice Chevalier* (1981)

8 Oh, to be seventy again!
   Georges Clemenceau 1841–1929: on seeing a pretty girl
   on his eightieth birthday; James Agate's diary, 19 April
   1938

9 I grow old . . . I grow old . . .
I shall wear the bottoms of my trousers rolled.
   T. S. Eliot 1888–1965: 'Love Song of J. Alfred Prufrock'
   (1917)

10 There's a fascination frantic
In a ruin that's romantic;
Do you think you are sufficiently decayed?
   W. S. Gilbert 1836–1911: *The Mikado* (1885)

11 Age does not make us childish, as men tell,
It merely finds us children still at heart.
   Johann Wolfgang von Goethe 1749–1832: *Faust* pt. 1
   (1808)

12 You will recognize, my boy, the first sign of old age: it is when you go out into the streets of London and realize for the first time how young the policemen look.

Seymour Hicks 1871–1949: C. R. D. Pulling *They Were Singing* (1952)

13 Nothing really wrong with him—only anno domini, but that's the most fatal complaint of all, in the end.

James Hilton 1900–54: *Goodbye, Mr Chips* (1934)

14 When I am an old woman I shall wear purple
With a red hat which doesn't go, and doesn't suit me.

Jenny Joseph 1932– : 'Warning' (1974)

15 Perhaps being old is having lighted rooms
Inside your head, and people in them, acting.
People you know, yet can't quite name.

Philip Larkin 1922–85: 'The Old Fools' (1974)

16 Will you still need me, will you still feed me,
When I'm sixty four?

John Lennon 1940–80 and **Paul McCartney** 1942– : 'When I'm Sixty Four' (1967 song)

17 Old people have one advantage compared with young ones. They have been young themselves, and young people haven't been old.

Lord Longford 1905– : attributed; in *Independent* 6 March 1999

18 Growing old is no more than a bad habit which a busy man has no time to form.

André Maurois 1885–1967: *The Art of Living* (1940)

19 The unending problem of growing old was not how he changed, but how things did.

Toni Morrison 1931– : *Tar Baby* (1981)

20 See how the world its veterans rewards!
A youth of frolics, an old age of cards.

Alexander Pope 1688–1744: 'To a Lady' (1735)

21 Growing old is like being increasingly penalized for a crime you haven't committed.

Anthony Powell 1905–2000: *Temporary Kings* (1973)

22 In a dream you are never eighty.

Anne Sexton 1928–74: 'Old' (1962)

23 How ill white hairs become a fool and jester!
   William Shakespeare 1564–1616: *Henry IV, Part 2* (1597)

24 Second childishness, and mere oblivion,
   Sans teeth, sans eyes, sans taste, sans everything.
   William Shakespeare 1564–1616: *As You Like It* (1599)

25 Every man desires to live long; but no man would be old.
   Jonathan Swift 1667–1745: *Thoughts on Various Subjects* (1727 ed.)

26 Do not go gentle into that good night,
   Old age should burn and rave at close of day;
   Rage, rage against the dying of the light.
   Dylan Thomas 1914–53: 'Do Not Go Gentle into that Good Night' (1952)

27 Old age is the most unexpected of all things that happen to a man.
   Leon Trotsky 1879–1940: diary, 8 May 1935

28 Time has shaken me by the hand and death is not far behind.
   John Wesley 1703–91: letter to Ezekiel Cooper, 1 February 1791

29 When you are old and grey and full of sleep,
   And nodding by the fire, take down this book
   And slowly read and dream of the soft look
   Your eyes had once, and of their shadows deep.
   W. B. Yeats 1865–1939: 'When You Are Old' (1893)

30 An aged man is but a paltry thing,
   A tattered coat upon a stick, unless
   Soul clap its hands and sing, and louder sing
   For every tatter in its mortal dress.
   W. B. Yeats 1865–1939: 'Sailing to Byzantium' (1928)

Opening Lines

1 It was a dark and stormy night.
   Edward Bulwer-Lytton 1803–73: *Paul Clifford* (1830)

2 It was the afternoon of my eighty-first birthday, and I was in bed with my catamite when Ali announced that the archbishop had come to see me.
Anthony Burgess 1917–93: *Earthly Powers* (1980)

3 *Gallia est omnis divisa in partes tres.*
Gaul as a whole is divided into three parts.
Julius Caesar 100–44 BC: *De Bello Gallico*

4 Whan that Aprill with his shoures soote
The droghte of March hath perced to the roote.
Geoffrey Chaucer *c.*1343–1400: *The Canterbury Tales*
'General Prologue'

5 *Nel mezzo del cammin di nostra vita.*
Midway along the path of our life.
Dante Alighieri 1265–1321: *Divina Commedia* 'Inferno'

6 'Is there anybody there?' said the Traveller,
Knocking on the moonlit door.
Walter de la Mare 1873–1956: 'The Listeners' (1912)

7 It was the best of times, it was the worst of times.
Charles Dickens 1812–70: *A Tale of Two Cities* (1859)

8 Last night I dreamt I went to Manderley again.
Daphne Du Maurier 1907–89: *Rebecca* (1938)

9 The boy stood on the burning deck
Whence all but he had fled.
Felicia Hemans 1793–1835: 'Casabianca' (1849)

10 Achilles' cursed anger sing, O goddess, that son of Peleus, which started a myriad sufferings for the Achaeans.
Homer 8th century BC: *The Iliad*

11 When Gregor Samsa awoke one morning from uneasy dreams he found himself transformed in his bed into a gigantic insect.
Franz Kafka 1883–1924: *The Metamorphosis* (1915)

12 Oh, what can ail thee knight at arms
Alone and palely loitering?
John Keats 1795–1821: 'La belle dame sans merci' (1820)

13 Of man's first disobedience, and the fruit
Of that forbidden tree, whose mortal taste

Brought death into the world, and all our woe,
With loss of Eden.
   John Milton 1608–74: *Paradise Lost* (1667)

14 Lolita, light of my life, fire of my loins. My sin, my soul.
Lo-lee-ta: the tip of the tongue taking a trip of three steps
down the palate to tap, at three, on the teeth. Lo. Lee. Ta.
   Vladimir Nabokov 1899–1977: *Lolita* (1955)

15 It was a bright cold day in April, and the clocks were
striking thirteen.
   George Orwell 1903–50: *Nineteen Eighty-Four* (1949)

16 O! for a Muse of fire, that would ascend
The brightest heaven of invention.
   William Shakespeare 1564–1616: *Henry V* (1599)

17 *Arma virumque cano.*

I sing of arms and the man.
   Virgil 70–19 BC: *Aeneid*

....

Opinion
....

1 Why should you mind being wrong if someone can show
you that you are?
   A. J. Ayer 1910–89: attributed

2 He that complies against his will,
Is of his own opinion still.
   Samuel Butler 1612–80: *Hudibras* pt. 3 (1680)

3 I trudge the streets rather than trade the soundbite. I . . .
would not know a focus group if I met one. I am unspun.
   Frank Dobson 1940– : in *Sunday Times* 27 February
   2000

4 They that approve a private opinion, call it opinion; but
they that mislike it, heresy: and yet heresy signifies no
more than private opinion.
   Thomas Hobbes 1588–1679: *Leviathan* (1651)

5 Every man has a right to utter what he thinks truth, and every other man has a right to knock him down for it. Martyrdom is the test.

    Samuel Johnson 1709–84: James Boswell *Life of Johnson* (1791) 1780

6 There are nine and sixty ways of constructing tribal lays, And—every—single—one—of—them—is—right!

    Rudyard Kipling 1865–1936: 'In the Neolithic Age' (1893)

7 Thank God, in these days of enlightenment and establishment, everyone has a right to his own opinions, and chiefly to the opinion that nobody else has a right to theirs.

    Ronald Knox 1888–1957: *Reunion All Round* (1914)

8 New opinions are always suspected, and usually opposed, without any other reason but because they are not already common.

    John Locke 1632–1704: *Essay concerning Human Understanding* (1690)

9 Opinion in good men is but knowledge in the making.

    John Milton 1608–74: *Areopagitica* (1644)

10 Some praise at morning what they blame at night; But always think the last opinion right.

    Alexander Pope 1688–1744: *An Essay on Criticism* (1711)

11 The opinions that are held with passion are always those for which no good ground exists; indeed the passion is the measure of the holder's lack of rational conviction.

    Bertrand Russell 1872–1970: *Sceptical Essays* (1928)

12 A man can brave opinion, a woman must submit to it.

    Mme de Staël 1766–1817: *Delphine* (1802)

Optimism and Pessimism

See also **Hope and Despair**

1 Where everything is bad it must be good to know the worst.

    F. H. Bradley 1846–1924: *Appearance and Reality* (1893)

2 The lark's on the wing;
The snail's on the thorn:
God's in his heaven—
All's right with the world!
  Robert Browning 1812–89: *Pippa Passes* (1841)

3 The optimist proclaims that we live in the best of all
possible worlds; and the pessimist fears this is true.
  James Branch Cabell 1879–1958: *The Silver Stallion*
  (1926)

4 I don't consider myself a pessimist. I think of a pessimist
as someone who is waiting for it to rain. And I feel soaked
to the skin.
  Leonard Cohen 1934– : in *Observer* 2 May 1993

5 I have known him come home to supper with a flood of
tears, and a declaration that nothing was now left but a
jail; and go to bed making a calculation of the expense of
putting bow-windows to the house, 'in case anything
turned up,' which was his favourite expression.
  Charles Dickens 1812–70: *David Copperfield* (1850) of Mr
  Micawber

6 Cheer up! the worst is yet to come!
  Philander Chase Johnson 1866–1939: *Everybody's
  Magazine* May 1920

7 Sin is behovely, but all shall be well and all shall be well
and all manner of thing shall be well.
  Julian of Norwich 1343–after 1416: *Revelations of Divine
  Love*

8 Man hands on misery to man.
It deepens like a coastal shelf.
Get out as early as you can,
And don't have any kids yourself.
  Philip Larkin 1922–85: 'This Be The Verse' (1974)

9 If we see light at the end of the tunnel,
It's the light of the oncoming train.
  Robert Lowell 1917–77: 'Since 1939' (1977)

10 an optimist is a guy
that has never had

much experience.
> **Don Marquis** 1878–1937: *archy and mehitabel* (1927)

11 Nothingness haunts being.
> **Jean-Paul Sartre** 1905–80: *Being and Nothingness* (1956)

12 In this best of possible worlds . . . all is for the best.
> **Voltaire** 1694–1778: *Candide* (1759); usually quoted 'All is for the best in the best of all possible worlds'

13 'Twixt the optimist and pessimist
The difference is droll:
The optimist sees the doughnut
But the pessimist sees the hole.
> **McLandburgh Wilson** 1892– : *Optimist and Pessimist*

Painting and Drawing

1 A product of the untalented, sold by the unprincipled to the utterly bewildered.
> **Al Capp** 1907–79: on abstract art, in *National Observer* 1 July 1963

2 Good painters imitate nature, bad ones spew it up.
> **Cervantes** 1547–1616: *El Licenciado Vidriera* in *Novelas Ejemplares* (1613)

3 Treat nature in terms of the cylinder, the sphere, the cone, all in perspective.
> **Paul Cézanne** 1839–1906: letter to Emile Bernard, 1904; Emile Bernard *Paul Cézanne* (1925)

4 In Claude's landscape all is lovely—all amiable—all is amenity and repose;—the calm sunshine of the heart.
> **John Constable** 1776–1837: lecture, 2 June 1836

5 Remark all these roughnesses, pimples, warts, and everything as you see me; otherwise I will never pay a farthing for it.
> **Oliver Cromwell** 1599–1658: to Lely, on the painting of his portrait; Horace Walpole *Anecdotes of Painting in England* (1763) (commonly quoted 'warts and all')

6 The King found her [Anne of Cleves] so different from her picture . . . that . . . he swore they had brought him a Flanders mare.
   Henry VIII 1491–1547: Tobias Smollett *Complete History of England* (3rd ed., 1759)

7 I rarely draw what I see—I draw what I feel in my body.
   Barbara Hepworth 1903–75: Alan Bowness *Barbara Hepworth—Drawings from a Sculptor's Landscape* (1966)

8 All painting, no matter what you're painting, is abstract in that it's got to be organized.
   David Hockney 1937– : *David Hockney* (1976)

9 *Le dessin est la probité de l'art.*
   Drawing is the true test of art.
   J. A. D. Ingres 1780–1867: *Pensées d'Ingres* (1922)

10 Art does not reproduce the visible; rather, it makes visible.
   Paul Klee 1879–1940: 'Creative Credo' (1920)

11 You should not paint the chair, but only what someone has felt about it.
   Edvard Munch 1863–1944: written *c.*1891; R. Heller *Munch* (1984)

12 I paint objects as I think them, not as I see them.
   Pablo Picasso 1881–1973: John Golding *Cubism* (1959)

13 An imitation in lines and colours on any surface of all that is to be found under the sun.
   Nicolas Poussin 1594–1665: of painting; letter to M. de Chambray, 1665

14 I have seen, and heard, much of Cockney impudence before now; but never expected to hear a coxcomb ask two hundred guineas for flinging a pot of paint in the public's face.
   John Ruskin 1819–1900: on Whistler's *Nocturne in Black and Gold*; *Fors Clavigera* (1871–84) Letter 79, 18 June 1877

15 Every time I paint a portrait I lose a friend.
   John Singer Sargent 1856–1925: N. Bentley and E. Esar *Treasury of Humorous Quotations* (1951)

16 I am a painter and I nail my pictures together.
  Kurt Schwitters 1887–1948: R. Hausmann *Am Anfang war Dada* (1972)

17 Painting is saying "Ta" to God.
  Stanley Spencer 1891–1959: letter from Spencer's daughter Shirin, in *Observer* 7 February 1988

18 No, I ask it for the knowledge of a lifetime.
  James McNeill Whistler 1834–1903: in his case against Ruskin, replying to the question: 'For two days' labour, you ask two hundred guineas?'; D. C. Seitz *Whistler Stories* (1913)

Parents

See also **Children**, **The Family**

1 Parents love their children more than children love their parents.
  Auctoritates Aristotelis: a compilation of medieval propositions

2 The joys of parents are secret, and so are their griefs and fears.
  Francis Bacon 1561–1626: *Essays* (1625) 'Of Parents and Children'

3 Honour thy father and thy mother.
  Bible: Exodus

4 A wise son maketh a glad father: but a foolish son is the heaviness of his mother.
  Bible: Proverbs

5 Having one child makes you a parent; having two you are a referee.
  David Frost 1939– : in *Independent* 16 September 1989

6 My father was frightened of his mother; I was frightened of my father, and I am damned well going to see to it that my children are frightened of me.
  George V 1865–1936: attributed, perhaps apocryphal; Randolph S. Churchill *Lord Derby* (1959)

7 Your children are not your children.
They are the sons and daughters of Life's longing for itself.
They came through you but not from you
And though they are with you yet they belong not to you.
   Kahlil Gibran 1883–1931: *The Prophet* (1923)

8 There are no illegitimate children, only illegitimate
parents.
   Edna Gladney: A. Loos *Kiss Hollywood Good-Bye* (1978);
   MGM paid her a large sum for the line for the 1941 film
   based on her life, 'Blossoms in the Dust'

9 If I'm more of an influence to your son as a rapper than
you are as a father . . . you got to look at yourself as a
parent.
   Ice Cube 1970– : in *Rolling Stone* 4 October 1990

10 If I were damned of body and soul,
I know whose prayers would make me whole,
Mother o' mine, O mother o' mine.
   Rudyard Kipling 1865–1936: *The Light That Failed* (1891)

11 They fuck you up, your mum and dad.
They may not mean to, but they do.
They fill you with the faults they had
And add some extra, just for you.
   Philip Larkin 1922–85: 'This Be The Verse' (1974)

12 Few misfortunes can befall a boy which bring worse
consequences than to have a really affectionate mother.
   W. Somerset Maugham 1874–1965: *A Writer's Notebook*
   (1949) (written in 1896)

13 Children aren't happy with nothing to ignore,
And that's what parents were created for.
   Ogden Nash 1902–71: 'The Parent' (1933)

14 If you bungle raising your children I don't think whatever
else you do well matters very much.
   Jacqueline Kennedy Onassis 1929–94: Theodore C.
   Sorenson *Kennedy* (1965)

15 A Jewish man with parents alive is a fifteen-year-old boy,
and will remain a fifteen-year-old boy until *they* die!
   Philip Roth 1933– : *Portnoy's Complaint* (1967)

16 The fundamental defect of fathers, in our competitive
society, is that they want their children to be a credit to
them.
   Bertrand Russell 1872–1970: *Sceptical Essays* (1928)

17 No matter how old a mother is she watches her middle-
aged children for signs of improvement.
   Florida Scott-Maxwell: *Measure of my Days* (1968)

18 It is a wise father that knows his own child.
   William Shakespeare 1564–1616: *The Merchant of
Venice* (1596–8)

19 Parentage is a very important profession, but no test of
fitness for it is ever imposed in the interest of the children.
   George Bernard Shaw 1856–1950: *Everybody's Political
What's What?* (1944)

20 The natural term of the affection of the human animal for
its offspring is six years.
   George Bernard Shaw 1856–1950: *Heartbreak House*
(1919)

21 The hand that rocks the cradle
Is the hand that rules the world.
   William Ross Wallace d. 1881: 'What rules the world'
(1865)

22 My children are ungrateful: they don't care. That is my
great reward. They are free.
   Fay Weldon 1931– : *Praxis* (1978)

23 Children begin by loving their parents; after a time they
judge them; rarely, if ever, do they forgive them.
   Oscar Wilde 1854–1900: *A Woman of No Importance*
(1893)

24 A slavish bondage to parents cramps every faculty of the
mind.
   Mary Wollstonecraft 1759–97: *A Vindication of the
Rights of Woman* (1792)

The Past

1 Even a god cannot change the past.
   Agathon b. *c.*445 BC: Aristotle *Nicomachaean Ethics*
   (literally 'The one thing which even a god cannot do is to
   make undone what has been done')

2 Nostalgia isn't what it used to be.
   Anonymous: graffito; taken as title of book by Simone
   Signoret, 1978

3 In every age 'the good old days' were a myth. No one ever
   thought they were good at the time. For every age has
   consisted of crises that seemed intolerable to the people
   who lived through them.
   Brooks Atkinson 1894–1984: *Once Around the Sun* (1951)

4 Antiquities are history defaced, or some remnants of
   history which have casually escaped the shipwreck of time.
   Francis Bacon 1561–1626: *The Advancement of Learning*
   (1605)

5 Stands the Church clock at ten to three?
   And is there honey still for tea?
   Rupert Brooke 1887–1915: 'The Old Vicarage,
   Grantchester' (1915)

6 The moving finger writes; and, having writ,
   Moves on: nor all thy piety nor wit
   Shall lure it back to cancel half a line,
   Nor all thy tears wash out a word of it.
   Edward Fitzgerald 1809–83: *The Rubáiyát of Omar
   Khayyám* (1859)

7 The past is a foreign country: they do things differently
   there.
   L. P. Hartley 1895–1972: *The Go-Between* (1953)

8 What are those blue remembered hills,
   What spires, what farms are those?
   That is the land of lost content,
   I see it shining plain,
   The happy highways where I went

And cannot come again.
    A. E. Housman 1859–1936: *A Shropshire Lad* (1896)

9 O God! Put back Thy universe and give me yesterday.
    Henry Arthur Jones 1851–1929 and **Henry Herman**
    1832–94: *The Silver King* (1907)

10 Yesterday, all my troubles seemed so far away,
Now it looks as though they're here to stay.
Oh I believe in yesterday.
    John Lennon 1940–80 and **Paul McCartney** 1942– :
    'Yesterday' (1965 song)

11 Think of it, soldiers; from the summit of these pyramids,
forty centuries look down upon you.
    Napoleon I 1769–1821: speech before the Battle of the
    Pyramids, 21 July 1798

12 Things ain't what they used to be.
    Ted Persons: title of song (1941)

13 I tell you the past is a bucket of ashes.
    Carl Sandburg 1878–1967: 'Prairie' (1918)

14 Those who cannot remember the past are condemned to
repeat it.
    George Santayana 1863–1952: *The Life of Reason* (1905)

15 What's gone and what's past help
Should be past grief.
    William Shakespeare 1564–1616: *The Winter's Tale*
    (1610–11)

16 O! call back yesterday, bid time return.
    William Shakespeare 1564–1616: *Richard II* (1595)

17 People who are always praising the past
And especially the times of faith as best
Ought to go and live in the Middle Ages
And be burnt at the stake as witches and sages.
    Stevie Smith 1902–71: 'The Past' (1957)

18 I think that today's youth have a tendency to live in the
present and work for the future—and to be totally ignorant
of the past.
    Steven Spielberg 1947– : in *Independent on Sunday* 22
    August 1999

19 The past is the only dead thing that smells sweet.
   Edward Thomas 1878–1917: 'Early one morning in May
   I set out' (1917)

20 *Mais où sont les neiges d'antan?*
   But where are the snows of yesteryear?
   François Villon b. 1431: 'Ballade des dames du temps
   jadis' (1461), tr. D. G. Rossetti

···

Patriotism
···

1   What pity is it
That we can die but once to serve our country!
   Joseph Addison 1672–1719: *Cato* (1713)

2 Patriotism is a lively sense of collective responsibility.
Nationalism is a silly cock crowing on its own dunghill.
   Richard Aldington 1892–1962: *The Colonel's Daughter*
   (1931)

3 A steady patriot of the world alone,
The friend of every country but his own.
   George Canning 1770–1827: of the Jacobin, in 'New
   Morality' (1821)

4 Patriotism is not enough. I must have no hatred or
bitterness towards anyone.
   Edith Cavell 1865–1915: on the eve of her execution, in
   The Times 23 October 1915

5   Be England what she will,
With all her faults, she is my country still.
   Charles Churchill 1731–64: *The Farewell* (1764)

6 Our country! In her intercourse with foreign nations, may
she always be in the right; but our country, right or wrong.
   Stephen Decatur 1779–1820: toast at Norfolk, Virginia,
   April 1816

7 If I had to choose between betraying my country and
betraying my friend, I hope I should have the guts to
betray my country.
   E. M. Forster 1879–1970: *Two Cheers for Democracy*
   (1951)

8 I may be uninspiring, but I'll be damned if I'm an alien!
   George V 1865–1936: on H. G. Wells's comment on 'an alien and uninspiring court'; Sarah Bradford *George VI* (1989); attributed, perhaps apocryphal

9 That this House will in no circumstances fight for its King and Country.
   D. M. Graham 1911–99: motion worded by Graham for a debate at the Oxford Union, 9 February 1933 (passed by 275 votes to 153)

10 I only regret that I have but one life to lose for my country.
   Nathan Hale 1755–76: prior to his execution by the British for spying, 22 September 1776

11 *Dulce et decorum est pro patria mori.*
   Lovely and honourable it is to die for one's country.
   Horace 65–8 BC: *Odes*

12 We don't want to fight, yet by jingo! if we do,
   We've got the ships, we've got the men, and got the money too.
   G. W. Hunt 1829?–1904: 'We Don't Want to Fight' (1878 song)

13 Patriotism is the last refuge of a scoundrel.
   Samuel Johnson 1709–84: James Boswell *Life of Johnson* (1791) 7 April 1775

14 I would die for my country but I would never let my country die for me.
   Neil Kinnock 1942– : speech at Labour party conference, 30 September 1986

15 These are the times that try men's souls. The summer soldier and the sunshine patriot will, in this crisis, shrink from the service of their country; but he that stands it *now*, deserves the love and thanks of men and women.
   Thomas Paine 1737–1809: *The Crisis* (December 1776)

16 My country, right or wrong; if right, to be kept right; and if wrong, to be set right!
   Carl Schurz 1829–1906: speech, US Senate, 29 February 1872

17 Breathes there the man, with soul so dead,
   Who never to himself hath said,

This is my own, my native land!
  Sir Walter Scott 1771–1832: *The Lay of the Last Minstrel*
  (1805)

18 You'll never have a quiet world till you knock the
  patriotism out of the human race.
    George Bernard Shaw 1856–1950: *O'Flaherty V.C.* (1919)

19 I vow to thee, my country—all earthly things above—
  Entire and whole and perfect, the service of my love.
    Cecil Spring-Rice 1859–1918: 'I Vow to Thee, My
    Country' (1918)

20 The cricket test—which side do they cheer for? . . . Are you
  still looking back to where you came from or where you
  are?
    Norman Tebbit 1931– : on the loyalties of Britain's
    immigrant population; interview in *Los Angeles Times*,
    reported in *Daily Telegraph* 20 April 1990

Peace

1 They shall beat their swords into plowshares, and their
  spears into pruninghooks: nation shall not lift up sword
  against nation, neither shall they learn war any more.
    Bible: Isaiah

2 The peace of God, which passeth all understanding, shall
  keep your hearts and minds through Christ Jesus.
    Bible: Philippians

3 Give peace in our time, O Lord.
    Book of Common Prayer 1662: *Morning Prayer*

4 This is the second time in our history that there has come
  back from Germany to Downing Street peace with honour.
  I believe it is peace for our time.
    Neville Chamberlain 1869–1940: speech from 10
    Downing Street, 30 September 1938

5 *E'n la sua volontade è nostra pace.*
  In His will is our peace.
    Dante Alighieri 1265–1321: *Divina Commedia* 'Paradiso'

6 Lord Salisbury and myself have brought you back peace—
but a peace I hope with honour.
  Benjamin Disraeli 1804–81: speech on returning from
  the Congress of Berlin, 16 July 1878

7 Go placidly amid the noise and the haste, and remember
what peace there may be in silence.
  Max Ehrmann 1872–1945: 'Desiderata' (1948); often
  wrongly dated to 1692, the date of foundation of a church
  in Baltimore whose vicar circulated the poem in 1956

8 I think that people want peace so much that one of these
days governments had better get out of the way and let
them have it.
  Dwight D. Eisenhower 1890–1969: broadcast discussion,
  31 August 1959

9 Kissinger brought peace to Vietnam the same way
Napoleon brought peace to Europe: by losing.
  Joseph Heller 1923–99: Good as Gold (1979)

10 Give peace a chance.
  John Lennon 1940–80 and **Paul McCartney** 1942– : title
  of song (1969)

11 You can't separate peace from freedom because no one can
be at peace unless he has his freedom.
  Malcolm X 1925–65: speech in New York, 7 January 1965

12 . . . Peace hath her victories
No less renowned than war.
  John Milton 1608–74: 'To the Lord General Cromwell'
  (written 1652)

13 You can't switch on peace like a light.
  Mo Mowlam 1949– : in Independent 6 September 1999

14 Enough of blood and tears. Enough.
  Yitzhak Rabin 1922–95: at the signing of the Israel-
  Palestine Declaration, Washington, 13 September 1993

15 . . . The naked, poor, and manglèd Peace,
Dear nurse of arts, plenties, and joyful births.
  William Shakespeare 1564–1616: Henry V (1599)

16 They make a wilderness and call it peace.
  Tacitus AD c.56–after 117: Agricola

17 *Qui desiderat pacem, praeparet bellum.*

Let him who desires peace, prepare for war.
    Vegetius fourth century AD: *Epitoma Rei Militaris*,
    usually quoted '*Si vis pacem, para bellum* [If you want
    peace, prepare for war]'

....

People
....

See also **Musicians**, **Poets**, **Politicians**,
Writers

1 He is gone, but his shadow still stands over all of us. It still
dictates to us and we, very often, obey.
    Svetlana Alliluyeva 1925– : of her father, Joseph Stalin;
    Twenty Letters to a Friend (1967)

2 To us he is no more a person
now but a whole climate of opinion.
    W. H. Auden 1907–73: 'In Memory of Sigmund Freud'
    (1940)

3 Rousseau was the first militant lowbrow.
    Isaiah Berlin 1909–97: in *Observer* 9 November 1952

4 She was the People's Princess, and that is how she will
stay . . . in our hearts and in our memories forever.
    Tony Blair 1953– : on hearing of the death of Diana,
    Princess of Wales, 31 August 1997

5 She's a gay man trapped in a woman's body.
    Boy George 1961– : of Madonna; *Take It Like a Man*
    (1995)

6 Thou large-brained woman and large-hearted man.
    Elizabeth Barrett Browning 1806–61: 'To George
    Sand—A Desire' (1844)

7 The seagreen Incorruptible.
    Thomas Carlyle 1795–1881: of Robespierre; *History of
    the French Revolution* (1837)

8 Macaulay is well for a while, but one wouldn't *live* under
Niagara.
    Thomas Carlyle 1795–1881: R. M. Milnes *Notebook* (1838)

9 Monet is only an eye, but what an eye!
   Paul Cézanne 1839–1906: attributed

10 In defeat unbeatable: in victory unbearable.
   Winston Churchill 1874–1965: of Viscount Montgomery;
   E. Marsh *Ambrosia and Small Beer* (1964)

11 Victor Hugo was a madman who thought he was Victor
   Hugo.
   Jean Cocteau 1889–1963: *Opium* (1930)

12 The mama of dada.
   Clifton Fadiman 1904– : of Gertrude Stein, *Party of One*
   (1955)

13 Even if I could be Shakespeare, I think I should still
   choose to be Faraday.
   Aldous Huxley 1894–1963: in 1925, attributed; Walter M.
   Elsasser *Memoirs of a Physicist in the Atomic Age* (1978)

14 And it seems to me you lived your life
   Like a candle in the wind.
   Elton John 1947– and **Bernie Taupin** 1950– : of
   Marilyn Monroe, later revised for Diana Princess of
   Wales; 'Candle in the Wind' (song, 1973)

15 An Archangel a little damaged.
   Charles Lamb 1775–1834: of Coleridge; letter to
   Wordsworth, 26 April 1816

16 Mad, bad, and dangerous to know.
   Lady Caroline Lamb 1785–1828: of Byron; diary, March
   1812

17 A good man fallen among Fabians.
   Lenin 1870–1924: of G. B. Shaw; A. Ransome *Six Weeks in
   Russia in 1919* (1919) 'Notes of Conversations with Lenin'

18 He seemed at ease and to have the look of the last
   gentleman in Europe.
   Ada Leverson 1865–1936: of Oscar Wilde, *Letters to the
   Sphinx* (1930)

19 Every word she writes is a lie, including 'and' and 'the'.
   Mary McCarthy 1912–89: quoting herself on Lillian
   Hellman in *New York Times* 16 February 1980

20 As he rose like a rocket, he fell like the stick.

Thomas Paine 1737–1809: on Edmund Burke losing the debate on the French Revolution to Charles James Fox, in the House of Commons; *Letter to the Addressers on the late Proclamation* (1792)

21 An elderly fallen angel travelling incognito.

Peter Quennell 1905–93: of André Gide, *The Sign of the Fish* (1960)

22 A doormat in a world of boots.

Jean Rhys *c.*1890–1979: describing herself; in *Guardian* 6 December 1990

23 The *éminence cerise*, the bolster behind the throne.

Will Self 1961– : of Queen Elizabeth the Queen Mother; in *Independent on Sunday* 8 August 1999

24 She would rather light a candle than curse the darkness, and her glow has warmed the world.

Adlai Stevenson 1900–65: on Eleanor Roosevelt; in *New York Times* 8 November 1962

25 Her conception of God was certainly not orthodox. She felt towards Him as she might have felt towards a glorified sanitary engineer; and in some of her speculations she seems hardly to distinguish between the Deity and the Drains.

Lytton Strachey 1880–1932: *Eminent Victorians* (1918) 'Florence Nightingale'

26 He was no striped frieze; he was shot silk.

Lytton Strachey 1880–1932: of Francis Bacon, *Elizabeth and Essex* (1928)

27 He snatched the lightning shaft from heaven, and the sceptre from tyrants.

A. R. J. Turgot 1727–81: inscription for a bust of Benjamin Franklin, inventor of the lightning conductor

28 What, when drunk, one sees in other women, one sees in Garbo sober.

Kenneth Tynan 1927–80: *Curtains* (1961)

29 A genius with the IQ of a moron.
    Gore Vidal 1925– : of Andy Warhol; in *Observer* 18 June 1989

30 As time requireth, a man of marvellous mirth and pastimes, and sometime of as sad gravity, as who say: a man for all seasons.
    Robert Whittington: of Sir Thomas More, in *Vulgaria* (1521)

31 He [Bernard Shaw] hasn't an enemy in the world, and none of his friends like him.
    Oscar Wilde 1854–1900: Bernard Shaw *Sixteen Self Sketches* (1949)

32   The statue stood
Of Newton, with his prism, and silent face:
The marble index of a mind for ever
Voyaging through strange seas of Thought, alone.
    William Wordsworth 1770–1850: *The Prelude* (1850)

Perfection

1 The pursuit of perfection, then, is the pursuit of sweetness and light . . . He who works for sweetness and light united, works to make reason and the will of God prevail.
    Matthew Arnold 1822–88: *Culture and Anarchy* (1869)

2 Pictures of perfection as you know make me sick and wicked.
    Jane Austen 1775–1817: letter to Fanny Knight, 23 March 1817

3 Faultless to a fault.
    Robert Browning 1812–89: *The Ring and the Book* (1868–9)

4 Perfection is the child of Time.
    Bishop Joseph Hall 1574–1656: *Works* (1625)

5 The best is the best, though a hundred judges have declared it so.
    Arthur Quiller-Couch 1863–1944: *Oxford Book of English Verse* (1900)

6 How many things by season seasoned are
  To their right praise and true perfection!
  William Shakespeare 1564–1616: *The Merchant of Venice* (1596–8)

7 No one can be perfectly free till all are free; no one can be perfectly moral till all are moral; no one can be perfectly happy till all are happy.
  Herbert Spencer 1820–1903: *Social Statics* (1850)

8 Finality is death. Perfection is finality.
  Nothing is perfect. There are lumps in it.
  James Stephens 1882–1950: *The Crock of Gold* (1912)

9 He is all fault who hath no fault at all:
  For who loves me must have a touch of earth.
  Alfred, Lord Tennyson 1809–92: *Idylls of the King* 'Lancelot and Elaine' (1859)

10 *Le mieux est l'ennemi du bien.*
  The best is the enemy of the good.
  Voltaire 1694–1778: *Contes* (1772), deriving from an Italian proverb

11 The intellect of man is forced to choose
  Perfection of the life, or of the work.
  W. B. Yeats 1865–1939: 'Coole Park and Ballylee, 1932' (1933)

Pessimism

see **Optimism and Pessimism**

Philosophy

1 The Socratic manner is not a game at which two can play.
  Max Beerbohm 1872–1956: *Zuleika Dobson* (1911)

2 Metaphysics is the finding of bad reasons for what we believe upon instinct.
  F. H. Bradley 1846–1924: *Appearance and Reality* (1893)

3 If it was so, it might be; and if it were so, it would be: but
as it isn't, it ain't. That's logic.
    Lewis Carroll 1832–98: *Through the Looking-Glass* (1872)

4 There is nothing so absurd but some philosopher has said
it.
    Cicero 106–43 BC: *De Divinatione*

5 When philosophy paints its grey on grey, then has a shape
of life grown old. By philosophy's grey on grey it cannot be
rejuvenated but only understood. The owl of Minerva
spreads its wings only with the falling of the dusk.
    G. W. F. Hegel 1770–1831: *Philosophy of Right* (1821) tr. T.
    M. Knox

6 I refute it *thus*.
    Samuel Johnson 1709–84: kicking a large stone by way
    of refuting Bishop Berkeley's theory of the non-existence
    of matter; James Boswell *Life of Johnson* (1791) 6 August
    1763

7 Philosophy will clip an Angel's wings.
    John Keats 1795–1821: 'Lamia' (1820)

8 The philosophers have only interpreted the world in
various ways; the point is to change it.
    Karl Marx 1818–83: *Theses on Feuerbach* (written 1845,
    published 1888)

9 How charming is divine philosophy!
Not harsh and crabbèd, as dull fools suppose,
But musical as is Apollo's lute,
    John Milton 1608–74: *Comus* (1637)

10 No more things should be presumed to exist than are
absolutely necessary.
    William of Occam *c.*1285–1349: not found in this form in
    his writings, although he frequently used similar
    expressions, e.g. 'Plurality should not be assumed
    unnecessarily'; *Quodlibeta* (*c.*1324)

11 The unexamined life is not worth living.
    Socrates 469–399 BC: in Plato *Apology*

12 The safest general characterization of the European philosophical tradition is that it consists of a series of footnotes to Plato.

Alfred North Whitehead 1861–1947: *Process and Reality* (1929)

13 Philosophy is a battle against the bewitchment of our intelligence by means of language.

Ludwig Wittgenstein 1889–1951: *Philosophische Untersuchungen* (1953)

Photography

1 A photograph is a secret about a secret. The more it tells you the less you know.

Diane Arbus 1923–71: Patricia Bosworth *Diane Arbus: a Biography* (1985)

2 I never cared for fashion much. Amusing little seams and witty little pleats. It was the girls I liked.

David Bailey 1938– : of his career as a photographer; in *Independent* 5 November 1990

3 Most things in life are moments of pleasure and a lifetime of embarrassment; photography is a moment of embarrassment and a lifetime of pleasure.

Tony Benn 1925– : in *Independent* 21 October 1989

4 If your pictures aren't good enough, you aren't close enough.

Robert Capa 1913–54: Russell Miller *Magnum: Fifty years at the Front Line of History* (1997)

5 To me, photography is the simultaneous recognition, in a fraction of a second, of the significance of an event as well as of a precise organization of forms which give that event its proper expression.

Henri Cartier-Bresson 1908– : *The Decisive Moment* (1952)

6 The paparazzi are nothing but dogs of war.
Catherine Deneuve 1943– : in *Daily Telegraph* 3
September 1997

7 The important thing is not the camera but the eye.
Alfred Eisenstaedt 1898–1995: in *New York Times* 26
September 1994

8 The photographer is like the cod which produces a million
eggs in order that one may reach maturity.
George Bernard Shaw 1856–1950: introduction to the
catalogue for an exhibition at the Royal Photographic
Society, 1906

Places

See also **America**, **Australia**, **Britain**,
Canada, **England**, **Europe**, **France**, **Ireland**,
London, **Scotland**, **Wales**

1 Whispering from her towers the last enchantments of the
Middle Age . . . Home of lost causes, and forsaken beliefs.
Matthew Arnold 1822–88: of Oxford, *Essays in Criticism*
(1865)

2 That sweet City with her dreaming spires.
Matthew Arnold 1822–88: of Oxford, 'Thyrsis' (1866)

3 One has no great hopes from Birmingham. I always say
there is something direful in the sound.
Jane Austen 1775–1817: *Emma* (1816)

4 Some refer to it as a cultural Chernobyl. I think of it as a
cultural Stalingrad.
J. G. Ballard 1930– : of Euro Disney; in *Daily Telegraph*
2 July 1994

5 STREETS FLOODED. PLEASE ADVISE.
Robert Benchley 1889–1945: telegraph message on
arriving in Venice

6 And this is good old Boston,
The home of the bean and the cod,

Where the Lowells talk to the Cabots
And the Cabots talk only to God.
John Collins Bossidy 1860–1928: verse spoken at Holy
Cross College alumni dinner in Boston, Massachusetts,
1910

7 For Cambridge people rarely smile,
Being urban, squat, and packed with guile.
Rupert Brooke 1887–1915: 'The Old Vicarage,
Grantchester' (1915)

8 While stands the Coliseum, Rome shall stand;
When falls the Coliseum, Rome shall fall;
And when Rome falls—the World.
Lord Byron 1788–1824: *Childe Harold's Pilgrimage*
(1812–18)

9 Venice is like eating an entire box of chocolate liqueurs in
one go.
Truman Capote 1924–84: in *Observer* 26 November 1961

10 A big hard-boiled city with no more personality than a
paper cup.
Raymond Chandler 1888–1959: of Los Angeles, *The
Little Sister* (1949)

11 I cannot forecast to you the action of Russia. It is a riddle
wrapped in a mystery inside an enigma.
Winston Churchill 1874–1965: radio broadcast, 1 October
1939

12 Poor Mexico, so far from God and so close to the United
States.
Porfirio Diaz 1830–1915: attributed

13 Kent, sir—everybody knows Kent—apples, cherries, hops,
and women.
Charles Dickens 1812–70: *Pickwick Papers* (1837) Jingle

14 The Alps, the Rockies and all other mountains are related
to the earth, the Himalayas to the heavens.
J. K. Galbraith 1908– : *A Life in our Times* (1981)

15 What cleanliness everywhere! You dare not throw your
cigarette into the lake. No graffiti in the urinals.
Switzerland is proud of this; but I believe this is just what
she lacks: manure.
　　André Gide 1869–1951: diary, Lucerne, 10 August 1917

16 The last time I saw Paris
　　Her heart was warm and gay,
　　I heard the laughter of her heart in ev'ry street café.
　　Oscar Hammerstein II 1895–1960: 'The Last Time I saw
Paris' (1940 song)

17 Paris is a movable feast.
　　Ernest Hemingway 1899–1961: *A Movable Feast* (1964)

18 The Netherlands have been for many years, as one may
say, the very cockpit of Christendom.
　　James Howell c.1594–1666: *Instructions for Foreign
Travel* (1642)

19 Italy is a geographical expression.
　　Prince Metternich 1773–1859: discussing the Italian
question with Palmerston in 1847

20 A trip through a sewer in a glass-bottomed boat.
　　Wilson Mizner 1876–1933: of Hollywood; A. Johnston *The
Legendary Mizners* (1953)

21 Russia has two generals in whom she can confide—
Generals Janvier [January] and Février [February].
　　Emperor Nicholas I of Russia 1796–1855: attributed

22 Hog Butcher for the World,
　　Tool Maker, Stacker of Wheat,
　　Player with Railroads and the Nation's Freight Handler;
　　Stormy, husky, brawling,
　　City of the Big Shoulders.
　　Carl Sandburg 1878–1967: 'Chicago' (1916)

23 Great God! this is an awful place.
　　Robert Falcon Scott 1868–1912: of the South Pole; diary,
17 January 1912

24 Let there be light! said Liberty,
　　And like sunrise from the sea,

Athens arose!
   Percy Bysshe Shelley 1792–1822: *Hellas* (1822)

25 It is from the midst of this putrid sewer that the greatest
river of human industry springs up and carries fertility to
the whole world. From this foul drain pure gold flows
forth.
   Alexis de Tocqueville 1805–59: of Manchester, *Voyage
en Angleterre et en Irlande de 1835* (1958)

26 Through reason Russia can't be known,
No common yardstick can avail you:
She has a nature all her own—
Have faith in her, all else will fail you.
   F. I. Tyutchev 1803–73: 'Through reason Russia can't be
known' (1866)

....

Pleasure
....

1 One half of the world cannot understand the pleasures of
the other.
   Jane Austen 1775–1817: *Emma* (1816)

2 The great pleasure in life is doing what people say you
cannot do.
   Walter Bagehot 1826–77: in *Prospective Review* 1853

3 I'm tired of Love: I'm still more tired of Rhyme.
But Money gives me pleasure all the time.
   Hilaire Belloc 1870–1953: 'Fatigued' (1923)

4 Let us have wine and women, mirth and laughter,
Sermons and soda-water the day after.
   Lord Byron 1788–1824: *Don Juan* (1819–24)

5 Life is a matter of passing the time enjoyably. There may
be other things in life, but I've been too busy passing my
time enjoyably to think very deeply about them.
   Peter Cook 1937–95: in *Guardian* 10 January 1994

6 Remorse, the fatal egg by pleasure laid.
   William Cowper 1731–1800: 'The Progress of Error'
(1782)

7 Ever let the fancy roam,
Pleasure never is at home.
   John Keats 1795–1821: 'Fancy' (1820)

8 A man enjoys the happiness he feels, a woman the
happiness she gives.
   Pierre Choderlos de Laclos 1741–1803: *Les Liaisons
   dangereuses* (1782)

9 The greatest pleasure I know, is to do a good action by
stealth, and to have it found out by accident.
   Charles Lamb 1775–1834: 'Table Talk by the late Elia' in
   The Athenaeum 4 January 1834

10 Who loves not woman, wine, and song
Remains a fool his whole life long.
   Martin Luther 1483–1546: attributed (later inscribed, in
   German, in the Luther room in the Wartburg)

11 The Puritan hated bear-baiting, not because it gave pain to
the bear, but because it gave pleasure to the spectators.
   Lord Macaulay 1800–59: *History of England* vol. 1 (1849)

12 It is a curious thing that people only ask if you are
enjoying yourself when you aren't.
   Edith Nesbit 1858–1924: *Five of Us, and Madeline* (1925)

13 Pleasure is nothing else but the intermission of pain.
   John Selden 1584–1654: *Table Talk* (1689) 'Pleasure'

14 Life would be very pleasant if it were not for its
enjoyments.
   R. S. Surtees 1805–64: *Mr Facey Romford's Hounds*
   (1865)

15 *Trahit sua quemque voluptas.*

Everyone is dragged on by their favourite pleasure.
   Virgil 70–19 BC: *Eclogues*

16 All the things I really like to do are either illegal, immoral,
or fattening.
   Alexander Woollcott 1887–1943: R. E. Drennan *Wit's
   End* (1973)

Poetry

1 It is barbarous to write a poem after Auschwitz.
   Theodor Adorno 1903–69: I. Buruma *Wages of Guilt*
   (1994)

2 The difference between genuine poetry and the poetry of
   Dryden, Pope, and all their school, is briefly this: their
   poetry is conceived and composed in their wits, genuine
   poetry is conceived and composed in the soul.
   Matthew Arnold 1822–88: *Essays in Criticism* (1888)

3 A poet's hope: to be,
   like some valley cheese,
   local, but prized elsewhere.
   W. H. Auden 1907–73: 'Shorts II' (1976)

4 Prose is when all the lines except the last go on to the end.
   Poetry is when some of them fall short of it.
   Jeremy Bentham 1748–1832: M. St. J. Packe *Life of John
   Stuart Mill* (1954)

5 That willing suspension of disbelief for the moment, which
   constitutes poetic faith.
   Samuel Taylor Coleridge 1772–1834: *Biographia
   Literaria* (1817)

6 Prose = words in their best order;—poetry = the *best* words
   in the best order.
   Samuel Taylor Coleridge 1772–1834: *Table Talk* (1835)
   12 July 1827

7   Wit will shine
   Through the harsh cadence of a rugged line.
   John Dryden 1631–1700: 'To the Memory of Mr Oldham'
   (1684)

8 Poetry is a subject as precise as geometry.
   Gustave Flaubert 1821–80: letter to Louise Colet, 14
   August 1853

9 I'd as soon write free verse as play tennis with the net
   down.
   Robert Frost 1874–1963: E. Lathem *Interviews with
   Robert Frost* (1966)

10 Like a piece of ice on a hot stove the poem must ride on its own melting. A poem may be worked over once it is in being, but may not be worried into being.

> **Robert Frost** 1874–1963: *Collected Poems* (1939) 'The Figure a Poem Makes'

11 As soon as war is declared it will be impossible to hold the poets back. Rhyme is still the most effective drum.

> **Jean Giraudoux** 1882–1944: *La Guerre de Troie n'aura pas lieu* (1935) tr. Christopher Fry as *Tiger at the Gates*, 1955

12 Skilled or unskilled, we all scribble poems.

> **Horace** 65–8 BC: *Epistles*

13 [BOSWELL:] Sir, what is poetry?

[JOHNSON:] Why Sir, it is much easier to say what it is not. We all *know* what light is; but it is not easy to *tell* what it is.

> **Samuel Johnson** 1709–84: James Boswell *Life of Johnson* (1791) 12 April 1776

14 If poetry comes not as naturally as the leaves to a tree it had better not come at all.

> **John Keats** 1795–1821: letter to Taylor, 27 February 1818

15 For twenty years I've stared my level best
To see if evening—any evening—would suggest
A patient etherized upon a table;
In vain. I simply wasn't able.

> **C. S. Lewis** 1898–1963: 'A Confession' (1964); on contemporary poetry

16 A poem should not mean
But be.

> **Archibald MacLeish** 1892–1982: 'Ars Poetica' (1926)

17 Writing a book of poetry is like dropping a rose petal down the Grand Canyon and waiting for the echo.

> **Don Marquis** 1878–1937: E. Anthony *O Rare Don Marquis* (1962)

18 Rhyme being . . . but the invention of a barbarous age, to set off wretched matter and lame metre.

> **John Milton** 1608–74: *Paradise Lost* (1667) 'The Verse' (preface, 1668)

19 Most people ignore most poetry
because
most poetry ignores most people.
Adrian Mitchell 1932– : *Poems* (1964)

20 All a poet can do today is warn.
Wilfred Owen 1893–1918: *Poems* (1963) preface (written 1918)

21 Of all the literary scenes
Saddest this sight to me:
The graves of little magazines
Who died to make verse free.
Keith Preston 1884–1927: 'The Liberators'

22 Poets are the unacknowledged legislators of the world.
Percy Bysshe Shelley 1792–1822: *A Defence of Poetry* (written 1821)

23 [The poet] cometh unto you, with a tale which holdeth children from play, and old men from the chimney corner.
Philip Sidney 1554–86: *The Defence of Poetry* (1595)

24 Poetry is the spontaneous overflow of powerful feelings: it takes its origin from emotion recollected in tranquillity.
William Wordsworth 1770–1850: *Lyrical Ballads* (2nd ed., 1802) preface

25 We make out of the quarrel with others, rhetoric, but of the quarrel with ourselves, poetry.
W. B. Yeats 1865–1939: *Essays* (1924)

Poets

1 In poetry, no less than in life, he is 'a beautiful and ineffectual angel, beating in the void his luminous wings in vain'.
Matthew Arnold 1822–88: *Essays in Criticism* (1888) 'Shelley'

2 He spoke, and loosed our heart in tears.
He laid us as we lay at birth

On the cool flowery lap of earth.
> **Matthew Arnold** 1822–88: of Wordsworth, 'Memorial
> Verses, April 1850' (1852)

3 You were silly like us; your gift survived it all:
The parish of rich women, physical decay,
Yourself. Mad Ireland hurt you into poetry.
> **W. H. Auden** 1907–73: 'In Memory of W. B. Yeats' (1940)

4 The reason Milton wrote in fetters when he wrote of
Angels and God, and at liberty when of Devils and Hell, is
because he was a true Poet, and of the Devil's party
without knowing it.
> **William Blake** 1757–1827: *The Marriage of Heaven and
> Hell* (1790–3)

5 Out-babying Wordsworth and out-glittering Keats.
> **Edward Bulwer-Lytton** 1803–73: of Tennyson, in *The
> New Timon* (1846)

6 All poets are mad.
> **Robert Burton** 1577–1640: *Anatomy of Melancholy*
> (1621–51) 'Democritus to the Reader'

7 We learn from Horace, Homer sometimes sleeps;
We feel without him: Wordsworth sometimes wakes.
> **Lord Byron** 1788–1824: *Don Juan* (1819–24)

8 There's nothing in the world for which a poet will give up
writing, not even when he is a Jew and the language of his
poems is German.
> **Paul Celan** 1920–70: letter to relatives, 2 August 1948

9 With Donne, whose muse on dromedary trots,
Wreathe iron pokers into true-love knots.
> **Samuel Taylor Coleridge** 1772–1834: 'On Donne's
> Poetry' (1818)

10 I used to think all poets were Byronic.
They're mostly wicked as a ginless tonic
And wild as pension plans.
> **Wendy Cope** 1945– : 'Triolet' (1986)

11 'Tis sufficient to say [of Chaucer], according to the
proverb, that here is God's plenty.
John Dryden 1631–1700: *Fables Ancient and Modern*
(1700)

12 He invades authors like a monarch; and what would be
theft in other poets, is only victory in him.
John Dryden 1631–1700: of Ben Jonson; *Essay of
Dramatic Poesy* (1668)

13 Immature poets imitate; mature poets steal.
T. S. Eliot 1888–1965: *The Sacred Wood* (1920)

14 Poets in our civilization, as it exists at present, must be
difficult.
T. S. Eliot 1888–1965: 'The Metaphysical Poets' (1921)

15 Dr Donne's verses are like the peace of God; they pass all
understanding.
James I 1566–1625: remark recorded by Archdeacon
Plume (1630–1704)

16 Milton, Madam, was a genius that could cut a Colossus
from a rock; but could not carve heads upon cherry-stones.
Samuel Johnson 1709–84: to Hannah More, who had
expressed a wonder that the poet who had written
Paradise Lost should write such poor sonnets; James
Boswell *Life of Johnson* (1791) 13 June 1784

17 Self-contempt, well-grounded.
F. R. Leavis 1895–1978: on the foundation of T. S. Eliot's
work, in *Times Literary Supplement* 21 October 1988

18 The poet is always indebted to the universe, paying
interest and fines on sorrow.
Vladimir Mayakovsky 1893–1930: 'Conversation with an
Inspector of Taxes about Poetry' (1926), tr. D. Obolensky

19 The high-water mark, so to speak, of Socialist literature is
W. H. Auden, a sort of gutless Kipling.
George Orwell 1903–50: *The Road to Wigan Pier* (1937)

20 Ev'n copious Dryden, wanted, or forgot,
The last and greatest art, the art to blot.
Alexander Pope 1688–1744: *Imitations of Horace* (1737)

21 Life's a curse, love's a blight, God's a blaggard, cherry
blossom is quite nice.

> **Tom Stoppard** 1937– : on A. E. Housman; *The Invention
> of Love* (1997)

....

Political Comment

....

See also **Government**, **Political Parties**,
Politics

1 We had better wait and see.

> **Herbert Asquith** 1852–1928: referring to the rumour
> that the House of Lords was to be flooded with new
> Liberal peers to ensure the passage of the Finance Bill,
> 1910

2 There are three classes which need sanctuary more than
others—birds, wild flowers, and Prime Ministers.

> **Stanley Baldwin** 1867–1947: in *Observer* 24 May 1925

3 If you carry this resolution you will send Britain's Foreign
Secretary naked into the conference chamber.

> **Aneurin Bevan** 1897–1960: speech at Labour Party
> Conference, 3 October 1957, against a motion proposing
> unilateral nuclear disarmament by the UK

4 My [foreign] policy is to be able to take a ticket at Victoria
Station and go anywhere I damn well please.

> **Ernest Bevin** 1881–1951: in *Spectator* 20 April 1951

5 This policy cannot succeed through speeches, and
shooting-matches, and songs; it can only be carried out
through blood and iron.

> **Otto von Bismarck** 1815–98: speech in the Prussian
> House of Deputies, 28 January 1886. In an earlier speech,
> 30 September 1862, Bismarck used the form 'iron and
> blood'

6 A gigantic system of outdoor relief for the aristocracy of
Great Britain.

> **John Bright** 1811–89: of British foreign policy; speech at
> Birmingham, 29 October 1858

7 I am for 'Peace, retrenchment, and reform', the watchword of the great Liberal party 30 years ago.
   John Bright 1811–89: speech at Birmingham, 28 April 1859

8 Meddle and muddle.
   Edward Stanley, 14th Earl of Derby 1799–1869: summarizing Earl Russell's foreign policy, in Speech on the Address, House of Lords, 4 February 1864

9 Think of it! A second Chamber selected by the Whips. A seraglio of eunuchs.
   Michael Foot 1913– : speech, House of Commons, 3 February 1969

10 The compact which exists between the North and the South is 'a covenant with death and an agreement with hell'.
   William Lloyd Garrison 1805–79: resolution adopted by the Massachusetts Anti-Slavery Society, 27 January 1843

11 We are all socialists now.
   William Harcourt 1827–1904: during the passage of Lord Goschen's 1888 budget, noted for the reduction of the national debt (attributed)

12 The unpleasant and unacceptable face of capitalism.
   Edward Heath 1916– : speech, House of Commons, 15 May 1973, on the Lonrho affair

13 And so, my fellow Americans: ask not what your country can do for you—ask what you can do for your country.
   John F. Kennedy 1917–63: inaugural address, 20 January 1961

14 With malice toward none; with charity for all; with firmness in the right, as God gives us to see the right, let us strive on to finish the work we are in.
   Abraham Lincoln 1809–65: second inaugural address, 4 March 1865

15 A mastiff? It is the right hon. Gentleman's poodle.
   David Lloyd George 1863–1945: on the House of Lords and Lord Balfour respectively; speech, House of Commons, 26 June 1907

16 Let us be frank about it: most of our people have never had it so good.

> **Harold Macmillan** 1894–1986: speech at Bedford, 20 July 1957 ('You Never Had It So Good' was the Democratic Party slogan during the 1952 US election campaign)

17 The wind of change is blowing through this continent, and, whether we like it or not, this growth of [African] national consciousness is a political fact.

> **Harold Macmillan** 1894–1986: speech at Cape Town, 3 February 1960

18 I was determined that no British government should be brought down by the action of two tarts.

> **Harold Macmillan** 1894–1986: comment on the Profumo affair, July 1963

19 There are three bodies no sensible man directly challenges: the Roman Catholic Church, the Brigade of Guards and the National Union of Mineworkers.

> **Harold Macmillan** 1894–1986: in *Observer* 22 February 1981

20 First of all the Georgian silver goes, and then all that nice furniture that used to be in the saloon. Then the Canalettos go.

> **Harold Macmillan** 1894–1986: speech on privatization to the Tory Reform Group, 8 November 1985

21 [Palmerston] once said that only three men in Europe had ever understood [the Schleswig-Holstein question], and of these the Prince Consort was dead, a Danish statesman (unnamed) was in an asylum, and he himself had forgotten it.

> **Lord Palmerston** 1784–1865: R. W. Seton-Watson *Britain in Europe 1789–1914* (1937)

22 We shall not be diverted from our course. To those waiting with bated breath for that favourite media catch-phrase, the U-turn, I have only this to say. 'You turn if you want; the lady's not for turning.'

> **Margaret Thatcher** 1925– : speech at Conservative Party Conference, 10 October 1980

23 Greater love hath no man than this, that he lay down his
friends for his life.
   Jeremy Thorpe 1929– : on Harold Macmillan sacking
   seven of his Cabinet on 13 July 1962

24 A week is a long time in politics.
   Harold Wilson 1916–95: probably first said at the time of
   the 1964 sterling crisis. See Nigel Rees *Sayings of the
   Century* (1984)

··

Political Parties
··

See also **Politicians**, **Politics**

1 The language of priorities is the religion of Socialism.
   Aneurin Bevan 1897–1960: speech at Labour Party
   Conference, 8 June 1949

2 God will not always be a Tory.
   Lord Byron 1788–1824: letter 2 February 1821

3 Then raise the scarlet standard high!
Within its shade we'll live or die.
Tho' cowards flinch and traitors sneer,
We'll keep the red flag flying here.
   James M. Connell 1852–1929: 'The Red Flag' (1889 song)

4 Damn your principles! Stick to your party.
   Benjamin Disraeli 1804–81: believed to have been said to
   Edward Bulwer-Lytton; attributed in E. Latham *Famous
   Sayings and their Authors* (1904)

5 There are some of us . . . who will fight and fight and fight
again to save the Party we love.
   Hugh Gaitskell 1906–63: speech at Labour Party
   Conference, 5 October 1960

6 A great party is not to be brought down because of a
scandal by a woman of easy virtue and a proved liar.
   Lord Hailsham 1907– : BBC television interview on the
   Profumo affair; in *The Times* 14 June 1963

7 If I could not go to Heaven but with a party, I would not go there at all.

Thomas Jefferson 1743–1826: letter to Francis Hopkinson, 13 March 1789

8 A dead or dying beast lying across a railway line and preventing other trains from getting through.

Roy Jenkins 1920– : of the Labour Party; in *Guardian* 16 May 1987

9 The longest suicide note in history.

Gerald Kaufman 1930– : on the Labour Party's election manifesto *New Hope for Britain* (1983); Denis Healey *The Time of My Life* (1989)

10 Loyalty is the Tory's secret weapon.

Lord Kilmuir 1900–67: Anthony Sampson *Anatomy of Britain* (1962)

11 I have only one firm belief about the American political system, and that is this: God is a Republican and Santa Claus is a Democrat.

P. J. O'Rourke 1947– : *Parliament of Whores* (1991)

12 Party-spirit, which at best is but the madness of many for the gain of a few.

Alexander Pope 1688–1744: letter to E. Blount, 27 August 1714

13 The mules of politics: without pride of ancestry, or hope of posterity.

John O'Connor Power 1848–1919: of the Liberal Unionists; H. H. Asquith *Memories and Reflections* (1928)

14 The more you read and observe about this Politics thing, you got to admit that each party is worse than the other. The one that's out always looks the best.

Will Rogers 1879–1935: *Illiterate Digest* (1924)

15 If they [the Republicans] will stop telling lies about the Democrats, we will stop telling the truth about them.

Adlai Stevenson 1900–65: speech during 1952 Presidential campaign

16 This party is a moral crusade or it is nothing.

Harold Wilson 1916–95: speech at the Labour Party Conference, 1 October 1962

Politicians

See also **Political Comment**, **Politics**

1 Being an MP is the sort of job all working-class parents
want for their children—clean, indoors and no heavy
lifting.
   Diane Abbott 1953– : in *Observer* 23 January 1994

2 This is a rotten argument, but it should be good enough
for their lordships on a hot summer afternoon.
   Anonymous: annotation to a ministerial brief, said to
   have been read out inadvertently in the House of Lords;
   Lord Home *The Way the Wind Blows* (1976)

3 A constitutional statesman is in general a man of common
opinion and uncommon abilities.
   Walter Bagehot 1826–77: *Biographical Studies* (1881)

4 I thought he was a young man of promise, but it appears
he is a young man of promises.
   Arthur James Balfour 1848–1930: describing Churchill;
   Winston Churchill *My Early Life* (1930)

5 [Winston Churchill] does not talk the language of the 20th
century but that of the 18th. He is still fighting Blenheim
all over again. His only answer to a difficult situation is
send a gun-boat.
   Aneurin Bevan 1897–1960: speech at Labour Party
   Conference, 2 October 1951

6 I am not going to spend any time whatsoever in attacking
the Foreign Secretary . . . If we complain about the tune,
there is no reason to attack the monkey when the organ
grinder is present.
   Aneurin Bevan 1897–1960: during a debate on the Suez
   crisis, House of Commons, 16 May 1957

7 Listening to a speech by Chamberlain is like paying a visit
to Woolworth's: everything in its place and nothing above
sixpence.
   Aneurin Bevan 1897–1960: Michael Foot *Aneurin Bevan*
   vol. 1 (1962)

8 A lath of wood painted to look like iron.
   Otto von Bismarck 1815–98: describing Lord Salisbury;
   attributed, but vigorously denied by Sidney Whitman in
   Personal Reminiscences of Prince Bismarck (1902)

9 Your representative owes you, not his industry only, but
   his judgement; and he betrays, instead of serving you, if he
   sacrifices it to your opinion.
   Edmund Burke 1729–97: speech, 3 November 1774

10 Not merely a chip of the old 'block', but the old block itself.
   Edmund Burke 1729–97: on the younger Pitt's maiden
   speech, February 1781

11 An honest politician is one who when he's bought stays
   bought.
   Simon Cameron 1799–1889: attributed

12 A minister who moves about in society is in a position to
   read the signs of the times even in a festive gathering, but
   one who remains shut up in his office learns nothing.
   Duc de Choiseul 1719–85: Jack F. Bernard *Talleyrand*
   (1973)

13 I have waited 50 years to see the boneless wonder [Ramsay
   Macdonald] sitting on the Treasury Bench.
   Winston Churchill 1874–1965: speech, House of
   Commons, 28 January 1931

14 It is the ability to foretell what is going to happen
   tomorrow, next week, next month, and next year. And to
   have the ability afterwards to explain why it didn't
   happen.
   Winston Churchill 1874–1965: on the qualifications for
   becoming a politician; B. Adler *Churchill Wit* (1965)

15 A sheep in sheep's clothing.
   Winston Churchill 1874–1965: of Clement Attlee; Lord
   Home *The Way the Wind Blows* (1976)

16 There are no true friends in politics. We are all sharks
   circling, and waiting, for traces of blood to appear in the
   water.
   Alan Clark 1928–99: diary, 30 November 1990

17 The only safe pleasure for a parliamentarian is a bag of
boiled sweets.
   Julian Critchley 1930– : *Listener* 10 June 1982

18 a politician is an arse upon
which everyone has sat except a man.
   e. e. cummings 1894–1962: *1 x 1* (1944) no. 10

19 It is not necessary that every time he rises he should give
his famous imitation of a semi-house-trained polecat.
   Michael Foot 1913– : of Norman Tebbit; speech, House
   of Commons, 2 March 1978

20 The prospect of a lot
Of dull MPs in close proximity,
All thinking for themselves is what
No man can face with equanimity.
   W. S. Gilbert 1836–1911: *Iolanthe* (1882)

21 Comrades, this man has a nice smile, but he's got iron
teeth.
   Andrei Gromyko 1909–89: on Mikhail Gorbachev; speech
   to Soviet Communist Party Central Committee, 11 March
   1985

22 'Do you pray for the senators, Dr Hale?' 'No, I look at the
senators and I pray for the country.'
   Edward Everett Hale 1822–1909: Van Wyck Brooks *New
   England Indian Summer* (1940)

23 Politicians are entitled to change their minds. But when
they adjust their principles some explanation is necessary.
   Roy Hattersley 1932– : in *Observer* 21 March 1999

24 Like being savaged by a dead sheep.
   Denis Healey 1917– : on being criticized by Geoffrey
   Howe in the House of Commons, 14 June 1978

25 If a due participation of office is a matter of right, how are
vacancies to be obtained? Those by death are few; by
resignation none.
   Thomas Jefferson 1743–1826: letter to E. Shipman and
   others, 12 July 1801 (usually quoted 'Few die and none
   resign')

26 He [Labouchere] did not object to the old man always
having a card up his sleeve, but he did object to his
insinuating that the Almighty had placed it there.
Henry Labouchere 1831–1912: on Gladstone's 'frequent
appeals to a higher power'; Earl Curzon *Modern
Parliamentary Eloquence* (1913)

27 The Stag at Bay with the mentality of a fox at large.
Bernard Levin 1928– : of Harold Macmillan; *The
Pendulum Years* (1970)

28 Forever poised between a cliché and an indiscretion.
Harold Macmillan 1894–1986: on the life of a Foreign
Secretary; in *Newsweek* 30 April 1956

29 What I want is men who will support me when I am in the
wrong.
Lord Melbourne 1779–1848: replying to a politician who
said 'I will support you as long as you are in the right';
Lord David Cecil *Lord M* (1954)

30 She has the eyes of Caligula, but the mouth of Marilyn
Monroe.
François Mitterrand 1916–96: comment to his new
European Minister Roland Dumas; in *Observer* 25
November 1990

31 A statesman is a politician who places himself at the
service of the nation. A politician is a statesman who
places the nation at his service.
Georges Pompidou 1911–74: in *Observer* 30 December
1973

32 All political lives, unless they are cut off in midstream at a
happy juncture, end in failure, because that is the nature
of politics and of human affairs.
Enoch Powell 1912–98: *Joseph Chamberlain* (1977)

33 We all know that Prime Ministers are wedded to the truth,
but like other married couples they sometimes live apart.
Saki (H. H. Munro) 1870–1916: *The Unbearable
Bassington* (1912)

34 Too clever by half.
Lord Salisbury 1893–1972: of Iain Macleod, Colonial
Secretary; speech, House of Lords, 7 March 1961

35   Get thee glass eyes;
And, like a scurvy politician, seem
To see the things thou dost not.
    William Shakespeare 1564–1616: *King Lear* (1605–6)

36 It is, I think, good evidence of life after death.
    Lord Soper 1903–98: on the quality of debate in the
House of Lords, in *Listener* 17 August 1978

37 A statesman is a politician who's been dead 10 or 15 years.
    Harry S. Truman 1884–1972: in *New York World
Telegram and Sun* 12 April 1958

38 A triumph of the embalmer's art.
    Gore Vidal 1925– : of Ronald Reagan, in *Observer* 26
April 1981

39 All those men have their price.
    Robert Walpole 1676–1745: of fellow parliamentarians;
W. Coxe *Memoirs of Sir Robert Walpole* (1798)

....

Politics

....

See also **Democracy**, **Government**, **Political
Comment**, **Political Parties**, **Politicians**,
Voting

1 In politics the middle way is none at all.
    John Adams 1735–1826: letter to Horatio Gates, 23
March 1776

2 Man is by nature a political animal.
    Aristotle 384–322 BC: *Politics*

3 [Russian Communism is] the illegitimate child of Karl
Marx and Catherine the Great.
    Clement Attlee 1883–1967: speech at Aarhus University,
11 April 1956

4 Politics is the art of the possible.
    Otto von Bismarck 1815–98: in conversation with Meyer
von Waldeck, 11 August 1867

5 A statesman . . . must wait until he hears the steps of God sounding through events; then leap up and grasp the hem of his garment.

Otto von Bismarck 1815–98: A. J. P. Taylor *Bismarck* (1955)

6 Magnanimity in politics is not seldom the truest wisdom; and a great empire and little minds go ill together.

Edmund Burke 1729–97: *On Conciliation with America* (1775)

7 In politics, there is no use looking beyond the next fortnight.

Joseph Chamberlain 1836–1914: letter from A. J. Balfour to 3rd Marquess of Salisbury, 24 March 1886

8 Safe is spelled D-U-L-L. Politics has got to be a fun activity, otherwise people turn their back on it.

Alan Clark 1928–99: on being selected as parliamentary candidate for Kensington and Chelsea, 24 January 1997

9 In politics, what begins in fear usually ends in folly.

Samuel Taylor Coleridge 1772–1834: *Table Talk* (1835) 5 October 1830

10 You campaign in poetry. You govern in prose.

Mario Cuomo 1932– : in *New Republic*, Washington, DC, 8 April 1985

11 International life is right-wing, like nature. The social contract is left-wing, like humanity.

Régis Debray 1940– : *Charles de Gaulle* (1994)

12 'Two nations; between whom there is no intercourse and no sympathy; who are as ignorant of each other's habits, thoughts, and feelings, as if they were dwellers in different zones, or inhabitants of different planets . . . ' 'You speak of—' said Egremont, hesitatingly, 'THE RICH AND THE POOR.'

Benjamin Disraeli 1804–81: *Sybil* (1845)

13 I never dared be radical when young
For fear it would make me conservative when old.

Robert Frost 1874–1963: 'Precaution' (1936)

14 Politics is not the art of the possible. It consists in choosing between the disastrous and the unpalatable.
   J. K. Galbraith 1908– : letter to President Kennedy, 2 March 1962

15 The great nations have always acted like gangsters, and the small nations like prostitutes.
   Stanley Kubrick 1928–99: in *Guardian* 5 June 1963

16 Who? Whom?
   Lenin 1870–1924: definition of political science, meaning 'Who will outstrip whom?'; in *Polnoe Sobranie Sochinenii* (1979) 17 October 1921, and elsewhere

17 Politics is a marathon, not a sprint.
   Ken Livingstone 1945– : in *New Statesman* 10 October 1997

18 If you want to succeed in politics, you must keep your conscience well under control.
   David Lloyd George 1863–1945: in Lord Riddell's diary, 23 April 1919

19 Events, dear boy. Events.
   Harold Macmillan 1894–1986: when asked what his biggest problem was; attributed

20 Politics is war without bloodshed while war is politics with bloodshed.
   Mao Tse-tung 1893–1976: lecture, 1938, in *Selected Works* (1965)

21 Political language . . . is designed to make lies sound truthful and murder respectable, and to give an appearance of solidity to pure wind.
   George Orwell 1903–50: *Shooting an Elephant* (1950) 'Politics and the English Language'

22 Politics is the art of preventing people from taking part in affairs which properly concern them.
   Paul Valéry 1871–1945: *Tel Quel 2* (1943)

23 Socialism can only arrive by bicycle.
   José Antonio Viera Gallo 1943– : Ivan Illich *Energy and Equity* (1974) epigraph

Pollution

See also **Environment**

1 Woe to her that is filthy and polluted, to the oppressing city!
  Bible: Zephaniah

2 NOISE, *n*. A stench in the ear . . . The chief product and authenticating sign of civilization.
  Ambrose Bierce 1842–*c*.1914: *Devil's Dictionary* (1911)

3 Man has been endowed with reason, with the power to create, so that he can add to what he's been given. But up to now he hasn't been a creator, only a destroyer. Forests keep disappearing, rivers dry up, wild life's become extinct, the climate's ruined and the land grows poorer and uglier every day.
  Anton Chekhov 1860–1904: *Uncle Vanya* (1897)

4 The river Rhine, it is well known,
  Doth wash your city of Cologne;
  But tell me, Nymphs, what power divine
  Shall henceforth wash the river Rhine?
  Samuel Taylor Coleridge 1772–1834: 'Cologne' (1834)

5 The sea is the universal sewer.
  Jacques Cousteau 1910–97: testimony before the House Committee on Science and Astronautics, 28 January 1971

6 Pollution knows no boundaries any more than do money or information.
  Peter F. Drucker 1909– : *Post-Capitalist Society* (1993)

7 Clear the air! clean the sky! wash the wind!
  T. S. Eliot 1888–1965: *Murder in the Cathedral* (1935)

8 The sanitary and mechanical age we are now entering makes up for the mercy it grants to our sense of smell by the ferocity with which it assails our sense of hearing. As usual, what we call 'progress' is the exchange of one nuisance for another nuisance.
  Havelock Ellis 1859–1939: *Impressions and Comments* (1914)

9 And all is seared with trade; bleared, smeared with toil;
And wears man's smudge and shares man's smell.
   Gerard Manley Hopkins 1844–89: 'God's Grandeur'
   (written 1877)

10 It goes so heavily with my disposition that this goodly
frame, the earth, seems to me a sterile promontory; this
most excellent canopy, the air, look you, this brave
o'erhanging firmament, this majestical roof fretted with
golden fire, why, it appears no other thing to me but a foul
and pestilent congregation of vapours.
   William Shakespeare 1564–1616: *Hamlet* (1601)

11 By avarice and selfishness, and a grovelling habit, from
which none of us is free, of regarding the soil as property
. . . the landscape is deformed.
   Henry David Thoreau 1817–62: *Walden* (1854) 'The Bean
   Field'

Poverty

1 Anyone who has ever struggled with poverty knows how
extremely expensive it is to be poor.
   James Baldwin 1924–87: *Nobody Knows My Name* (1961)

2 Come away; poverty's catching.
   Aphra Behn 1640–89: *The Rover* pt. 2 (1681)

3 What mean ye that ye beat my people to pieces, and grind
the faces of the poor?
   Bible: Isaiah

4 When I give food to the poor they call me a saint. When I
ask why the poor have no food they call me a communist.
   Helder Camara 1909–99: attributed

5 The poor are Europe's blacks.
   Nicolas-Sébastien Chamfort 1741–94: *Maximes et
   Pensées* (1796)

6 People don't resent having nothing nearly as much as too
little.
   Ivy Compton-Burnett 1884–1969: *A Family and a
   Fortune* (1939)

7 The murmuring poor, who will not fast in peace.
  George Crabbe 1754–1832: 'The Newspaper' (1785)

8 Give me not poverty lest I steal.
  Daniel Defoe 1660–1731: *Moll Flanders* (1721)

9 There is no scandal like rags, nor any crime so shameful
as poverty.
  George Farquhar 1678–1707: *The Beaux' Stratagem*
  (1707)

10 I want there to be no peasant in my kingdom so poor that
he is unable to have a chicken in his pot every Sunday.
  Henri IV 1553–1610: H. de Péréfixe *Histoire de Henri le*
  Grand (1681)

11 Oh! God! that bread should be so dear,
And flesh and blood so cheap!
  Thomas Hood 1799–1845: 'The Song of the Shirt' (1843)

12 It's easy to be independent when you've got money. But to
be independent when you haven't got a thing—that's the
Lord's test.
  Mahalia Jackson 1911–72: *Movin' On Up* (with Evan
  McLoud Wylie 1966)

13 Resolve not to be poor: whatever you have, spend less.
Poverty is a great enemy to human happiness; it certainly
destroys liberty, and it makes some virtues impracticable,
and others extremely difficult.
  Samuel Johnson 1709–84: letter to James Boswell,
  7 December 1782

14 The misfortunes of poverty carry with them nothing
harder to bear than that it makes men ridiculous.
  Juvenal AD *c.*60–*c.*130: *Satires*

15 Battles and sex are the only free diversions in slum life.
Couple them with drink, which costs money, and you have
the three principal outlets for that escape complex which
is for ever working in the tenement dweller's subconscious
mind.
  Alexander McArthur and **H. Kingsley Long**: *No Mean*
  City (1935)

16 I never saw a beggar yet who would recognise guilt if it bit him on his unwashed ass.
Tony Parsons 1953– : *Dispatches from the Front Line of Popular Culture* (1994)

17 The greatest of evils and the worst of crimes is poverty.
George Bernard Shaw 1856–1950: *Major Barbara* (1907) preface

18 Poverty is no disgrace to a man, but it is confoundedly inconvenient.
Sydney Smith 1771–1845: J. Potter Briscoe *Sidney Smith: His Wit and Wisdom* (1900)

19 Sixteen tons, what do you get?
Another day older and deeper in debt.
Say brother, don't you call me 'cause I can't go
I owe my soul to the company store.
Merle Travis 1917–83: 'Sixteen Tons' (1947 song)

Power

1 Power tends to corrupt and absolute power corrupts absolutely.
Lord Acton 1834–1902: letter to Bishop Mandell Creighton, 3 April 1887

2 When he laughed, respectable senators burst with laughter,
And when he cried the little children died in the streets
W. H. Auden 1907–73: 'Epitaph on a Tyrant' (1940)

3 All rising to great place is by a winding stair.
Francis Bacon 1561–1626: *Essays* (1625) 'Of Great Place'

4 Whatever happens we have got
The Maxim Gun, and they have not.
Hilaire Belloc 1870–1953: *The Modern Traveller* (1898)

5 Every dictator uses religion as a prop to keep himself in power.
Benazir Bhutto 1953– : interview on *60 Minutes*, CBS-TV, 8 August 1986

6 The most potent weapon in the hands of the oppressor is the mind of the oppressed.
   Steve Biko 1946–77: statement as witness, 3 May 1976

7 Power is so apt to be insolent and Liberty to be saucy, that they are very seldom upon good terms.
   George Savile, Marquess of Halifax 1633–95: *Political, Moral, and Miscellaneous Thoughts* (1750)

8 A man may build himself a throne of bayonets, but he cannot sit on it.
   Dean Inge 1860–1954: *Philosophy of Plotinus* (1923), quoted by Boris Yeltsin at the time of the failed military coup in Russia, August 1991

9 Power is the great aphrodisiac.
   Henry Kissinger 1923– : in *New York Times* 19 January 1971

10 Power? It's like a Dead Sea fruit. When you achieve it, there is nothing there.
   Harold Macmillan 1894–1986: Anthony Sampson *The New Anatomy of Britain* (1971)

11 Political power grows out of the barrel of a gun.
   Mao Tse-tung 1893–1976: speech, 6 November 1938

12 Who controls the past controls the future: who controls the present controls the past.
   George Orwell 1903–50: *Nineteen Eighty-Four* (1949)

13   Man, proud man,
Drest in a little brief authority.
   William Shakespeare 1564–1616: *Measure for Measure* (1604)

14 You only have power over people as long as you don't take *everything* away from them. But when you've robbed a man of *everything* he's no longer in your power—he's free again.
   Alexander Solzhenitsyn 1918– : *The First Circle* (1968)

15 The Pope! How many divisions has *he* got?
  Joseph Stalin 1879–1953: on being asked to encourage
  Catholicism in Russia by way of conciliating the Pope, 13
  May 1935

16 The hand that signed the treaty bred a fever,
  And famine grew, and locusts came;
  Great is the hand that holds dominion over
  Man by a scribbled name.
  Dylan Thomas 1914–53: 'The hand that signed the paper
  felled a city' (1936)

....

Practicality
....

1 It's grand, and you canna expect to be baith grand and
  comfortable.
  J. M. Barrie 1860–1937: *The Little Minister* (1891)

2 Put your trust in God, my boys, and keep your powder dry.
  Valentine Blacker 1728–1823: 'Oliver's Advice' (1856),
  often attributed to Oliver Cromwell himself

3 Whenever our neighbour's house is on fire, it cannot be
  amiss for the engines to play a little on our own.
  Edmund Burke 1729–97: *Reflections on the Revolution in
  France* (1790)

4 Life is too short to stuff a mushroom.
  Shirley Conran 1932– : *Superwoman* (1975)

5 The colour of the cat doesn't matter as long as it catches
  the mice.
  Deng Xiaoping 1904–97: in *Financial Times* 18 December
  1986; quoting a Chinese proverb

6 Common sense is the best distributed commodity in the
  world, for every man is convinced that he is well supplied
  with it.
  René Descartes 1596–1650: *Le Discours de la méthode*
  (1637)

7 Common sense is nothing more than a deposit of
prejudices laid down in the mind before you reach
eighteen.
Albert Einstein 1879–1955: Lincoln Barnett *The Universe
and Dr Einstein* (1950 ed.)

8 Praise the Lord and pass the ammunition.
Howell Forgy 1908–83: at Pearl Harbor, 7 December 1941,
while sailors passed ammunition by hand to the deck;
later title of song by Frank Loesser, 1942

9 So I really think that American gentlemen are the best
after all, because kissing your hand may make you feel
very very good but a diamond and safire bracelet lasts
forever.
Anita Loos 1893–1981: *Gentlemen Prefer Blondes* (1925)

10 Common sense is not so common.
Voltaire 1694–1778: *Dictionnaire philosophique* (1765)
'Sens Commun'

Praise

1 It has been well said that 'the arch-flatterer with whom all
the petty flatterers have intelligence is a man's self.'
Francis Bacon 1561–1626: *Essays* (1625) 'Of Love'

2 He who discommendeth others obliquely commendeth
himself.
Sir Thomas Browne 1605–82: *Christian Morals* (1716)

3 The advantage of doing one's praising for oneself is that
one can lay it on so thick and exactly in the right places.
Samuel Butler 1835–1902: *The Way of All Flesh* (1903)

4 Imitation is the sincerest of flattery.
Charles Caleb Colton *c.*1780–1832: *Lacon* (1820)

5 All censure of a man's self is oblique praise. It is in order
to shew how much he can spare.
Samuel Johnson 1709–84: James Boswell *Life of
Johnson* (1791) 25 April 1778

6 And even the ranks of Tuscany
Could scarce forbear to cheer.
   Lord Macaulay 1800–59: *Lays of Ancient Rome* (1842)
   'Horatius'

7 Damn with faint praise, assent with civil leer,
And without sneering, teach the rest to sneer.
   Alexander Pope 1688–1744: 'An Epistle to Dr Arbuthnot'
   (1735)

8 But when I tell him he hates flatterers,
He says he does, being then most flattered.
   William Shakespeare 1564–1616: *Julius Caesar* (1599)

9 I suppose flattery hurts no one, that is, if he doesn't inhale.
   Adlai Stevenson 1900–65: television broadcast, 30 March
   1952

Prayer

1 Bernard always had a few prayers in the hall and some
whiskey afterwards as he was rarther pious but Mr
Salteena was not very addicted to prayers so he marched
up to bed.
   Daisy Ashford 1881–1972: *The Young Visiters* (1919)

2 O Lord! thou knowest how busy I must be this day: if I
forget thee, do not thou forget me.
   Jacob Astley 1579–1652: prayer before the Battle of
   Edgehill

3 The wish for prayer is a prayer in itself.
   Georges Bernanos 1888–1948: *Journal d'un curé de
   campagne* (1936)

4 Ask, and it shall be given you; seek, and ye shall find;
knock, and it shall be opened unto you.
   Bible: St Matthew

5 And lips say, 'God be pitiful,'
Who ne'er said, 'God be praised.'
   Elizabeth Barrett Browning 1806–61: 'The Cry of the
   Human' (1844)

6 He prayeth best, who loveth best
All things both great and small.
Samuel Taylor Coleridge 1772–1834: 'The Rime of the
Ancient Mariner' (1798)

7 I throw myself down in my Chamber, and I call in, and
invite God, and his Angels thither, and when they are
there, I neglect God and his Angels, for the noise of a fly,
for the rattling of a coach, for the whining of a door.
John Donne 1572–1631: sermon, 12 December 1626

8 To lift up the hands in prayer gives God glory, but a man
with a dungfork in his hand, a woman with a slop-pail,
give him glory too.
Gerard Manley Hopkins 1844–89: 'The Principle or
Foundation' (1882)

9 The prayers of the dying are especially precious to God,
because they will soon be in His presence.
Basil Hume 1923–99: in *Independent* 18 June 1999

10 One single grateful thought raised to heaven is the most
perfect prayer.
G. E. Lessing 1729–81: *Minna von Barnhelm* (1767)

11 Often when I pray I wonder if I am not posting letters to a
non-existent address.
C. S. Lewis 1898–1963: letter to Arthur Greeves, 24
December 1930

12 Christ beside me,
Christ before me,
Christ behind me,
Christ within me,
Christ beneath me,
Christ above me.
St Patrick fl. 5th cent.: 'St Patrick's Breastplate'

13 The family that prays together stays together.
Al Scalpone: motto devised for the Roman Catholic
Family Rosary Crusade, 1947

14 My words fly up, my thoughts remain below:
Words without thoughts never to heaven go.
William Shakespeare 1564–1616: *Hamlet* (1601)

15 I am just going to pray for you at St Paul's, but with no
very lively hope of success.
   Sydney Smith 1771–1845: H. Pearson *The Smith of
   Smiths* (1934)

16 If thou shouldst never see my face again,
Pray for my soul. More things are wrought by prayer
Than this world dreams of.
   Alfred, Lord Tennyson 1809–92: *Idylls of the King* 'The
   Passing of Arthur' (1869)

17 Whatever a man prays for, he prays for a miracle. Every
prayer reduces itself to this: Great God, grant that twice
two be not four.
   Ivan Turgenev 1818–83: *Poems in Prose* (1881) 'Prayer'

18 You can't pray a lie.
   Mark Twain 1835–1910: *Adventures of Huckleberry Finn*
   (1885)

Prejudice

See also **Race**

1 It comes as a great shock around the age of 5, 6 or 7 to
discover that the flag to which you have pledged
allegiance, along with everybody else, has not pledged
allegiance to you. It comes as a great shock to see Gary
Cooper killing off the Indians and, although you are
rooting for Gary Cooper, that the Indians are you.
   James Baldwin 1924–87: speech at Cambridge
   University, 17 February 1965

2 But not so odd
As those who choose
A Jewish God,
But spurn the Jews.
   Cecil Browne 1932– : reply to verse by William Norman
   Ewer

3 Bigotry may be roughly defined as the anger of men who
have no opinions.

   G. K. Chesterton 1874–1936: *Heretics* (1905)

4 Being a star has made it possible for me to get insulted in
places where the average Negro could never *hope* to go and
get insulted.

   Sammy Davis Jnr. 1925–90: *Yes I Can* (1965)

5 Minds are like parachutes. They only function when they
are open.

   James Dewar 1842–1923: attributed

6 If my theory of relativity is proven correct, Germany will
claim me as a German and France will declare that I am a
citizen of the world. Should my theory prove untrue,
France will say that I am a German and Germany will
declare that I am a Jew.

   Albert Einstein 1879–1955: address at the Sorbonne,
   Paris, possibly early December 1929; in *New York Times*
   16 February 1930

7 How odd
Of God
To choose
The Jews.

   William Norman Ewer 1885–1976: in *Week-End Book*
   (1924)

8 Make hatred hated!

   Anatole France 1844–1924: speech to public school
   teachers in Tours, August 1919

9 Drive out prejudices through the door, and they will return
through the window.

   Frederick the Great 1712–86: letter to Voltaire, 19
   March 1771

10 Without the aid of prejudice and custom, I should not be
able to find my way across the room.

   William Hazlitt 1778–1830: 'On Prejudice' (1830)

11 And wherefore is he wearing such a conscience-stricken
air?

Oh they're taking him to prison for the colour of his hair.
A. E. Housman 1859–1936: *Collected Poems* (1939)
'Additional Poems' no. 18

12 Four legs good, two legs bad.
George Orwell 1903–50: *Animal Farm* (1945)

13 We should therefore claim, in the name of tolerance, the
right not to tolerate the intolerant.
Karl Popper 1902–94: *The Open Society and Its Enemies*
(1945)

14 Who's 'im, Bill?
A stranger!
'Eave 'arf a brick at 'im.
Punch: 1854

15 When people feel deeply, impartiality is bias.
Lord Reith 1889–1971: *Into the Wind* (1945)

16 You call me misbeliever, cut-throat dog,
And spit upon my Jewish gabardine,
And all for use of that which is mine own.
William Shakespeare 1564–1616: *The Merchant of
Venice* (1596–8)

17 The only good Indian is a dead Indian.
Philip Henry Sheridan 1831–88: at Fort Cobb, January
1869 (attributed)

18 Bigotry tries to keep truth safe in its hand
With a grip that kills it.
Rabindranath Tagore 1861–1941: *Fireflies* (1928)

19 Am I not a man and a brother.
Josiah Wedgwood 1730–95: legend on Wedgwood
cameo, depicting a kneeling Negro slave in chains;
reproduced in facsimile in E. Darwin *The Botanic
Garden* pt. 1 (1791)

. . . .

The Present
. . . .

1 Can ye not discern the signs of the times?
Bible: St Matthew

2 Take therefore no thought for the morrow: for the morrow
shall take thought for the things of itself. Sufficient unto
the day is the evil thereof.
  Bible: St Matthew

3 Exhaust the little moment. Soon it dies.
And be it gash or gold it will not come
Again in this identical disguise.
  Gwendolyn Brooks 1917– : 'Exhaust the little moment'
  (1949)

4 The rule is, jam to-morrow and jam yesterday—but never
jam today.
  Lewis Carroll 1832–98: *Through the Looking-Glass* (1872)

5 The present is the funeral of the past,
And man the living sepulchre of life.
  John Clare 1793–1864: 'The present is the funeral of the
  past' (written 1845)

6 Ah, fill the cup:—what boots it to repeat
How time is slipping underneath our feet:
Unborn TO-MORROW, and dead YESTERDAY,
Why fret about them if TO-DAY be sweet!
  Edward Fitzgerald 1809–83: *The Rubáiyát of Omar
  Khayyám* (1859)

7 *Carpe diem, quam minimum credula postero.*

  Seize the day, put no trust in the future.
  Horace 65–8 BC: *Odes*

8 I *see* it is the whitest, frothiest, blossomiest blossom that
there ever could be, and I can see it. Things are both more
trivial than they ever were, and more important than they
ever were, and the difference between the trivial and the
important doesn't seem to matter. But the nowness of
everything is absolutely wondrous.
  Dennis Potter 1935–94: *Seeing the Blossom* (1994)

9 What is love? 'tis not hereafter;
Present mirth hath present laughter;

What's to come is still unsure.
  William Shakespeare 1564–1616: *Twelfth Night* (1601)

The Presidency

1 My country has in its wisdom contrived for me the most
  insignificant office that ever the invention of man
  contrived or his imagination conceived.
    John Adams 1735–1826: of the vice-presidency; letter to
    Abigail Adams, 19 December 1793

2 The US presidency is a Tudor monarchy plus telephones.
    Anthony Burgess 1917–93: George Plimpton (ed.)
    Writers at Work 4th Series (1977)

3 I'm President of the United States, and I'm not going to eat
  any more broccoli!
    George Bush 1924– : in *New York Times* 23 March 1990

4 No easy problems ever come to the President of the United
  States. If they are easy to solve, somebody else has solved
  them.
    Dwight D. Eisenhower 1890–1969: in *Parade Magazine* 8
    April 1962

5 All the security around the American president is just to
  make sure the man who shoots him gets caught.
    Norman Mailer 1923– : in *Sunday Telegraph* 4 March
    1990

6 When the President does it, that means that it is not
  illegal.
    Richard Nixon 1913–94: David Frost *I Gave Them a
    Sword* (1978)

7 I have got such a bully pulpit!
    Theodore Roosevelt 1858–1919: in *Outlook* (New York)
    27 February 1909

8 The answer to the runaway Presidency is not the
  messenger-boy Presidency. The American democracy must
  discover a middle way between making the President a

tsar and making him a puppet.
> **Arthur M. Schlesinger Jr.** 1917– : *The Imperial Presidency* (1973); preface

9 Ronald Reagan . . . is attempting a great breakthrough in political technology—he has been perfecting the Teflon-coated Presidency. He sees to it that nothing sticks to him.
> **Patricia Schroeder** 1940– : speech in the US House of Representatives, 2 August 1983

Pride

1 To be commonly above others, still more to think yourself above others, is to be below them every now and then, and sometimes much below.
> **Walter Bagehot** 1826–77: in *National Review* July 1859 'John Milton'

2 Pride goeth before destruction, and an haughty spirit before a fall.
> **Bible**: Proverbs

3 For whosoever exalteth himself shall be abased; and he that humbleth himself shall be exalted.
> **Bible**: St Luke. See also St Matthew

4 He that is down needs fear no fall,
He that is low no pride.
He that is humble ever shall
Have God to be his guide.
> **John Bunyan** 1628–88: *The Pilgrim's Progress* (1684) 'Shepherd Boy's Song'

5 If I'm ever feeling a bit uppity, whenever I get on my high horse, I go and take another look at my dear Mam's mangle that has pride of place in the dining-room.
> **Brian Clough** 1935– : *Clough: The Autobiography* (1994)

6 And the Devil did grin, for his darling sin
Is pride that apes humility.
> **Samuel Taylor Coleridge** 1772–1834: 'The Devil's Thoughts' (1799)

7 We are so very 'umble.
   Charles Dickens 1812–70: *David Copperfield* (1850)
   Uriah Heep

8 I can trace my ancestry back to a protoplasmal primordial
   atomic globule. Consequently, my family pride is
   something in-conceivable. I can't help it. I was born
   sneering.
   W. S. Gilbert 1836–1911: *The Mikado* (1885)

9 In 1969 I published a small book on Humility. It was a
   pioneering work which has not, to my knowledge, been
   superseded.
   Lord Longford 1905– : in *Tablet* 22 January 1994

10 PLEASE ACCEPT MY RESIGNATION. I DON'T WANT TO BELONG TO
   ANY CLUB THAT WILL ACCEPT ME AS A MEMBER.
   Groucho Marx 1895–1977: *Groucho and Me* (1959)

11 No one can make you feel inferior without your consent.
   Eleanor Roosevelt 1884–1962: in *Catholic Digest* August
   1960

12 As for conceit, what man will do any good who is not
   conceited? Nobody holds a good opinion of a man who has
   a low opinion of himself.
   Anthony Trollope 1815–82: *Orley Farm* (1862)

Progress

1 Belief in progress is a doctrine of idlers and Belgians. It is
   the individual relying upon his neighbours to do his work.
   Charles Baudelaire 1821–67: *Journaux intimes* (1887), tr.
   Christopher Isherwood

2 We are like dwarfs on the shoulders of giants, so that we
   can see more than they, and things at a greater distance,
   not by virtue of any sharpness of sight on our part, or any
   physical distinction, but because we are carried high and
   raised up by their giant size.
   Bernard of Chartres d. *c.*1130: John of Salisbury *The
   Metalogicon* (1159)

3 Want is one only of five giants on the road of
reconstruction . . . the others are Disease, Ignorance,
Squalor and Idleness.
   William Henry Beveridge 1879–1963: *Social Insurance
   and Allied Services* (1942)

4 The thing that hath been, it is that which shall be; and
that which is done is that which shall be done: and there is
no new thing under the sun.
   Bible: Ecclesiastes

5 Man aspires to the stars. But if he can get his sewage and
refuse distributed and utilised in orderly fashion he will
be doing very well.
   Roy Bridger: in *The Times* 13 July 1959

6 Progress, man's distinctive mark alone,
Not God's, and not the beasts': God is, they are,
Man partly is and wholly hopes to be.
   Robert Browning 1812–89: 'A Death in the Desert' (1864)

7 What have the Romans ever done for us?
   Graham Chapman 1941–89 et al.: *Monty Python's Life of
   Brian* (1979 film)

8 pity this busy monster, manunkind,
not. Progress is a comfortable disease.
   e. e. cummings 1894–1962: *1 x 1* (1944) no. 14

9 The European talks of progress because by an ingenious
application of some scientific acquirements he has
established a society which has mistaken comfort for
civilization.
   Benjamin Disraeli 1804–81: *Tancred* (1847)

10 As it will be in the future, it was at the birth of Man—
There are only four things certain since Social Progress
   began:
That the Dog returns to his Vomit and the Sow returns to
   her Mire,
And the burnt Fool's bandaged finger goes wabbling back
   to the Fire.
   Rudyard Kipling 1865–1936: 'The Gods of the Copybook
   Headings' (1919)

11 Is it progress if a cannibal uses knife and fork?
  Stanislaw Lec 1909–66: *Unkempt Thoughts* (1962)

12 One step forward two steps back.
  Lenin 1870–1924: title of book (1904)

13 If I have seen further it is by standing on the shoulders of giants.
  Isaac Newton 1642–1727: letter to Robert Hooke, 5 February 1676

14 'Change' is scientific, 'progress' is ethical; change is indubitable, whereas progress is a matter of controversy.
  Bertrand Russell 1872–1970: *Unpopular Essays* (1950) 'Philosophy and Politics'

15 The reasonable man adapts himself to the world: the unreasonable one persists in trying to adapt the world to himself. Therefore all progress depends on the unreasonable man.
  George Bernard Shaw 1856–1950: *Man and Superman* (1903)

16 And he gave it for his opinion, that whoever could make two ears of corn or two blades of grass to grow upon a spot of ground where only one grew before, would deserve better of mankind, and do more essential service to his country than the whole race of politicians put together.
  Jonathan Swift 1667–1745: *Gulliver's Travels* (1726)

Punishment

see **Crime and Punishment**

Quotations

1 The surest way to make a monkey of a man is to quote him.
  Robert Benchley 1889–1945: *My Ten Years in a Quandary* (1936)

2 It is a good thing for an uneducated man to read books of quotations.
   Winston Churchill 1874–1965: *My Early Life* (1930)

3 I know heaps of quotations, so I can always make quite a fair show of knowledge.
   O. Douglas 1877–1948: *The Setons* (1917)

4 I hate quotation. Tell me what you know.
   Ralph Waldo Emerson 1803–82: diary, May 1849

5 Windbags can be right. Aphorists can be wrong. It is a tough world.
   James Fenton 1949– : in *Times* 21 February 1985

6 An anthology is like all the plums and orange peel picked out of a cake.
   Walter Raleigh 1861–1922: letter to Mrs Robert Bridges, 15 January 1915

7 I always have a quotation for everything—it saves original thinking.
   Dorothy L. Sayers 1893–1957: *Have His Carcase* (1932)

8 Famous remarks are very seldom quoted correctly.
   Simeon Strunsky 1879–1948: *No Mean City* (1944)

9 What a good thing Adam had. When he said a good thing he knew nobody had said it before.
   Mark Twain 1835–1910: *Notebooks* (1935)

10 OSCAR WILDE: How I wish I had said that.
   WHISTLER: You will, Oscar, you will.
   James McNeill Whistler 1834–1903: R. Ellman *Oscar Wilde* (1987)

11 The nice thing about quotes is that they give us a nodding acquaintance with the originator which is often socially impressive.
   Kenneth Williams 1926–88: *Acid Drops* (1980)

12 Some for renown on scraps of learning dote,
   And think they grow immortal as they quote.
   Edward Young 1683–1765: *The Love of Fame* (1725–8)

Race

See also **Equality, Prejudice**

1 Black is beautiful.
Anonymous: slogan of American civil rights
campaigners, mid-1960s

2 My mother bore me in the southern wild,
And I am black, but O! my soul is white;
White as an angel is the English child:
But I am black as if bereaved of light.
William Blake 1757–1827: 'The Little Black Boy' (1789)

3 You have seen how a man was made a slave; you shall see
how a slave was made a man.
Frederick Douglass c.1818–95: *Narrative of the Life of
Frederick Douglass* (1845)

4 Irish Americans are about as Irish as black Americans are
African.
Bob Geldof 1954– : in *Observer* 22 June 1986

5 I herewith commission you to carry out all preparations
with regard to . . . a *total solution* of the Jewish question
in those territories of Europe which are under German
influence.
Hermann Goering 1893–1946: instructions to Heydrich,
31 July 1941

6 Though it be a thrilling and marvellous thing to be merely
young and gifted in such times, it is doubly so, doubly
dynamic—to be young, gifted and *black*.
Lorraine Hansberry 1930–65: *To be young, gifted and
black: Lorraine Hansberry in her own words* (1969)
adapted by Robert Nemiroff

7 And if the white man thought that Asians were a low,
filthy nation, Asians could still smile with relief—at least,
they were not Africans. And if the white man thought that
Africans were a low, filthy nation, Africans in southern
Africa could still smile—at least, they were not bushmen.
They all have their monsters.
Bessie Head 1937–86: *Maru* (1971)

8 Southern trees bear strange fruit,
Blood on the leaves and blood at the root,
Black bodies swinging in the Southern breeze,
Strange fruit hanging from the poplar trees.
   Billie Holiday 1915–59: 'Strange Fruit' (1939)

9 I, too, sing America.
I am the darker brother.
They send me to eat in the kitchen
When company comes.
   Langston Hughes 1902–67: 'I, Too' (1925)

10 When I look out at this convention, I see the face of
America, red, yellow, brown, black, and white. We are all
precious in God's sight—the real rainbow coalition.
   Jesse Jackson 1941– : speech at Democratic National
   Convention, Atlanta, 19 July 1988

11 There are no 'white' or 'coloured' signs on the foxholes or
graveyards of battle.
   John F. Kennedy 1917–63: message to Congress on
   proposed Civil Rights Bill, 19 June 1963

12 I have a dream that my four little children will one day
live in a nation where they will not be judged by the
colour of their skin but by the content of their character.
   Martin Luther King 1929–68: speech at Civil Rights
   March in Washington, 28 August 1963

13 There are no 'mixed' marriages. It just looks that way.
People don't mix races; they abandon them or pick them.
   Toni Morrison 1931– : *Tar Baby* (1981)

14 There are very few Eskimos, but millions of Whites, just
like mosquitoes. It is something very special and
wonderful to be an Eskimo—they are like the snow geese.
If an Eskimo forgets his language and Eskimo ways, he
will be nothing but just another mosquito.
   Abraham Okpik: attributed

15 Our mistreatment was just not right, and I was tired of it.
   Rosa Parks 1913– : of her refusal, on 1 December 1955,
   to surrender her seat on a segregated bus in Alabama to
   a white man; *Quiet Strength* (1994)

16 Where today are the Pequot? Where are the Narragansett, the Mohican, the Pokanoket, and many other once powerful tribes of our people? They have vanished before the avarice and oppression of the white man, as snow before the summer sun.

   Tecumseh 1768–1813: Dee Brown *Bury My Heart at Wounded Knee* (1970)

17 Growing up, I came up with this name: I'm a Cablinasian.

   Tiger Woods 1975– : explaining his rejection of 'African-American' as the term to describe his Caucasian, Afro-American, Native American, Thai, and Chinese ancestry; interview, 21 April 1997

··

Reading

··

See also **Books**

1 He was wont to say that if he had read as much as other men, he should have known no more than other men.

   John Aubrey 1626–97: *Brief Lives* 'Thomas Hobbes'

2 In science, read, by preference, the newest works; in literature, the oldest.

   Edward Bulwer-Lytton 1803–73: *Caxtoniana* (1863) 'Hints on Mental Culture'

3 The reading or non-reading a book—will never keep down a single petticoat.

   Lord Byron 1788–1824: letter to Richard Hoppner, 29 October 1819

4 Choose an author as you choose a friend.

   Wentworth Dillon, Earl of Roscommon c.1633–1685: *Essay on Translated Verse* (1684)

5 What do we ever get nowadays from reading to equal the excitement and the revelation in those first fourteen years?

   Graham Greene 1904–91: *The Lost Childhood and Other Essays* (1951)

6 A man ought to read just as inclination leads him; for
what he reads as a task will do him little good.
  Samuel Johnson 1709–84: James Boswell *Life of
  Johnson* (1791) 14 July 1763

7 Much have I travelled in the realms of gold,
And many goodly states and kingdoms seen.
  John Keats 1795–1821: 'On First Looking into
  Chapman's Homer' (1817)

8 Curiously enough, one cannot *read* a book: one can only
reread it. A good reader, a major reader, an active and
creative reader is a rereader.
  Vladimir Nabokov 1899–1977: *Lectures on Literature*
  (1980)

9 The bookful blockhead, ignorantly read,
With loads of learned lumber in his head.
  Alexander Pope 1688–1744: *An Essay on Criticism* (1711)

10 POLONIUS: What do you read, my lord?
HAMLET: Words, words, words.
  William Shakespeare 1564–1616: *Hamlet* (1601)

11 People say that life is the thing, but I prefer reading.
  Logan Pearsall Smith 1865–1946: *Afterthoughts* (1931)
  'Myself'

12 Reading is to the mind what exercise is to the body.
  Richard Steele 1672–1729: in *Tatler* 18 March 1710

Reality

1 It's as large as life, and twice as natural!
  Lewis Carroll 1832–98: *Through the Looking-Glass* (1872)

2 Reality goes bounding past the satirist like a cheetah
laughing as it lopes ahead of the greyhound.
  Claud Cockburn 1904–81: *Crossing the Line* (1958)

3   Human kind
Cannot bear very much reality.
  T. S. Eliot 1888–1965: *Four Quartets* 'Burnt Norton' (1936)

4 All theory, dear friend, is grey, but the golden tree of actual life springs ever green.

> **Johann Wolfgang von Goethe** 1749–1832: *Faust* pt. 1 (1808)

5 What is rational is actual and what is actual is rational.

> **G. W. F. Hegel**.1770–1831: *Grundlinien der Philosophie des Rechts* (1821)

6 The camera makes everyone a tourist in other people's reality, and eventually in one's own.

> **Susan Sontag** 1933– : in *New York Review of Books* 18 April 1974

7 They said, 'You have a blue guitar,
You do not play things as they are.'

The man replied, 'Things as they are
Are changed upon the blue guitar.'

> **Wallace Stevens** 1879–1955: 'The Man with the Blue Guitar' (1937)

8 The nineteenth century dislike of Realism is the rage of Caliban seeing his own face in the glass.

> **Oscar Wilde** 1854–1900: *The Picture of Dorian Gray* (1891)

9 BLANCHE: I don't want realism.
MITCH: Naw, I guess not.
BLANCHE: I'll tell you what I want. Magic!

> **Tennessee Williams** 1911–83: *A Streetcar Named Desire* (1947)

Religion

See also **The Bible**, **The Church**, **God**, **Prayer**

1 Render therefore unto Caesar the things which are Caesar's; and unto God the things that are God's.

> **Bible**: St Matthew

2 Faith is the substance of things hoped for, the evidence of
things not seen.
Bible: Hebrews

3 SAINT, *n*. A dead sinner revised and edited.
Ambrose Bierce 1842–c.1914: *The Devil's Dictionary*
(1911)

4 Men have lost their reason in nothing so much as their
religion, wherein stones and clouts make martyrs.
Sir Thomas Browne 1605–82: *Hydriotaphia* (Urn Burial,
1658)

5 They are for religion when in rags and contempt; but I am
for him when he walks in his golden slippers, in the
sunshine and with applause.
John Bunyan 1628–88: *The Pilgrim's Progress* (1678) Mr
By-Ends

6 One religion is as true as another.
Robert Burton 1577–1640: *Anatomy of Melancholy*
(1621–51)

7 Christians have burnt each other, quite persuaded
That all the Apostles would have done as they did.
Lord Byron 1788–1824: *Don Juan* (1819–24)

8 Putting moral virtues at the highest, and religion at the
lowest, religion must still be allowed to be a collateral
security, at least, to virtue; and every prudent man will
sooner trust to two securities than to one.
Lord Chesterfield 1694–1773: *Letters to his Son* (1774) 8
January 1750

9 Thou shalt have one God only; who
Would be at the expense of two?
Arthur Hugh Clough 1819–61: 'The Latest Decalogue'
(1862)

10 Wherever God erects a house of prayer,
The Devil always builds a chapel there;
And 'twill be found, upon examination,
The latter has the largest congregation.
Daniel Defoe 1660–1731: *The True-Born Englishman*
(1701)

11 Science without religion is lame, religion without science
is blind.
   Albert Einstein 1879–1955: *Science, Philosophy and
   Religion* (1941)

12 The various modes of worship, which prevailed in the
Roman world, were all considered by the people as equally
true; by the philosopher, as equally false; and by the
magistrate, as equally useful. And thus toleration
produced not only mutual indulgence, but even religious
concord.
   Edward Gibbon 1737–94: *Decline and Fall of the Roman
   Empire* (1776–88)

13 In vain with lavish kindness
The gifts of God are strown;
The heathen in his blindness
Bows down to wood and stone.
   Bishop Reginald Heber 1783–1826: 'From Greenland's
   icy mountains' (1821 hymn)

14 A verse may find him, who a sermon flies,
And turn delight into a sacrifice.
   George Herbert 1593–1633: 'The Church Porch' (1633)

15 In all ages of the world, priests have been enemies of
liberty.
   David Hume 1711–76: *Essays, Moral, Political, and
   Literary* (1875) 'Of the Parties of Great Britain' (1741–2)

16 'Twas only fear first in the world made gods.
   Ben Jonson c.1573–1637: *Sejanus* (1603)

17 Religion is the frozen thought of men out of which they
build temples.
   Jiddu Krishnamurti 1895–1986: in *Observer* 22 April
   1928

18 *Tantum religio potuit suadere malorum.*
So much wrong could religion induce.
   Lucretius c.94–55 BC: *De Rerum Natura*

19 Better authentic mammon than a bogus god.
   Louis MacNeice 1907–63: *Autumn Journal* (1939)

20 I count religion but a childish toy,
And hold there is no sin but ignorance.
　　Christopher Marlowe 1564–93: *The Jew of Malta* (c.1592)

21 Religion . . . is the opium of the people.
　　Karl Marx 1818–83: *A Contribution to the Critique of Hegel's Philosophy of Right* (1843–4)

22 Things have come to a pretty pass when religion is allowed to invade the sphere of private life.
　　Lord Melbourne 1779–1848: on hearing an evangelical sermon; G. W. E. Russell *Collections and Recollections* (1898)

23 If I am obliged to bring religion into after-dinner toasts (which indeed does not seem quite the thing) I shall drink . . . to Conscience first, and to the Pope afterwards.
　　Cardinal Newman 1801–90: *Letter Addressed to the Duke of Norfolk . . .* (1875)

24 It is convenient that there be gods, and, as it is convenient, let us believe that there are.
　　Ovid 43 BC–AD c.17: *Ars Amatoria*

25 My country is the world, and my religion is to do good.
　　Thomas Paine 1737–1809: *The Rights of Man* pt. 2 (1792)

26 Is that which is holy loved by the gods because it is holy, or is it holy because it is loved by the gods?
　　Plato 429–347 BC: *Euthyphro*

27 Religion to me has always been the wound, not the bandage.
　　Dennis Potter 1935–94: *Seeing the Blossom* (1994)

28 Religion may in most of its forms be defined as the belief that the gods are on the side of the Government.
　　Bertrand Russell 1872–1970: attributed

29 'Men of sense are really but of one religion.' . . . 'Pray, my lord, what religion is that which men of sense agree in?' 'Madam,' says the earl immediately, 'men of sense never tell it.'
　　1st Earl of Shaftesbury 1621–83: Bishop Gilbert Burnet *History of My Own Time* vol. 1 (1724)

30 Had I but served my God with half the zeal
I served my king, he would not in mine age

Have left me naked to mine enemies.
   William Shakespeare 1564–1616: *Henry VIII* (with John
   Fletcher, 1613)

31 The dust of creeds outworn.
   Percy Bysshe Shelley 1792–1822: *Prometheus Unbound*
   (1820)

32 We have just enough religion to make us hate, but not
enough to make us love one another.
   Jonathan Swift 1667–1745: *Thoughts on Various Subjects*
   (1711)

33 There is no expeditious road
To pack and label men for God,
And save them by the barrel-load.
Some may perchance, with strange surprise,
Have blundered into Paradise.
   Francis Thompson 1859–1907: 'A Judgement in Heaven'
   (1913)

34 Orthodoxy is my doxy; heterodoxy is another man's doxy.
   Bishop William Warburton 1698–1779: Joseph Priestley
   Memoirs (1807)

35 I went to America to convert the Indians; but oh, who shall
convert me?
   John Wesley 1703–91: diary, 24 January 1738

36 So many gods, so many creeds,
So many paths that wind and wind,
While just the art of being kind
Is all the sad world needs.
   Ella Wheeler Wilcox 1855–1919: 'The World's Need'

37 Scratch the Christian and you find the pagan—spoiled.
   Israel Zangwill 1864–1926: *Children of the Ghetto* (1892)

Revenge

1 Revenge is a kind of wild justice, which the more man's
nature runs to, the more ought law to weed it out.
   Francis Bacon 1561–1626: *Essays* (1625) 'Of Revenge'

2 Vengeance is mine; I will repay, saith the Lord.
   Bible: Romans

3 Sweet is revenge—especially to women.
   Lord Byron 1788–1824: *Don Juan* (1819–24)

4 It may be that vengeance is sweet, and that the gods
   forbade vengeance to men because they reserved for
   themselves so delicious and intoxicating a drink. But no
   one should drain the cup to the bottom. The dregs are
   often filthy-tasting.
   Winston Churchill 1874–1965: *The River War* (1899)

5 Heaven has no rage, like love to hatred turned,
   Nor Hell a fury, like a woman scorned.
   William Congreve 1670–1729: *The Mourning Bride* (1697)

6 The Germans . . . are going to be squeezed as a lemon is
   squeezed—until the pips squeak.
   Eric Geddes 1875–1937: speech at Cambridge, 10
   December 1918

7 Nobody ever forgets where he buried a hatchet.
   Frank McKinney ('Kin') Hubbard 1868–1930: *Abe
   Martin's Broadcast* (1930)

8 Get your retaliation in first.
   Carwyn James 1929–83: attributed, 1971

9 Men should be either treated generously or destroyed,
   because they take revenge for slight injuries—for heavy
   ones they cannot.
   Niccolò Machiavelli 1469–1527: *The Prince* (1513)

Revolution and Rebellion

1 Better to abolish serfdom from above than to wait till it
   begins to abolish itself from below.
   Tsar Alexander II 1818–81: speech in Moscow, 30 March
   1856

2 The most radical revolutionary will become a conservative on the day after the revolution.
Hannah Arendt 1906–75: in *New Yorker* 12 September 1970

3 Those who have served the cause of the revolution have ploughed the sea.
Simón Bolívar 1783–1830: attributed

4 Revolutions are celebrated when they are no longer dangerous.
Pierre Boulez 1925– : in *Guardian* 13 January 1989

5 Rebellion to tyrants is obedience to God.
John Bradshaw 1602–59: suppositious epitaph

6 Would it not be easier
In that case for the government
To dissolve the people
And elect another?
Bertolt Brecht 1898–1956: 'The Solution' (1953); on the 1953 uprising in East Germany

7 Kings will be tyrants from policy when subjects are rebels from principle.
Edmund Burke 1729–97: *Reflections on the Revolution in France* (1790)

8 All modern revolutions have ended in a reinforcement of the State.
Albert Camus 1913–60: *The Rebel* (1953)

9 While there is a lower class, I am in it; while there is a criminal element, I am of it; while there is a soul in prison, I am not free.
Eugene Victor Debs 1855–1926: speech at his trial for sedition in Cleveland, Ohio, 14 September 1918

10 All civilization has from time to time become a thin crust over a volcano of revolution.
Havelock Ellis 1859–1939: *Little Essays of Love and Virtue* (1922)

11 A desperate disease requires a dangerous remedy.
Guy Fawkes 1570–1606: 6 November 1605

12 How much the greatest event it is that ever happened in the world! and how much the best!
   Charles James Fox 1749–1806: on the fall of the Bastille; letter to R. Fitzpatrick, 30 July 1789

13 I will die like a true-blue rebel. Don't waste any time in mourning—organize.
   Joe Hill 1879–1915: farewell telegram prior to his death by firing squad; in *Salt Lake* (Utah) *Tribune* 19 November 1915

14 A little rebellion now and then is a good thing.
   Thomas Jefferson 1743–1826: letter to James Madison, 30 January 1787

15 A share in two revolutions is living to some purpose.
   Thomas Paine 1737–1809: E. Foner *Tom Paine and Revolutionary America* (1976)

16 *Après nous le déluge.*
   After us the deluge.
   Madame de Pompadour 1721–64: Mme du Hausset *Mémoires* (1824)

17 *J'ai vécu.*
   I survived.
   Abbé Emmanuel Joseph Sieyès 1748–1836: when asked what he had done during the French Revolution

18 I have seen the future; and it works.
   Lincoln Steffens 1866–1936: following a visit to the Soviet Union in 1919, in *Letters* (1938)

19 Bliss was it in that dawn to be alive,
   But to be young was very heaven!
   William Wordsworth 1770–1850: 'The French Revolution, as it Appeared to Enthusiasts' (1809); also *The Prelude* (1850)

Royalty

1 He is the fountain of honour.
   Francis Bacon 1561–1626: *An Essay of a King* (1642)

2 We must not let in daylight upon magic.
    Walter Bagehot 1826–77: *The English Constitution* (1867)

3 The Sovereign has, under a constitutional monarchy such
as ours, three rights—the right to be consulted, the right to
encourage, the right to warn.
    Walter Bagehot 1826–77: *The English Constitution* (1867)

4 It has been said, not truly, but with a possible
approximation to truth, that in 1802 every hereditary
monarch was insane.
    Walter Bagehot 1826–77: *The English Constitution* (1867)

5 To be Prince of Wales is not a position. It is a predicament.
    Alan Bennett 1934– : *The Madness of King George* (1995
film)

6 A subject and a sovereign are clean different things.
    Charles I 1600–49: speech on the scaffold, 30 January
1649

7 Titles are shadows, crowns are empty things,
The good of subjects is the end of kings.
    Daniel Defoe 1660–1731: *The True-Born Englishman*
(1701)

8 I'd like to be a queen in people's hearts but I don't see
myself being Queen of this country.
    Diana, Princess of Wales 1961–97: interview on
Panorama, BBC1 TV, 20 November 1995

9 Everyone likes flattery; and when you come to Royalty you
should lay it on with a trowel.
    Benjamin Disraeli 1804–81: G. W. E. Russell *Collections
and Recollections* (1898)

10 At long last I am able to say a few words of my own . . .
you must believe me when I tell you that I have found it
impossible to carry the heavy burden of responsibility and
to discharge my duties as King as I would wish to do
without the help and support of the woman I love.
    Edward VIII 1894–1972: radio broadcast following his
abdication, 11 December 1936

11 I know I have the body of a weak and feeble woman, but I have the heart and stomach of a king, and of a king of England too.
>**Elizabeth I** 1533–1603: speech to the troops at Tilbury on the approach of the Armada, 1588

12 It is a very curious thing that no matter where I go, in whatever country, the children always think I should be wearing a silver dress and a golden crown. They must all be bitterly disappointed. Maybe I should.
>**Elizabeth II** 1926– : remark on tour of China, 1985

13 We could not go anywhere without sending word ahead so that life might be put on parade for us.
>**Infanta Eulalia of Spain** 1864–1958: *Court Life from Within* (1915)

14 Soon there will be only five Kings left—the King of England, the King of Spades, the King of Clubs, the King of Hearts and the King of Diamonds.
>**King Farouk** 1920–65: comment in Cairo, 1948

15 *L'État c'est moi.*
I am the State.
>**Louis XIV** 1638–1715: before the Parlement de Paris, 13 April 1655; probably apocryphal

16 For seventeen years he did nothing at all but kill animals and stick in stamps.
>**Harold Nicolson** 1886–1968: of King George V; diary, 17 August 1949

17 Royalty is the gold filling in a mouthful of decay.
>**John Osborne** 1929– : 'They call it cricket' in T. Maschler (ed.) *Declaration* (1957)

18 The Right Divine of Kings to govern wrong.
>**Alexander Pope** 1688–1744: *The Dunciad* (1742)

19 Uneasy lies the head that wears a crown.
>**William Shakespeare** 1564–1616: *Henry IV, Part 2* (1597)

20 Not all the water in the rough rude sea
Can wash the balm from an anointed king.
>**William Shakespeare** 1564–1616: *Richard II* (1595)

21 Monarchy is only the string that ties the robber's bundle.
   Percy Bysshe Shelley 1792–1822: *A Philosophical View of Reform* (written 1819–20)

22 I will be good.
   Queen Victoria 1819–1901: on being shown a chart of the line of succession, 11 March 1830; Theodore Martin *The Prince Consort* (1875)

23 To walk five paces behind his far more important wife—that's so difficult for this poor man.
   Sarah, Duchess of York 1959– : on Prince Philip; in *Independent* 8 April 2000

··

Satisfaction and Discontent

··

1 A book of verses underneath the bough,
A jug of wine, a loaf of bread—and Thou
Beside me singing in the wilderness—
And wilderness were paradise enow.
   Edward Fitzgerald 1809–83: *The Rubáiyát of Omar Khayyám* (1879 ed.)

2 These are the days when men of all social disciplines and all political faiths seek the comfortable and the accepted . . . in minor modification of the scriptural parable, the bland lead the bland.
   J. K. Galbraith 1908– : *The Affluent Society* (1958)

3 He who thinks to realize when he is older the hopes and desires of youth is always deceiving himself, for every decade of a man's life possesses its own kind of happiness, its own hopes and prospects.
   Johann Wolfgang von Goethe 1749–1832: *Elective Affinities* (1809)

4   It is a flaw
In happiness, to see beyond our bourn—
It forces us in summer skies to mourn:
It spoils the singing of the nightingale.
   John Keats 1795–1821: 'To J. H. Reynolds, Esq.' (written 1818)

5 If one cannot catch the bird of paradise, better take a wet hen.
Nikita Khrushchev 1894–1971: in *Time* 6 January 1958

6 He is well paid that is well satisfied.
William Shakespeare 1564–1616: *The Merchant of Venice* (1596–8)

7 'Tis just like a summer birdcage in a garden; the birds that are without despair to get in, and the birds that are within despair, and are in a consumption, for fear they shall never get out.
John Webster *c.*1580–*c.*1625: *The White Devil* (1612)

8 He spoke with a certain what-is-it in his voice, and I could see that, if not actually disgruntled, he was far from being gruntled.
P. G. Wodehouse 1881–1975: *The Code of the Woosters* (1938)

9 Plain living and high thinking are no more:
The homely beauty of the good old cause
Is gone.
William Wordsworth 1770–1850: 'O friend! I know not which way I must look' (1807)

Science

See also **Inventions and Discoveries, Life Sciences, Technology**

1 When I find myself in the company of scientists, I feel like a shabby curate who has strayed by mistake into a drawing room full of dukes.
W. H. Auden 1907–73: *The Dyer's Hand* (1963)

2 Anybody who is not shocked by this subject has failed to understand it.
Niels Bohr 1885–1962: of quantum mechanics; attributed

3 Basic research is what I am doing when I don't know what I am doing.
    Werner von Braun 1912–77: R. L. Weber *A Random Walk in Science* (1973)

4 The aim of science is not to open the door to infinite wisdom, but to set a limit to infinite error.
    Bertolt Brecht 1898–1956: *Life of Galileo* (1939)

5 The essence of science: ask an impertinent question, and you are on the way to a pertinent answer.
    Jacob Bronowski 1908–74: *The Ascent of Man* (1973)

6 There was a young lady named Bright,
Whose speed was far faster than light;
She set out one day
In a relative way
And returned on the previous night.
    Arthur Buller 1874–1944: 'Relativity' (1923)

7 If an elderly but distinguished scientist says that something is possible he is almost certainly right, but if he says that it is impossible he is very probably wrong.
    Arthur C. Clarke 1917– : in *New Yorker* 9 August 1969

8 In science the credit goes to the man who convinces the world, not to the man to whom the idea first occurs.
    Francis Darwin 1848–1925: in *Eugenics Review* April 1914

9 It is more important to have beauty in one's equations than to have them fit experiment.
    Paul Dirac 1902–84: in *Scientific American* May 1963

10 I ask you to look both ways. For the road to a knowledge of the stars leads through the atom; and important knowledge of the atom has been reached through the stars.
    Arthur Eddington 1882–1944: *Stars and Atoms* (1928)

11 Science without religion is lame, religion without science is blind.
    Albert Einstein 1879–1955: *Science, Philosophy and Religion* (1941)

12 The grand aim of all science [is] to cover the greatest
number of empirical facts by logical deduction from the
smallest possible number of hypotheses or axioms.
   Albert Einstein 1879–1955: Lincoln Barnett *The Universe
   and Dr Einstein* (1950 ed.)

13 We do not know why they [elementary particles] have the
masses they do; we do not know why they transform into
another the way they do; we do not know anything! The
one concept that stands like the Rock of Gibraltar in our
sea of confusion is the Pauli [exclusion] principle.
   George Gamow 1904–68: in *Scientific American* July
   1959

14 The great tragedy of Science—the slaying of a beautiful
hypothesis by an ugly fact.
   T. H. Huxley 1825–95: *Collected Essays* (1893–4)
   'Biogenesis and Abiogenesis'

15 Science is nothing but trained and organized common
sense, differing from the latter only as a veteran may
differ from a raw recruit: and its methods differ from
those of common sense only as far as the guardsman's cut
and thrust differ from the manner in which a savage
wields his club.
   T. H. Huxley 1825–95: *Collected Essays* (1893–4) 'The
   Method of Zadig'

16 If we assume that the last breath of, say, Julius Caesar has
by now become thoroughly scattered through the
atmosphere, then the chances are that each of us inhales
one molecule of it with every breath we take.
   James Jeans 1877–1946: now usually quoted as the
   'dying breath of Socrates'; *An Introduction to the Kinetic
   Theory of Gases* (1940)

17 It is a good morning exercise for a research scientist to
discard a pet hypothesis every day before breakfast.
   Konrad Lorenz 1903–89: *On Aggression* (1966)

18 It may be so, there is no arguing against facts and
experiments.
   Isaac Newton 1642–1727: when told of an experiment
   which appeared to destroy his theory, as reported by

John Conduit, 1726; D. Brewster *Memoirs of Sir Isaac Newton* (1855)

19 The physicists have known sin; and this is a knowledge which they cannot lose.
J. Robert Oppenheimer 1904–67: lecture at Massachusetts Institute of Technology, 25 November 1947

20 Where observation is concerned, chance favours only the prepared mind.
Louis Pasteur 1822–95: address, 7 December 1854

21 A new scientific truth does not triumph by convincing its opponents and making them see the light, but rather because its opponents eventually die, and a new generation grows up that is familiar with it.
Max Planck 1858–1947: *A Scientific Autobiography* (1949)

22 Science is built up of facts, as a house is built of stones; but an accumulation of facts is no more a science than a heap of stones is a house.
Henri Poincaré 1854–1912: *Science and Hypothesis* (1905)

23 Nature, and Nature's laws lay hid in night.
God said, *Let Newton be!* and all was light.
Alexander Pope 1688–1744: 'Epitaph: Intended for Sir Isaac Newton' (1730)

24 Aristotle maintained that women have fewer teeth than men; although he was twice married, it never occurred to him to verify this statement by examining his wives' mouths.
Bertrand Russell 1872–1970: *Impact of Science on Society* (1952)

25 All science is either physics or stamp collecting.
Ernest Rutherford 1871–1937: J. B. Birks *Rutherford at Manchester* (1962)

26 We haven't got the money, so we've got to think!
Ernest Rutherford 1871–1937: in *Bulletin of the Institute of Physics* (1962), as recalled by R. V. Jones

27 It did not last: the Devil howling 'Ho!
Let Einstein be!' restored the status quo.
J. C. Squire 1884–1958: 'In continuation of Pope on Newton' (1926)

28 It is much easier to make measurements than to know exactly what you are measuring.
J. W. N. Sullivan 1886–1937: comment, 1928; R. L. Weber *More Random Walks in Science* (1982)

29 He had been eight years upon a project for extracting sunbeams out of cucumbers, which were to be put into vials hermetically sealed, and let out to warm the air in raw inclement summers.
Jonathan Swift 1667–1745: *Gulliver's Travels* (1726)

30 Neutrinos, they are very small
They have no charge and have no mass
And do not interact at all.
John Updike 1932– : 'Cosmic Gall' (1964)

31 Science means simply the aggregate of all the recipes that are always successful. The rest is literature.
Paul Valéry 1871–1945: *Moralités* (1932)

32 The outcome of any serious research can only be to make two questions grow where one question grew before.
Thorstein Veblen 1857–1929: *University of California Chronicle* (1908)

33 *Felix qui potuit rerum cognoscere causas.*
Lucky is he who has been able to understand the causes of things.
Virgil 70–19 BC: *Georgics*

Scotland and the Scots

1 There are few more impressive sights in the world than a Scotsman on the make.
J. M. Barrie 1860–1937: *What Every Woman Knows* (1908)

2 Scotland, land of the omnipotent No.
Alan Bold 1943– : 'A Memory of Death' (1969)

3 My heart's in the Highlands, my heart is not here;
My heart's in the Highlands a-chasing the deer.
   Robert Burns 1759–96: 'My Heart's in the Highlands'
   (1790)

4 Scots, wha hae wi' Wallace bled,
Scots, wham Bruce has aften led,
Welcome to your gory bed,—
Or to victorie.
   Robert Burns 1759–96: 'Robert Bruce's March to
   Bannockburn' (1799)

5 A land of meanness, sophistry, and mist.
   Lord Byron 1788–1824: 'The Curse of Minerva' (1812)

6 From the lone shieling of the misty island
Mountains divide us, and the waste of seas—
Yet still the blood is strong, the heart is Highland,
And we in dreams behold the Hebrides!
   John Galt 1779–1839: 'Canadian Boat Song', attributed

7 It came with a lass, and it will pass with a lass.
   James V 1512–42: of the crown of Scotland, on learning
   of the birth of Mary Queen of Scots, December 1542;
   Robert Lindsay of Pitscottie (c.1500–65) *History of
   Scotland* (1728)

8 The noblest prospect which a Scotchman ever sees, is the
high road that leads him to England!
   Samuel Johnson 1709–84: James Boswell *Life of
   Johnson* (1791) 6 July 1763

9 Who owns this landscape?
The millionaire who bought it or
the poacher staggering downhill in the early morning
with a deer on his back?
   Norman McCaig 1910–96: 'A Man in Assynt' (1969)

10 Now there's ane end of ane old song.
   James Ogilvy, 1st Earl of Seafield 1664–1730: as he
   signed the engrossed exemplification of the Act of Union,
   1706, in *The Lockhart Papers* (1817)

11 O Caledonia! stern and wild,
Meet nurse for a poetic child!
   Sir Walter Scott 1771–1832: *The Lay of the Last Minstrel*
   (1805)

12 Stands Scotland where it did?
   William Shakespeare 1564–1616: *Macbeth* (1606)

13 It's nae good blamin' it oan the English fir colonising us.
Ah don't hate the English. They're just wankers. We can't
even pick a decent vibrant, healthy culture to be colonised
by.
   Irvine Welsh 1957– : *Trainspotting* (1994)

14 O flower of Scotland, when will we see your like again,
that fought and died for your bit hill and glen
and stood against him, proud Edward's army,
and sent him homeward tae think again.
   Roy Williamson 1936–90: 'O Flower of Scotland' (1968)

The Sea

1 A willing foe and sea room.
   Anonymous: naval toast in the time of Nelson

2 They that go down to the sea in ships: and occupy their
business in great waters.
   Bible: Psalm 107

3 Be pleased to receive into thy Almighty and most gracious
protection the persons of us thy servants, and the Fleet in
which we serve.
   Book of Common Prayer 1662: *Forms of Prayer to be
   Used at Sea*

4 Roll on, thou deep and dark blue Ocean—roll!
Ten thousand fleets sweep over thee in vain;
Man marks the earth with ruin—his control
Stops with the shore.
   Lord Byron 1788–1824: *Childe Harold's Pilgrimage*
   (1812–18)

5 Don't talk to me about naval tradition. It's nothing but
rum, sodomy, and the lash.
   Winston Churchill 1874–1965: P. Gretton *Former Naval
   Person* (1968)

6 Water, water, everywhere,
And all the boards did shrink;
Water, water, everywhere,
Nor any drop to drink.
   Samuel Taylor Coleridge 1772–1834: 'The Rime of the
   Ancient Mariner' (1798)

7 No man will be a sailor who has contrivance enough to get
himself into a jail; for being in a ship is being in a jail,
with the chance of being drowned . . . A man in a jail has
more room, better food, and commonly better company.
   Samuel Johnson 1709–84: James Boswell *Life of
   Johnson* (1791) 16 March 1759

8 It is an interesting biological fact that all of us have in our
veins the exact same percentage of salt in our blood that
exists in the ocean, and therefore, we have salt in our
blood, in our sweat, in our tears. We are tied to the ocean.
And when we go back to the sea—whether it is to sail or to
watch it—we are going back from whence we came.
   John F. Kennedy 1917–63: speech, Newport, Rhode
   Island, 14 September 1962

9 If blood be the price of admiralty,
Lord God, we ha' paid in full!
   Rudyard Kipling 1865–1936: 'The Song of the Dead'
   (1896)

10 I must go down to the sea again, to the lonely sea and the
sky,
And all I ask is a tall ship and a star to steer her by.
   John Masefield 1878–1967: 'Sea Fever' (misprinted 'I
   must down to the seas' in the 1902 original)

11 The sea hates a coward!
   Eugene O'Neill 1888–1953: *Mourning becomes Electra*
   (1931)

12 The sea has such extraordinary moods that sometimes you feel this is the only sort of life—and 10 minutes later you're praying for death.

    Prince Philip, Duke of Edinburgh 1921– : in *Independent* 31 December 1998

13 Full fathom five thy father lies;
Of his bones are coral made:
Those are pearls that were his eyes:
Nothing of him that doth fade,
But doth suffer a sea-change
Into something rich and strange.

    William Shakespeare 1564–1616: *The Tempest* (1611)

14 Rocked in the cradle of the deep.

    Emma Hart Willard 1787–1870: title of song (1840), inspired by a prospect of the Bristol Channel

The Seasons

1 Sumer is icumen in,
Lhude sing cuccu!
Groweth sed, and bloweth med,
And springeth the wude nu.

    Anonymous: 'Cuckoo Song' (*c*.1250)

2 Coldly, sadly descends
The autumn evening. The Field
Strewn with its dank yellow drifts
Of withered leaves, and the elms,
Fade into dimness apace.

    Matthew Arnold 1822–88: 'Rugby Chapel, November 1857' (1867)

3 Early autumn—
rice field, ocean,
one green.

    Matsuo Basho 1644–94: translated by Lucien Stryk

4 In fact, it is about five o'clock in an evening that the first hour of spring strikes—autumn arrives in the early morning, but spring at the close of a winter day.

    Elizabeth Bowen 1899–1973: *Death of the Heart* (1938)

5 The English winter—ending in July,
  To recommence in August.
     Lord Byron 1788–1824: *Don Juan* (1819–24)

6 April is the cruellest month, breeding
  Lilacs out of the dead land.
     T. S. Eliot 1888–1965: *The Waste Land* (1922)

7 June is bustin' out all over.
     Oscar Hammerstein II 1895–1960: title of song (1945)

8 Summer time an' the livin' is easy,
  Fish are jumpin' an' the cotton is high.
     Du Bose Heyward 1885–1940 and **Ira Gershwin**
     1896–1983: 'Summertime' (1935 song)

9 No shade, no shine, no butterflies, no bees,
  No fruits, no flowers, no leaves, no birds,—
  November!
     Thomas Hood 1799–1845: 'No!' (1844)

10 Loveliest of trees, the cherry now
   Is hung with bloom along the bough,
   And stands about the woodland ride
   Wearing white for Eastertide.
      A. E. Housman 1859–1936: *A Shropshire Lad* (1896)

11 Season of mists and mellow fruitfulness,
   Close bosom-friend of the maturing sun;
   Conspiring with him how to load and bless
   With fruit the vines that round the thatch-eaves run.
      John Keats 1795–1821: 'To Autumn' (1820)

12 The autumn always gets me badly, as it breaks into
   colours. I want to get south, where there is no autumn,
   where the cold doesn't crouch over one like a snow-leopard
   waiting to pounce. The heart of the North is dead, and the
   fingers of cold are corpse fingers.
      D. H. Lawrence 1885–1930: letter to J. Middleton Murry,
      3 October 1924

13 What of October, that ambiguous month, the month of
   tension, the unendurable month?
      Doris Lessing 1919– : *Martha Quest* (1952)

14 Winter is icumen in,
   Lhude sing Goddamm,

Raineth drop and staineth slop,
And how the wind doth ramm!
    Ezra Pound 1885–1972: 'Ancient Music' (1917)

15 In the bleak mid-winter
Frosty wind made moan,
Earth stood hard as iron,
Water like a stone.
    Christina Rossetti 1830–94: 'Mid-Winter' (1875)

16 When icicles hang by the wall,
And Dick the shepherd blows his nail,
And Tom bears logs into the hall,
And milk comes frozen home in pail.
    William Shakespeare 1564–1616: *Love's Labour's Lost*
(1595)

17 O wild West Wind, thou breath of Autumn's being,
Thou, from whose unseen presence the leaves dead
Are driven, like ghosts from an enchanter fleeing.
    Percy Bysshe Shelley 1792–1822: 'Ode to the West
Wind' (1819)

18 In winter I get up at night
And dress by yellow candle-light.
In summer, quite the other way,—
I have to go to bed by day.
    Robert Louis Stevenson 1850–94: 'Bed in Summer'
(1885)

19 The way to ensure summer in England is to have it framed
and glazed in a comfortable room.
    Horace Walpole 1717–97: letter to Revd William Cole, 28
May 1774

Secrets

1 I shall be but a short time tonight. I have seldom spoken
with greater regret, for my lips are not yet unsealed. Were
these troubles over I would make a case, and I guarantee

that not a man would go into the lobby against us.
Stanley Baldwin 1867–1947: speech, House of Commons,
10 December 1935 (usually quoted 'My lips are sealed')

2 When thou doest alms, let not thy left hand know what thy
right hand doeth.
Bible: St Matthew

3 In the culture I grew up in you did your work and you did
not put your arm around it to stop other people from
looking—you took the earliest possible opportunity to
make knowledge available.
James Black 1924– : on modern medical research; in
Daily Telegraph 11 December 1995

4 Nothing attracts me like a closed door. I cannot let my
camera rest until I have pried it open.
Margaret Bourke-White 1906–71: *Portrait of Myself*
(1964)

5 The truth is out there.
Chris Carter 1957– : catchphrase; *The X Files* (American
television series, 1993–)

6 The small man said to the other: 'Where does a wise man
hide a pebble?' And the tall man answered in a low voice:
'On the beach.'
G. K. Chesterton 1874–1936: *The Innocence of Father
Brown* (1911)

7 I know that's a secret, for it's whispered every where.
William Congreve 1670–1729: *Love for Love* (1695)

8 For secrets are edged tools,
And must be kept from children and from fools.
John Dryden 1631–1700: *Sir Martin Mar-All* (1667)

9 I would not open windows into men's souls.
Elizabeth I 1533–1603: oral tradition, the words possibly
originating in a letter drafted by Bacon

10 We dance round in a ring and suppose,
But the Secret sits in the middle and knows.
Robert Frost 1874–1963: 'The Secret Sits' (1942)

11 Once the toothpaste is out of the tube, it is awfully hard to get it back in.

> **H. R. Haldeman** 1929– : comment on the Watergate affair, 8 April 1973

12 Love and a cough cannot be hid.

> **George Herbert** 1593–1633: *Outlandish Proverbs* (1640)

13 It is public scandal that constitutes offence, and to sin in secret is not to sin at all.

> **Molière** 1622–73: *Le Tartuffe* (1669)

....

The Self
....

1 The image of myself which I try to create in my own mind in order that I may love myself is very different from the image which I try to create in the minds of others in order that they may love me.

> **W. H. Auden** 1907–73: *The Dyer's Hand* (1963)

2 Some thirty inches from my nose
The frontier of my Person goes,
And all the untilled air between
Is private *pagus* or demesne.

> **W. H. Auden** 1907–73: 'Prologue: the Birth of Architecture' (1966)

3 Through the Thou a person becomes I.

> **Martin Buber** 1878–1965: *Ich und Du* (1923)

4 'You' your joys and your sorrows, your memories and ambitions, your sense of personal identity and free will, are in fact no more than the behaviour of a vast assembly of nerve cells and their associated molecules.

> **Francis Crick** 1916– : *The Astonishing Hypothesis: The Scientific Search for the Soul* (1994)

5 I am the master of my fate:
I am the captain of my soul.

> **W. E. Henley** 1849–1903: 'Invictus. In Memoriam R.T.H.B.' (1888)

6 If I am not for myself who is for me; and being for my own
self what am I?
Hillel 'The Elder' *c.*60 BC–AD *c.*9: *Pirqe Aboth*

7 It is not contrary to reason to prefer the destruction of the
whole world to the scratching of my finger.
David Hume 1711–76: *A Treatise upon Human Nature*
(1739)

8 I am not a number, I am a free man!
Patrick McGoohan 1928– et al.: Number Six, in *The
Prisoner* (TV series 1967–68)

9 The self is hateful.
Blaise Pascal 1623–62: *Pensées* (1670)

10 Thus God and nature linked the gen'ral frame,
And bade self-love and social be the same.
Alexander Pope 1688–1744: *An Essay on Man* Epistle 3
(1733)

11 Personal isn't the same as important.
Terry Pratchett 1948– : *Men at Arms* (1993)

12 Who is it that can tell me who I am?
William Shakespeare 1564–1616: *King Lear* (1605–6)

13 It is easy—terribly easy—to shake a man's faith in himself.
To take advantage of that to break a man's spirit is devil's
work.
George Bernard Shaw 1856–1950: *Candida* (1898)

14 Rose is a rose is a rose is a rose, is a rose.
Gertrude Stein 1874–1946: *Sacred Emily* (1913)

15 If a man does not keep pace with his companions, perhaps
it is because he hears a different drummer. Let him step to
the music which he hears, however measured or far away.
Henry David Thoreau 1817–62: *Walden* (1854)

16 Do I contradict myself?
Very well then I contradict myself,
(I am large, I contain multitudes.)
Walt Whitman 1819–92: 'Song of Myself' (written 1855)

Self-Knowledge

1 Know thyself.
   Anonymous: inscribed on the temple of Apollo at
   Delphi; Plato ascribes the saying to the Seven Wise Men

2 The tragedy of a man who has found himself out.
   J. M. Barrie 1860–1937: *What Every Woman Knows* (1908)

3 Why beholdest thou the mote that is in thy brother's eye,
   but considerest not the beam that is in thine own eye?
   Bible: St Matthew

4 O wad some Pow'r the giftie gie us
   To see oursels as others see us!
   It wad frae mony a blunder free us,
      And foolish notion.
   Robert Burns 1759–96: 'To a Louse' (1786)

5 How little do we know that which we are!
   How less what we may be!
   Lord Byron 1788–1824: *Don Juan* (1819–24)

6 I do not know whether I was then a man dreaming I was a
   butterfly, or whether I am now a butterfly dreaming I am a
   man.
   Chuang-tzu (or Zhuangzi) *c.*369–286 BC: *Chuang Tzu*
   (1889) tr. H. A. Giles

7 But I do nothing upon my self, and yet I am mine own
   Executioner.
   John Donne 1572–1631: *Devotions upon Emergent
   Occasions* (1624)

8 I do not know myself, and God forbid that I should.
   Johann Wolfgang von Goethe 1749–1832: J. P.
   Eckermann *Gespräche mit Goethe* (1836–48) 10 April 1829

9 All our knowledge is, ourselves to know.
   Alexander Pope 1688–1744: *An Essay on Man* Epistle 4
   (1734)

10 This above all: to thine own self be true,
   And it must follow, as the night the day,
   Thou canst not then be false to any man.
   William Shakespeare 1564–1616: *Hamlet* (1601)

11 There are few things more painful than to recognise one's own faults in others.
   John Wells 1936– : in *Observer* 23 May 1982

....

Sex
....

See also **Love**, **Marriage**

1 That [sex] was the most fun I ever had without laughing.
   Woody Allen 1935– : *Annie Hall* (1977 film, with Marshall Brickman)

2 Don't knock masturbation. It's sex with someone I love.
   Woody Allen 1935– : *Annie Hall* (1977 film, with Marshall Brickman)

3 On bisexuality: It immediately doubles your chances for a date on Saturday night.
   Woody Allen 1935– : in *New York Times* 1 December 1975

4 Give me chastity and continency—but not yet!
   St Augustine of Hippo AD 354–430: *Confessions* (AD 397–8)

5 This trivial and vulgar way of coition; it is the foolishest act a wise man commits in all his life, nor is there any thing that will more deject his cooled imagination, when he shall consider what an odd and unworthy piece of folly he hath committed.
   Sir Thomas Browne 1605–82: *Religio Medici* (1643)

6 It doesn't matter what you do in the bedroom as long as you don't do it in the street and frighten the horses.
   Mrs Patrick Campbell 1865–1940: D. Fielding *Duchess of Jermyn Street* (1964)

7 The pleasure is momentary, the position ridiculous, and the expense damnable.
   Lord Chesterfield 1694–1773: of sex; attributed

8 I have never yet seen anyone whose desire to build up his moral power was as strong as sexual desire.
   Confucius 551–479 BC: *Analects*

9 Licence my roving hands, and let them go,
Behind, before, above, between, below.
O my America, my new found land,
My kingdom, safeliest when with one man manned.
   John Donne 1572–1631: 'To His Mistress Going to Bed'
   (c.1595)

10 Seduction is often difficult to distinguish from rape. In
seduction, the rapist bothers to buy a bottle of wine.
   Andrea Dworkin 1946– : speech to women at *Harper &
   Row*, 1976; *Letters from a War Zone* (1988)

11 I'll have what she's having.
   Nora Ephron 1941– : said by woman to waiter, seeing
   Sally acting an orgasm; *When Harry Met Sally* (1989 film)

12 Personally I know nothing about sex because I've always
been married.
   Zsa Zsa Gabor 1919– : in *Observer* 16 August 1987

13 But did thee feel the earth move?
   Ernest Hemingway 1899–1961: *For Whom the Bell Tolls*
   (1940)

14 When I hear his steps outside my door I lie down on my
bed, close my eyes, open my legs, and think of England.
   Lady Hillingdon 1857–1940: diary, 1912 (original
   untraced, perhaps apocryphal); J. Gathorne-Hardy *The
   Rise and Fall of the British Nanny* (1972)

15 I'll come no more behind your scenes, David; for the silk
stockings and white bosoms of your actresses excite my
amorous propensities.
   Samuel Johnson 1709–84: James Boswell *Life of
   Johnson* (1791) 1750

16 Sex and taxes are in many ways the same. Tax does to
cash what males do to genes. It dispenses assets among the
population as a whole. Sex, not death, is the great leveller.
   Steve Jones 1944– : speech to the Royal Society; in
   Independent 25 January 1997

17 The only unnatural sex act is that which you cannot
perform.
   Alfred Kinsey 1894–1956: attributed; in *Time* 21 January
   1966

18 'Tisn't beauty, so to speak, nor good talk necessarily. It's just It. Some women'll stay in a man's memory if they once walked down a street.
  Rudyard Kipling 1865–1936: *Traffics and Discoveries* (1904)

19 Sexual intercourse began
In nineteen sixty-three
(Which was rather late for me)—
Between the end of the *Chatterley* ban
And the Beatles' first LP.
  Philip Larkin 1922–85: 'Annus Mirabilis' (1974)

20 Pornography is the attempt to insult sex, to do dirt on it.
  D. H. Lawrence 1885–1930: *Phoenix* (1936) 'Pornography and Obscenity'

21 The Duke returned from the wars today and did pleasure me in his top-boots.
  Sarah, Duchess of Marlborough 1660–1744: attributed in various forms. See I. Butler *Rule of Three* (1967)

22 The orgasm has replaced the Cross as the focus of longing and the image of fulfilment.
  Malcolm Muggeridge 1903–90: *Tread Softly* (1966)

23 Not tonight, Josephine.
  Napoleon I 1769–1821: attributed, but probably apocryphal

24 Delight of lust is gross and brief
And weariness treads on desire.
  Petronius d. AD 65: A. Baehrens *Poetae Latini Minores* (1882), tr. H. Waddell

25 Love is two minutes fifty-two seconds of squishing noises.
  Johnny Rotten 1957– : in *Daily Mirror*, 1983

26 Die: die for adultery! No:
The wren goes to't, and the small gilded fly
Does lecher in my sight.
Let copulation thrive.
  William Shakespeare 1564–1616: *King Lear* (1605–6)

27 Is it not strange that desire should so many years outlive performance?
> **William Shakespeare** 1564–1616: *Henry IV, Part 2* (1597)

28 Someone asked Sophocles, 'How is your sex-life now? Are you still able to have a woman?' He replied, 'Hush, man; most gladly indeed am I rid of it all, as though I had escaped from a mad and savage master.'
> **Sophocles** *c.*496–406 BC: Plato *Republic*

29 Is that a gun in your pocket, or are you just glad to see me?
> **Mae West** 1892–1980: Joseph Weintraub *Peel Me a Grape* (1975); usually quoted as 'Is that a pistol in your pocket . . . '

Shakespeare

See also **Acting and the Theatre**

1 Others abide our question. Thou art free.
We ask and ask: Thou smilest and art still,
Out-topping knowledge.
> **Matthew Arnold** 1822–88: 'Shakespeare' (1849)

2 Was there ever such stuff as great part of Shakespeare? Only one must not say so!
> **George III** 1738–1820: Fanny Burney's diary, 19 December 1785

3 His mind and hand went together: And what he thought, he uttered with that easiness, that we have scarce received from him a blot.
> **John Heming** 1556–1630 and **Henry Condell** d. 1627: First Folio Shakespeare (1623) preface

4 Shakespeare is so tiring. You never get a chance to sit down unless you're a king.
> **Josephine Hull** ?1886–1957: in *Time* 16 November 1953

5 Thou hadst small Latin, and less Greek.
> **Ben Jonson** *c.*1573–1637: 'To the Memory of . . . Shakespeare' (1623)

6 He was not of an age, but for all time!
    Ben Jonson c.1573–1637: 'To the Memory of . . .
    Shakespeare' (1623)

7 When I read Shakespeare I am struck with wonder
    That such trivial people should muse and thunder
    In such lovely language.
    D. H. Lawrence 1885–1930: 'When I Read Shakespeare'
    (1929)

8 With the single exception of Homer, there is no eminent
    writer, not even Sir Walter Scott, whom I can despise so
    entirely as I despise Shakespeare when I measure my mind
    against his.
    George Bernard Shaw 1856–1950: in *Saturday Review*
    26 September 1896

9 He had read Shakespeare and found him weak in
    chemistry.
    H. G. Wells 1866–1946: 'Lord of the Dynamos' (1927)

Sickness

See also **Medicine**

1 I know the colour rose, and it is lovely,
    But not when it ripens in a tumour;
    And healing greens, leaves and grass, so springlike,
    In limbs that fester are not springlike.
    Dannie Abse 1923– : 'Pathology of Colours' (1968)

2 A man's illness is his private territory and, no matter how
    much he loves you and how close you are, you stay an
    outsider. You are healthy.
    Lauren Bacall 1924– : *By Myself* (1978)

3 She is not sailing into the dark: the voyage is over, and
    under the dark escort of Alzheimer's she has arrived
    somewhere.
    John Bayley 1925– : *Iris: A memoir of Iris Murdoch*
    (1998)

4 If a lot of cures are suggested for a disease, it means that
the disease is incurable.
>   **Anton Chekhov** 1860–1904: *The Cherry Orchard* (1904),
>   tr. E. Fen

5 and I swear sometimes
when I put my head to his chest
I can hear the virus humming
like a refrigerator.
>   **Mark Doty** 1953– : 'Atlantis' (1996); of Aids

6 Venerable Mother Toothache
Climb down from the white battlements,
Stop twisting in your yellow fingers
The fourfold rope of nerves.
>   **John Heath-Stubbs** 1918– : 'A Charm Against the
>   Toothache' (1954)

7 Human nature seldom walks up to the word 'cancer'.
>   **Rudyard Kipling** 1865–1936: *Debits and Credits* (1926)

8 Illness is not something a person *has*; it's another way of
being.
>   **Jonathan Miller** 1934– : *The Body in Question* (1978)

9 Cured yesterday of my disease,
I died last night of my physician.
>   **Matthew Prior** 1664–1721: 'The Remedy Worse than the
>   Disease' (1727)

10 I now begin the journey that will lead me into the sunset
of my life.
>   **Ronald Reagan** 1911– : statement to the American
>   people revealing that he had Alzheimer's disease, 1994

11   Diseases desperate grown,
By desperate appliances are relieved
Or not at all.
>   **William Shakespeare** 1564–1616: *Hamlet* (1601)

12 The biggest disease today is not leprosy or tuberculosis,
but rather the feeling of being unwanted, uncared for and
deserted by everybody.
>   **Mother Teresa** 1910–97: in *Observer* 3 October 1971

Silence

1 Silence is the virtue of fools.
    Francis Bacon 1561–1626: *De Dignitate et Augmentis Scientiarum* (1623)

2 If we had a keen vision and feeling of all ordinary human life, it would be like hearing the grass grow and the squirrel's heart beat, and we should die of that roar which lies on the other side of silence.
    George Eliot 1819–80: *Middlemarch* (1871–2)

3 Elected Silence, sing to me
And beat upon my whorlèd ear.
    Gerard Manley Hopkins 1844–89: 'The Habit of Perfection' (written 1866)

4 Thou still unravished bride of quietness,
Thou foster-child of silence and slow time.
    John Keats 1795–1821: 'Ode on a Grecian Urn' (1820)

5 People talking without speaking
People hearing without listening . . .
'Fools,' said I, 'You do not know
Silence like a cancer grows.'
    Paul Simon 1942– : 'Sound of Silence' (1964 song)

Singing

See also **Music**

1 Today if something is not worth saying, people sing it.
    Pierre-Augustin Caron de Beaumarchais 1732–99: *The Barber of Seville* (1775)

2 The exercise of singing is delightful to Nature, and good to preserve the health of man. It doth strengthen all parts of the breast, and doth open the pipes.
    William Byrd 1543–1623: *Psalms, Sonnets and Songs* (1588)

3 Swans sing before they die: 'twere no bad thing
Should certain persons die before they sing.
> **Samuel Taylor Coleridge** 1772–1834: 'On a Volunteer
> Singer' (1834)

4 Every tone [of the songs of the slaves] was a testimony
against slavery, and a prayer to God for deliverance from
chains.
> **Frederick Douglass** c.1818–95: *Narrative of the Life of
> Frederick Douglass* (1845)

5 In writing songs I've learned as much from Cézanne as I
have from Woody Guthrie.
> **Bob Dylan** 1941– : Clinton Heylin *Dylan: Behind the
> Shades* (1991)

6 If a man were permitted to make all the ballads, he need
not care who should make the laws of a nation.
> **Andrew Fletcher of Saltoun** 1655–1716: 'Conversation
> concerning a Right Regulation of Government . . . '
> (1704)

7 Opera is when a guy gets stabbed in the back and, instead
of bleeding, he sings.
> **Ed Gardner** 1901–63: in *Duffy's Tavern* (US radio
> programme, 1940s)

8 It's the only song I've ever written where I get goose
bumps every time I play it.
> **Elton John** 1947– : of 'Candle in the Wind'; in *Daily
> Telegraph* 9 September 1997

9 You think that's noise—you ain't heard nuttin' yet!
> **Al Jolson** 1886–1950: in a café, competing with the din
> from a neighbouring building site, 1906

10 Sing 'em muck! It's all they can understand!
> **Dame Nellie Melba** 1861–1931: advice to Dame Clara
> Butt, prior to her departure for Australia; W. H. Ponder
> *Clara Butt* (1928)

11 An unalterable and unquestioned law of the musical world
required that the German text of French operas sung by
Swedish artists should be translated into Italian for the
clearer understanding of English-speaking audiences.
> **Edith Wharton** 1862–1937: *The Age of Innocence* (1920)

The Skies

1 Beautiful! Beautiful! Magnificent desolation.
   Buzz Aldrin 1930– : on landing on the moon, 21 July
   1969

2 Slowly, silently, now the moon
   Walks the night in her silver shoon.
   Walter de la Mare 1873–1956: 'Silver' (1913)

3 Busy old fool, unruly sun,
   Why dost thou thus,
   Through windows, and through curtains call on us?
   John Donne 1572–1631: 'The Sun Rising'

4 *Eppur si muove.*
   But it does move.
   Galileo Galilei 1564–1642: attributed to Galileo after his
   recantation, that the earth moves around the sun, in 1632

5 Look at the stars! look, look up at the skies!
   O look at all the fire-folk sitting in the air!
   The bright boroughs, the circle-citadels there!
   Gerard Manley Hopkins 1844–89: 'The Starlight Night'
   (written 1877)

6 Oh! I have slipped the surly bonds of earth
   And danced the skies on laughter-silvered wings; . . .
   And, while with silent lifting mind I've trod
   The high, untrespassed sanctity of space,
   Put out my hand and touched the face of God.
   John Gillespie Magee 1922–41: 'High Flight' (1943)

7 . . . The evening star,
   Love's harbinger.
   John Milton 1608–74: *Paradise Lost* (1667)

8 The eternal silence of these infinite spaces [the heavens]
   terrifies me.
   Blaise Pascal 1623–62: *Pensées* (1670)

9   The moon's an arrant thief,
   And her pale fire she snatches from the sun.
   William Shakespeare 1564–1616: *Timon of Athens* (1607)

10 And like a dying lady, lean and pale,
    Who totters forth, wrapped in a gauzy veil.
    Percy Bysshe Shelley 1792–1822: 'The Waning Moon'
    (1824)

....

Sleep and Dreams

....

1 Have you noticed . . . there is never any third act in a
    nightmare? They bring you to a climax of terror and then
    leave you there. They are the work of poor dramatists.
    Max Beerbohm 1872–1956: S. N. Behrman *Conversations
    with Max* (1960)

2 The sleep of a labouring man is sweet.
    Bible: Ecclesiastes

3 The armoured cars of dreams, contrived to let us do
    so many a dangerous thing.
    Elizabeth Bishop 1911–79: 'Sleeping Standing Up' (1946)

4 . . . The cool kindliness of sheets, that soon
    Smooth away trouble; and the rough male kiss
    Of blankets.
    Rupert Brooke 1887–1915: 'The Great Lover' (1914)

5 That children dream not in the first half year, that men
    dream not in some countries, are to me sick men's dreams,
    dreams out of the ivory gate, and visions before midnight.
    Sir Thomas Browne 1605–82: 'On Dreams'

6 All the things one has forgotten scream for help in dreams.
    Elias Canetti 1905–94: *Die Provinz der Menschen* (1973)

7 The interpretation of dreams is the royal road to a
    knowledge of the unconscious activities of the mind.
    Sigmund Freud 1856–1939: *The Interpretation of Dreams*
    (2nd ed., 1909)

8 When you're lying awake with a dismal headache, and
    repose is taboo'd by anxiety,
    I conceive you may use any language you choose to
    indulge in, without impropriety.
    W. S. Gilbert 1836–1911: *Iolanthe* (1882)

9 Sleep is when all the unsorted stuff comes flying out as
from a dustbin upset in a high wind.
William Golding 1911–93: *Pincher Martin* (1956)

10 The dream of reason produces monsters.
Goya 1746–1828: *Los Caprichos* (1799)

11 What hath night to do with sleep?
John Milton 1608–74: *Comus* (1637)

12 And so to bed.
Samuel Pepys 1633–1703: diary, 20 April 1660

13 O God! I could be bounded in a nut-shell, and count myself
a king of infinite space, were it not that I have bad dreams.
William Shakespeare 1564–1616: *Hamlet* (1601)

14 Methought I heard a voice cry, 'Sleep no more!
Macbeth does murder sleep,' the innocent sleep,
Sleep that knits up the ravelled sleave of care.
William Shakespeare 1564–1616: *Macbeth* (1606)

15   The quick Dreams,
The passion-wingèd Ministers of thought.
Percy Bysshe Shelley 1792–1822: *Adonais* (1821)

16 Tired Nature's sweet restorer, balmy sleep!
Edward Young 1683–1765: *Night Thoughts* (1742–5)

Society

1 Hunger allows no choice
To the citizen or the police;
We must love one another or die.
W. H. Auden 1907–73: 'September 1, 1939' (1940)

2 We started off trying to set up a small anarchist
community, but people wouldn't obey the rules.
Alan Bennett 1934– : *Getting On* (1972)

3 The greatest happiness of the greatest number is the
foundation of morals and legislation.
Jeremy Bentham 1748–1832: *Commonplace Book*.
Bentham claimed that either Joseph Priestley (1733–1804)
or Cesare Beccaria (1738–94) passed on 'the sacred truth'

4 Society is indeed a contract . . . it becomes a partnership
not only between those who are living, but between those
who are living, those who are dead, and those who are to
be born.
Edmund Burke 1729–97: *Reflections on the Revolution in
France* (1790)

5 No man is an Island, entire of it self.
John Donne 1572–1631: *Devotions upon Emergent
Occasions* (1624)

6 Only in the state does man have a rational existence . . .
Man owes his entire existence to the state, and has his
being within it alone.
G. W. F. Hegel 1770–1831: *Lectures on the Philosophy of
World History: Introduction* (1830), tr. H. B. Nisbet

7 In a consumer society there are inevitably two kinds of
slaves: the prisoners of addiction and the prisoners of envy.
Ivan Illich 1926– : *Tools for Conviviality* (1973)

8 From each according to his abilities, to each according to
his needs.
Karl Marx 1818–83: *Critique of the Gotha Programme*
(written 1875, but of earlier origin)

9 The city is not a concrete jungle, it is a human zoo.
Desmond Morris 1928– : *The Human Zoo* (1969)

10 *La propriété c'est le vol.*
Property is theft.
Pierre-Joseph Proudhon 1809–65: *Qu'est-ce que la
propriété?* (1840)

11 There is no such thing as Society. There are individual
men and women, and there are families.
Margaret Thatcher 1925– : in *Woman's Own* 31 October
1987

12 The Social Contract is nothing more or less than a vast
conspiracy of human beings to lie to and humbug
themselves and one another for the general Good. Lies are
the mortar that bind the savage individual man into the
social masonry.
H. G. Wells 1866–1946: *Love and Mr Lewisham* (1900)

Solitude

1 He who is unable to live in society, or who has no need because he is sufficient for himself, must be either a beast or a god.
  Aristotle 384–322 BC: *Politics*

2 Yes! in the sea of life enisled,
  With echoing straits between us thrown,
  Dotting the shoreless watery wild,
  We mortal millions live *alone*.
  Matthew Arnold 1822–88: 'To Marguerite—Continued' (1852)

3 He [Barrymore] would quote from Genesis the text which says, 'It is not good for man to be alone,' and then add, 'But O my God, what a relief.'
  John Barrymore 1882–1942: A. Power-Waters *John Barrymore* (1941)

4 It is not good that the man should be alone; I will make him an help meet for him.
  Bible: Genesis

5 To fly from, need not be to hate, mankind.
  Lord Byron 1788–1824: *Childe Harold's Pilgrimage* (1812–18)

6 I am monarch of all I survey,
  My right there is none to dispute.
  William Cowper 1731–1800: 'Verses Supposed to be Written by Alexander Selkirk' (1782)

7 I want to be alone.
  Greta Garbo 1905–90: *Grand Hotel* (1932 film)

8 If you are idle, be not solitary; if you are solitary, be not idle.
  Samuel Johnson 1709–84: letter to Boswell, 27 October 1779

9 Down to Gehenna or up to the Throne,
  He travels the fastest who travels alone.
  Rudyard Kipling 1865–1936: *The Story of the Gadsbys* (1890)

10 All the lonely people, where do they all come from?
    John Lennon 1940–80 and **Paul McCartney** 1942– :
    'Eleanor Rigby' (1966 song)

11 Ships that pass in the night, and speak each other in
    passing;
    Only a signal shown and a distant voice in the darkness;
    So on the ocean of life we pass and speak one another,
    Only a look and a voice; then darkness again and a silence.
    Henry Wadsworth Longfellow 1807–82: *Tales of a
    Wayside Inn* pt. 3 (1874)

12 A man should keep for himself a little back shop, all his
    own, quite unadulterated, in which he establishes his true
    freedom and chief place of seclusion and solitude.
    Montaigne 1533–92: *Essais* (1580)

13 Never less alone than when alone.
    Samuel Rogers 1763–1855: 'Human Life' (1819)

14 Man goes into the noisy crowd to drown his own clamour
    of silence.
    Rabindranath Tagore 1861–1941: 'Stray Birds' (1916)

15 God created man and, finding him not sufficiently alone,
    gave him a companion to make him feel his solitude more
    keenly.
    Paul Valéry 1871–1945: *Tel Quel 1* (1941)

16 Laugh and the world laughs with you;
    Weep, and you weep alone;
    For the sad old earth must borrow its mirth,
    But has trouble enough of its own.
    Ella Wheeler Wilcox 1855–1919: 'Solitude'

Sorrow

See also **Suffering**

1 Sob, heavy world,
    Sob as you spin
    Mantled in mist, remote from the happy.
    W. H. Auden 1907–73: *The Age of Anxiety* (1947)

2 O my son Absalom, my son, my son Absalom! would God I
had died for thee, O Absalom, my son, my son!
　　Bible: II Samuel

3 By the waters of Babylon we sat down and wept: when we
remembered thee, O Sion.
　　Bible: Psalm 137

4 For a tear is an intellectual thing;
And a sigh is the sword of an Angel King.
　　William Blake 1757–1827: *Jerusalem* (1815)

5 I tell you, hopeless grief is passionless.
　　Elizabeth Barrett Browning 1806–61: 'Grief' (1844)

6 Silence augmenteth grief, writing increaseth rage,
Staled are my thoughts, which loved and lost, the wonder
of our age.
　　Edward Dyer d. 1607: 'Elegy on the Death of Sir Philip
Sidney' (1593)

7 We do not expect people to be deeply moved by what is not
unusual. That element of tragedy which lies in the very
fact of frequency, has not yet wrought itself into the coarse
emotion of mankind.
　　George Eliot 1819–80: *Middlemarch* (1871–2)

8 How small and selfish is sorrow. But it bangs one about
until one is senseless.
　　Queen Elizabeth, the Queen Mother 1900– : letter to
Edith Sitwell, 1952; Victoria Glendinning *Edith Sitwell*
(1983)

9 He felt the loyalty we all feel to unhappiness—the sense
that that is where we really belong.
　　Graham Greene 1904–91: *The Heart of the Matter* (1948)

10 Now laughing friends deride tears I cannot hide,
So I smile and say 'When a lovely flame dies,
Smoke gets in your eyes.'
　　Otto Harbach 1873–1963: 'Smoke Gets in your Eyes'
(1933 song)

11 Grief is a species of idleness.
   Samuel Johnson 1709–84: letter to Mrs Thrale, 17
   March 1773

12 Then glut thy sorrow on a morning rose.
   John Keats 1795–1821: 'Ode on Melancholy' (1820)

13 Tragedy ought really to be a great kick at misery.
   D. H. Lawrence 1885–1930: letter to A. W. McLeod, 6
   October 1912

14 No one ever told me that grief felt so like fear.
   C. S. Lewis 1898–1963: *A Grief Observed* (1961)

15 When sorrows come, they come not single spies,
   But in battalions.
   William Shakespeare 1564–1616: *Hamlet* (1601)

16 Give sorrow words: the grief that does not speak
   Whispers the o'er-fraught heart, and bids it break.
   William Shakespeare 1564–1616: *Macbeth* (1606)

17 Tears, idle tears, I know not what they mean,
   Tears from the depth of some divine despair.
   Alfred, Lord Tennyson 1809–92: *The Princess* (1847)
   song (added 1850)

18 *Sunt lacrimae rerum et mentem mortalia tangunt.*
   There are tears shed for things and mortality touches the
   heart.
   Virgil 70–19 BC: *Aeneid*

19 Total grief is like a minefield. No knowing when one will
   touch the tripwire.
   Sylvia Townsend Warner 1893–1978: diary 11 December
   1969

20 For of all sad words of tongue or pen,
   The saddest are these: 'It might have been!'
   John Greenleaf Whittier 1807–92: 'Maud Muller' (1854)

21 He first deceased; she for a little tried
   To live without him: liked it not, and died.
   Henry Wotton 1568–1639: 'Upon the Death of Sir
   Albertus Moreton's Wife' (1651)

Speech and Speeches

See also **Conversation**

1 I do not object to people looking at their watches when I am speaking. But I strongly object when they start shaking them to make certain they are still going.
   Lord Birkett 1883–1962: in *Observer* 30 October 1960

2 Grasp the subject, the words will follow.
   Cato the Elder 234–149 BC: Caius Julius Victor *Ars Rhetorica*

3 And adepts in the speaking trade
   Keep a cough by them ready made.
   Charles Churchill 1731–64: *The Ghost* (1763)

4 He [Lord Charles Beresford] is one of those orators of whom it was well said, 'Before they get up, they do not know what they are going to say; when they are speaking, they do not know what they are saying; and when they have sat down, they do not know what they have said.'
   Winston Churchill 1874–1965: speech, House of Commons, 20 December 1912

5 When you have nothing to say, say nothing.
   Charles Caleb Colton c.1780–1832: *Lacon* (1820)

6 Humming, Hawing and Hesitation are the three Graces of contemporary Parliamentary oratory.
   Julian Critchley 1930– : *Westminster Blues* (1985)

7 When asked what was first in oratory, [he] replied to his questioner, 'action,' what second, 'action,' and again third, 'action'.
   Demosthenes c.384—c.322 BC: Cicero *Brutus*

8 Public speaking is like the winds of the desert: it blows constantly without doing any good.
   Faisal: when asked, at the inception of the UN in 1945, why he (as Saudi Arabian minister) was the only delegate not to have delivered a speech; Y. Karsh *Karsh: A 50-Year Retrospective* (1983)

9 Human speech is like a cracked kettle on which we tap crude rhythms for bears to dance to, while we long to make music that will melt the stars.
  Gustave Flaubert 1821–80: *Madame Bovary* (1857)

10 A speech from Ernest Bevin on a major occasion had all the horrific fascination of a public execution. If the mind was left immune, eyes and ears and emotions were riveted.
  Michael Foot 1913– : *Aneurin Bevan* vol. 1 (1962)

11 I absorb the vapour and return it as a flood.
  W. E. Gladstone 1809–98: on public speaking, in Lord Riddell *Some Things That Matter* (1927 ed.)

12 To Trinity Church, Dorchester. The rector in his sermon delivers himself of mean images in a very sublime voice, and the effect is that of a glowing landscape in which clothes are hung up to dry.
  Thomas Hardy 1840–1928: *Notebooks* 1 February 1874

13 A . . . sharp tongue is the only edged tool that grows keener with constant use.
  Washington Irving 1783–1859: *The Sketch Book* (1820) 'Rip Van Winkle'

14 The finest eloquence is that which gets things done and the worst is that which delays them.
  David Lloyd George 1863–1945: speech at Paris Peace Conference, 18 January 1919

15 Speech is civilisation itself. The word, even the most contradictory word, preserves contact—it is silence which isolates.
  Thomas Mann 1875–1955: *The Magic Mountain* (1924)

16 But all was false and hollow; though his tongue
  Dropped manna, and could make the worse appear
  The better reason.
  John Milton 1608–74: *Paradise Lost* (1667)

17 He [Winston Churchill] mobilized the English language and sent it into battle to steady his fellow countrymen and hearten those Europeans upon whom the long dark night of tyranny had descended.
  Ed Murrow 1908–65: broadcast, 30 November 1954

18 I do not much dislike the matter, but
The manner of his speech.
   William Shakespeare 1564–1616: *Antony and Cleopatra*
   (1606–7)

19 Friends, Romans, countrymen, lend me your ears.
   William Shakespeare 1564–1616: *Julius Caesar* (1599)

20 It is impossible for an Englishman to open his mouth
without making some other Englishman hate or despise
him.
   George Bernard Shaw 1856–1950: *Pygmalion* (1916)

21 If I reprehend any thing in this world, it is the use of my
oracular tongue, and a nice derangement of epitaphs!
   Richard Brinsley Sheridan 1751–1816: *The Rivals* (1775)

22 Do you remember that in classical times when Cicero had
finished speaking, the people said, 'How well he spoke', but
when Demosthenes had finished speaking, they said, 'Let
us march.'
   Adlai Stevenson 1900–65: introducing John F. Kennedy
   in 1960; Bert Cochran *Adlai Stevenson* (1969)

23 What can be said at all can be said clearly; and whereof
one cannot speak thereof one must be silent.
   Ludwig Wittgenstein 1889–1951: *Tractatus Logico-
   Philosophicus* (1922)

24 The reason why we have two ears and only one mouth is
that we may listen the more and talk the less.
   Zeno 333–261 BC: Diogenes Laertius *Lives of the
   Philosophers*

....

Sport
....

1 Float like a butterfly, sting like a bee.
   Muhammad Ali 1942– : summary of his boxing strategy,
   in G. Sullivan *Cassius Clay Story* (1964), probably
   originated by Drew 'Bundini' Brown

2 I'm the greatest.
   Muhammad Ali 1942– : catch-phrase used from 1962

3 The great fallacy is that the game is first and last about winning. It is nothing of the kind. The game is about glory, it is about doing things in style and with a flourish, about going out and beating the lot, not waiting for them to die of boredom.

    Danny Blanchflower 1926–93: attributed, 1972

4 Boxing's just showbusiness with blood.

    Frank Bruno 1961– : in *Observer* 29 December 1991

5 I call tennis the McDonald's of sport—you go in, they make a quick buck out of you, and you're out.

    Pat Cash 1965– : in *Independent on Sunday* 4 July 1999

6 As the race wore on . . . his oar was dipping into the water nearly *twice* as often as any other.

    Desmond Coke 1879–1931: *Sandford of Merton* (1903), usually misquoted 'All rowed fast, but none so fast as stroke'

7 The important thing in life is not the victory but the contest; the essential thing is not to have won but to have fought well.

    Baron Pierre de Coubertin 1863–1937: speech in London on the Olympic Games; 24 July 1908

8 Honey, I just forgot to duck.

    Jack Dempsey 1895–1983: to his wife, on losing the World Heavyweight title, 23 September 1926. After a failed attempt on his life in 1981, Ronald Reagan quipped 'I forgot to duck'

9 There is plenty of time to win this game, and to thrash the Spaniards too.

    Francis Drake *c.*1540–96: attributed

10 Nice guys. Finish last.

    Leo Durocher 1906–91: casual remark at a practice ground, July 1946; in *Nice Guys Finish Last* (as the remark generally is quoted, 1975)

11 The bigger they are, the further they have to fall.

    Robert Fitzsimmons 1862–1917: prior to a boxing match, in *Brooklyn Daily Eagle* 11 August 1900 (similar forms found in proverbs since the 15th century)

12 Football is an art more central to our culture than
anything the Arts Council deigns to recognize.
   Germaine Greer 1939– : in *Independent* 28 June 1996

13 If you watch a game, it's fun. If you play it, it's recreation.
If you work at it, it's golf.
   Bob Hope 1903– : in *Reader's Digest* October 1958

14 It's more than a game. It's an institution.
   Thomas Hughes 1822–96: of cricket; *Tom Brown's
   Schooldays* (1857)

15 We was robbed!
   Joe Jacobs 1896–1940: after Jack Sharkey beat Max
   Schmeling (of whom Jacobs was manager) in the
   heavyweight title fight, 21 June 1932

16 Fly fishing may be a very pleasant amusement; but angling
or float fishing I can only compare to a stick and a string,
with a worm at one end and a fool at the other.
   Samuel Johnson 1709–84: attributed, in Hawker
   Instructions to Young Sportsmen (1859); attributed to
   Jonathan Swift in *The Indicator* 27 October 1819

17 . . . *Duas tantum res anxius optat,*
Panem et circenses.

Only two things does he [the modern citizen] anxiously
wish for—bread and circuses.
   Juvenal AD *c.*60–*c.*130: *Satires*

18 The flannelled fools at the wicket or the muddied oafs at
the goals.
   Rudyard Kipling 1865–1936: 'The Islanders' (1903)

19 Cricket—a game which the English, not being a spiritual
people, have invented in order to give themselves some
conception of eternity.
   Lord Mancroft 1914–87: *Bees in Some Bonnets* (1979)

20 Oh, he's football crazy, he's football mad
And the football it has robbed him o' the wee bit sense he
had.
And it would take a dozen skivvies, his clothes to wash
and scrub,

Since our Jock became a member of that terrible football
club.
Jimmy McGregor: 'Football Crazy' (1960 song)

21   Chaos umpire sits,
And by decision more embroils the fray.
John Milton 1608–74: *Paradise Lost* (1667)

22 There's a breathless hush in the Close to-night—
Ten to make and the match to win—
A bumping pitch and a blinding light,
An hour to play and the last man in.
Henry Newbolt 1862–1938: 'Vitaï Lampada' (1897)

23 Play up! play up! and play the game!
Henry Newbolt 1862–1938: 'Vitaï Lampada' (1897)

24 Take me out to the ball game,
Take me out with the crowd.
Buy me some peanuts and cracker-jack—
I don't care if I never get back.
Jack Norworth 1879–1959: 'Take Me Out to the Ball
Game' (1908 song)

25 Eclipse first, the rest nowhere.
Dennis O'Kelly *c.*1720–87: comment at Epsom, 3 May
1769

26 Serious sport has nothing to do with fair play. It is bound
up with hatred, jealousy, boastfulness, and disregard of all
the rules.
George Orwell 1903–50: *Shooting an Elephant* (1950)
'I Write as I Please'

27 Football? It's the beautiful game.
Pelé 1940– : attributed; his autobiography (1977) was *My
Life and the Beautiful Game*

28 To say that these men paid their shillings to watch twenty-
two hirelings kick a ball is merely to say that a violin is
wood and catgut, that *Hamlet* is so much paper and ink.
For a shilling the Bruddersford United AFC offered you
Conflict and Art.
J. B. Priestley 1894–1984: *The Good Companions* (1929)

29 For when the One Great Scorer comes to mark against
your name,

He writes—not that you won or lost—but how you played the Game.
Grantland Rice 1880–1954: 'Alumnus Football' (1941)

30 To play billiards well is a sign of an ill-spent youth.
Charles Roupell: attributed, in D. Duncan *Life of Herbert Spencer* (1908)

31 Sure, winning isn't everything. It's the only thing.
Henry 'Red' Sanders: in *Sports Illustrated* 26 December 1955 (often attributed to Vince Lombardi)

32 When we have matched our rackets to these balls,
We will in France, by God's grace, play a set
Shall strike his father's crown into the hazard.
William Shakespeare 1564–1616: *Henry V* (1599)

33 Some people think football is a matter of life and death . . . I can assure them it is much more serious than that.
Bill Shankly 1914–81: in *Sunday Times* 4 October 1981

34 As no man is born an artist, so no man is born an angler.
Izaak Walton 1593–1683: *The Compleat Angler* (1653)

··

Statistics
··

1 [The War Office kept three sets of figures:] one to mislead the public, another to mislead the Cabinet, and the third to mislead itself.
Herbert Asquith 1852–1928: A. Horne *Price of Glory* (1962)

2 A witty statesman said, you might prove anything by figures.
Thomas Carlyle 1795–1881: *Chartism* (1839)

3 There are three kinds of lies: lies, damned lies and statistics.
Benjamin Disraeli 1804–81: attributed to Disraeli in Mark Twain *Autobiography* (1924)

4 From the fact that there are 400,000 species of beetles on this planet, but only 8,000 species of mammals, he [Haldane] concluded that the Creator, if He exists, has a special preference for beetles.

J. B. S. Haldane 1892–1964: report of lecture, 7 April 1951

5 We are just statistics, born to consume resources.

Horace 65–8 BC: *Epistles*

6 He uses statistics as a drunken man uses lampposts—for support rather than for illumination.

Andrew Lang 1844–1912: attributed

7 If your experiment needs statistics, you ought to have done a better experiment.

Ernest Rutherford 1871–1937: Norman T. J. Bailey *The Mathematical Approach to Biology and Medicine* (1967)

8 The so-called science of poll-taking is not a science at all but a mere necromancy. People are unpredictable by nature, and although you can take a nation's pulse, you can't be sure that the nation hasn't just run up a flight of stairs.

E. B. White 1899–1985: in *New Yorker* 13 November 1948

Style

1 Have something to say, and say it as clearly as you can. That is the only secret of style.

Matthew Arnold 1822–88: G. W. E. Russell *Collections and Recollections* (1898)

2 It is rustic all through. It is moorish, and wild, and knotty as a root of heath.

Charlotte Brontë 1816–55: on the setting of Emily Brontë's *Wuthering Heights*, in her own preface to the 1850 edition

3 Style is the man.

Comte de Buffon 1707–88: *Discours sur le style* (1753)

4 One had as good be out of the world, as out of the fashion.
   Colley Cibber 1671–1757: *Love's Last Shift* (1696)

5 The Mandarin style . . . is beloved by literary pundits, by
   those who would make the written word as unlike as
   possible to the spoken one.
   Cyril Connolly 1903–74: *Enemies of Promise* (1938)

6 Style is life! It is the very life-blood of thought!
   Gustave Flaubert 1821–80: letter to Louise Colet,
   7 September 1853

7 I strive to be brief, and I become obscure.
   Horace 65–8 BC: *Ars Poetica*

8 When we see a natural style, we are quite surprised and
   delighted, for we expected to see an author and we find a
   man.
   Blaise Pascal 1623–62: *Pensées* (1670)

9 True wit is Nature to advantage dressed,
   What oft was thought, but ne'er so well expressed.
   Alexander Pope 1688–1744: *An Essay on Criticism* (1711)

10 Too many flowers . . . too little fruit.
   Sir Walter Scott 1771–1832: of Felicia Hemans's literary
   style; letter to Joanna Baillie, 18 July 1823

11 Proper words in proper places, make the true definition of
   a style.
   Jonathan Swift 1667–1745: *Letter to a Young Gentleman
   lately entered into Holy Orders* (9 January 1720)

12 'Feather-footed through the plashy fen passes the questing
   vole' . . . 'Yes,' said the Managing Editor. 'That must be
   good style.'
   Evelyn Waugh 1903–66: *Scoop* (1938)

13 I don't wish to sign my name, though I am afraid
   everybody will know who the writer is: one's style is one's
   signature always.
   Oscar Wilde 1854–1900: letter to the *Daily Telegraph*,
   2 February 1891

Success and Failure

1 'Tis not in mortals to command success,
But we'll do more, Sempronius; we'll deserve it.
Joseph Addison 1672–1719: *Cato* (1713)

2 History to the defeated
May say Alas but cannot help or pardon.
W. H. Auden 1907–73: 'Spain 1937' (1937)

3 Ever tried. Ever failed. No matter. Try again. Fail again.
Fail better.
Samuel Beckett 1906–89: *Worstward Ho* (1983)

4 The race is not to the swift, nor the battle to the strong.
Bible: Ecclesiastes

5 For what shall it profit a man, if he shall gain the whole
world, and lose his own soul?
Bible: St Mark. See also St Matthew

6 The conduct of a losing party never appears right: at least
it never can possess the only infallible criterion of wisdom
to vulgar judgements—success.
Edmund Burke 1729–97: *Letter to a Member of the
National Assembly* (1791)

7 *Veni, vidi, vici.*

I came, I saw, I conquered.
Julius Caesar 100–44 BC: inscription displayed in
Caesar's Pontic triumph, according to Suetonius *Lives of
the Caesars*; or, according to Plutarch *Parallel Lives*,
written in a letter by Caesar, announcing the victory of
Zela which concluded the Pontic campaign

8 You ask, what is our aim? I can answer in one word:
Victory, victory at all costs, victory in spite of all terror;
victory, however long and hard the road may be; for
without victory, there is no survival.
Winston Churchill 1874–1965: speech, House of
Commons, 13 May 1940

9 Victory has a hundred fathers, but no-one wants to recognise defeat as his own.
Count Galeazzo Ciano 1903–44: diary, 9 September 1942

10 I have climbed to the top of the greasy pole.
Benjamin Disraeli 1804–81: on becoming Prime Minister; W. Monypenny and G. Buckle *Life of Disraeli* (1916)

11 She knows there's no success like failure
And that failure's no success at all.
Bob Dylan 1941– : 'Love Minus Zero / No Limit' (1965 song)

12 If *A* is a success in life, then *A* equals *x* plus *y* plus *z*. Work is *x*; *y* is play; and *z* is keeping your mouth shut.
Albert Einstein 1879–1955: in *Observer* 15 January 1950

13 Success is relative:
It is what we can make of the mess we have made of things.
T. S. Eliot 1888–1965: *The Family Reunion* (1939)

14 For a writer, success is always temporary, success is only a delayed failure. And it is incomplete.
Graham Greene 1904–91: *A Sort of Life* (1971)

15 Winning is everything. The only ones who remember you when you come second are your wife and your dog.
Damon Hill 1960– : in *Sunday Times* 18 December 1994

16 The moral flabbiness born of the exclusive worship of the bitch-goddess *success*.
William James 1842–1910: letter to H. G. Wells, 11 September 1906

17 If you can meet with triumph and disaster
And treat those two imposters just the same.
Rudyard Kipling 1865–1936: 'If—' (1910)

18 *Vae victis.*

Down with the defeated!
Livy 59 BC–AD 17: cry (already proverbial) of the Gallic King, Brennus, on capturing Rome in 390 BC; in *Ab Urbe Condita*

19 Be nice to people on your way up because you'll meet 'em on your way down.
Wilson Mizner 1876–1933: A. Johnston *The Legendary Mizners* (1953)

20 There is only one step from the sublime to the ridiculous.
Napoleon I 1769–1821: following the retreat from Moscow in 1812; D. G. De Pradt *Histoire de l'Ambassade dans le grand-duché de Varsovie en 1812* (1815)

21 Failure is human, after all, and you grow up by making mistakes. I've made a ton of them, but as long as I keep on failing better, I don't mind.
Joely Richardson 1965– : in *Observer* 14 May 2000

22   We fail!
But screw your courage to the sticking-place,
And we'll not fail.
William Shakespeare 1564–1616: *Macbeth* (1606)

23 Success makes life easier. It doesn't make *living* easier.
Bruce Springsteen 1949– : in *Q Magazine* August 1992

24 *Deos fortioribus adesse.*
The gods are on the side of the stronger.
Tacitus AD *c*.56–after 117: *Histories*

25 All you need in this life is ignorance and confidence; then success is sure.
Mark Twain 1835–1910: letter to Mrs Foote, 2 December 1887

26 We are not interested in the possibilities of defeat; they do not exist.
Queen Victoria 1819–1901: on the Boer War during 'Black Week', December 1899

27 It is not enough to succeed. Others must fail.
Gore Vidal 1925– : G. Irvine *Antipanegyric for Tom Driberg* 8 December 1976

28 These success encourages: they can because they think they can.
Virgil 70–19 BC: *Aeneid*

Suffering

1 Children's talent to endure stems from their ignorance of alternatives.

Maya Angelou 1928– : *I Know Why The Caged Bird Sings* (1969)

2 Even the dreadful martyrdom must run its course
Anyhow in a corner, some untidy spot
Where the dogs go on with their doggy life and the torturer's horse
Scratches its innocent behind on a tree.

W. H. Auden 1907–73: 'Musée des Beaux Arts' (1940)

3 Nothing happens to anybody which he is not fitted by nature to bear.

Marcus Aurelius AD 121–80: *Meditations*

4 Some people like being burdened. It gives them an interest.

Beryl Bainbridge 1933– : *An Awfully Big Adventure* (1989)

5 To each his suff'rings, all are men,
Condemned alike to groan;
The tender for another's pain,
Th' unfeeling for his own.

Thomas Gray 1716–71: *Ode on a Distant Prospect of Eton College* (1747)

6 If suffer we must, let's suffer on the heights.

Victor Hugo 1802–85: *Contemplations* (1856)

7 Scars have the strange power to remind us that our past is real.

Cormac McCarthy 1933– : *All the Pretty Horses* (1993)

8 Thank you, madam, the agony is abated.

Lord Macaulay 1800–59: aged four, having had hot coffee spilt over his legs; G. O. Trevelyan *Life and Letters of Lord Macaulay* (1876)

9 It is not true that suffering ennobles the character; happiness does that sometimes, but suffering, for the most part, makes men petty and vindictive.

W. Somerset Maugham 1874–1965: *Moon and Sixpence* (1919)

10 What does not kill me makes me stronger.
   Friedrich Nietzsche 1844–1900: *Twilight of the Idols* (1889)

11   The worst is not,
So long as we can say, 'This is the worst.'
   William Shakespeare 1564–1616: *King Lear* (1605–6)

12 He jests at scars, that never felt a wound.
   William Shakespeare 1564–1616: *Romeo and Juliet* (1595)

13   I am a man
More sinned against than sinning.
   William Shakespeare 1564–1616: *King Lear* (1605–6)

14 When times get rough,
And friends just can't be found
Like a bridge over troubled water
I will lay me down.
   Paul Simon 1942– : 'Bridge over Troubled Water' (1970 song)

15 Nothing begins, and nothing ends,
That is not paid with moan;
For we are born in other's pain,
And perish in our own.
   Francis Thompson 1859–1907: 'Daisy' (1913)

16 Those who have courage to love should have courage to suffer.
   Anthony Trollope 1815–82: *The Bertrams* (1859)

17 O you who have borne even heavier things, God will grant an end to these too.
   Virgil 70–19 BC: *Aeneid*

18 Too long a sacrifice
Can make a stone of the heart.
   W. B. Yeats 1865–1939: 'Easter, 1916' (1921)

The Supernatural

1 Up the airy mountain,
Down the rushy glen,

We daren't go a-hunting,
For fear of little men.
  William Allingham 1824–89: 'The Fairies' (1850)

2 From ghoulies and ghosties and long-leggety beasties
And things that go bump in the night,
  Good Lord, deliver us!
  Anonymous: 'The Cornish or West Country Litany', in
  F. T. Nettleinghame *Polperro Proverbs and Others* (1926)

3 I always knew the living talked rot, but it's nothing to the
rot the dead talk.
  Margot Asquith 1864–1945: on spiritualism; Henry
  'Chips' Channon, diary, 20 December 1937

4 Then a spirit passed before my face; the hair of my flesh
stood up.
  Bible: Job

5 For we wrestle not against flesh and blood, but against
principalities, against powers, against the rulers of the
darkness of this world, against spiritual wickedness in
high places.
  Bible: Ephesians

6 I wants to make your flesh creep.
  Charles Dickens 1812–70: *Pickwick Papers* (1837) The
  Fat Boy

7 There are fairies at the bottom of our garden!
  Rose Fyleman 1877–1957: 'The Fairies' (1918)

8 Superstition is the poetry of life.
  Johann Wolfgang von Goethe 1749–1832: *Maximen und
  Reflexionen* (1819)

9 All argument is against it; but all belief is for it.
  Samuel Johnson 1709–84: of the existence of ghosts;
  James Boswell *Life of Johnson* (1791) 31 March 1778

10 Double, double toil and trouble;
Fire burn and cauldron bubble.
  William Shakespeare 1564–1616: *Macbeth* (1606)

11 Superstition sets the whole world in flames; philosophy
quenches them.
  Voltaire 1694–1778: *Dictionnaire philosophique* (1764)

Taxes

1 To tax and to please, no more than to love and to be wise, is not given to men.
   Edmund Burke 1729–97: *On American Taxation* (1775)

2 Read my lips: no new taxes.
   George Bush 1924– : campaign pledge on taxation, in *New York Times* 19 August 1988

3 In this world nothing can be said to be certain, except death and taxes.
   Benjamin Franklin 1706–90: letter to Jean Baptiste Le Roy, 13 November 1789

4 All taxes must, at last, fall upon agriculture.
   Edward Gibbon 1737–94: quoting Artaxerxes, in *The Decline and Fall of the Roman Empire* (1776–88)

5 Only the little people pay taxes.
   Leona Helmsley *c*.1920– : addressed to her housekeeper in 1983, and reported at her trial for tax evasion; in *New York Times* 12 July 1989

6 *Excise.* A hateful tax levied upon commodities.
   Samuel Johnson 1709–84: *Dictionary of the English Language* (1755)

7 Taxation without representation is tyranny.
   James Otis 1725–83: watchword (coined *c*.1761) of the American Revolution

8 Income Tax has made more Liars out of the American people than Golf.
   Will Rogers 1879–1935: *The Illiterate Digest* (1924)

9 There is no art which one government sooner learns of another than that of draining money from the pockets of the people.
   Adam Smith 1723–90: *Wealth of Nations* (1776)

10 *Pecunia non olet.*
   Money has no smell.
   Emperor Vespasian AD 9–79: quashing an objection to a tax on public lavatories; Suetonius *Lives of the Caesars*

11 The art of government is to make two-thirds of a nation
pay all it possibly can pay for the benefit of the other third.
   Voltaire 1694–1778: attributed; Walter Bagehot *The
   English Constitution* (1867)

Teaching

See also **Education**

1 A teacher affects eternity; he can never tell where his
influence stops.
   Henry Brooks Adams 1838–1918: *The Education of
   Henry Adams* (1907)

2 There is no such whetstone, to sharpen a good wit and
encourage a will to learning, as is praise.
   Roger Ascham 1515–68: *The Schoolmaster* (1570)

3 For precept must be upon precept, precept upon precept;
line upon line, line upon line; here a little, and there a
little.
   Bible: Isaiah

4 Be a governess! Better be a slave at once!
   Charlotte Brontë 1816–55: *Shirley* (1849)

5 A man who reviews the old so as to find out the new is
qualified to teach others.
   Confucius 551–479 BC: *Analects*

6 We teachers can only help the work going on, as servants
wait upon a master.
   Maria Montessori 1870–1952: *The Absorbent Mind* (1949)

7 Men must be taught as if you taught them not,
And things unknown proposed as things forgot.
   Alexander Pope 1688–1744: *An Essay on Criticism* (1711)

8 For every person who wants to teach there are
approximately thirty who don't want to learn—much.
   W. C. Sellar 1898–1951 and **R. J. Yeatman** 1898–1968:
   And Now All This (1932)

9 *Homines dum docent discunt.*

Even while they teach, men learn.

> **Seneca ('the Younger')** *c.*4 BC–AD 65: *Epistulae Morales*

10 He who can, does. He who cannot, teaches.

> **George Bernard Shaw** 1856–1950: *Man and Superman* (1903)

11 Give me a girl at an impressionable age, and she is mine for life.

> **Muriel Spark** 1918– : *The Prime of Miss Jean Brodie* (1961)

12 Delightful task! to rear the tender thought,
To teach the young idea how to shoot.

> **James Thomson** 1700–48: *The Seasons* (1746) 'Spring'

Technology

See also **Inventions and Discoveries, Science**

1 Science finds, industry applies, man conforms.

> **Anonymous**: subtitle of guidebook to 1933 Chicago World's Fair

2 Give me but one firm spot on which to stand, and I will move the earth.

> **Archimedes** *c.*287–212 BC: on the action of a lever; Pappus *Synagoge*

3 Your worship is your furnaces,
Which, like old idols, lost obscenes,
Have molten bowels; your vision is
Machines for making more machines.

> **Gordon Bottomley** 1874–1948: 'To Ironfounders and Others' (1912)

4 I sell here, Sir, what all the world desires to have—POWER.

> **Matthew Boulton** 1728–1809: speaking to Boswell of his engineering works; in James Boswell *Life of Samuel Johnson* (1791)

5 Any sufficiently advanced technology is indistinguishable from magic.
  Arthur C. Clarke 1917– : *Profiles of the Future* (1962)

6 For a successful technology, reality must take precedence over public relations, for nature cannot be fooled.
  Richard Phillips Feynman 1918–88: Appendix to the *Rogers Commission Report on the Space Shuttle Challenger Accident* 6 June 1986

7 Technology . . . the knack of so arranging the world that we need not experience it.
  Max Frisch 1911–91: *Homo Faber* (1957)

8 Technology happens. It's not good, it's not bad. Is steel good or bad?
  Andrew Grove 1936– : in *Time* 29 December 1997

9 The thing with high-tech is that you always end up using scissors.
  David Hockney 1937– : in *Observer* 10 July 1994

10 This is not the age of pamphleteers. It is the age of the engineers. The spark-gap is mightier than the pen.
  Lancelot Hogben 1895–1975: *Science for the Citizen* (1938)

11 One machine can do the work of fifty ordinary men. No machine can do the work of one extraordinary man.
  Elbert Hubbard 1859–1915: *Thousand and One Epigrams* (1911)

12 Communism is Soviet power plus the electrification of the whole country.
  Lenin 1870–1924: Report to 8th Congress, 1920

13 The new electronic interdependence recreates the world in the image of a global village.
  Marshall McLuhan 1911–80: *The Gutenberg Galaxy* (1962)

14 The medium is the message.
  Marshall McLuhan 1911–80: *Understanding Media* (1964)

15 When this circuit learns your job, what are you going to do?
   Marshall McLuhan 1911–80: *The Medium is the Massage* (1967)

16 When you see something that is technically sweet, you go ahead and do it and you argue about what to do about it only after you have had your technical success. That is the way it was with the atomic bomb.
   J. Robert Oppenheimer 1904–67: in *In the Matter of J. Robert Oppenheimer, USAEC Transcript of Hearing Before Personnel Security Board* (1954)

17 One servant is worth a thousand gadgets.
   Joseph Alois Schumpeter 1883–1950: J. K. Galbraith *A Life in our Times* (1981)

18 Her own mother lived the latter years of her life in the horrible suspicion that electricity was dripping invisibly all over the house.
   James Thurber 1894–1961: *My Life and Hard Times* (1933)

19 Thanks to modern technology . . . history now comes equipped with a fast-forward button.
   Gore Vidal 1925– : *Screening History* (1992)

20 The Britain that is going to be forged in the white heat of this revolution will be no place for restrictive practices or for outdated methods on either side of industry.
   Harold Wilson 1916–95: speech at the Labour Party Conference, 1 October 1963; usually quoted 'the white heat of the technological revolution'

Temptation

1 Watch and pray, that ye enter not into temptation: the spirit indeed is willing but the flesh is weak.
   Bible: St Matthew

2 From all the deceits of the world, the flesh, and the devil,
Good Lord, deliver us.
Book of Common Prayer 1662: *The Litany*

3 What's done we partly may compute,
But know not what's resisted.
Robert Burns 1759–96: 'Address to the Unco Guid' (1787)

4 Who was it said a temptation resisted is a true measure of
character? Certainly no one in Beverly Hills.
Joan Collins 1933– : in *Independent* 18 July 1998

5 The Lord above made liquor for temptation—but
With a little bit of luck . . .
When temptation comes you'll give right in!
Alan Jay Lerner 1918–86: 'With a Little Bit of Luck'
(1956 song)

6 This extraordinary pride in being exempt from temptation
that you have not yet risen to the level of! Eunuchs
boasting of their chastity!
C. S. Lewis 1898–1963: 'Unreal Estates' in Kingsley Amis
and Robert Conquest (eds.) *Spectrum IV* (1965)

7 If we are to be punished for the sins we have committed, at
least we should be praised for our yearning for the sins we
have not committed.
Jawaharlal Nehru 1889–1964: paraphrasing the poet
Mirza Ghalib (1797–1849); letter to Indira Gandhi, 7 May
1943

8   Is this her fault or mine?
The tempter or the tempted, who sins most?
William Shakespeare 1564–1616: *Measure for Measure*
(1604)

9 There are several good protections against temptations,
but the surest is cowardice.
Mark Twain 1835–1910: *Following the Equator* (1897)

10 I can resist everything except temptation.
Oscar Wilde 1854–1900: *Lady Windermere's Fan* (1892)

The Theatre

see **Acting and the Theatre**

Thinking

See also **Ideas**, **The Mind**

1 To change your mind and to follow him who sets you right is to be nonetheless the free agent that you were before.
Marcus Aurelius AD 121–80: *Meditations*

2 Never express yourself more clearly than you think.
Niels Bohr 1885–1962: Abraham Pais *Einstein Lived Here* (1994)

3 *Cogito, ergo sum.*
I think, therefore I am.
René Descartes 1596–1650: *Le Discours de la méthode* (1637)

4 It is a capital mistake to theorize before you have all the evidence. It biases the judgement.
Arthur Conan Doyle 1859–1930: *A Study in Scarlet* (1888)

5 What was once thought can never be unthought.
Friedrich Dürrenmatt 1921– : *The Physicists* (1962)

6 Reasons are not like garments, the worse for wearing.
Robert Devereux, 2nd Earl of Essex 1566–1601: letter to Lord Willoughby, 4 January 1599

7 I'll not listen to reason . . . Reason always means what someone else has got to say.
Elizabeth Gaskell 1810–65: *Cranford* (1853)

8 Logical consequences are the scarecrows of fools and the beacons of wise men.
T. H. Huxley 1825–95: *Science and Culture and Other Essays* (1881)

9 I'm Irish. We think sideways.
Spike Milligan 1918– : in *Independent on Sunday* 20 June 1999

10 *Doublethink* means the power of holding two contradictory
beliefs in one's mind simultaneously, and accepting both of
them.
   George Orwell 1903–50: *Nineteen Eighty-Four* (1949)

11 I don't mind your thinking slowly: I mind your publishing
faster than you think.
   Wolfgang Pauli 1900–58: attributed

12 How comes it to pass, then, that we appear such cowards
in reasoning, and are so afraid to stand the test of
ridicule?
   3rd Earl of Shaftesbury 1671–1713: *A Letter Concerning
   Enthusiasm* (1708)

13 Yond Cassius has a lean and hungry look;
He thinks too much: such men are dangerous.
   William Shakespeare 1564–1616: *Julius Caesar* (1599)

14 The real question is not whether machines think but
whether men do.
   B. F. Skinner 1904–90: *Contingencies of Reinforcement*
   (1969)

15 Heretics are the only bitter remedy against the entropy of
human thought.
   Yevgeny Zamyatin 1884–1937: 'Literature, Revolution
   and Entropy' quoted in *The Dragon and other Stories*
   (1967, tr. M. Ginsberg) introduction

Time

1 Time is the measure of movement.
   Auctoritates Aristotelis: a compilation of medieval
   propositions

2 Every instant of time is a pinprick of eternity.
   Marcus Aurelius AD 121–80: *Meditations*

3 VLADIMIR: That passed the time.
ESTRAGON: It would have passed in any case.

VLADIMIR: Yes, but not so rapidly.
Samuel Beckett 1906–89: *Waiting for Godot* (1955)

4 I am Time grown old to destroy the world,
Embarked on the course of world annihilation.
Bhagavad Gita 250 BC–AD 250: ch. 11

5 To every thing there is a season, and a time to every
purpose under the heaven:
A time to be born, and a time to die . . .
A time to weep, and a time to laugh; a time to mourn, and
a time to dance.
Bible: Ecclesiastes

6 Men talk of killing time, while time quietly kills them.
Dion Boucicault 1820–90: *London Assurance* (1841)

7 What's not destroyed by Time's devouring hand?
Where's Troy, and where's the Maypole in the Strand?
James Bramston c.1694–1744: *The Art of Politics* (1729)

8 I recommend to you to take care of minutes: for hours will
take care of themselves.
Lord Chesterfield 1694–1773: *Letters to his Son* (1774) 6
November 1747

9 I shall use the phrase 'time's arrow' to express this one-
way property of time which has no analogue in space.
Arthur Eddington 1882–1944: *The Nature of the Physical
World* (1928)

10 The distinction between past, present and future is only an
illusion, however persistent.
Albert Einstein 1879–1955: letter to Michelangelo Besso,
21 March 1955

11 Time present and time past
Are both perhaps present in time future,
And time future contained in time past.
T. S. Eliot 1888–1965: *Four Quartets* 'Burnt Norton' (1936)

12 I have measured out my life with coffee spoons.
T. S. Eliot 1888–1965: 'Love Song of J. Alfred Prufrock'
(1917)

13 Time is . . . Time was . . . Time is past.
> **Robert Greene** c.1560–92: *Friar Bacon and Friar Bungay* (1594)

14 Time, you old gipsy man,
Will you not stay,
Put up your caravan
Just for one day?
> **Ralph Hodgson** 1871–1962: 'Time, You Old Gipsy Man' (1917)

15 *In the long run* we are all dead.
> **John Maynard Keynes** 1883–1946: *A Tract on Monetary Reform* (1923)

16 Nothing puzzles me more than time and space; and yet nothing troubles me less, as I never think about them.
> **Charles Lamb** 1775–1834: letter to Thomas Manning, 2 January 1810

17 The sunlight on the garden
Hardens and grows cold,
We cannot cage the minute
Within its net of gold.
> **Louis MacNeice** 1907–63: 'Sunlight on the Garden' (1938)

18 But at my back I always hear
Time's wingèd chariot hurrying near:
And yonder all before us lie
Deserts of vast eternity.
> **Andrew Marvell** 1621–78: 'To His Coy Mistress' (1681)

19 *Tempus edax rerum.*

Time the devourer of everything.
> **Ovid** 43 BC–AD c.17: *Metamorphoses*

20 Even such is Time, which takes in trust
Our youth, our joys, and all we have,
And pays us but with age and dust.
> **Walter Ralegh** c.1552–1618: written the night before his death

21 Half our life is spent trying to find something to do with
the time we have rushed through life trying to save.
   Will Rogers 1879–1935: letter in *New York Times* 29 April
   1930

22 Three o'clock is always too late or too early for anything
you want to do.
   Jean-Paul Sartre 1905–80: *La Nausée* (Nausea, 1938)

23 Ah! the clock is always slow;
It is later than you think.
   Robert W. Service 1874–1958: 'It Is Later Than You
   Think' (1921)

24 To-morrow, and to-morrow, and to-morrow,
Creeps in this petty pace from day to day,
To the last syllable of recorded time;
And all our yesterdays have lighted fools
The way to dusty death.
   William Shakespeare 1564–1616: *Macbeth* (1606)

25 Time hath, my lord, a wallet at his back,
Wherein he puts alms for oblivion.
   William Shakespeare 1564–1616: *Troilus and Cressida*
   (1602)

26 The woods decay, the woods decay and fall,
The vapours weep their burthen to the ground,
Man comes and tills the field and lies beneath,
And after many a summer dies the swan.
   Alfred, Lord Tennyson 1809–92: 'Tithonus' (1860,
   revised 1864)

27 As if you could kill time without injuring eternity.
   Henry David Thoreau 1817–62: *Walden* (1854)

28 Time is
Too slow for those who wait,
Too swift for those who fear,
Too long for those who grieve,
Too short for those who rejoice;
But for those who love,

Time is eternity.

> **Henry Van Dyke** 1852–1933: 'Time is too slow for those who wait' (1905), read at the funeral of Diana, Princess of Wales; the original form of the last line is 'Time is not'

29 *Sed fugit interea, fugit inreparabile tempus.*

But meanwhile it is flying, irretrievable time is flying.

> **Virgil** 70–19 BC: *Georgics* (usually quoted '*tempus fugit* [time flies]')

30 Time, like an ever-rolling stream,
Bears all its sons away.

> **Isaac Watts** 1674–1748: 'O God, our help in ages past' (1719 hymn)

....

Titles

....

1 Not a reluctant peer but a persistent commoner.

> **Tony Benn** 1925– : of his ultimately successful fight to disclaim his inherited title of Viscount Stansgate; at a press conference, 23 November 1960

2 The rank is but the guinea's stamp,
The man's the gowd for a' that!

> **Robert Burns** 1759–96: 'For a' that and a' that' (1790)

3 A medal glitters, but it also casts a shadow.

> **Winston Churchill** 1874–1965: on the envy caused by the award of honours, in 1941; Kenneth Rose *King George V* (1983)

4 A fully-equipped duke costs as much to keep up as two Dreadnoughts; and dukes are just as great a terror and they last longer.

> **David Lloyd George** 1863–1945: speech at Newcastle, 9 October 1909

5 An aristocracy in a republic is like a chicken whose head has been cut off: it may run about in a lively way, but in fact it is dead.

> **Nancy Mitford** 1904–73: *Noblesse Oblige* (1956)

6 When I want a peerage, I shall buy it like an honest man.

> **Lord Northcliffe** 1865–1922: Tom Driberg *Swaff* (1974)

7 There is no stronger craving in the world than that of the rich for titles, except perhaps that of the titled for riches.
   Hesketh Pearson 1887–1964: *The Pilgrim Daughters* (1961)

8 Titles distinguish the mediocre, embarrass the superior, and are disgraced by the inferior.
   George Bernard Shaw 1856–1950: *Man and Superman* (1903)

9 She needed no royal title to continue to generate her particular brand of magic.
   Lord Spencer 1964– : of his sister, Diana, Princess of Wales, at her funeral, 7 September 1997

10 What harm have I ever done to the Labour Party?
   R. H. Tawney 1880–1962: on declining the offer of a peerage, in *Evening Standard* 18 January 1962

11 Kind hearts are more than coronets,
   And simple faith than Norman blood.
   Alfred, Lord Tennyson 1809–92: 'Lady Clara Vere de Vere' (1842)

12 People fail you, children disappoint you, thieves break in, moths corrupt, but an OBE goes on for ever.
   Fay Weldon 1931– : *Praxis* (1978)

The Town

see **The Country and the Town**

Transience

1 *Sic transit gloria mundi.*
   Thus passes the glory of the world.
   Anonymous: said at the coronation of a new Pope, while flax is burned; used at the coronation of Alexander V, 1409, but earlier in origin

2 All flesh is as grass, and all the glory of man as the flower
of grass. The grass withereth, and the flower thereof
falleth away.
   Bible: I Peter

3 He who binds to himself a joy
Doth the winged life destroy
But he who kisses the joy as it flies
Lives in Eternity's sunrise.
   William Blake 1757–1827: *MS Note-Book*

4 The reputation which the world bestows
is like the wind, that shifts now here now there,
its name changed with the quarter whence it blows.
   Dante Alighieri 1265–1321: *Divina Commedia*
   'Purgatorio'

5 Look thy last on all things lovely,
Every hour.
   Walter de la Mare 1873–1956: 'Fare Well' (1918)

6 A little rule, a little sway,
A sunbeam in a winter's day,
Is all the proud and mighty have
Between the cradle and the grave.
   John Dyer 1700–58: *Grongar Hill* (1726)

7 Gather ye rosebuds while ye may,
Old Time is still a-flying:
And this same flower that smiles to-day,
To-morrow will be dying.
   Robert Herrick 1591–1674: 'To the Virgins, to Make
   Much of Time' (1648)

8 Like that of leaves is a generation of men.
   Homer 8th century BC: *The Iliad*

Transport

1 This is the Night Mail crossing the Border,
Bringing the cheque and the postal order,
Letters for the rich, letters for the poor,

The shop at the corner, the girl next door.
   W. H. Auden 1907–73: 'Night Mail' (1936)

2 I myself see the car crash as a tremendous sexual event really: a liberation of human and machine libido (if there is such a thing).
   J. G. Ballard 1930– : in *Penthouse* September 1970

3 I think that cars today are almost the exact equivalent of the great Gothic cathedrals: I mean the supreme creation of an era.
   Roland Barthes 1915–80: *Mythologies* (1957)

4 Before the Roman came to Rye or out to Severn strode,
The rolling English drunkard made the rolling English road.
   G. K. Chesterton 1874–1936: 'The Rolling English Road' (1914)

5 [There are] only two classes of pedestrians in these days of reckless motor traffic—the quick, and the dead.
   Lord Dewar 1864–1930: George Robey *Looking Back on Life* (1933)

6 Railway termini. They are our gates to the glorious and the unknown. Through them we pass out into adventure and sunshine, to them, alas! we return.
   E. M. Forster 1879–1970: *Howards End* (1910)

7 Sir, Saturday morning, although recurring at regular and well-foreseen intervals, always seems to take this railway by surprise.
   W. S. Gilbert 1836–1911: letter to the station-master at Baker Street, on the Metropolitan line; John Julius Norwich *Christmas Crackers* (1980)

8 There is *nothing*—absolutely nothing—half so much worth doing as simply messing about in boats.
   Kenneth Grahame 1859–1932: *The Wind in the Willows* (1908)

9 The poetry of motion! The *real* way to travel! The *only* way to travel! Here today—in next week tomorrow!
   Kenneth Grahame 1859–1932: on the car; *The Wind in the Willows* (1908)

10 There is no class of person more moved by hatred than the
motorist and the policeman is a convenient receptacle for
his feeling.
    C. W. Hewitt: speech to the Lawyers' Club of the
    London School of Economics, 22 October 1959

11 What good is speed if the brain has oozed out on the way?
    Karl Kraus 1874–1936: in *Die Fackel* September 1909

12 The car has become an article of dress without which we
feel uncertain, unclad and incomplete in the urban
compound.
    Marshall McLuhan 1911–80: *Understanding Media* (1964)

13 Beneath this slab
John Brown is stowed.
He watched the ads,
And not the road.
    Ogden Nash 1902–71: 'Lather as You Go' (1942)

14 You have your own company, your own temperature
control, your own music—and don't have to put up with
dreadful human beings sitting alongside you.
    Steven Norris 1945– : on cars compared to public
    transport; comment to Commons Environment Select
    Committee, in *Daily Telegraph* 9 February 1995

15 I did not fully understand the dread term 'terminal illness'
until I saw Heathrow for myself.
    Dennis Potter 1935–94: in *Sunday Times* 4 June 1978

16 No other man-made device since the shields and lances of
ancient knights fulfils a man's ego like an automobile.
    Lord Rootes 1894–1964: attributed, 1958

17 After the first powerful plain manifesto
The black statement of pistons, without more fuss
But gliding like a queen, she leaves the station.
    Stephen Spender 1909– : 'The Express' (1933)

18 There are only two emotions in a plane: boredom and
terror.
    Orson Welles 1915–85: in *The Times* 6 May 1985

19 Commuter—one who spends his life
In riding to and from his wife;
A man who shaves and takes a train,

And then rides back to shave again.
    E. B. White 1899–1985: 'The Commuter' (1982)

....

Travel

....

1 Travel, in the younger sort, is a part of education; in the
  elder, a part of experience. He that travelleth into a
  country before he hath some entrance into the language,
  goeth to school, and not to travel.
      Francis Bacon 1561–1626: *Essays* (1625) 'Of Travel'

2 See one promontory (said Socrates of old), one mountain,
  one sea, one river, and see all.
      Robert Burton 1577–1640: *The Anatomy of Melancholy*
      (1621–51)

3 Men travel faster now, but I do not know if they go to
  better things.
      Willa Cather 1873–1947: *Death Comes for the Archbishop*
      (1927)

4 A cold coming we had of it,
  Just the worst time of the year
  For a journey, and such a long journey:
  The ways deep and the weather sharp,
  The very dead of winter.
      T. S. Eliot 1888–1965: 'Journey of the Magi' (1927)

5 Worth seeing, yes; but not worth going to see.
      Samuel Johnson 1709–84: of the Giant's Causeway;
      James Boswell *Life of Johnson* (1791) 12 October 1779

6 Of all noxious animals, too, the most noxious is a tourist.
  And of all tourists the most vulgar, ill-bred, offensive and
  loathsome is the British tourist.
      Francis Kilvert 1840–79: diary, 5 April 1870

7 A good traveller is one who does not know where he is
  going to, and a perfect traveller does not know where he
  came from.
      Lin Yutang 1895–1976: *The Importance of Living* (1938)

8 Whenever I prepare for a journey I prepare as though for death. Should I never return, all is in order.
  Katherine Mansfield 1888–1923: diary, 29 January 1922

9 A man travels the world in search of what he needs and returns home to find it.
  George Moore 1852–1933: *The Brook Kerith* (1916)

10 That life-quickening atmosphere of a big railway station where everything is something trembling on the brink of something else.
  Vladimir Nabokov 1899–1977: *Spring in Fialta and other stories* (1956)

11 In the middle ages people were tourists because of their religion, whereas now they are tourists because tourism is their religion.
  Robert Runcie 1921–2000: speech in London, 6 December 1988

12 To travel hopefully is a better thing than to arrive, and the true success is to labour.
  Robert Louis Stevenson 1850–94: *Virginibus Puerisque* (1881)

13 I always love to begin a journey on Sundays, because I shall have the prayers of the church, to preserve all that travel by land, or by water.
  Jonathan Swift 1667–1745: *Polite Conversation* (1738)

14 There is no land unhabitable nor sea innavigable.
  Robert Thorne d. 1527: Richard Hakluyt *The Principal Navigations, Voyages, and Discoveries of the English Nation* (1589)

Trust and Treachery

1 He that is surety for a stranger shall smart for it.
  Bible: Proverbs

2 Just for a handful of silver he left us,
  Just for a riband to stick in his coat.
  Robert Browning 1812–89: 'The Lost Leader' (1845), of Wordsworth

3 Anyone can rat, but it takes a certain amount of ingenuity to re-rat.

> **Winston Churchill** 1874–1965: on rejoining the Conservatives twenty years after leaving them for the Liberals, c.1924; Kay Halle *Irrepressible Churchill* (1966)

4 I know what it is to be a subject, and what to be a Sovereign. Good neighbours I have had, and I have met with bad: and in trust I have found treason.

> **Elizabeth I** 1533–1603: speech to a Parliamentary deputation at Richmond, 12 November 1586, as reported in Camden's *Annals* (1615). A report 'which the queen herself heavily amended in her own hand' omits the concluding words

5 Anyone who hasn't experienced the ecstasy of betrayal knows nothing about ecstasy at all.

> **Jean Genet** 1910–86: *Prisoner of Love* (1986)

6 Treason doth never prosper, what's the reason?
For if it prosper, none dare call it treason.

> **John Harington** 1561–1612: *Epigrams* (1618)

7 And I said to the man who stood at the gate of the year:
'Give me a light that I may tread safely into the unknown.'
And he replied:
'Go out into the darkness and put your hand into the Hand of God. That shall be to you better than light and safer than a known way.'

> **Minnie Louise Haskins** 1875–1957: 'God Knows' (1908); quoted by George VI in his Christmas broadcast, 1939

8 It is better to suffer wrong than to do it, and happier to be sometimes cheated than not to trust.

> **Samuel Johnson** 1709–84: in *Rambler* 18 December 1750

9 *Quis custodiet ipsos custodes?*

Who is to guard the guards themselves?

> **Juvenal** AD c.60–c.130: *Satires*

10 To betray, you must first belong.

> **Kim Philby** 1912–88: in *Sunday Times* 17 December 1967

11 But I'm always true to you, darlin', in my fashion.
Yes I'm always true to you, darlin', in my way.
Cole Porter 1891–1964: 'Always True to You in my
Fashion' (1949 song)

12   *Equo ne credite, Teucri,*
Quidquid est, timeo Danaos et dona ferentes.
Do not trust the horse, Trojans. Whatever it is, I fear the
Greeks even when they bring gifts.
Virgil 70–19 BC: *Aeneid*

13 Having watched the form of our traitors for a number of
years, I cannot think that espionage can be recommended
as a technique for building an impressive civilization. It's
a lout's game.
Rebecca West 1892–1983: *The Meaning of Treason* (1982
ed.)

Truth

See also **Lies and Lying**

1 The truth is often a terrible weapon of aggression. It is
possible to lie, and even to murder, for the truth.
Alfred Adler 1870–1937: *The Problems of Neurosis* (1929)

2 The truth which makes men free is for the most part the
truth which men prefer not to hear.
Herbert Agar 1897–1980: *A Time for Greatness* (1942)

3 Plato is dear to me, but dearer still is truth.
Aristotle 384–322 BC: attributed

4 It contains a misleading impression, not a lie. It was being
economical with the truth.
Robert Armstrong 1927– : during the 'Spycatcher' trial,
Supreme Court, New South Wales, in *Daily Telegraph* 19
November 1986

5 What is truth? said jesting Pilate; and would not stay for
an answer.
Francis Bacon 1561–1626: *Essays* (1625) 'Of Truth'

6 And ye shall know the truth, and the truth shall make you free.
  Bible: St John

7 Great is Truth, and mighty above all things.
  Bible (Apocrypha): I Esdras

8 A truth that's told with bad intent
Beats all the lies you can invent.
  William Blake 1757–1827: 'Auguries of Innocence' (*c.*1803)

9 One of the favourite maxims of my father was the distinction between the two sorts of truths, profound truths recognized by the fact that the opposite is also a profound truth, in contrast to trivialities where opposites are obviously absurd.
  Niels Bohr 1885–1962: S. Rozental *Niels Bohr* (1967)

10 Many from . . . an inconsiderate zeal unto truth, have too rashly charged the troops of error, and remain as trophies unto the enemies of truth.
  Sir Thomas Browne 1605–82: *Religio Medici* (1643)

11 'Tis strange—but true; for truth is always strange; Stranger than fiction.
  Lord Byron 1788–1824: *Don Juan* (1819–24)

12 What I tell you three times is true.
  Lewis Carroll 1832–98: *The Hunting of the Snark* (1876)

13 It is commonly said, and more particularly by Lord Shaftesbury, that ridicule is the best test of truth.
  Lord Chesterfield 1694–1773: *Letters to his Son* (1774) 6 February 1752

14 When you have eliminated the impossible, whatever remains, *however improbable*, must be the truth.
  Arthur Conan Doyle 1859–1930: *The Sign of Four* (1890)

15 Nothing is too wonderful to be true, if it be consistent with the laws of nature, and in such things as these, experiment is the best test of such consistency.
  Michael Faraday 1791–1867: diary, 19 March 1849

16 An exaggeration is a truth that has lost its temper.
 Kahlil Gibran 1883–1931: *Sand and Foam* (1926)

17 Truth is not merely what we are thinking, but also why, to whom and under what circumstances we say it.
 Václav Havel 1936– : *Temptation* (1985)

18 True and False are attributes of speech, not of things. And where speech is not, there is neither Truth nor Falsehood.
 Thomas Hobbes 1588–1679: *Leviathan* (1651)

19 It is the customary fate of new truths to begin as heresies and to end as superstitions.
 T. H. Huxley 1825–95: *Science and Culture and Other Essays* (1881)

20 In lapidary inscriptions a man is not upon oath.
 Samuel Johnson 1709–84: James Boswell *Life of Johnson* (1791) 1775

21 Honesty is praised and left to shiver.
 Juvenal AD c.60–c.130: *Satires*

22 I maintain that Truth is a pathless land, and you cannot approach it by any path whatsoever, by any religion, by any sect.
 Jiddu Krishnamurti 1895–1986: remark, 1929; L. Heber *Krishnamurti* (1931)

23 It is one thing to show a man that he is in error, and another to put him in possession of truth.
 John Locke 1632–1704: *Essay concerning Human Understanding* (1690)

24 But, my dearest Agathon, it is truth which you cannot contradict; you can without any difficulty contradict Socrates.
 Socrates 469–399 BC: Plato *Symposium*

25 There was things which he stretched, but mainly he told the truth.
 Mark Twain 1835–1910: *The Adventures of Huckleberry Finn* (1884)

26 I can't tell a lie, Pa; you know I can't tell a lie. I did cut it
with my hatchet.
   George Washington 1732–99: M. L. Weems *Life of
   George Washington* (10th ed., 1810)

27 The truth is rarely pure, and never simple.
   Oscar Wilde 1854–1900: *The Importance of Being Earnest*
   (1895)

28 A thing is not necessarily true because a man dies for it.
   Oscar Wilde 1854–1900: *Sebastian Melmoth* (1904 ed.)

The Twentieth Century

1 Will the last generation of the twentieth century differ
very much from the first? Will they be healthier and
longer-lived, wiser, better, and more intelligent, or will
they remain substantially the same as the people we have
known and the people whom history has portrayed to us?
   Anonymous: in *The Times* 1 January 1901

2 Everything is becoming science fiction. From the margins
of an almost invisible literature has sprung the intact
reality of the 20th century.
   J. G. Ballard 1930– : 'Fictions of Every Kind' in *Books
   and Bookmen* February 1971

3 The light may be fading on the 20th century, but the sun is
still rising on America.
   Bill Clinton 1946– : in *Sunday Times* 2 January 2000

4 Mankind has probably done more damage to the earth in
the 20th century than in all of previous human history.
   Jacques Cousteau 1910–97: in *New Perspectives
   Quarterly* Summer 1996

5 For 80 per cent of humanity the Middle Ages ended
suddenly in the 1950s; or perhaps better still, they were *felt*
to end in the 1960s.
   Eric Hobsbawm 1917– : *Age of Extremes* (1994)

6 The American century—and the European half
millennium—is coming to an end. The world century is
beginning.
   Rosabeth Moss Kanter 1943– : *World Class* (1995)

7 If the nineteenth century was the age of the editorial chair,
ours is the century of the psychiatrist's couch.
   Marshall McLuhan 1911–80: *Understanding Media* (1964)

8 We close the century with most people still languishing in
poverty, subjected to hunger, preventable disease, illiteracy
and insufficient shelter.
   Nelson Mandela 1918– : at a ceremony at his former
   prison cell on Robben Island; in *Observer* 2 January 2000

9 The culture of the 1990s can be summed up by Neighbours
and football.
   Spike Milligan 1918– : in *Sunday Times* 2 January 2000

10 Our gadget-filled paradise suspended in a hell of
international insecurity.
   Reinhold Niebuhr 1892–1971: *Pious and Secular America*
   (1957)

11 It was she [the Chelsea Girl] who established the fact that
this latter half of the twentieth century belongs to Youth.
   Mary Quant 1934– : *Quant by Quant* (1966)

12 Suppose . . . that Lenin had died of typhus in Siberia in
1895 and Hitler had been killed on the western front in
1916. What would the twentieth century have looked like
now?
   Arthur M. Schlesinger Jr. 1917– : *The Cycles of
   American History* (1986)

13 The twentieth century decorates life like a Christmas cake,
but it still cannot do anything about the basic ingredients.
   Derek Tangye 1912–96: *A Gull on the Roof* (1961)

14 The twentieth century will be remembered chiefly, not as
an age of political conflicts and technical inventions, but
as an age in which human society dared to think of the
health of the whole human race as a practical objective.
   Arnold Toynbee 1889–1975: attributed

Unbelief

see **Belief and Unbelief**

The Universe

1 Had I been present at the Creation, I would have given some useful hints for the better ordering of the universe.
Alfonso 'the Wise', King of Castile 1221–84: on studying the Ptolemaic system (attributed)

2 For one of those gnostics, the visible universe was an illusion or, more precisely, a sophism. Mirrors and fatherhood are abominable because they multiply it and extend it.
Jorge Luis Borges 1899–1986: *Tlön, Uqbar, Orbis Tertius* (1941)

3 'Gad! she'd better!'
Thomas Carlyle 1795–1881: on hearing that Margaret Fuller 'accept[ed] the universe'; William James *Varieties of Religious Experience* (1902)

4 The eternal mystery of the world is its comprehensibility . . . The fact that it is comprehensible is a miracle.
Albert Einstein 1879–1955: in *Franklin Institute Journal* March 1936; usually quoted as 'The most incomprehensible fact about the universe is that it is comprehensible'

5 The world is disgracefully managed, one hardly knows to whom to complain.
Ronald Firbank 1886–1926: *Vainglory* (1915)

6 Now, my own suspicion is that the universe is not only queerer than we suppose, but queerer than we *can* suppose.
J. B. S. Haldane 1892–1964: *Possible Worlds* (1927)

7 If we find the answer to that [why it is that we and the universe exist], it would be the ultimate triumph of human reason—for then we would know the mind of God.
Stephen Hawking 1942– : *A Brief History of Time* (1988)

8 This, now, is the judgement of our scientific age—the third
reaction of man upon the universe! This universe is not
hostile, nor yet is it friendly. It is simply indifferent.
John H. Holmes 1879–1964: *The Sensible Man's View of
Religion* (1932)

9 There is a coherent plan to the universe, though I don't
know what it's a plan for.
Fred Hoyle 1915– : attributed

10 From the intrinsic evidence of his creation, the Great
Architect of the Universe now begins to appear as a pure
mathematician.
James Jeans 1877–1946: *The Mysterious Universe* (1930)

11 How is it that hardly any major religion has looked at
science and concluded, 'This is better than we thought!
The Universe is much bigger than our prophets said,
grander, more subtle, more elegant'?
Carl Sagan 1934–96: *Pale Blue Dot* (1995)

12 There are more things in heaven and earth, Horatio,
Than are dreamt of in your philosophy.
William Shakespeare 1564–1616: *Hamlet* (1601)

13 We milk the cow of the world, and as we do
We whisper in her ear, 'You are not true.'
Richard Wilbur 1921– : 'Epistemology' (1950)

14 The world is everything that is the case.
Ludwig Wittgenstein 1889–1951: *Tractatus Logico-
Philosophicus* (1922)

Vice

see **Virtue and Vice**

Violence

1 Keep violence in the mind
Where it belongs.
Brian Aldiss 1925– : 'Charteris' (1969)

2 Pale Ebenezer thought it wrong to fight,
But Roaring Bill (who killed him) thought it right.
   Hilaire Belloc 1870–1953: 'The Pacifist' (1938)

3 All they that take the sword shall perish with the sword.
   Bible: St Matthew

4 I say violence is necessary. It is as American as cherry pie.
   H. Rap Brown 1943– : speech, 27 July 1967

5 A riot is at bottom the language of the unheard.
   Martin Luther King 1929–68: *Where Do We Go From Here?* (1967)

6   Who overcomes
By force, hath overcome but half his foe.
   John Milton 1608–74: *Paradise Lost* (1667)

7 If you strike a child take care that you strike it in anger,
even at the risk of maiming it for life. A blow in cold blood
neither can nor should be forgiven.
   George Bernard Shaw 1856–1950: *Man and Superman* (1903)

8 Where force is necessary, there it must be applied boldly,
decisively and completely. But one must know the
limitations of force; one must know when to blend force
with a manoeuvre, a blow with an agreement.
   Leon Trotsky 1879–1940: *What Next?* (1932)

9 The quietly pacifist peaceful
always die
to make room for men
who shout.
   Alice Walker 1944– : 'The QPP' (1973)

10 It's very unfashionable to say this, but rape actually isn't
the worst thing that can happen to a woman if you're safe,
alive and unmarked after the event.
   Fay Weldon 1931– : in *Radio Times* 4 July 1998

Virtue and Vice

See also **Good and Evil**

1 Virtue is like a rich stone, best plain set.
   Francis Bacon 1561–1626: *Essays* (1625) 'Of Beauty'

2 He that is without sin among you, let him first cast a stone at her.
   Bible: St John

3 Terrible is the temptation to be good.
   Bertolt Brecht 1898–1956: *The Caucasian Chalk Circle* (1948)

4 Vice came in always at the door of necessity, not at the door of inclination.
   Daniel Defoe 1660–1731: *Moll Flanders* (1721)

5   What after all
   Is a halo? It's only one more thing to keep clean.
   Christopher Fry 1907– : *The Lady's not for Burning* (1949)

6 But if he does really think that there is no distinction between virtue and vice, why, Sir, when he leaves our houses, let us count our spoons.
   Samuel Johnson 1709–84: in James Boswell *Life of Johnson* (1791) 14 July 1763

7 No one ever suddenly became depraved.
   Juvenal AD *c*.60–*c*.130: *Satires*

8 Be good, sweet maid, and let who will be clever.
   Charles Kingsley 1819–75: 'A Farewell' (1858)

9 Our intentions make blackguards of us all; our weakness in carrying them out we call probity.
   Pierre Choderlos de Laclos 1741–1803: *Les Liaisons Dangereuses* (1782) letter 66

10 An orgy looks particularly alluring seen through the mists of righteous indignation.
   Malcolm Muggeridge 1903–90: *The Most of Malcolm Muggeridge* (1966)

11 Virtue she finds too painful an endeavour,
Content to dwell in decencies for ever.
  Alexander Pope 1688–1744: 'To a Lady' (1735)

12 Dost thou think, because thou art virtuous, there shall be
no more cakes and ale?
  William Shakespeare 1564–1616: *Twelfth Night* (1601)

13 How far that little candle throws his beams!
So shines a good deed in a naughty world.
  William Shakespeare 1564–1616: *The Merchant of
  Venice* (1596–8)

14 What is virtue but the Trade Unionism of the married?
  George Bernard Shaw 1856–1950: *Man and Superman*
  (1903)

15   Change in a trice
The lilies and languors of virtue
For the raptures and roses of vice.
  Algernon Charles Swinburne 1837–1909: 'Dolores'
  (1866)

16 Would that we had spent one whole day well in this world!
  Thomas à Kempis c.1380–1471: *De Imitatione Christi*

17 Virtue knows to a farthing what it has lost by not having
been vice.
  Horace Walpole 1717–97: L. Kronenberger *The
  Extraordinary Mr Wilkes* (1974)

Voting

See also **Democracy**

1 Elections are won by men and women chiefly because most
people vote against somebody rather than for somebody.
  Franklin P. Adams 1881–1960: *Nods and Becks* (1944)

2 Vote early and vote often.
  Anonymous: US election slogan, already current when
  quoted by William Porcher Miles in the House of
  Representatives, 31 March 1858

3 The accursed power which stands on Privilege
(And goes with Women, and Champagne, and Bridge)
Broke—and Democracy resumed her reign:
(Which goes with Bridge, and Women and Champagne).
   Hilaire Belloc 1870–1953: 'On a Great Election' (1923)

4 Woman stock is rising in the market. I shall not live to see
women vote, but I'll come and rap at the ballot box.
   Lydia Maria Child 1802–80: letter to Sarah Shaw, 3
   August 1856

5 An election is coming. Universal peace is declared, and the
foxes have a sincere interest in prolonging the lives of the
poultry.
   George Eliot 1819–80: *Felix Holt* (1866)

6 Hell, I never vote *for* anybody. I always vote *against*.
   W. C. Fields 1880–1946: R. L. Taylor *W. C. Fields* (1950)

7 I always voted at my party's call,
And I never thought of thinking for myself at all.
   W. S. Gilbert 1836–1911: *HMS Pinafore* (1878)

8 To give victory to the right, not bloody bullets, but
peaceful ballots only, are necessary.
   Abraham Lincoln 1809–65: speech, 18 May 1858; usually
   quoted 'The ballot is stronger than the bullet'

9 If voting changed anything, they'd abolish it.
   Ken Livingstone 1945– : title of book, 1987

10 It's not the voting that's democracy, it's the counting.
   Tom Stoppard 1937– : *Jumpers* (1972)

....

Wales
....

1 It profits a man nothing to give his soul for the whole
world . . . But for Wales—!
   Robert Bolt 1924–95: *A Man for All Seasons* (1960)

2 Who dare compare the English, the most degraded of all
the races under heaven, with the Welsh?
   Giraldus Cambrensis 1146?–1220?: attributed

3 Wales, Wales, sweet are thy hills and vales,
  Thy speech, thy song,
  To thee belong,
  O may they live ever in Wales.
    Evan James: 'Land of My Fathers' (1856)

4 Though it appear a little out of fashion,
  There is much care and valour in this Welshman.
    William Shakespeare 1564–1616: *Henry V* (1599)

5 The land of my fathers. My fathers can have it.
    Dylan Thomas 1914–53: in *Adam* December 1953

6 I wanted a play that would paint the full face of sensuality,
  rebellion and revivalism. In South Wales these three
  phenomena have played second fiddle only to Rugby Union
  which is a distillation of all three.
    Gwyn Thomas 1913–81: introduction to *Jackie the
    Jumper* (1962)

7 There is no present in Wales,
  And no future;
  There is only the past,
  Brittle with relics . . .
  And an impotent people,
  Sick with inbreeding,
  Worrying the carcase of an old song.
    R. S. Thomas 1913– : 'Welsh Landscape' (1955)

8 The Welsh remain the only race whom you can vilify
  without being called a racist.
    A. N. Wilson 1950– : in *Sunday Times* 23 April 2000

War

See also **The Army**

1 A bayonet is a weapon with a worker at each end.
    Anonymous: British pacifist slogan (1940)

2 When war enters a country
It produces lies like sand.
   Anonymous: epigraph to A. Ponsonby *Falsehood in
   Wartime* (1928)

3 We make war that we may live in peace.
   Aristotle 384–322 BC: *Nicomachean Ethics*

4 The bomber will always get through. The only defence is
in offence, which means that you have to kill more women
and children more quickly than the enemy if you want to
save yourselves.
   Stanley Baldwin 1867–1947: speech, House of Commons,
   10 November 1932

5 Not worth the healthy bones of a single Pomeranian
grenadier.
   Otto von Bismarck 1815–98: of possible German
   involvement in the Balkans; George O. Kent *Bismarck
   and his Times* (1978)

6 They have gone too long without a war here. Where is
morality to come from in such a case, I ask? Peace is
nothing but slovenliness, only war creates order.
   Bertolt Brecht 1898–1956: *Mother Courage* (1939)

7 As you know, God is usually on the side of the big
squadrons against the small.
   Comte de Bussy-Rabutin 1618–93: letter to the Comte
   de Limoges, 18 October 1677

8 In war, whichever side may call itself the victor, there are
no winners, but all are losers.
   Neville Chamberlain 1869–1940: speech at Kettering, 3
   July 1938

9 Laws are silent in time of war.
   Cicero 106–43 BC: *Pro Milone*

10 War is nothing but a continuation of politics with the
admixture of other means.
   Karl von Clausewitz 1780–1831: *On War* (1832–4)
   commonly rendered 'War is the continuation of politics
   by other means'

11 Everything is very simple in war, but the simplest thing is difficult. These difficulties accumulate and produce a friction which no man can imagine exactly who has not seen war.

Karl von Clausewitz 1780–1831: *On War* (1832–4)

12 War is too serious a matter to entrust to military men.

Georges Clemenceau 1841–1929: attributed to Clemenceau, e.g. in H. Jackson *Clemenceau and the Third Republic* (1946), but also to Briand and Talleyrand

13 I love the smell of napalm in the morning. It smells like victory.

Francis Ford Coppola 1939– : *Apocalypse Now* (1979 film, with John Milius)

14 War is the most exciting and dramatic thing in life. In fighting to the death you feel terribly relaxed when you manage to come through.

Moshe Dayan 1915–81: in *Observer* 13 February 1972

15 The sword is the axis of the world and its power is absolute.

Charles de Gaulle 1890–1970: *Vers l'armée de métier* (1934)

16 I am not only a pacifist but a militant pacifist. I am willing to fight for peace. Nothing will end war unless the people themselves refuse to go to war.

Albert Einstein 1879–1955: interview with G. S. Viereck, January 1931

17 There never was a good war, or a bad peace.

Benjamin Franklin 1706–90: letter to Josiah Quincy, 11 September 1783

18 If we are attacked we can only defend ourselves with guns not with butter.

Joseph Goebbels 1897–1945: speech in Berlin, 17 January 1936

19 Would you rather have butter or guns? . . . preparedness makes us powerful. Butter merely makes us fat.

Hermann Goering 1893–1946: speech at Hamburg, 1936, in W. Frischauer *Goering* (1951).

20 War is hell, and all that, but it has a good deal to recommend it. It wipes out all the small nuisances of peace-time.
 Ian Hay 1876–1952: *The First Hundred Thousand* (1915)

21 Among the calamities of war may be jointly numbered the diminution of the love of truth, by the falsehoods which interest dictates and credulity encourages.
 Samuel Johnson 1709–84: *The Idler* 11 November 1758; possibly the source of 'When war is declared, Truth is the first casualty', epigraph to Arthur Ponsonby's *Falsehood in Wartime* (1928); attributed also to Hiram Johnson, speaking in the US Senate, 1918

22 It is well that war is so terrible. We should grow too fond of it.
 Robert E. Lee 1807–70: after the battle of Fredericksburg, December 1862 (attributed)

23 He knew that the essence of war is violence, and that moderation in war is imbecility.
 Lord Macaulay 1800–59: *Essays Contributed to the Edinburgh Review* (1843) 'John Hampden'

24 War hath no fury like a non-combatant.
 C. E. Montague 1867–1928: *Disenchantment* (1922)

25 Rule 1, on page 1 of the book of war, is: 'Do not march on Moscow' . . . [Rule 2] is: 'Do not go fighting with your land armies in China.'
 Field Marshal Montgomery 1887–1976: speech, House of Lords, 30 May 1962

26 Probably the battle of Waterloo *was* won on the playing-fields of Eton, but the opening battles of all subsequent wars have been lost there.
 George Orwell 1903–50: *The Lion and the Unicorn* (1941)

27 My subject is War, and the pity of War.
 The Poetry is in the pity.
 Wilfred Owen 1893–1918: *Poems* (1963) preface (written 1918)

28 History is littered with the wars which everybody knew would never happen.
 Enoch Powell 1912–98: speech, 19 October 1967

29 A man who is good enough to shed his blood for the
country is good enough to be given a square deal
afterwards.
   Theodore Roosevelt 1858–1919: speech, 4 June 1903

30 Little girl . . . Sometime they'll give a war and nobody will
come.
   Carl Sandburg 1878–1967: *The People, Yes* (1936);
   'Suppose They Gave a War and Nobody Came?' was the
   title of a 1970 film

31 Once more unto the breach, dear friends, once more;
Or close the wall up with our English dead!
In peace there's nothing so becomes a man
As modest stillness and humility:
But when the blast of war blows in our ears,
Then imitate the action of the tiger.
   William Shakespeare 1564–1616: *Henry V* (1599)

32 There is many a boy here to-day who looks on war as all
glory, but, boys, it is all hell.
   General Sherman 1820–91: speech at Columbus, Ohio,
   11 August 1880

33 War is capitalism with the gloves off.
   Tom Stoppard 1937– : *Travesties* (1975)

34 Next to a battle lost, the greatest misery is a battle gained.
   Duke of Wellington 1769–1852: in *Diary of Frances, Lady
   Shelley 1787–1817* (ed. R. Edgcumbe)

Wars

1 Men said openly that Christ and His saints slept.
   Anonymous: of twelfth-century England during the civil
   war between Stephen and Matilda; *Anglo-Saxon
   Chronicle* for 1137

2 *Ils ne passeront pas.*
They shall not pass.
   Anonymous: slogan of the French army at the defence
   of Verdun, 1916; variously attributed to Marshal Pétain
   and to General Robert Nivelle

3 It became necessary to destroy the town to save it.
   Anonymous: statement issued by US Army, referring to
   Ben Tre in Vietnam; in *New York Times* 8 February 1968

4 The Somme is like the Holocaust. It revealed things about
   mankind that we cannot come to terms with and cannot
   forget. It can never become the past.
   Pat Barker 1943– : on winning the Booker Prize,
   November 1995

5 If there is ever another war in Europe, it will come out of
   some damned silly thing in the Balkans.
   Otto von Bismarck 1815–98: quoted in the House of
   Commons, 16 August 1945

6 The Falklands thing was a fight between two bald men
   over a comb.
   Jorge Luis Borges 1899–1986: in *Time* 14 February 1983

7 The angel of death has been abroad throughout the land;
   you may almost hear the beating of his wings.
   John Bright 1811–89: on the effects of the Crimean war;
   speech, House of Commons, 23 February 1855

8 I think we might be going a bridge too far.
   Frederick Browning 1896–1965: expressing reservations
   about the Arnhem 'Market Garden' operation, 10
   September 1944

9 We shall not flag or fail. We shall go on to the end. We
   shall fight in France, we shall fight on the seas and oceans,
   we shall fight with growing confidence and growing
   strength in the air, we shall defend our island, whatever
   the cost may be. We shall fight on the beaches, we shall
   fight on the landing grounds, we shall fight in the fields
   and in the streets, we shall fight in the hills; we shall
   never surrender.
   Winston Churchill 1874–1965: speech, House of
   Commons, 4 June 1940

10 Let us therefore brace ourselves to our duty, and so bear
   ourselves that, if the British Empire and its
   Commonwealth lasts for a thousand years, men will still

say, 'This was their finest hour.'

> **Winston Churchill** 1874–1965: speech, House of
> Commons, 18 June 1940

11 Never in the field of human conflict was so much owed by
so many to so few.

> **Winston Churchill** 1874–1965: on the Battle of Britain;
> speech, House of Commons, 20 August 1940

12 Give us the tools and we will finish the job.

> **Winston Churchill** 1874–1965: radio broadcast, 9
> February 1941

13 My home policy: I wage war; my foreign policy: I wage
war. All the time I wage war.

> **Georges Clemenceau** 1841–1929: speech to French
> Chamber of Deputies, 8 March 1918

14 I'm glad we've been bombed. It makes me feel I can look
the East End in the face.

> **Queen Elizabeth, the Queen Mother** 1900– : to a
> London policeman, 13 September 1940

15 My centre is giving way, my right is retreating, situation
excellent, I am attacking.

> **Ferdinand Foch** 1851–1929: message during the first
> Battle of the Marne, September 1914

16 This is not a peace treaty, it is an armistice for twenty
years.

> **Ferdinand Foch** 1851–1929: at the signing of the Treaty
> of Versailles, 1919; in P. Reynaud *Mémoires* (1963)

17 I counted them all out and I counted them all back.

> **Brian Hanrahan** 1949– : on the number of British
> aeroplanes joining the raid on Port Stanley; BBC
> broadcast report, 1 May 1982

18 *No pasarán.*

They shall not pass.

> **Dolores Ibarruri** 1895–1989: radio broadcast, Madrid, 19
> July 1936

19 We're going to bomb them back into the Stone Age.

> **Curtis E. LeMay** 1906–90: on the North Vietnamese, in
> *Mission with LeMay* (1965)

20 I hope we may say that thus, this fateful morning, came to
an end all wars.
   David Lloyd George 1863–1945: speech, House of
   Commons, 11 November 1918

21 All quiet along the Potomac.
   General George B. McClellan 1826–85: said at the time
   of the American Civil War (attributed)

22 In Flanders fields the poppies blow
Between the crosses, row on row.
   John McCrae 1872–1918: 'In Flanders Fields' (1915)

23 Anyone who isn't confused doesn't really understand the
situation.
   Ed Murrow 1908–65: on the Vietnam War; Walter Bryan
   The Improbable Irish (1969)

24 I have only one eye,—I have a right to be blind sometimes
. . . I really do not see the signal!
   Horatio, Lord Nelson 1758–1805: at the battle of
   Copenhagen; R. Southey *Life of Nelson* (1813)

25 *Guerra a cuchillo.*
War to the knife.
   José de Palafox 1780–1847: at the siege of Saragossa, 4
   August 1808, replying to the suggestion that he should
   surrender (as reported). He actually said '*Guerra y
   cuchillo* [War and the knife]'

26 We must be the great arsenal of democracy.
   Franklin D. Roosevelt 1882–1945: broadcast, 29
   December 1940

27 The First World War had begun—imposed on the
statesmen of Europe by railway timetables.
   A. J. P. Taylor 1906–90: *The First World War* (1963)

28 They now *ring* the bells, but they will soon *wring* their
hands.
   Robert Walpole 1676–1745: on the declaration of war
   with Spain, 1739; W. Coxe *Memoirs of Sir Robert Walpole*
   (1798)

29 Up Guards and at them!
   Duke of Wellington 1769–1852: in *The Battle of Waterloo*
   by a Near Observer [J. Booth] (1815), later denied by
   Wellington

30 Hard pounding this, gentlemen; let's see who will pound
   longest.
   Duke of Wellington 1769–1852: at the Battle of Waterloo;
   in Sir Walter Scott *Paul's Letters* (1816)

31 The battle of Waterloo was won on the playing fields of
   Eton.
   Duke of Wellington 1769–1852: oral tradition, but not
   found in this form of words

Wealth

See also **Money**

1 Riches are a good handmaid, but the worst mistress.
   Francis Bacon 1561–1626: *De Dignitate et Augmentis*
   Scientiarum (1623)

2 It is easier for a camel to go through the eye of a needle,
   than for a rich man to enter into the kingdom of God.
   Bible: St Matthew

3 Greed is all right . . . Greed is healthy. You can be greedy
   and still feel good about yourself.
   Ivan F. Boesky 1937– : commencement address,
   Berkeley, California, 18 May 1986

4 The man who dies . . . rich dies disgraced.
   Andrew Carnegie 1835–1919: *North American Review*
   June 1889

5 Let me tell you about the very rich. They are different
   from you and me.
   F. Scott Fitzgerald 1896–1940: to which Ernest
   Hemingway replied, 'Yes, they have more money'; *All the*
   Sad Young Men (1926)

6 In every well-governed state, wealth is a sacred thing; in democracies it is the only sacred thing.
   Anatole France 1844–1924: *L'Île des pingouins* (1908)

7 We are all Adam's children but silk makes the difference.
   Thomas Fuller 1654–1734: *Gnomologia* (1732)

8 The greater the wealth, the thicker will be the dirt.
   J. K. Galbraith 1908– : *The Affluent Society* (1958)

9 If you can actually count your money, then you are not really a rich man.
   J. Paul Getty 1892–1976: in *Observer* 3 November 1957

10 We are not here to sell a parcel of boilers and vats, but the potentiality of growing rich, beyond the dreams of avarice.
   Samuel Johnson 1709–84: at the sale of Thrale's brewery; James Boswell *Life of Johnson* (1791) 6 April 1781

11 Will the people in the cheaper seats clap your hands? All the rest of you, if you'll just rattle your jewellery.
   John Lennon 1940–80: at Royal Variety Performance, 4 November 1963

12   Let none admire
That riches grow in hell; that soil may best
Deserve the precious bane.
   John Milton 1608–74: *Paradise Lost* (1667)

13 I spend my life ministering to the swinish luxury of the rich.
   William Morris 1834–96: attributed, *c.*1877; W. R. Lethaby *Philip Webb* (1935)

14 Having money is rather like being a blonde. It is more fun but not vital.
   Mary Quant 1934– : in *Observer* 2 November 1986

15 A kiss on the hand may be quite continental,
But diamonds are a girl's best friend.
   Leo Robin 1900– : 'Diamonds are a Girl's Best Friend' (1949 song); from the film *Gentlemen Prefer Blondes*

16 The chief enjoyment of riches consists in the parade of riches.
   Adam Smith 1723–90: *Wealth of Nations* (1776)

17 How many things I can do without!

    Socrates 469–399 BC: on looking at a multitude of wares exposed for sale; Diogenes Laertius *Lives of the Philosophers*

18 It was very prettily said, that we may learn the little value of fortune by the persons on whom heaven is pleased to bestow it.

    Richard Steele 1672–1729: *The Tatler* 27 July 1710

19 I've been rich and I've been poor: rich is better.

    Sophie Tucker 1884–1966: attributed

Weather

1 Rainy days—
silkworms droop
on mulberries.

    Matsuo Basho 1644–94: translated by Lucien Stryk

2 The rain, it raineth on the just
And also on the unjust fella:
But chiefly on the just, because
The unjust steals the just's umbrella.

    Lord Bowen 1835–94: W. Sichel *Sands of Time* (1923)

3 When men were all asleep the snow came flying,
In large white flakes falling on the city brown,
Stealthily and perpetually settling and loosely lying,
Hushing the latest traffic of the drowsy town.

    Robert Bridges 1844–1930: 'London Snow' (1890)

4 Every time it rains, it rains
Pennies from heaven.
Don't you know each cloud contains
Pennies from heaven?

    Johnny Burke 1908–64: 'Pennies from Heaven' (1936 song)

5 The frost performs its secret ministry,
Unhelped by any wind.

    Samuel Taylor Coleridge 1772–1834: 'Frost at Midnight' (1798)

6 This is a London particular . . . A fog, miss.
 Charles Dickens 1812–70: *Bleak House* (1853)

7 A woman rang to say she heard there was a hurricane on
 the way. Well don't worry, there isn't.
 Michael Fish 1944– : weather forecast on the night
 before serious gales in southern England; BBC TV, 15
 October 1987

8 Children are dumb to say how hot the day is,
 How hot the scent is of the summer rose.
 Robert Graves 1895–1985: 'The Cool Web' (1927)

9 This is the weather the cuckoo likes,
 And so do I;
 When showers betumble the chestnut spikes,
 And nestlings fly.
 Thomas Hardy 1840–1928: 'Weathers' (1922)

10 When two Englishmen meet, their first talk is of the
 weather.
 Samuel Johnson 1709–84: in *The Idler* 24 June 1758

11 It is impossible to live in a country which is continually
 under hatches . . . Rain! Rain! Rain!
 John Keats 1795–1821: letter to Reynolds from Devon, 10
 April 1818

12 No one can tell me,
 Nobody knows,
 Where the wind comes from,
 Where the wind goes.
 A. A. Milne 1882–1956: 'Wind on the Hill' (1927)

13 The first fall of snow is not only an event, but it is a
 magical event. You go to bed in one kind of world and
 wake up to find yourself in another quite different, and if
 this is not enchantment, then where is it to be found?
 J. B. Priestley 1894–1984: *Apes and Angels* (1928) 'First
 Snow'

14 The fog comes
 on little cat feet.
 It sits looking
 over harbour and city
 on silent haunches

and then moves on.
Carl Sandburg 1878–1967: 'Fog' (1916)

15 So foul and fair a day I have not seen.
William Shakespeare 1564–1616: *Macbeth* (1606)

16 The best sun we have is made of Newcastle coal.
Horace Walpole 1717–97: letter to George Montagu, 15 June 1768

17 It was the wrong kind of snow.
Terry Worrall: explaining disruption on British Rail, in *The Independent* 16 February 1991

....
Woman's Role
....
See also **Men and Women**

1 If all men are born free, how is it that all women are born slaves?
Mary Astell 1668–1731: *Some Reflections upon Marriage* (1706 ed.)

2 The freedom women were supposed to have found in the Sixties largely boiled down to easy contraception and abortion: things to make life easier for men, in fact.
Julie Burchill 1960– : *Damaged Goods* (1986)

3 I could have stayed home and baked cookies and had teas. But what I decided was to fulfil my profession, which I entered before my husband was in public life.
Hillary Rodham Clinton 1947– : comment on questions raised by rival Democratic contender Edmund G. Brown Jr.; in *Albany Times-Union* 17 March 1992

4 The worker is the slave of capitalist society, the female worker is the slave of that slave.
James Connolly 1868–1916: *The Re-conquest of Ireland* (1915)

5 One is not born a woman: one becomes one.
Simone de Beauvoir 1908–86: *The Second Sex* (1949)

6 Today the problem that has no name is how to juggle work,
love, home and children.
　　Betty Friedan 1921– : *The Second Stage* (1987)

7 I didn't fight to get women out from behind the vacuum
cleaner to get them onto the board of Hoover.
　　Germaine Greer 1939– : in *Guardian* 27 October 1986

8 My mother said it was simple to keep a man, you must be
a maid in the living room, a cook in the kitchen and a
whore in the bedroom. I said I'd hire the other two and
take care of the bedroom bit.
　　Jerry Hall: in *Observer* 6 October 1985

9 A woman's preaching is like a dog's walking on his hinder
legs. It is not done well; but you are surprised to find it
done at all.
　　Samuel Johnson 1709–84: James Boswell *Life of
　　Johnson* (1791) 31 July 1763

10 A man is in general better pleased when he has a good
dinner upon his table, than when his wife talks Greek.
　　Samuel Johnson 1709–84: John Hawkins (ed.) *The
　　Works of Samuel Johnson* (1787) 'Apophthegms,
　　Sentiments, Opinions, etc.'

11 The First Blast of the Trumpet Against the Monstrous
Regiment of Women.
　　John Knox c.1505–72: title of pamphlet (1558)

12 But if God had wanted us to think just with our wombs,
why did He give us a brain?
　　Clare Booth Luce 1903– : in *Life* 16 October 1970

13 Feminism is the most revolutionary idea there has ever
been. Equality for women demands a change in the human
psyche more profound then anything Marx dreamed of. It
means valuing parenthood as much as we value banking.
　　Polly Toynbee 1946– : in *Guardian* 19 January 1987

14 The Queen is most anxious to enlist every one who can
speak or write to join in checking this mad, wicked folly of
'Woman's Rights', with all its attendant horrors, on which
her poor feeble sex is bent, forgetting every sense of

womanly feeling and propriety.
Queen Victoria 1819–1901: letter to Theodore Martin, 29 May 1870

15 I do not wish them [women] to have power over men; but over themselves.
Mary Wollstonecraft 1759–97: *A Vindication of the Rights of Woman* (1792)

....

Women

....

See also **Men and Women**

1 The weaker sex, to piety more prone.
William Alexander, Earl of Stirling *c.*1567–1640: 'Doomsday' 5th Hour (1637)

2 All the privilege I claim for my own sex . . . is that of loving longest, when existence or when hope is gone.
Jane Austen 1775–1817: *Persuasion* (1818)

3 Who can find a virtuous woman? for her price is far above rubies.
Bible: Proverbs

4 Good women always think it is their fault when someone else is being offensive. Bad women never take the blame for anything.
Anita Brookner 1938– : *Hotel du Lac* (1984)

5 In her first passion woman loves her lover,
In all the others all she loves is love.
Lord Byron 1788–1824: *Don Juan* (1819–24)

6 Women, then, are only children of a larger growth.
Lord Chesterfield 1694–1773: *Letters to his Son* (1774) 5 September 1748

7 The prime truth of woman, the universal mother . . . that if a thing is worth doing, it is worth doing badly.
G. K. Chesterton 1874–1936: *What's Wrong with the World* (1910)

8 She knows her man, and when you rant and swear,
Can draw you to her *with a single hair*.
    John Dryden 1631–1700: translation of Persius *Satires*

9 She takes just like a woman, yes, she does
She makes love just like a woman, yes, she does
And she aches just like a woman
But she breaks like a little girl.
    Bob Dylan 1941– : 'Just Like a Woman' (1966 song)

10 The happiest women, like the happiest nations, have no
history.
    George Eliot 1819–80: *The Mill on the Floss* (1860)

11 What does a woman want?
    Sigmund Freud 1856–1939: letter to Marie Bonaparte, E.
Jones *Sigmund Freud* (1955)

12 Eternal Woman draws us upward.
    Johann Wolfgang von Goethe 1749–1832: *Faust* pt. 2
(1832)

13 Being a woman is of special interest only to aspiring male
transsexuals. To actual women, it is merely a good excuse
not to play football.
    Fran Lebowitz 1946– : *Metropolitan Life* (1978)

14 She's the sort of woman who lives for others—you can
always tell the others by their hunted expression.
    C. S. Lewis 1898–1963: *The Screwtape Letters* (1942)

15 So this gentleman said a girl with brains ought to do
something with them besides think.
    Anita Loos 1893–1981: *Gentlemen Prefer Blondes* (1925)

16 A woman will always sacrifice herself if you give her the
opportunity. It is her favourite form of self-indulgence.
    W. Somerset Maugham 1874–1965: *Circle* (1921)

17 Woman was God's second blunder.
    Friedrich Nietzsche 1844–1900: *Der Antichrist* (1888)

18 Woman is the nigger of the world.
    Yoko Ono 1933– : interview for *Nova* magazine (1968);
adopted by John Lennon as song title (1972)

19 Slamming their doors, stamping their high heels, banging their irons and saucepans—the eternal flaming racket of the female.
    John Osborne 1929– : *Look Back in Anger* (1956)

20 The greatest glory of a woman is to be least talked about by men.
    Pericles c.495–429 BC: Thucydides *History of the Peloponnesian War*

21 Every woman adores a Fascist,
The boot in the face, the brute
Brute heart of a brute like you.
    Sylvia Plath 1932–63: 'Daddy' (1963)

22 *Elle flotte, elle hésite; en un mot, elle est femme.*
She floats, she hesitates; in a word, she's a woman.
    Jean Racine 1639–99: *Athalie* (1691)

23 O Woman! in our hours of ease,
Uncertain, coy, and hard to please . . .
When pain and anguish wring the brow,
A ministering angel thou!
    Sir Walter Scott 1771–1832: *Marmion* (1808)

24   Frailty, thy name is woman!
    William Shakespeare 1564–1616: *Hamlet* (1601)

25 Age cannot wither her, nor custom stale
Her infinite variety; other women cloy
The appetites they feed, but she makes hungry
Where most she satisfies.
    William Shakespeare 1564–1616: *Antony and Cleopatra* (1606–7)

26 Vitality in a woman is a blind fury of creation.
    George Bernard Shaw 1856–1950: *Man and Superman* (1903)

27 Here's to the maiden of bashful fifteen
Here's to the widow of fifty
Here's to the flaunting, extravagant quean;
And here's to the housewife that's thrifty.
    Richard Brinsley Sheridan 1751–1816: *The School for Scandal* (1777)

28 The great and almost only comfort about being a woman is
that one can always pretend to be more stupid than one is
and no one is surprised.

    Freya Stark 1893–1993: *The Valleys of the Assassins*
(1934)

29 We are becoming the men we wanted to marry.

    Gloria Steinem 1934– : *Ms* July/August 1982

30 From birth to 18 a girl needs good parents. From 18 to 35,
she needs good looks. From 35 to 55, good personality.
From 55 on, she needs good cash.

    Sophie Tucker 1884–1966: M. Freedland *Sophie* (1978)

31 When once a woman has given you her heart, you can
never get rid of the rest of her body.

    John Vanbrugh 1664–1726: *The Relapse* (1696)

32   *Varium et mutabile semper*
Femina.

Fickle and changeable always is woman.

    Virgil 70–19 BC: *Aeneid*

Words

See also **Language**, **Meaning**

1 The Greeks had a word for it.

    Zoë Akins 1886–1958: title of play (1930)

2 Words are the tokens current and accepted for conceits, as
moneys are for values.

    Francis Bacon 1561–1626: *The Advancement of Learning*
(1605)

3 There is no use indicting words, they are no shoddier than
what they peddle.

    Samuel Beckett 1906–89: *Malone Dies* (1958)

4 'When *I* use a word,' Humpty Dumpty said in a rather
scornful tone, 'it means just what I choose it to mean—
neither more nor less.'

    Lewis Carroll 1832–98: *Through the Looking-Glass* (1872)

5 It cannot in the opinion of His Majesty's Government be classified as slavery in the extreme acceptance of the word without some risk of terminological inexactitude.

Winston Churchill 1874–1965: speech, House of Commons, 22 February 1906

6 A man who could make so vile a pun would not scruple to pick a pocket.

John Dennis 1657–1734: *The Gentleman's Magazine* (1781), editorial note

7   Words strain,
Crack and sometimes break, under the burden,
Under the tension, slip, slide, perish,
Decay with imprecision, will not stay in place,
Will not stay still.

T. S. Eliot 1888–1965: *Four Quartets* 'Burnt Norton' (1936)

8 Dialect words—those terrible marks of the beast to the truly genteel.

Thomas Hardy 1840–1928: *The Mayor of Casterbridge* (1886)

9 And once sent out, a word takes wing beyond recall.

Horace 65–8 BC: *Epistles*

10 *Lexicographer*. A writer of dictionaries, a harmless drudge.

Samuel Johnson 1709–84: *Dictionary of the English Language* (1755)

11 I am not yet so lost in lexicography as to forget that words are the daughters of earth, and that things are the sons of heaven. Language is only the instrument of science, and words are but the signs of ideas.

Samuel Johnson 1709–84: *Dictionary of the English Language* (1755) preface

12 Words are, of course, the most powerful drug used by mankind.

Rudyard Kipling 1865–1936: speech, 14 February 1923

13 In my youth there were words you couldn't say in front of a girl; now you can't say 'girl'.

Tom Lehrer 1928– : interview in *The Oldie*, 1996

14 Woord is but wynd; leff woord and tak the dede.
John Lydgate c.1370–c.1451: *Secrets of Old Philosophers*

15 Syllables govern the world.
John Selden 1584–1654: *Table Talk* (1689) 'Power: State'

16 What's in a name? that which we call a rose
By any other name would smell as sweet.
William Shakespeare 1564–1616: *Romeo and Juliet*
(1595)

17 But words are words; I never yet did hear
That the bruised heart was piercèd through the ear.
William Shakespeare 1564–1616: *Othello* (1602–4)

18 In a world full of audio visual marvels, may words matter
to you and be full of magic.
Godfrey Smith 1926– : letter to a new grandchild, in
Sunday Times 5 July 1987

Work

1 *Arbeit macht frei.*

Work liberates.
Anonymous: words inscribed on the gates of Dachau
concentration camp, 1933, and subsequently on those of
Auschwitz

2 In the sweat of thy face shalt thou eat bread.
Bible: Genesis

3 For the labourer is worthy of his hire.
Bible: St Luke

4 By working faithfully eight hours a day, you may
eventually get to be a boss and work twelve hours a day.
Robert Frost 1874–1963: attributed

5 Work is love made visible.
Kahlil Gibran 1883–1931: *The Prophet* (1923)

6 That state is a state of slavery in which a man does what he likes to do in his spare time and in his working time that which is required of him.

Eric Gill 1882–1940: *Art-nonsense and Other Essays* (1929) 'Slavery and Freedom'.

7 The pornography industry is virtually the only employer that pays women very much better than men.

Germaine Greer 1939– : in *Observer* 12 March 2000

8 I have long been of the opinion that if work were such a splendid thing the rich would have kept more of it for themselves.

Bruce Grocott 1940– : *Observer* 22 May 1988

9 I like work: it fascinates me. I can sit and look at it for hours. I love to keep it by me: the idea of getting rid of it nearly breaks my heart.

Jerome K. Jerome 1859–1927: *Three Men in a Boat* (1889)

10 Why should I let the toad *work*
Squat on my life?
Can't I use my wit as a pitchfork
And drive the brute off?

Philip Larkin 1922–85: 'Toads' (1955)

11 Blessèd are the horny hands of toil!

James Russell Lowell 1819–91: 'A Glance Behind the Curtain' (1844)

12 Work expands so as to fill the time available for its completion.

C. Northcote Parkinson 1909–93: *Parkinson's Law* (1958)

13 We spend our midday sweat, our midnight oil;
We tire the night in thought, the day in toil.

Francis Quarles 1592–1644: *Emblems* (1635)

14 It's true hard work never killed anybody, but I figure why take the chance?

Ronald Reagan 1911– : in *Guardian* 31 March 1987

15 If you have great talents, industry will improve them: if you have but moderate abilities, industry will supply their deficiency.

   Joshua Reynolds 1723–92: *Discourses on Art* (11 December 1769)

16 Which of us . . . is to do the hard and dirty work for the rest—and for what pay? Who is to do the pleasant and clean work, and for what pay?

   John Ruskin 1819–1900: *Sesame and Lilies* (1865)

17 One of the symptoms of approaching nervous breakdown is the belief that one's work is terribly important, and that to take a holiday would bring all kinds of disaster.

   Bertrand Russell 1872–1970: *Conquest of Happiness* (1930)

18 The labour we delight in physics pain.

   William Shakespeare 1564–1616: *Macbeth* (1606)

19 Work was like a stick. It had two ends. When you worked for the knowing you gave them quality; when you worked for a fool you simply gave him eye-wash.

   Alexander Solzhenitsyn 1918– : *One Day in the Life of Ivan Denisovich* (1962)

20 Work to survive, survive by consuming, survive to consume: the hellish cycle is complete.

   Raoul Vaneigem 1934– : *The Revolution of Everyday Life* (1967)

21 Work is the curse of the drinking classes.

   Oscar Wilde 1854–1900: in H. Pearson *Life of Oscar Wilde* (1946)

Writers

See also **Poets**, **Shakespeare**

1 Shaw's plays are the price we pay for Shaw's prefaces.

   James Agate 1877–1947: diary 10 March 1933

2 Writers, like teeth, are divided into incisors and grinders.
  Walter Bagehot 1826–77: *Estimates of some Englishmen
  and Scotchmen* (1858)

3 He describes London like a special correspondent for
  posterity.
  Walter Bagehot 1826–77: in *National Review* 7 October
  1858 'Charles Dickens'

4 When I am dead, I hope it may be said:
  'His sins were scarlet, but his books were read.'
  Hilaire Belloc 1870–1953: 'On His Books' (1923)

5 The writer's only responsibility is to his art. He will be
  completely ruthless if he is a good one . . . If a writer has
  to rob his mother, he will not hesitate; the *Ode on a
  Grecian Urn* is worth any number of old ladies.
  William Faulkner 1897–1962: in *Paris Review* Spring 1956

6 A dogged attempt to cover the universe with mud, an
  inverted Victorianism, an attempt to make crossness and
  dirt succeed where sweetness and light failed.
  E. M. Forster 1879–1970: of James Joyce's *Ulysses*;
  Aspects of the Novel (1927)

7 Another damned, thick, square book! Always scribble,
  scribble, scribble! Eh! Mr Gibbon?
  Duke of Gloucester 1743–1805: in Henry Best *Personal
  and Literary Memorials* (1829) also attributed to the Duke
  of Cumberland and George III

8 The work of Henry James has always seemed divisible by a
  simple dynastic arrangement into three reigns: James I,
  James II, and the Old Pretender.
  Philip Guedalla 1889–1944: *Supers and Supermen* (1920)

9 No man but a blockhead ever wrote, except for money.
  Samuel Johnson 1709–84: James Boswell *Life of
  Johnson* (1791) 5 April 1776

10 He has the look of a man who has been in hell and seen
  there, not a hopeless suffering, but meanness and frippery.
  W. Somerset Maugham 1874–1965: on Dostoevsky; *A
  Writer's Notebook* (1949) written in 1917

11 I think like a genius, I write like a distinguished author, and I speak like a child.
   Vladimir Nabokov 1899–1977: *Strong Opinions* (1973)

12 English literature's performing flea.
   Sean O'Casey 1880–1964: P. G. Wodehouse *Performing Flea* (1953), describing the author

13 The shelf life of the modern hardback writer is somewhere between the milk and the yoghurt.
   Calvin Trillin 1935– : in *Sunday Times* 9 June 1991 (attributed)

14 A woman must have money and a room of her own if she is to write fiction.
   Virginia Woolf 1882–1941: *A Room of One's Own* (1929)

....

Writing
....

See also **Books**, **Literature**, **Poetry**, **Style**

1 If you can't annoy somebody with what you write, I think there's little point in writing.
   Kingsley Amis 1922–95: in *Radio Times* 1 May 1971

2 Let other pens dwell on guilt and misery. I quit such odious subjects as soon as I can.
   Jane Austen 1775–1817: *Mansfield Park* (1814)

3 Beneath the rule of men entirely great
   The pen is mightier than the sword.
   Edward Bulwer-Lytton 1803–73: *Richelieu* (1839)

4 You praise the firm restraint with which they write—
   I'm with you there, of course:
   They use the snaffle and the curb all right,
   But where's the bloody horse?
   Roy Campbell 1901–57: 'On Some South African Novelists' (1930)

5 When in doubt have a man come through the door with a gun in his hand.
   Raymond Chandler 1888–1959: attributed

6 A writer must be as objective as a chemist: he must abandon the subjective line; he must know that dung-heaps play a very reasonable part in a landscape, and that evil passions are as inherent in life as good ones.

    Anton Chekhov 1860–1904: letter to M. V. Kiselev, 14 January 1887

7 They shut me up in prose—
As when a little girl
They put me in the closet—
Because they liked me 'still'.

    Emily Dickinson 1830–86: 'They shut me up in prose' (c.1862)

8 We must beat the iron while it is hot, but we may polish it at leisure.

    John Dryden 1631–1700: *Aeneis* (1697)

9 The test of a round character is whether it is capable of surprising in a convincing way. If it never surprises, it is flat. If it does not convince, it is flat pretending to be round.

    E. M. Forster 1879–1970: *Aspects of the Novel* (1927)

10 Only connect! . . . Only connect the prose and the passion.

    E. M. Forster 1879–1970: *Howards End* (1910)

11 The business of the poet and novelist is to show the sorriness underlying the grandest things, and the grandeur underlying the sorriest things.

    Thomas Hardy 1840–1928: notebook entry for 19 April 1885

12 The most essential gift for a good writer is a built-in, shock-proof shit detector. This is the writer's radar and all great writers have had it.

    Ernest Hemingway 1899–1961: in *Paris Review* Spring 1958

13 I am a camera with its shutter open, quite passive, recording, not thinking.

    Christopher Isherwood 1904–86: *Goodbye to Berlin* (1939) 'Berlin Diary' Autumn 1930

14 A man may write at any time, if he will set himself
doggedly to it.
  Samuel Johnson 1709–84: James Boswell *Life of
  Johnson* (1791) March 1750

15 Read over your compositions, and where ever you meet
with a passage which you think is particularly fine, strike
it out.
  Samuel Johnson 1709–84: in James Boswell *Life of
  Johnson* (1791) 30 April 1773; quoting a college tutor

16 A writer's ambition should be . . . to trade a hundred
contemporary readers for ten readers in ten years' time
and for one reader in a hundred years.
  Arthur Koestler 1905–83: in *New York Times Book
  Review* 1 April 1951

17 When my sonnet was rejected, I exclaimed, 'Damn the age;
I will write for Antiquity!'
  Charles Lamb 1775–1834: letter to B. W. Proctor 22
  January 1829

18 If you try to nail anything down in the novel, either it kills
the novel, or the novel gets up and walks away with the
nail.
  D. H. Lawrence 1885–1930: *Phoenix* (1936) 'Morality and
  the Novel'

19 There is no need for the writer to eat a whole sheep to be
able to tell you what mutton tastes like. It is enough if he
eats a cutlet. But he should do that.
  W. Somerset Maugham 1874–1965: *A Writer's Notebook*
  (1949) written in 1941

20 Things unattempted yet in prose or rhyme.
  John Milton 1608–74: *Paradise Lost* (1667)

21   What in me is dark
Illumine, what is low raise and support;
That to the height of this great argument
I may assert eternal providence,
And justify the ways of God to men.
  John Milton 1608–74: *Paradise Lost* (1667)

22 If you steal from one author, it's plagiarism; if you steal from many, it's research.
   Wilson Mizner 1876–1933: A. Johnston *The Legendary Mizners* (1953)

23 The last thing one knows in constructing a work is what to put first.
   Blaise Pascal 1623–62: *Pensées* (1670)

24 But those who cannot write, and those who can,
   All rhyme, and scrawl, and scribble, to a man.
   Alexander Pope 1688–1744: *Imitations of Horace* (1737)

25 And, as imagination bodies forth
   The forms of things unknown, the poet's pen
   Turns them to shapes, and gives to airy nothing
   A local habitation and a name.
   William Shakespeare 1564–1616: *A Midsummer Night's Dream* (1595–6)

26 Writing is not a profession but a vocation of unhappiness.
   Georges Simenon 1903–89: in *Paris Review* Summer 1955

27 Not that the story need be long, but it will take a long while to make it short.
   Henry David Thoreau 1817–62: letter to Harrison Blake, 16 November 1857

28 The composition of a tragedy requires *testicles*.
   Voltaire 1694–1778: on being asked why no woman had ever written 'a tolerable tragedy'; letter from Byron to John Murray, 2 April 1817

29 I come from a backward place: your duty is supplied by life around you. One guy plants bananas; another plants cocoa; I'm a writer, I plant lines. There's the same clarity of occupation, and the sense of devotion.
   Derek Walcott 1930– : in *Guardian* 12 July 1997

30 Never forget what I believe was observed to you by Coleridge, that every great and original writer, in proportion as he is great and original, must himself create the taste by which he is to be relished.
   William Wordsworth 1770–1850: letter to Lady Beaumont, 21 May 1807

Youth

See also **The Generation Gap**

1 I'm not young enough to know everything.
  J. M. Barrie 1860–1937: *The Admirable Crichton*
  (performed 1902, published 1914)

2 Youth is something very new: twenty years ago no one
  mentioned it.
  Coco Chanel 1883–1971: M. Haedrich *Coco Chanel, Her
  Life, Her Secrets* (1971)

3 It is better to waste one's youth than to do nothing with it
  at all.
  Georges Courteline 1858–1929: *La Philosophie de
  Georges Courteline* (1948)

4 A boy's will is the wind's will
  And the thoughts of youth are long, long thoughts.
  Henry Wadsworth Longfellow 1807–82: 'My Lost
  Youth' (1858)

5 Youth is vivid rather than happy, but memory always
  remembers the happy things.
  Bernard Lovell 1913– : in *The Times* 20 August 1993

6 Whom the gods love dies young.
  Menander 342–c.292 BC: *Dis Exapaton*

7 The atrocious crime of being a young man . . . I shall
  neither attempt to palliate nor deny.
  William Pitt 1708–78: speech, House of Commons,
  2 March 1741

8 Being young is greatly overestimated . . . Any failure
  seems so total. Later on you realize you can have another
  go.
  Mary Quant 1934– : in *Observer* 5 May 1996

9   My salad days,
  When I was green in judgement.
  William Shakespeare 1564–1616: *Antony and Cleopatra*
  (1606–7)

10 What music is more enchanting than the voices of young
people, when you can't hear what they say?

Logan Pearsall Smith 1865–1946: *Afterthoughts* (1931)

11 The force that through the green fuse drives the flower
Drives my green age.

Dylan Thomas 1914–53: 'The force that through the
green fuse' (1934)

12 Heaven lies about us in our infancy!
Shades of the prison-house begin to close
Upon the growing boy.

William Wordsworth 1770–1850: 'Ode. Intimations of
Immortality' (1807)

Index of Authors

Abbott, Diane
(1953–)
Politicians 1

Abse, Dannie (1923–)
Men 1
Sickness 1

Accius (170–*c*.86 BC)
Government 1

Acheson, Dean
(1893–1971)
Britain 1
Bureaucracy 1
Careers 1

Acton, Lord
(1834–1902)
Power 1

Adams, Abigail
(1744–1818)
Character 1

Adams, Douglas
(1952–)
Life 1

Adams, Franklin P.
(1881–1960)
Middle Age 1
Voting 1

**Adams, Henry
Brooks** (1838–1918)
Education 1
Experience 1
Meaning 1
Morality 1
Teaching 1

Adams, John
(1735–1826)
Government 2
Letters 1
Politics 1
Presidency 1

Adamson, Harold
(1906–80)
Crises 1

Addison, Joseph
(1672–1719)
Business 1
Future 1
Gardens 1
Happiness 1
Humour 1
Patriotism 1
Success 1

Ade, George
(1866–1944)
Marriage 1

Adenauer, Konrad
(1876–1967)
Character 2

Adler, Alfred
(1870–1937)
Truth 1

Adorno, Theodor
(1903–69)
Poetry 1

Agar, Herbert
(1897–1980)
Truth 2

Agate, James
(1877–1947)
Certainty 1
Writers 1

Agathon (b. *c*.445 BC)
Past 1

Agee, James
(1909–55)
Nature 1

Agesilaus (444–400 BC)
Action 1

Aitken, Jonathan
(1942–)
Justice 1

Akins, Zoë (1886–1958)
Words 1

Alain (1868–1951)
Ideas 1

Alcuin (*c*.735–804)
Minorities 1

Aldington, Richard
(1892–1962)
Patriotism 2

Aldiss, Brian (1925–)
Violence 1

Aldrin, Buzz (1930–)
Skies 1

**Alexander, Cecil
Frances** (1818–95)
Animals 1
Class 1

Alexander II, Tsar
(1818–81)
Revolution 1

**Alexander, William,
Earl of Stirling**
(*c*.1567–1640)
Women 1

**Alfonso 'the Wise',
King of Castile**
(1221–84)
Universe 1

Ali, Muhammad
(1942–)
Sport 1, 2

Ali ibn-Abi-Talib
(*c*.602–661)
Enemies 1

Allen, Fred
(1894–1956)
America 1
Management 1

Allen, Woody (1935–)
Death 1
Sex 1, 2, 3

Alliluyeva, Svetlana
(1925–)
People 1

Allingham, William
(1824–89)
Supernatural 1

Ambrose, St
(*c*.339–97)
Behaviour 1
**American
Declaration of
Independence** (1776)
Human Rights 1
Ames, Fisher
(1758–1808)
Government 3
Amies, Hardy (1909–)
Dress 1
Amis, Kingsley
(1922–95)
Death 2
Men and Women 1
Writing 1
Amis, Martin (1949–)
Middle Age 2
Anacharsis (6th
century BC)
Law 1
**Andrewes, Bishop
Lancelot** (1555–1626)
Church 1
Angelou, Maya
(1928–)
Suffering 1
Anka, Paul (1941–)
Living 1
Annan, Kofi (1938–)
Cooperation 1
Anonymous
Alcohol 1
Army 1
Birds 1
Business 2
Computers 1
Crises 2
Death 3
Determination 1, 2
Economics 1
Education 2
Epitaphs 1, 2, 3, 4
Experience 2
Fame 1

Fools 1
Friendship 1
God 1
Gossip 1, 2
Government 4
Heroes 1
Human Rights 2
Ideas 2
Intelligence 1
Ireland 1
Justice 2, 3
Knowledge 1
Liberty 1
Lies 1
Living 2
Madness 1
Mathematics 1, 2
Moderation 1
Money 1
Music 1
News 1
Past 2
Politicians 2
Race 1
Sea 1
Seasons 1
Self-Knowledge 1
Supernatural 2
Technology 1
Transience 1
Twentieth Century 1
Voting 2
War 1, 2
Wars 1, 2, 3
Work 1
Anouilh, Jean
(1910–87)
Fate 1
Love 1
**Apollinaire,
Guillaume** (1880–1918)
Custom 1
Inventions 1
Memory 1
**Appleton, Thomas
Gold** (1812–84)
America 2, 3

Arbus, Diane
(1923–71)
Photography 1
Arbuthnot, Dr
(1667–1735)
Law 2
Archilochus (7th
century BC)
Knowledge 2
Archimedes
(*c*.287–212 BC)
Inventions 2
Technology 2
Arden, Elizabeth
(1876–1966)
Money 2
Arendt, Hannah
(1906–75)
Good 1
Revolution 2
Aristotle (384–322 BC)
Acting 1
Certainty 2
Friendship 2
Good 2
Nature 2
Politics 2
Solitude 1
Truth 3
War 3
Armstrong, Louis
(1901–71)
Music 2, 3
Armstrong, Neil
(1930–)
Achievement 1
Armstrong, Robert
(1927–)
Truth 4
Arnald-Amaury
(d. 1225)
Cynicism 1
Arnold, Matthew
(1822–88)
Belief 1
Change 1
Leadership 1

Memory 2
Middle Age 3
Perfection 1
Places 1, 2
Poetry 2
Poets 1, 2
Seasons 2
Shakespeare 1
Solitude 2
Style 1
Arnold, Thomas
(1795–1842)
Crime 1
Ascham, Roger
(1515–68)
Education 3
Teaching 2
Ashford, Daisy
(1881–1972)
Middle Age 4
Prayer 1
Asimov, Isaac
(1920–92)
Health 1
Asquith, Herbert
(1852–1928)
Political Comment 1
Statistics 1
Asquith, Margot
(1864–1945)
Supernatural 3
Astell, Mary
(1668–1731)
Woman's Role 1
Astley, Jacob
(1579–1652)
Prayer 2
Astor, Nancy
(1879–1964)
Alcohol 2
Atkinson, Brooks
(1894–1984)
Democracy 1
Past 3
Attenborough, David
(1926–)
Animals 2

Attlee, Clement
(1883–1967)
Democracy 2
Politics 3
Aubrey, John
(1626–97)
Gossip 3
Reading 1
**Auctoritates
Aristotelis**
Argument 1
Parents 1
Time 1
Auden, W. H.
(1907–73)
Art 1
Behaviour 2
Body 1
Books 1
Death 4
Generation Gap 1
Good 3
Heart 1
Humour 2
Intelligence 2
Letters 2
People 2
Poetry 3
Poets 3
Power 1
Science 1
Self 1, 2
Society 1
Sorrow 1
Success 2
Suffering 2
Transport 1
Augarten, Stan
Computers 2
**Augustine, St of
Hippo** (AD 354–430)
Good 4
Justice 4
Living 3
Moderation 2
Sex 4

Aung San Suu Kyi
(1945–)
Men and Women 2
Aurelius, Marcus
(AD 121–80)
Suffering 3
Thinking 1
Time 2
Austen, Jane
(1775–1817)
Advice 1
Conversation 1
Gifts 1
Gossip 4
Happiness 2
Humour 3
Idleness 1
Ignorance 1
Literature 1
Marriage 2
Men 2
Money 3
Morality 2
Perfection 3
Places 3
Pleasure 1
Women 2
Writing 2
Awdry, Revd W.
(1911–97)
Church 1
Ayer, A. J. (1910–89)
Opinion 1
Ayres, Pam (1947–)
Medicine 1

Babel, Isaac
(1894–1940)
Fear 1
Bacall, Lauren
(1924–)
Sickness 2
Bacon, Francis
(1561–1626)
Action 2
Anger 1
Beauty 1

Bacon, Francis
(cont.)
  Belief 2
  Books 2
  Certainty 3
  Change 2
  Children 1
  Dance 1
  Death 5
  Diplomacy 1
  Education 4
  Fame 2
  Family 1
  Friendship 3
  Gardens 2
  Indifference 1
  Inventions 3
  Knowledge 3
  Life 2
  Marriage 3
  Medicine 2, 3
  Misfortune 1
  Money 4
  Old Age 1
  Parents 2
  Past 4
  Power 3
  Praise 1
  Revenge 1
  Royalty 1
  Silence 1
  Travel 1
  Truth 5
  Virtue 1
  Wealth 1
  Words 2
Bacon, Roger
(c.1220–c.1292)
  Mathematics 3
Bagehot, Walter
(1826–77)
  Bureaucracy 2
  Languages 1
  Leadership 2
  Marriage 4
  News 2
  Pleasure 2

  Politicians 3
  Pride 1
  Royalty 2, 3, 4
  Writers 2, 3
Bailey, David (1938–)
  Photography 2
Bainbridge, Beryl
(1933–)
  Suffering 4
Bairnsfather, Bruce
(1888–1959)
  Advice 2
Bakunin, Michael
(1814–76)
  Musicians 1
Baldwin, James
(1924–87)
  Money 5
  Poverty 1
  Prejudice 1
Baldwin, Stanley
(1867–1947)
  Political Comment 2
  Secrets 1
  War 4
**Balfour, Arthur
James** (1848–1930)
  Politicians 4
Ballard, J. G. (1930–)
  Places 4
  Transport 2
  Twentieth Century 2
Barker, Pat (1943–)
  Wars 4
**Barnard, Frederick
R.**
  Language 1
Barnes, Julian
(1946–)
  Books 3
  Britain 3
  History 1
Barnum, Phineas T.
(1810–91)
  Fools 2

Barrie, J. M.
(1860–1937)
  Belief 3
  Charm 1
  Death 6
  Life 3
  Memory 3
  Practicality 1
  Scotland 1
  Self-Knowledge 2
  Youth 1
Barrymore, John
(1882–1942)
  Solitude 3
Barth, Karl
(1886–1968)
  Musicians 2
Barthes, Roland
(1915–80)
  Transport 3
Baruch, Bernard
(1870–1965)
  Old Age 2
Barzun, Jacques
(1907–)
  Life 4
Basho, Matsuo
(1644–94)
  Animals 3
  Seasons 3
  Weather 1
**Bates, Katherine
Lee** (1859–1929)
  America 4
Baudelaire, Charles
(1821–67)
  Class 2
  Inventions 4
  Progress 1
Baudrillard, Jean
(1929–)
  America 5
Baxter, Richard
(1615–91)
  Behaviour 3
Bayley, John (1925–)
  Sickness 3

Beaumarchais, Pierre-Augustin Caron de (1732–99)
Human Race 1
Humour 4
Singing 1

Beaverbrook, Lord (1879–1964)
Inventions 5

Beckett, Samuel (1906–89)
Bores 1
Custom 2
Death 7
Human Race 2
Life 5
Success 3
Time 3
Words 3

Becon, Thomas (1512–67)
Alcohol 3

Bede, The Venerable (AD 673–735)
Life 6

Beecham, Thomas (1879–1961)
Music 4
Musicians 3

Beerbohm, Max (1872–1956)
Imagination 1
Philosophy 1
Sleep 1

Beethoven, Ludwig van (1770–1827)
Fate 2
Musicians 4

Beeton, Mrs (1836–65)
Management 2

Behan, Brendan (1923–64)
Absence 1
Fame 3

Behn, Aphra (1640–89)
Money 6
Poverty 2

Bellarmine, Cardinal Robert (1542–1621)
Memory 4

Belloc, Hilaire (1870–1953)
Certainty 4
Class 3
Life Sciences 1
Medicine 4
Misfortune 3
Pleasure 3
Power 4
Violence 2
Voting 3
Writers 4

Benchley, Robert (1889–1945)
Places 5
Quotations 1

Benn, Tony (1925–)
Belief 4
Future 2
Photography 3
Titles 1

Bennett, Alan (1934–)
Acting 2
Family 2
Memory 5
Morality 3
Royalty 5
Society 2

Bennett, Arnold (1867–1931)
Idealism 1
Justice 5
Marriage 5
News 3

Bennett, Jill (1931–90)
Marriage 6

Bensley, Connie (1929–)
Body 2

Bentham, Jeremy (1748–1832)
Animals 4
Crime 2
Human Rights 3
Poetry 4
Society 3

Bentley, Edmund Clerihew (1875–1956)
Biography 1

Beresford, Lord Charles (1846–1919)
Apology 1

Berkeley, Bishop George (1685–1753)
Knowledge 4
Mathematics 4

Berlin, Irving (1888–1989)
Acting 3
America 6
Christmas 1
Dance 2

Berlin, Isaiah (1909–97)
Liberty 2
People 3

Bernal, J. D. (1901–71)
Life Sciences 2

Bernanos, Georges (1888–1948)
Heaven 1
Prayer 3

Bernard, Claude (1813–78)
Life Sciences 3

Bernard of Chartres (d. c.1130)
Progress 2

Berners, Lord (1883–1950)
Fame 4

Berra, Yogi (1925–)
Beginnings 1
Future 3

Berryman, John
(1914–72)
Bores 2
Fear 2
Betjeman, John
(1906–84)
Christmas 2
Education 5
Environment 1
Bevan, Aneurin
(1897–1960)
Management 3
Moderation 3
News 4
Political Comment 3
Political Parties 1
Politicians 5, 6, 7
**Beveridge, William
Henry** (1879–1963)
Progress 3
Bevin, Ernest
(1881–1951)
Enemies 2
Political Comment 4
Bhagavad Gita
(250 BC–AD 250)
Time 4
Bhutto, Benazir
(1953–)
Power 5
Bible
Absence 2
Alcohol 4
Anger 2
Animals 5
Argument 2
Beauty 2
Beginnings 2
Belief 5
Birth 1
Body 3
Books 4
Careers 2
Chance 1
Change 3
Children 2, 3
Christmas 3

Cooperation 2
Crime 3, 4
Death 8, 9
Enemies 3
Environment 2
Envy 1
Epitaphs 5
Equality 1
Fame 5
Family 3
Fate 3
Food 1
Fools 3, 4
Forgiveness 1
Friendship 4
Gardens 3
Gifts 2, 3, 4
God 2, 3
Good 5, 6
Greatness 1
Hatred 1
Heaven 2
Hope 1
Hypocrisy 1
Idealism 2
Idleness 2
Inventions 6
Justice 6, 7
Knowledge 5, 6
Language 2
Law 3
Leadership 3
Life 7, 8
Living 4, 5
Love 2, 3, 4, 5, 6
Manners 1
Marriage 7
Medicine 5
Misfortune 3
Moderation 4
Money 7
Murder 1
News 5, 6
Old Age 3
Parents 3, 4
Peace 1, 2
Pollution 1

Poverty 3
Prayer 4
Present 1, 2
Pride 2, 3
Progress 4
Religion 1, 2
Revenge 2
Sea 2
Secrets 2
Self-Knowledge 3
Sleep 2
Solitude 4
Sorrow 2, 3
Success 4, 5
Supernatural 4, 5
Teaching 3
Temptation 1
Time 5
Transience 2
Trust 1
Truth 6
Violence 3
Virtue 2
Wealth 2
Women 3
Work 2, 3
Bible (Apocrypha)
Business 2
Medicine 6
Truth 7
Bidault, Georges
(1899–1983)
Mistakes 1
Bierce, Ambrose
(1842–c.1914)
Pollution 2
Religion 3
Biko, Steve (1946–77)
Power 6
Billings, Josh
(1818–85)
Knowledge 7
Binyon, Laurence
(1869–1943)
Epitaphs 6
Bion (c.325–c.255 BC)
Cruelty 1

Birkett, Lord
(1883–1962)
  Speech 1
Birrell, Augustine
(1850–1933)
  History 2
Bishop, Elizabeth
(1911–79)
  Sleep 3
Bismarck, Otto von
(1815–98)
  Europe 1
  Political Comment 5
  Politicians 8
  Politics 4, 5
  War 5
  Wars 5
Björk (1965–)
  Music 5
Black, James
(1924–)
  Secrets 3
Blacker, Valentine
(1728–1823)
  Practicality 2
Blackstone, William
(1723–80)
  Justice 8
Blair, Tony (1953–)
  Action 3
  Crime 5
  Education 6
  Leadership 4
  People 4
Blake, Eubie
(1883–1983)
  Old Age 4
Blake, William
(1757–1827)
  Anger 3
  Animals 6
  Cruelty 2
  England 1
  Environment 3
  Fools 5
  Good 7
  Human Race 3, 4

Imagination 2
Knowledge 8
Love 7
Men and Women 3
Poets 4
Race 2
Sorrow 4
Transience 3
Truth 8
Blanchflower, Danny
(1926–93)
  Sport 3
Bliss, Arthur
(1891–1975)
  Old Age 5
**Blücher, Gebhard
Lebrecht** (1742–1819)
  London 1
Bly, Robert (1926–)
  Men 3
Blythe, Ronald
(1922–)
  Country 1
Boesky, Ivan F.
(1937–)
  Wealth 3
Boethius
(AD c.476–524)
  Misfortune 4
Bogart, John B.
(1848–1921)
  News 7
Bohr, Niels
(1885–1962)
  Belief 6
  Science 2
  Thinking 2
  Truth 9
Bold, Alan (1943–)
  Scotland 2
**Bolingbroke, Henry
St John, 1st
Viscount** (1678–1751)
  Mistakes 2
Bolívar, Simón
(1783–1830)
  Revolution 3

Bolt, Robert (1924–95)
  Wales 1
Bonhoeffer, Dietrich
(1906–45)
  Character 3
**Book of Common
Prayer** (1662)
  Conscience 1
  Day 1
  Death 10, 11
  Environment 4
  Languages 2
  Marriage 8, 9
  Peace 3
  Sea 3
  Temptation 2
Boothroyd, Betty
(1929–)
  Ambition 1
Boren, James H.
(1925–)
  Bureaucracy 3
Borges, Jorge Luis
(1899–1986)
  Languages 3
  Universe 2
  Wars 6
Borgia, Cesare
(1476–1507)
  Ambition 2
Borrow, George
(1803–81)
  Literature 2
Bosquet, Pierre
(1810–61)
  Army 2
**Bossidy, John
Collins** (1860–1928)
  Places 6
Boswell, James
(1740–95)
  Manners 2
Bottomley, Gordon
(1874–1948)
  Technology 3

Boucicault, Dion
(1820–90)
Time 6

**Boulay, Antoine de
la Meurthe**
(1761–1840)
Mistakes 3

Boulez, Pierre
(1925–)
Revolution 4

Boulton, Matthew
(1728–1809)
Technology 4

**Bourke-White,
Margaret** (1906–71)
Secrets 4

Bowen, Elizabeth
(1899–1973)
Absence 3
Envy 2
Experience 3
Fate 4
Ireland 2
Seasons 4

Bowen, Lord (1835–94)
Justice 9
Weather 2

Boy George (1961–)
Character 4
People 5

Brackett, Charles
(1892–1969) and
Wilder, Billy (1906–)
Cinema 1

Bradford, John
(c.1510–55)
Chance 2

Bradley, F. H.
(1846–1924)
Optimism 1
Philosophy 2

Bradshaw, John
(1602–59)
Revolution 5

Bramah, Ernest
(1868–1942)
Conversation 2

Bramston, James
(c.1694–1744)
Time 7

Braque, Georges
(1882–1963)
Art 2

Brasher, Christopher
Drugs 1

Braun, Werner von
(1912–77)
Science 3

Brecht, Bertolt
(1898–1956)
Dress 2
Heroes 2
Morality 4
Revolution 6
Science 4
Virtue 3
War 6

Brenan, Gerald
(1894–1987)
Bores 3
Leisure 1

Brenner, Sydney
(1927–)
Computers 3

Brereton, Jane
(1685–1740)
Fools 6

Bridger, Roy
Progress 5

Bridges, Robert
(1844–1930)
Weather 3

Bright, John (1811–89)
Government 5
Political Comment 6,
7
Wars 7

**Brillat-Savarin,
Anthelme** (1755–1826)
Food 2, 3
Inventions 7

Brockbank, Russell
(1913–)
Europe 2

Brodrick, St John
(1856–1942)
Manners 3

Brodsky, Joseph
(1940–96)
Literature 3

Bronowski, Jacob
(1908–74)
Action 4
Cruelty 3
Health 2
Science 5

Brontë, Charlotte
(1816–55)
Action 5
Style 2
Teaching 4

Brontë, Emily
(1818–48)
Courage 1

Brooke, Rupert
(1887–1915)
Death 12
Flowers 1
Past 5
Places 2
Sleep 4

Brookner, Anita
(1938–)
Women 4

Brooks, Gwendolyn
(1917–)
Present 3

Brooks, J.
Animals 7

Brown, H. Rap
(1943–)
Violence 4

Brown, Lew
(1893–1958)
Life 9

Brown, T. E. (1830–97)
Gardens 4

Brown, Thomas
(1663–1704)
Hatred 2

Browne, Cecil
(1932–)
  Prejudice 2
Browne, Sir Thomas
(1605–82)
  Human Race 5
  Mathematics 5
  Medicine 7
  Nature 3
  Praise 2
  Religion 4
  Sex 5
  Sleep 5
  Truth 10
**Browning, Elizabeth
Barrett** (1806–61)
  People 6
  Prayer 5
  Sorrow 5
Browning, Frederick
(1896–1965)
  Wars 8
Browning, Robert
(1812–89)
  Ambition 3
  Beauty 3
  Bible 1
  Birds 2
  Choice 1
  Cynicism 2
  Determination 3
  England 2
  God 4
  Ignorance 2
  Optimism 2
  Perfection 3
  Progress 6
  Trust 2
Bruce, Lenny
(1925–66)
  Drugs 2
Brummell, Beau
(1778–1840)
  Dress 3
**Brundtland, Gro
Harlem** (1939–)
  Environment 5

Bruno, Frank (1961–)
  Sport 4
Buber, Martin
(1878–1965)
  Self 3
Buchman, Frank
(1878–1961)
  Economics 2
Buffon, Comte de
(1707–88)
  Genius 1
  Style 3
Buller, Arthur
(1874–1944)
  Science 6
**Bulwer-Lytton,
Edward** (1803–73)
  Friendship 5
  Opening Lines 1
  Poets 5
  Reading 2
  Writing 3
Bunting, Basil
(1900–85)
  Environment 6
Bunyan, John
(1628–88)
  Pride 4
  Religion 5
Burchill, Julie
(1960–)
  Woman's Role 2
Burgess, Anthony
(1917–93)
  Opening Lines 2
  Presidency 2
Burke, Edmund
(1729–97)
  Ambition 4
  Cooperation 3
  Custom 3
  Determination 4
  Europe 3
  Family 4
  Fear 3
  Future 4
  Good 8

  Government 6
  Human Rights 4
  Law 4
  Liberty 3
  Politicians 9, 10
  Politics 6
  Practicality 3
  Revolution 7
  Society 4
  Success 6
  Taxes 1
Burke, Johnny
(1908–64)
  Weather 4
Burns, John
(1858–1943)
  England 3
Burns, Robert
(1759–96)
  Animals 8
  Chance 3
  Cruelty 4
  Equality 2
  Food 4
  Friendship 6
  Love 8
  Scotland 3, 4
  Self-Knowledge 4
  Temptation 3
  Titles 2
**Burroughs, William
S.** (1914–97)
  Drugs 3
  Good 9
Burton, Robert
(1577–1640)
  Love 9
  Poets 6
  Religion 6
  Travel 2
**Busenbaum,
Hermann** (1600–68)
  Morality 5
Bush, George
(1924–)
  Bores 4
  Idealism 3

Bush, George (*cont.*)
Presidency 3
Taxes 2
**Bussy-Rabutin,
Comte de** (1618–93)
War 7
**Butler, Nicholas
Murray** (1862–1947)
Knowledge 9
Butler, Samuel
(1612–80)
Cynicism 3
Hypocrisy 2
Opinion 2
Butler, Samuel
(1835–1902)
Art 3
Canada 1
Conscience 2
Dogs 1
Language 3
Life 10
Life Sciences 4
Meeting 1
Men 4
Praise 3
Byatt, A. S. (1936–)
Books 5
Byrd, William
(1543–1623)
Singing 2
Byron, Lord
(1788–1824)
Beauty 4
Behaviour 4
Bores 5
Censorship 1
Critics 1
Dance 3
Dogs 2
Fame 6
Food 5
Hatred 3
Hope 2
Lies 2
Literature 4
Marriage 10, 11

Men and Women 4
Nature 4
Places 8
Pleasure 4
Poets 7
Political Parties 2
Reading 3
Religion 7
Revenge 3
Scotland 5
Sea 4
Seasons 5
Self-Knowledge 5
Solitude 5
Truth 11
Women 5
Bywater, Michael
Britain 3

**Cabell, James
Branch** (1879–1958)
Optimism 3
Caesar, Julius
(100–44 BC)
Ambition 5
Behaviour 5
Choice 2
Opening Lines 3
Success 7
Caine, Michael
(1933–)
Class 4
Callimachus
(c.305–c.240 BC)
Books 6
**Calonne, Charles
Alexandre de**
(1734–1802)
Achievement 2
Camara, Helder
(1909–99)
Poverty 4
Cameron, Simon
(1799–1889)
Politicians 11

**Campbell, Mrs
Patrick** (1865–1940)
Marriage 12
Sex 6
Campbell, Roy
(1901–57)
Human Race 6
Writing 4
Campbell, Thomas
(1777–1844)
Books 7
Country 2
Environment 7
Camus, Albert
(1913–60)
Charm 2
Imagination 3
Intelligence 3
Lies 3
Morality 6
Revolution 8
Canetti, Elias
(1905–94)
Sleep 6
Canning, George
(1770–1827)
Friendship 7
Patriotism 3
Cantona, Eric
(1966–)
News 8
Capa, Robert
(1913–54)
Photography 4
Capone, Al
(1899–1947)
Crime 6
Capote, Truman
(1924–84)
Places 9
Capp, Al (1907–79)
Painting 1
Capra, Frank
(1897–1991)
Cinema 2

**Caracciolo,
Francesco** (1752–99)
England 4

Carey, George
(1935–)
Church 3

Carlyle, Thomas
(1795–1881)
Biography 2
Civilization 1
France 1
History 3
Idleness 3
Libraries 1
People 7, 8
Statistics 2
Universe 3

Carnegie, Andrew
(1835–1919)
Wealth 4

Carroll, Lewis
(1832–98)
Achievement 3
Beginnings 3
Belief 7
Books 8
Conversation 3
Education 7
Gifts 5
Justice 10
Language 4
Manners 4
Meaning 2
Philosophy 3
Present 4
Reality 1
Truth 12
Words 4

Carson, Rachel
(1907–64)
Environment 8

Carter, Chris (1957–)
Secrets 5

Carter, Henry
(d. 1806)
Australia 1

Carter, Howard
(1874–1939)
Inventions 8

Cartier, Jacques
(1491–1557)
Canada 2

**Cartier-Bresson,
Henri** (1908–)
Photography 5

Cartwright, John
(1740–1824)
Democracy 3

Casals, Pablo
(1876–1973)
Old Age 6

Cash, Pat (1965–)
Sport 5

Cassandre, A. M.
(1901–68)
Advertising 1

Castle, Barbara
(1910–)
Determination 5

Castro, Fidel (1927–)
Economics 3

Cather, Willa
(1873–1947)
Management 4
Travel 3

**Catherine, Empress
the Great** (1729–96)
Forgiveness 2

Cato the Elder
(234–149 BC)
Speech 5

Catullus (c.84–c.54 BC)
Meeting 2

Cavell, Edith
(1865–1915)
Patriotism 4

Ceaușescu, Nicolae
(1918–89)
Enemies 4

Cecil, Lord Hugh
(1869–1956)
Church 4

Celan, Paul (1920–70)
Death 13
Poets 8

Centlivre, Susannah
(c.1669–1723)
Money 8

Cervantes (1547–1616)
Food 6
Painting 2

Cézanne, Paul
(1839–1906)
Painting 3
People 9

**Chamberlain,
Joseph** (1836–1914)
Politics 7

Chamberlain, Neville
(1869–1940)
Peace 4
War 8

**Chamfort, Nicolas-
Sébastien** (1741–94)
Poverty 5

Chandler, Raymond
(1888–1959)
Crime 7
Heroes 3
Language 5
Places 10
Writing 5

Chanel, Coco
(1883–1971)
Europe 4
Youth 2

**Channon, Henry
'Chips'** (1897–1958)
Diaries 1

Chaplin, Charlie
(1889–1977)
Cinema 3

Chapman, George
(c.1559–1634)
England 5

Chapman, Graham
(1941–89) et al.
Change 4
Death 14

Chapman, Graham
(*cont.*)
  Progress 7
Charles I (1600–49)
  Apology 2
  Royalty 6
Charles II (1630–85)
  Last Words 1
Charles V, Emperor
(1500–58)
  Languages 4
Charles, Hugh
(1907–) see Parker,
Ross and Charles,
Hugh
**Charles, Prince of
Wales** (1948–)
  Architecture 1
Chaucer, Geoffrey
(*c*.1343–1400)
  Beauty 5
  Behaviour 6
  Birds 3
  Education 8, 9
  Flowers 2
  Hypocrisy 3
  Love 10
  Murder 2
  Opening Lines 4
Chekhov, Anton
(1860–1904)
  Acting 4
  Beauty 6
  Friendship 8
  Hatred 4
  Men and Women 5
  Pollution 3
  Sickness 4
  Writing 6
Chesterfield, Lord
(1694–1773)
  Advice 3
  Chance 4
  Conversation 4
  Enemies 5
  Idleness 4
  Knowledge 10

  Manners 5
  Religion 8
  Sex 7
  Time 7
  Truth 13
  Women 6
Chesterton, G. K.
(1874–1936)
  Crime 8
  Custom 4
  God 5
  Government 7
  Ideas 3
  Ireland 3
  Knowledge 11
  Literature 5
  Memory 6
  Prejudice 3
  Secrets 6
  Transport 4
  Women 7
Chevalier, Maurice
(1888–1972)
  Old Age 7
Child, Lydia Maria
(1802–80)
  Voting 4
Choiseul, Duc de
(1719–85)
  Politicians 12
Chomsky, Noam
(1928–)
  Computers 4
  Language 6
**Chuang-tzu (or
Zhuangzi)**
(*c*.369–286 BC)
  Self-Knowledge 6
**Church, Francis
Pharcellus** (1839–1906)
  Christmas 4
Churchill, Charles
(1731–64)
  Achievement 4
  Hypocrisy 4
  Patriotism 5
  Speech 3

**Churchill, Lord
Randolph** (1849–94)
  Ireland 4
  Mathematics 6
Churchill, Winston
(1874–1965)
  Alcohol 5
  Animals 9
  Beginnings 4
  Britain 4
  Certainty 5
  Democracy 4
  Diplomacy 2
  Europe 5
  Food 7
  Future 5
  Language 7
  People 10
  Places 11
  Politicians 13, 14, 15
  Quotations 2
  Revenge 4
  Sea 5
  Speech 4
  Success 8
  Titles 3
  Trust 3
  Wars 9, 10, 11, 12
  Words 5
**Ciano, Count
Galeazzo** (1903–44)
  Success 9
Cibber, Colley
(1671–1757)
  Marriage 13
  Style 4
Cicero (106–43 BC)
  Behaviour 7
  Law 5, 6
  Mistakes 4
  Money 9
  Philosophy 4
  War 9
Cioran, E. M.
(1911–95)
  Idleness 5

Clare, John
(1793–1864)
Present 5

Clark, Alan (1928–99)
Bureaucracy 4
Character 5
Politicians 16
Politics 8

Clarke, Arthur C.
(1917–)
Environment 9
Science 7
Technology 5

Clarke, John (d. 1658)
Home 1

Clausewitz, Karl von
(1780–1831)
War 10, 11

Clayton, Tubby
(1885–1972)
Gifts 6

Cleaver, Eldridge
(1935–98)
Management 5

**Clemenceau,
Georges** (1841–1929)
Old Age 8
War 12
Wars 13

Clinton, Bill (1946–)
Drugs 4
Life Sciences 5
Meaning 3
Twentieth Century 3

**Clinton, Hillary
Rodham** (1947–)
Children 4
Woman's Role 3

Clough, Arthur Hugh
(1819–61)
Crime 9
Determination 6
Envy 3
Fear 4
Murder 3
Religion 9

Clough, Brian (1935–)
Pride 5

Cobbett, William
(1762–1835)
London 2

Cockburn, Claud
(1904–81)
News 9
Reality 2

Cocteau, Jean
(1889–1963)
Books 9
Life 11
People 11

Cohen, John (1911–)
Language 8

Cohen, Leonard
(1934–)
Body 4
Optimism 4

Coke, Desmond
(1879–1931)
Sport 6

Coke, Edward
(1552–1634)
Business 4
Home 2

**Coleridge, Samuel
Taylor** (1772–1834)
Acting 5
Birth 2
Chance 5
Day 2
Hope 3
Humour 5
Men and Women 6
Poetry 5, 6
Poets 9
Politics 9
Pollution 4
Prayer 6
Pride 6
Sea 6
Singing 3
Weather 5

Collins, Joan (1933–)
Temptation 4

**Colman, George, the
Elder** (1732–94) and
Garrick, David
(1717–79)
Love 11

**Colton, Charles
Caleb** (c.1780–1832)
Country 3
Education 10
Praise 4
Speech 5

Comden, Betty
(1919–) and **Green,
Adolph** (1915–)
Beginnings 5

**Compton-Burnett,
Ivy** (1884–1969)
Men and Women 7
Poverty 6

Condell, Henry
(d. 1627) see Heming,
John and Condell,
Henry

Confucius
(551–479 BC)
Education 11
Human Race 7
Sex 8
Teaching 5

Congreve, William
(1670–1729)
Gossip 5
Love 12
Marriage 14, 15
Music 6
Revenge 5
Secrets 7

Conlon, Gerry
(1954–)
Justice 11

Connell, James M.
(1852–1929)
Political Parties 3

Connolly, Billy
(1942–)
Marriage 16

Connolly, Cyril
(1903–74)
  Charm 3
  Children 5
  Country 4
  Critics 2
  Memory 7
  Men and Women 8
  Style 5
Connolly, James
(1868–1916)
  Woman's Role 4
Conrad, Joseph
(1857–1924)
  Ambition 6
  Apology 3
Conran, Shirley
(1932–)
  Home 3
  Practicality 4
Constable, John
(1776–1837)
  Beauty 7
  Painting 4
Constant, Benjamin
(1767–1834)
  Art 4
**Constitution of the
United States** (1787)
  Crime 10
Cook, Dan
  Beginnings 6
Cook, Peter (1937–95)
  Pleasure 5
Coolidge, Calvin
(1872–1933)
  Civilization 2
  Determination 7
Cope, Wendy (1945–)
  Poets 10
Copland, Aaron
(1900–90)
  Music 7
**Coppola, Francis
Ford** (1939–)
  War 13

Cornes, Ralph
  Computers 5
Cornford, Francis M.
(1874–1943)
  Lies 4
Cornuel, Mme
(1605–94)
  Heroes 4
Coronation Service
(1689)
  Bible 2
**Coubertin, Baron
Pierre de** (1863–1937)
  Sport 7
Coué, Émile
(1857–1926)
  Medicine 8
Coupland, Douglas
(1961–)
  Careers 3
Courteline, Georges
(1858–1929)
  Youth 3
Cousteau, Jacques
(1910–97)
  Pollution 5
  Twentieth Century 4
Coward, Noël
(1899–1973)
  Acting 6
  Behaviour 8
  Class 5
  England 6
  London 3
  Music 8
Cowley, Abraham
(1618–67)
  Life 12
Cowper, William
(1731–1800)
  Change 5
  Country 5
  God 6
  Pleasure 6
  Solitude 6

Crabbe, George
(1754–1832)
  Custom 5
  Poverty 7
Crashaw, Richard
(c.1612–49)
  Marriage 17
**Creighton, Bishop
Mandell** (1843–1901)
  Good 10
Crick, Francis
(1916–)
  Life Sciences 6
  Self 4
Crisp, Quentin
(1908–99)
  Biography 3
  Home 4
Critchley, Julian
(1930–)
  Politicians 17
  Speech 6
Cromwell, Oliver
(1599–1658)
  Achievement 5
  Last Words 2
  Meeting 3
  Mistakes 5
  Painting 5
Crossman, Richard
(1907–74)
  Bureaucracy 5
Crowley, Aleister
(1875–1947)
  Living 6
**Cumberland, Bishop
Richard** (1631–1718)
  Idleness 6
cummings, e. e.
(1894–1962)
  Body 5
  Politicians 18
  Progress 8
Cuomo, Mario
(1932–)
  Politics 10

Cupitt, Don (1934–)
  Christmas 5
Curran, John Philpot
(1750–1817)
  Liberty 4
Curtiz, Michael
(1888–1962)
  Cinema 4
Cyprian, St
(AD c.200–258)
  Church 5

Dali, Salvador
(1904–89)
  Ambition 7
Dante Alighieri
(1265–1321)
  Conscience 3
  Gossip 6
  Heaven 3
  Love 13
  Misfortune 5
  Opening Lines 5
  Peace 5
  Transience 4
**Danton, Georges
Jacques** (1759–94)
  Courage 2
Darnell, Bill
  Environment 10
Darrow, Clarence
(1857–1938)
  Belief 8
Darwin, Charles
(1809–82)
  Animals 10
  Language 9
  Life Sciences 7
  Nature 5
Darwin, Francis
(1848–1925)
  Science 8
Davies, Robertson
(1913–95)
  Biography 4
  Canada 3

Davies, Scrope
(c.1783–1852)
  Madness 2
Davies, Sir John
(1569–1626)
  Dance 4
Davies, W. H.
(1871–1940)
  Birds 4
  Leisure 2
Davis, Sammy Jnr.
(1925–90)
  Prejudice 4
Dawkins, Richard
(1941–)
  Death 15
  Life Sciences 8
**Dawson,
Christopher**
(1889–1970)
  Good 11
Day, Robin (1923–2000)
  Broadcasting 1
Dayan, Moshe
(1915–81)
  War 14
de Beauvoir, Simone
(1908–86)
  Woman's Role 5
de Bernières, Louis
(1954–)
  Achievement 6
  Heart 2
  Love 14
Debray, Régis
(1940–)
  Politics 11
Debs, Eugene Victor
(1855–1926)
  Revolution 9
Decatur, Stephen
(1779–1820)
  Patriotism 6
Defoe, Daniel
(1660–1731)
  Church 6
  Custom 6

  Poverty 8
  Religion 10
  Royalty 7
  Virtue 4
Degas, Edgar
(1834–1917)
  Art 5
de Gaulle, Charles
(1890–1970)
  Canada 4
  Censorship 2
  Diplomacy 3
  France 2
  War 15
de la Mare, Walter
(1873–1956)
  Flowers 3
  Opening Lines 6
  Skies 2
  Transience 5
**de Leon, Walter and
Jones, Paul M.**
  Life 13
Delius, Frederick
(1862–1934)
  Music 9
de Mille, Agnes
(1908–)
  Dance 5
Demosthenes
(c.384–c.322 BC)
  Speech 7
Dempsey, Jack
(1895–1983)
  Sport 8
Deneuve, Catherine
(1943–)
  Men 5
  Photography 6
Deng Xiaoping
(1904–97)
  Practicality 5
Dennis, John
(1657–1734)
  Words 6

De Quincey, Thomas
(1785–1859)
    Drugs 5
    Murder 4
**Derby, Edward
Stanley, 14th Earl of**
(1799–1869)
    Political Comment 8
Derrida, Jacques
(1930–)
    Critics 3
Descartes, René
(1596–1650)
    Practicality 6
    Thinking 3
**Destouches,
Philippe Néricault**
(1680–1754)
    Absence 4
Dewar, James
(1842–1923)
    Prejudice 5
Dewar, Lord
(1864–1930)
    Transport 5
Diamond, John
    Health 3
**Diana, Princess of
Wales** (1961–97)
    Food 8
    Marriage 18
    Royalty 8
Diaz, Porfirio
(1830–1915)
    Places 12
Dickens, Charles
(1812–70)
    Bureaucracy 6
    Business 5
    Chance 6
    Christmas 6
    Class 6
    Education 12
    Food 9
    Knowledge 12
    Last Words 3
    Law 7, 8

Letters 3
Love 15
Minorities 2
Money 10
Opening Lines 7
Optimism 5
Places 13
Pride 7
Supernatural 6
Weather 6
Dickinson, Emily
(1830–86)
    Meeting 4
    Writing 7
**Dillon, Wentworth,
Earl of Roscommon**
(c.1633–1685)
    Reading 4
Dinesen, Isak
(1885–1962)
    Human Race 8
Diogenes (404–323 BC)
    Cynicism 4
**Dionysius of
Halicarnassus** (fl.
30–7 BC)
    History 4
Dirac, Paul (1902–84)
    Science 9
Disraeli, Benjamin
(1804–81)
    Apology 4
    Biography 5
    Careers 4
    Experience 4
    Government 8
    Human Race 9
    Ireland 5
    Justice 12
    Lies 5
    Life 14
    Minorities 3
    Peace 6
    Political Parties 4
    Politics 12
    Progress 9
    Royalty 9

Statistics 3
Success 10
Dobson, Frank
(1940–)
    Opinion 3
Dodd, Ken (1931–)
    Humour 6
Donne, John
(1572–1631)
    Animals 11
    Death 16, 17
    Fools 7
    Imagination 4
    Letters 4
    Love 16, 17
    Men and Women 9
    Prayer 7
    Self-Knowledge 7
    Sex 9
    Skies 3
    Society 5
Dors, Diana (1931–84)
    Letters 5
Dostoevsky, Fedor
(1821–81)
    Beauty 8
Doty, Mark (1953–)
    Sickness 5
Douglas, Keith
(1920–44)
    Misfortune 6
Douglas, Lord Alfred
(1870–1945)
    Love 18
Douglas, O.
(1877–1948)
    Letters 6
    Quotations 3
Douglass, Frederick
(c.1818–95)
    Human Rights 5
    Race 3
    Singing 4
Dowson, Ernest
(1867–1900)
    Memory 8

Doyle, Arthur Conan
(1859–1930)
  Country 6
  Crime 11
  Genius 2
  Imagination 5
  Intelligence 4
  Libraries 2
  Thinking 4
  Truth 14
Drabble, Margaret
(1939–)
  England 7
Drake, Francis
(c.1540–96)
  Achievement 7
  Sport 9
Drayton, Michael
(1563–1631)
  Meeting 5
  News 10
Drucker, Peter F.
(1909–)
  Pollution 6
Dryden, John
(1631–1700)
  Anger 4
  Genius 3
  Government 9
  Happiness 3
  Humour 7
  Idleness 7
  Love 19
  Men 6
  Minorities 4
  Mistakes 6
  Poetry 7
  Poets 11, 12
  Secrets 8
  Women 8
  Writing 8
Du Bellay, Joachim
(1522–60)
  France 3
Du Deffand, Mme
(1697–1780)
  Achievement 8

Dumas, Alexandre
(1802–70)
  Cooperation 4
Dumas, Alexandre
(1824–95)
  Marriage 19
Du Maurier, Daphne
(1907–89)
  Opening Lines 8
Dumouriez, General
(1739–1823)
  Behaviour 9
Duport, James
(1606–79)
  Madness 3
Durocher, Leo
(1906–91)
  Sport 10
Durrell, Lawrence
(1912–90)
  Church 7
**Dürrenmatt,
Friedrich** (1921–)
  Thinking 5
Dworkin, Andrea
(1946–)
  Birth 3
  Sex 10
Dyer, Edward
(d. 1607)
  Sorrow 6
Dyer, John (1700–58)
  Transience 6
Dylan, Bob (1941–)
  Generation Gap 2
  Heroes 5
  Money 11
  Singing 5
  Success 11
  Women 9

Eddington, Arthur
(1882–1944)
  Chance 7
  Science 10
  Time 9

**Edison, Thomas
Alva** (1847–1931)
  Genius 4
**Edmonds, John
Maxwell** (1875–1958)
  Epitaphs 7
Edward VIII
(1894–1972)
  Royalty 10
Edwards, John
  Business 6
Edwards, Jonathan
(1703–58)
  Death 18
Ehrenreich, Barbara
(1941–)
  Health 4
Ehrmann, Max
(1872–1945)
  Peace 7
Einstein, Albert
(1879–1955)
  Chance 8
  Future 6
  God 7
  Intelligence 5
  Mathematics 7
  Practicality 7
  Prejudice 6
  Religion 11
  Science 11, 12
  Success 12
  Time 10
  Universe 4
  War 16
**Eisenhower, Dwight
D.** (1890–1969)
  Army 3
  Peace 8
  Presidency 4
Eisenstaedt, Alfred
(1898–1995)
  Photography 7
Elgar, Edward
(1857–1934)
  Art 6

Elgar, Edward (*cont.*)
Music 10
Eliot, George
(1819–80)
Gossip 7
Hope 4
Humour 8
Marriage 20
Silence 2
Sorrow 7
Voting 5
Women 10
Eliot, T. S. (1888–1965)
Beginnings 7, 8
Cats 1
Day 3
Death 19
Experience 5
Fear 5
Forgiveness 3
Heaven 4
Knowledge 13
Life 15
Medicine 9
Memory 9
Morality 7
Old Age 9
Poets 13, 14
Pollution 7
Reality 3
Seasons 6
Success 13
Time 11, 12
Travel 4
Words 7
Elizabeth I (1533–1603)
Ambition 8
Birth 4
Forgiveness 4
Government 10
Last Words 4
Royalty 11
Secrets 9
Trust 4
Elizabeth II (1926–)
Misfortune 7
Royalty 12

Elizabeth, Queen, the Queen Mother
(1900–)
Sorrow 8
Wars 14
Ellis, Alice Thomas
(1932–)
Character 6
Ellis, Havelock
(1859–1939)
Pollution 8
Revolution 10
Elton, Ben (1959–)
Leadership 5
Emerson, Ralph Waldo (1803–82)
Achievement 9
Ambition 9
Children 6
Conversation 5
Education 13
Friendship 9
Gardens 5
Greatness 2
Heroes 6
Honour 1
Justice 13
Language 10
Quotations 4
Empson, William
(1906–84)
Literature 6
Engels, Friedrich
(1820–95) see Marx, Karl and Engels, Friedrich
Ephron, Nora (1941–)
Sex 11
Epicurus (341–271 BC)
Death 20
Erhard, Ludwig
(1897–1977)
Europe 6
Ertz, Susan
(1894–1985)
Bores 6

Essex, Robert Devereux, 2nd Earl of (1566–1601)
Thinking 6
Estienne, Henri
(1531–98)
Generation Gap 3
Euclid (fl. *c.*300 BC)
Mathematics 8
Eulalia, Infanta of Spain (1864–1958)
Royalty 13
Euripides
(*c.*485–*c.*406 BC)
Fate 5
Hypocrisy 5
Evans, Abel
(1679–1737)
Epitaphs 8
Ewer, William Norman (1885–1976)
Prejudice 7

Fadiman, Clifton
(1904–)
Food 10
People 12
Faisal
Speech 8
Falkland, Lucius Cary, Viscount
(1610–43)
Change 6
Faraday, Michael
(1791–1867)
Inventions 9
Truth 15
Farouk, King
(1920–65)
Royalty 14
Farquhar, George
(1678–1707)
Poverty 9
Faulkner, William
(1897–1962)
Writers 5

Fawkes, Guy
(1570–1606)
  Revolution 11
Fenton, James
(1949–)
  Quotations 5
**Ferdinand I,
Emperor** (1503–64)
  Justice 14
Fermi, Enrico
(1901–54)
  Ignorance 3
**Feynman, Richard
Phillips** (1918–88)
  Technology 6
Field, Frank (1942–)
  Certainty 6
Fielding, Henry
(1707–54)
  Envy 4
  Gossip 8
Fields, Dorothy
(1905–74)
  Determination 8
Fields, W. C.
(1880–1946)
  Epitaphs 9
  Fools 8
  Humour 9
  Voting 6
Finney, Albert
(1936–)
  Equality 3
Firbank, Ronald
(1886–1926)
  Universe 5
Fish, Michael (1944–)
  Weather 7
Fitzgerald, Edward
(1809–83)
  Flowers 4
  Past 6
  Present 6
  Satisfaction 1
Fitzgerald, F. Scott
(1896–1940)
  Hope 5

  Intelligence 6
  Middle Age 5
  Wealth 5
Fitzsimmons, Robert
(1862–1917)
  Sport 11
Flaubert, Gustave
(1821–80)
  Art 7
  Enemies 6
  Poetry 8
  Speech 9
  Style 6
Flecker, James Elroy
(1884–1915)
  Knowledge 14
Fleming, Ian (1908–64)
  Chance 9
**Fletcher, Andrew of
Saltoun** (1655–1716)
  Singing 6
**Florian, Jean-Pierre
Claris de** (1755–94)
  Love 20
Foch, Ferdinand
(1851–1929)
  Wars 15, 16
Foley, J. (1906–70)
  Army 4
Foot, Michael (1913–)
  Political Comment 9
  Politicians 19
  Speech 10
Foote, Samuel
(1720–77)
  Bores 7
Forbes, Miss C. F.
(1817–1911)
  Dress 4
Ford, Gerald (1909–)
  Government 11
Ford, Henry
(1863–1947)
  Choice 3
  Good 12
  Health 5
  History 5

Forgy, Howell
(1908–83)
  Practicality 8
Forster, E. M.
(1879–1970)
  Critics 4
  Cynicism 5
  Death 21
  Democracy 5
  Gossip 9
  Literature 7
  Manners 6
  Music 11
  Patriotism 7
  Transport 6
  Writers 6
  Writing 9, 10
Forster, Margaret
(1938–)
  Biography 6
Forsyth, Frederick
(1938–)
  Memory 10
Fox, Charles James
(1749–1806)
  Revolution 12
France, Anatole
(1844–1924)
  Behaviour 10
  Government 12
  Lies 6
  Prejudice 8
  Wealth 6
Frank, Anne (1929–45)
  Diaries 2
Franklin, Benjamin
(1706–90)
  Business 7, 8
  Cooperation 5
  Hope 6
  Human Race 10
  Inventions 10
  Taxes 3
  War 17
Frederick the Great
(1712–86)
  Government 13

Frederick the Great
(*cont.*)
Prejudice 9

Freeman, E. A.
(1823–92)
History 6

French, Marilyn
(1929–)
Family 5
Men 7

Freud, Sigmund
(1856–1939)
Body 6
Life 16
Sleep 7
Women 11

Friedan, Betty
(1921–)
Woman's Role 6

Friedman, Milton
(1912–)
Economics 4

Frisch, Max (1911–91)
Technology 7

Frohman, Charles
(1860–1915)
Last Words 5

Frost, David (1939–)
Parents 5

Frost, Robert
(1874–1963)
Change 7
Choice 4
Determination 9
Happiness 4
Home 6
Poetry 9, 10
Politics 13
Secrets 10
Work 4

Fry, Christopher
(1907–)
Home 6
Language 11
Virtue 5

Fry, Elizabeth
(1780–1845)
Crime 12

Fry, Stephen (1957–)
Body 7

Fuentes, Carlos
(1928–)
Future 7

Fukuyama, Francis
(1952–)
Computers 6

**Fuller, R.
Buckminster**
(1895–1983)
Environment 11

Fuller, Thomas
(1608–61)
Architecture 2

Fuller, Thomas
(1654–1734)
Gardens 6
Wealth 7

Fyleman, Rose
(1877–1957)
Supernatural 7

Gabor, Zsa Zsa
(1919–)
Hatred 5
Sex 12

**Gainsborough,
Thomas** (1727–88)
Last Words 6

Gaitskell, Hugh
(1906–63)
Country 7
Europe 7
Political Parties 5

Galbraith, J. K.
(1908–)
Advertising 2
Crises 3
Economics 5
Mistakes 7
Places 14
Politics 14
Satisfaction 2

Wealth 8

Galen (AD 129–199)
Life Sciences 9

Galileo Galilei
(1564–1642)
Mathematics 9
Skies 4

Gallagher, Noel
(1967–)
Drugs 6
Indifference 2
Men 8

Galsworthy, John
(1867–1933)
Beauty 9

Galt, John (1779–1839)
Scotland 6

Gamow, George
(1904–68)
Science 13

Gandhi, Mahatma
(1869–1948)
Civilization 3

Garbo, Greta
(1905–90)
Solitude 7

Gardiner, Richard
(b. c.1533)
Gardens 7

Gardner, Ed (1901–63)
Singing 7

Garrick, David
(1717–79)
Food 11

Garrick, David
(1717–79) see Colman,
George, the Elder and
Garrick, David

**Garrison, William
Lloyd** (1805–79)
Political Comment 10

Gaskell, Elizabeth
(1810–65)
Men 9
Thinking 7

Gay, John (1685–1732)
  Choice 5
  Enemies 7
  Epitaphs 10
  Marriage 21
Geddes, Eric
(1875–1937)
  Revenge 6
Geldof, Bob (1954–)
  Musicians 5
  Race 4
Genet, Jean (1910–86)
  Hatred 6
  Trust 5
George II (1683–1760)
  Madness 4
George III (1738–1820)
  Shakespeare 2
George V (1865–1936)
  Last Words 7
  Parents 6
  Patriotism 8
George VI (1895–1952)
  Diplomacy 4
Gershwin, Ira
(1896–1983) see
Heyward, Du Bose and
Gershwin, Ira
Getty, J. Paul
(1892–1976)
  Wealth 9
Gibbon, Edward
(1737–94)
  Crime 13
  History 7
  Languages 5
  London 4
  Religion 12
  Taxes 4
Gibran, Kahlil
(1883–1931)
  Marriage 22
  Parents 7
  Truth 16
  Work 5

Gide, André
(1869–1951)
  Places 15
Gilbert, W. S.
(1836–1911)
  Crime 14, 15
  Equality 4
  Language 12
  Law 9
  Meaning 4
  Men 10
  Old Age 10
  Politicians 20
  Pride 8
  Sleep 8
  Transport 7
  Voting 7
Gill, Eric (1882–1940)
  Work 6
Giovanni, Nikki
(1943–)
  Mistakes 8
Giraldus Cambrensis
(1146?–1220?)
  Wales 2
Giraudoux, Jean
(1882–1944)
  Law 10
  Poetry 11
Gladney, Edna
  Parents 8
Gladstone, W. E.
(1809–98)
  Crises 4
  Democracy 6
  Economics 6
  Future 8
  Government 14
  Speech 11
Glasse, Hannah (fl.
1747)
  Food 12
Gloucester, Duke of
(1743–1805)
  Writers 7

Godard, Jean-Luc
(1930–)
  Cinema 5, 6
Godwin, William
(1756–1836)
  Crises 5
Goebbels, Joseph
(1897–1945)
  Argument 3
  War 18
Goering, Hermann
(1893–1946)
  Race 5
  War 19
**Goethe, Johann
Wolfgang von**
(1749–1832)
  Art 8
  Character 7
  Fame 7
  Last Words 8
  Love 21
  Mathematics 10
  Old Age 11
  Reality 4
  Satisfaction 3
  Self-Knowledge 8
  Supernatural 8
  Women 12
Golding, William
(1911–93)
  Humour 10
  Sleep 9
Goldsmith, Oliver
(1728–74)
  Knowledge 15
  Law 11
  Life 17
  Marriage 23
Goldwater, Barry
(1909–98)
  Moderation 5
Goldwyn, Sam
(1882–1974)
  Certainty 7
  Cinema 7, 8
  Law 12

Goodman, Amy
(1957–)
　News 11
Gorky, Maxim
(1868–1936)
　Art 9
Gould, Stephen Jay
(1941–)
　Greatness 3
Goya (1746–1828)
　Sleep 10
Grade, Lew (1906–98)
　Cinema 9
Graham, D. M.
(1911–99)
　Patriotism 9
Graham, Martha
(1894–1991)
　Dance 6
Grahame, Kenneth
(1859–1932)
　Transport 8, 9
Grant, Ulysses S.
(1822–85)
　Law 13
Graves, Robert
(1895–1985)
　Love 22
　Weather 8
Gray, John Chipman
(1839–1915)
　Home 7
Gray, Thomas
(1716–71)
　Children 7
　Day 4
　Fame 8
　Ignorance 4
　Suffering 5
Greeley, Horace
(1811–72)
　America 7
Green, Adolph
(1915–) see Comden,
Betty and Green,
Adolph

Greene, Graham
(1904–91)
　Children 8
　Good 13
　Happiness 5
　Indifference 3
　Reading 5
　Sorrow 9
　Success 14
Greene, Robert
(c.1560–92)
　Time 13
Greer, Germaine
(1939–)
　Australia 2
　Beauty 10
　Men and Women 10
　Sport 12
　Woman's Role 7
　Work 7
Grellet, Stephen
(1773–1855)
　Good 14
Grey, Lord of
Fallodon (1862–1933)
　Civilization 4
Grierson, John
(1888–1972)
　Art 10
Griffith-Jones,
Mervyn (1909–79)
　Censorship 3
Grocott, Bruce
(1940–)
　Work 8
Gromyko, Andrei
(1909–89)
　Politicians 21
Grossmith, George
(1847–1912) and
Grossmith, Weedon
(1854–1919)
　Home 8
　Misfortune 8
Grossmith, Weedon
(1854–1919) see
Grossmith, George and

Grossmith, Weedon
Grove, Andrew
(1936–)
　Business 9
　Technology 8
Guedalla, Philip
(1889–1944)
　Writers 8
Gurney, Dorothy
Frances (1858–1932)
　Gardens 8
Guthrie, Woody
(1912–67)
　America 8

Hailsham, Lord
(1907–)
　Political Parties 6
Hakuin (1686–1769)
　Cooperation 6
Haldane, J. B. S.
(1892–1964)
　Life Sciences 10
　Statistics 4
　Universe 6
Haldeman, H. R.
(1929–)
　Secrets 11
Hale, Edward
Everett (1822–1909)
　Politicians 22
Hale, Nathan
(1755–76)
　Patriotism 10
Halifax, George
Savile, Marquess of
(1633–95)
　Crime 16
　Power 7
Hall, Bishop Joseph
(1574–1656)
　Perfection 4
Hall, Jerry
　Woman's Role 8
Hamilton, Alex
(1936–)
　Character 8

Hamilton, William
(1788–1856)
Mind 1

Hammerstein II, Oscar (1895–1960)
Hope 7
Music 12
Places 16
Seasons 7

Hanrahan, Brian
(1949–)
Wars 17

Hansberry, Lorraine
(1930–65)
Race 6

Harbach, Otto
(1873–1963)
Sorrow 10

Harcourt, William
(1827–1904)
Political Comment 11

Hardy, Godfrey Harold (1877–1947)
Mathematics 11

Hardy, Thomas
(1840–1928)
Body 8
History 8
Hope 8
Speech 12
Weather 9
Words 8
Writing 11

Hare, Maurice Evan
(1886–1967)
Fate 6

Harington, John
(1561–1612)
Trust 6

Harlech, Lord
(1918–85)
Britain 5

Harman, Lord Justice (1894–1970)
Business 10

Harris, Thomas
(1940–) and **Tally, Ted** (1952–)
Food 13

Hart, Lorenz
(1895–1943)
Behaviour 11

Harte, Bret
(1836–1902)
Chance 10

Hartley, L. P.
(1895–1972)
Past 7

Haskins, Minnie Louise (1875–1957)
Trust 7

Hattersley, Roy
(1932–)
Politicians 23

Havel, Václav
(1936–)
Hope 9
Nature 6
Truth 17

Hawking, Stephen
(1942–)
Mathematics 12
Universe 7

Hay, Ian (1876–1952)
Humour 11
War 20

Hazlitt, William
(1778–1830)
Conversation 6
Country 8
Hatred 7
Manners 7
Prejudice 10

Head, Bessie
(1937–86)
Race 7

Healey, Denis
(1917–)
Politicians 24

Heaney, Seamus
(1939–)
Ireland 6

Hearst, William Randolph (1863–1951)
News 12

Heath, Edward
(1916–)
Political Comment 12

Heath-Stubbs, John
(1918–)
Sickness 6

Heber, Bishop Reginald (1783–1826)
Religion 13

Hegel, G. W. F.
(1770–1831)
History 9
Philosophy 5
Reality 5
Society 6

Heine, Heinrich
(1797–1856)
Censorship 4
Last Words 9

Heisenberg, Werner
(1901–76)
Mistakes 9

Heller, Joseph
(1923–99)
Madness 5
Peace 9

Hellman, Lillian
(1905–84)
Conscience 4
Cynicism 6

Helmsley, Leona
(c.1920–)
Taxes 5

Hemans, Felicia
(1793–1835)
Opening Lines 9

Heming, John
(1556–1630) and
Condell, Henry
(d. 1627)
Shakespeare 3

Hemingway, Ernest
(1899–1961)
Courage 3

Hemingway, Ernest
(*cont.*)
  Places 17
  Sex 13
  Writing 12
Henley, W. E.
(1849–1903)
  Determination 10
  Self 5
Henri IV (1553–1610)
  Cynicism 7
  Poverty 10
Henry VIII (1491–1547)
  Painting 6
Henry, Patrick
(1736–99)
  Liberty 5
Hepworth, Barbara
(1903–75)
  Painting 7
Heraclitus
(*c.*540–*c.*480 BC)
  Change 8
  Character 9
Herbert, A. P.
(1890–1971)
  Country 9
  Humour 12
  Marriage 24
Herbert, George
(1593–1633)
  Hope 10
  Religion 14
  Secrets 12
Herman, Henry
(1832–94) see Jones,
Henry Arthur and
Herman, Henry
Herrick, Robert
(1591–1674)
  Body 9
  Dress 5
  Marriage 25
  Transience 7
Hervey, Lord
(1696–1743)
  Lies 7

Heseltine, Michael
(1933–)
  Courage 4
Hesse, Hermann
(1877–1962)
  Class 7
  Hatred 8
Heston, Charlton
(1924–)
  Apology 5
  Murder 5
Hewart, Lord
(1870–1943)
  Justice 15
Hewitt, C. W.
  Transport 10
Heyward, Du Bose
(1885–1940) and
Gershwin, Ira
(1896–1983)
  Seasons 8
Hicks, J. R. (1904–)
  Business 11
Hicks, Seymour
(1871–1949)
  Old Age 12
Hightower, Jim
  Moderation 6
Hill, Aaron (1685–1750)
  Courage 5
Hill, Damon (1960–)
  Success 15
Hill, Joe (1879–1915)
  Revolution 13
Hill, Rowland
(1744–1833)
  Music 13
Hillel 'The Elder'
(*c.*60 BC–AD *c.*9)
  Self 6
Hillingdon, Lady
(1857–1940)
  Sex 14
Hilton, James
(1900–54)
  Old Age 13

Hippocrates
(*c.*460–357 BC)
  Art 11
  Medicine 10
Hirst, Damien
(1965–)
  Art 12
Hitchcock, Alfred
(1899–1980)
  Acting 5
  Broadcasting 2
  Cinema 10
  Fear 6
Hitler, Adolf
(1889–1945)
  Leadership 6
  Lies 8
Hobbes, Thomas
(1588–1679)
  Last Words 10
  Life 18
  Opinion 4
  Truth 18
Hobsbawm, Eric
(1917–)
  Twentieth Century 5
Hockney, David
(1937–)
  Painting 8
  Technology 9
Hodgson, Ralph
(1871–1962)
  Animals 12
  Time 14
Hogben, Lancelot
(1895–1975)
  Technology 10
Holiday, Billie
(1915–59)
  Drugs 7
  Race 8
Holland, Henry
Scott (1847–1918)
  Death 22
Holmes, John H.
(1879–1964)
  Universe 8

Holmes, Oliver Wendell (1809–94)
  Conversation 7
Homer (8th century BC)
  Death 23
  Opening Lines 10
  Transience 8
Hood, Thomas (1799–1845)
  Poverty 11
  Seasons 9
Hope, A. D. (1907–)
  Australia 3
Hope, Anthony (1863–1933)
  Children 9
  Epitaphs 11
Hope, Bob (1903–)
  Money 12
  Sport 13
Hopkins, Gerard Manley (1844–89)
  Beauty 11
  Birds 5
  Environment 12
  Hope 11
  Mind 2
  Pollution 9
  Prayer 8
  Silence 3
  Skies 5
Horace (65–8 BC)
  Achievement 10
  Anger 5
  Crises 6
  Death 24
  Fame 9
  Fools 9
  Happiness 6
  Hope 12
  Literature 8
  Mistakes 10
  Moderation 7
  Money 13
  Nature 7
  Patriotism 11

  Poetry 12
  Present 7
  Statistics 5
  Style 7
  Words 9
Horne, Donald Richmond (1921–)
  Australia 4
Housman, A. E. (1859–1936)
  Alcohol 6
  Nature 8
  Past 8
  Prejudice 11
  Seasons 10
Howell, James (c.1594–1666)
  Places 18
Hoyle, Fred (1915–)
  Universe 9
Hubbard, Elbert (1859–1915)
  Genius 5
  Life 19
  News 13
  Technology 11
Hubbard, Frank McKinney ('Kin') (1868–1930)
  Revenge 7
Hughes, Langston (1902–67)
  Race 9
Hughes, Ted (1930–98)
  Birds 6
Hughes, Thomas (1822–96)
  Sport 14
Hugo, Victor (1802–85)
  God 8
  Ideas 4
  Suffering 6
Hull, Josephine (?1886–1957)
  Shakespeare 4
Hume, Basil (1923–99)
  Prayer 9

Hume, David (1711–76)
  Beauty 12
  Custom 7
  Money 14
  Religion 15
  Self 7
Hunt, G. W. (1829?–1904)
  Patriotism 12
Huxley, Aldous (1894–1963)
  Apology 6
  Change 9
  Critics 5
  Education 14
  Experience 6
  Happiness 7
  Manners 8
  People 13
Huxley, Julian (1887–1975)
  God 9
Huxley, T. H. (1825–95)
  Certainty 8
  Knowledge 16
  Science 14, 15
  Thinking 8
  Truth 19
Hytner, Nicholas (1956–)
  Cinema 11
Ibarruri, Dolores (1895–1989)
  Liberty 6
  Wars 18
Ibsen, Henrik (1828–1906)
  Dress 6
  Minorities 5
Ice Cube (1970–)
  Parents 9
Ice-T (1958–)
  Language 13
Illich, Ivan (1926–)
  Society 7

Inge, Dean (1860–1954)
  Argument 4
  Liberty 7
  Power 8
Ingersoll, Robert G.
(1833–99)
  God 10
Ingham, Bernard
(1932–)
  Government 15
  News 14
Ingres, J. A. D.
(1780–1867)
  Painting 9
Irving, John (1942–)
  Memory 11
Irving, Washington
(1783–1859)
  Change 10
  Speech 13
Isaacson, Walter
(1952–)
  Computers 7
Isherwood,
Christopher (1904–86)
  Writing 13
Issigonis, Alec
(1906–88)
  Management 6

Jackson, Andrew
(1767–1845)
  Courage 6
Jackson, Jesse
(1941–)
  Race 10
Jackson, Mahalia
(1911–72)
  Poverty 12
Jacobs, Joe
(1896–1940)
  Sport 15
James I (1566–1625)
  Poets 15
James V (1512–42)
  Scotland 7

James, Carwyn
(1929–83)
  Revenge 8
James, Clive (1939–)
  Broadcasting 3
James, Evan
  Wales 3
James, Henry
(1843–1916)
  Art 13
  Critics 6
  Day 5
  Life 20
  Literature 9
  Living 7
James, William
(1842–1910)
  Alcohol 7
  Lies 9
  Success 16
Jarrell, Randall
(1914–65)
  Ideas 5
  Manners 9
Jean-Baptiste,
Marianne
  Britain 6
Jeans, James
(1877–1946)
  Life Sciences 11
  Science 16
  Universe 10
Jefferson, Thomas
(1743–1826)
  Civilization 5
  Gardens 9
  Health 6
  Liberty 8
  Morality 8
  Political Parties 7
  Politicians 25
  Revolution 14
Jeffrey, Francis,
Lord (1773–1850)
  Critics 7

Jenkins, David,
Bishop of Durham
(1925–)
  God 11
Jenkins, Roy (1920–)
  Political Parties 8
Jennings, Elizabeth
(1926–)
  Animals 13
Jerome, Jerome K.
(1859–1927)
  Idleness 8
  Medicine 11
  Work 9
Jerrold, Douglas
(1803–57)
  France 4
Jewel, Bishop John
(1522–71)
  Church 8
Joad, C. E. M.
(1891–1953)
  Meaning 5
John, Elton (1947–)
  Singing 8
John, Elton (1947–)
and Taupin, Bernie
(1950–)
  People 14
John Paul II, Pope
(1920–)
  Church 10
Johnson, Amy
(1903–41)
  Achievement 11
Johnson, Dorothy
(1905–84)
  Heroes 7
Johnson, Lyndon
Baines (1908–73)
  Enemies 8
  Intelligence 8
Johnson, Philander
Chase (1866–1939)
  Optimism 6

Johnson, Samuel
(1709–84)
  Achievement 12
  Advertising 3
  Alcohol 8
  Behaviour 12
  Biography 7
  Books 10
  Careers 5
  Change 11
  Conversation 8
  Critics 8
  Death 25
  Equality 5
  Food 14
  Friendship 10
  Genius 6
  Ignorance 5
  Imagination 6
  Intelligence 7
  Justice 16
  Knowledge 17
  Language 14
  Languages 6
  Libraries 3
  Life 21
  Living 8
  London 5
  Marriage 26
  Music 14
  Opinion 5
  Patriotism 13
  Philosophy 6
  Poetry 13
  Poets 16
  Poverty 13
  Praise 5
  Reading 6
  Scotland 8
  Sea 7
  Sex 15
  Solitude 8
  Sorrow 11
  Sport 16
  Supernatural 9
  Taxes 6
  Travel 5

  Trust 8
  Truth 20
  Virtue 6
  War 21
  Wealth 10
  Weather 10
  Woman's Role 9, 10
  Words 10, 11
  Writers 9
  Writing 14, 15
John XXIII, Pope
(1881–1963)
  Church 9
Johst, Hanns
(1890–1978)
  Civilization 6
Jolson, Al (1886–1950)
  Singing 9
Jones, Henry Arthur
(1851–1929) and
Herman, Henry
(1832–94)
  Past 9
Jones, Paul M. see
de Leon, Walter and
Jones, Paul M.
Jones, Steve (1944–)
  Chance 11
  Sex 16
Jonson, Ben
(c.1573–1637)
  Epitaphs 12
  Lies 10
  Men and Women 11
  Religion 16
  Shakespeare 5, 6
Joseph II (1741–90)
  Musicians 6
Joseph, Jenny
(1932–)
  Idleness 9
  Old Age 14
Jowett, Benjamin
(1817–93)
  Lies 11

Joyce, James
(1882–1941)
  Art 14
  Ireland 7
Julian of Norwich
(1343–after 1416)
  Optimism 7
Jung, Carl Gustav
(1875–1961)
  Children 10
  Drugs 8
  Heart 3
  Life 22
  Middle Age 6
Justice, Donald
(1925–)
  Middle Age 7
Juvenal (AD c.60–c.130)
  Children 11
  Crime 17
  Health 7
  Poverty 14
  Sport 17
  Trust 9
  Truth 21
  Virtue 7

Kafka, Franz
(1883–1924)
  Law 14
  Opening Lines 11
Kalmar, Bert
(1884–1947) et al.
  Honour 2
  Meeting 6
Kant, Immanuel
(1724–1804)
  Happiness 8
  Human Race 11
  Morality 9
**Kanter, Rosabeth
Moss** (1943–)
  Twentieth Century 6
Karr, Alphonse
(1808–90)
  Change 12

Karr, Alphonse (*cont.*)
  Crime 18
Kaufman, Gerald
(1930–)
  Political Parties 9
Keats, John
(1795–1821)
  Alcohol 9
  Beauty 13, 14
  Death 26
  Epitaphs 13
  Imagination 7
  Inventions 11
  Love 23
  Music 15
  Nature 9
  Opening Lines 12
  Philosophy 7
  Pleasure 7
  Poetry 14
  Reading 7
  Satisfaction 4
  Seasons 11
  Silence 4
  Sorrow 12
  Weather 11
Keenan, Brian
(1950–)
  Liberty 9
Keillor, Garrison
(1942–)
  Men 11
Keller, Helen
(1880–1968)
  Language 15
Kennedy, John F.
(1917–63)
  Beginnings 9
  Cooperation 7
  Diplomacy 5
  Liberty 10
  Political Comment 13
  Race 11
  Sea 8
Kennedy, Joseph P.
(1888–1969)
  Determination 11

Keynes, John
Maynard (1883–1946)
  Government 16
  Time 15
Khrushchev, Nikita
(1894–1971)
  Satisfaction 5
Kierkegaard, Sören
(1813–1855)
  Life 23
Kilmuir, Lord
(1900–67)
  Political Parties 10
Kilvert, Francis
(1840–79)
  Travel 6
King, Martin Luther
(1929–68)
  Cooperation 8
  Equality 6
  Idealism 4
  Justice 17
  Race 12
  Violence 5
King, Stephen
(1947–)
  Fear 7
King, William Lyon
Mackenzie (1874–1950)
  Canada 5
Kingsley, Charles
(1819–75)
  Bible 3
  Virtue 8
Kinnock, Neil (1942–)
  Patriotism 14
Kinsey, Alfred
(1894–1956)
  Sex 17
Kipling, Rudyard
(1865–1936)
  Army 5
  Art 15
  Cats 2
  Character 10
  Crises 7
  England 8

  Gardens 10
  Knowledge 18
  Madness 6
  Men and Women 12
  News 15
  Opinion 6
  Parents 10
  Progress 10
  Sea 9
  Sex 18
  Sickness 7
  Solitude 9
  Sport 18
  Success 17
  Words 12
Kissinger, Henry
(1923–)
  Management 7
  Power 9
Klee, Paul (1879–1940)
  Painting 10
Klopstock, Friedrich
(1724–1803)
  Meaning 6
Knox, John (*c.*1505–72)
  Woman's Role 11
Knox, Ronald
(1888–1957)
  Opinion 7
Koestler, Arthur
(1905–83)
  God 12
  Writing 16
Kohl, Helmut (1930–)
  Europe 8
Kraus, Karl
(1874–1936)
  Transport 11
Krishnamurti, Jiddu
(1895–1986)
  Happiness 9
  Religion 17
  Truth 22
Kronecker, Leopold
(1823–91)
  Mathematics 13

Krutch, Joseph
Wood (1893–1970)
  Cats 3
Kubrick, Stanley
(1928–99)
  Politics 15
Kundera, Milan
(1929–)
  Intelligence 9

Labouchere, Henry
(1831–1912)
  Politicians 26
la Bruyère, Jean de
(1645–96)
  Life 24
Laclos, Pierre
Choderlos de
(1741–1803)
  Pleasure 8
  Virtue 9
Lacroix, Christian
(1951–)
  Dress 7
Laforgue, Jules
(1860–87)
  Life 25
Lahr, John (1941–)
  Advertising 4
Laing, R. D. (1927–89)
  Madness 7
Lamb, Charles
(1775–1834)
  Gardens 11
  Humour 13
  Libraries 4
  People 15
  Pleasure 9
  Time 16
  Writing 17
Lamb, Lady Caroline
(1785–1828)
  People 16
Lamont, Norman
(1942–)
  Business 12
  Economics 7

  Government 18
Lance, Bert (1931–)
  Management 8
Lang, Andrew
(1844–1912)
  Statistics 6
Lang, Fritz (1890–1976)
  America 9
Lang, Julia (1921–)
  Beginnings 10
Lao Tzu
(c.604–c.531 BC)
  Beginnings 11
Larkin, Philip
(1922–85)
  Books 11
  Bores 8
  Day 6
  Life 26
  London 6
  Old Age 15
  Optimism 8
  Parents 11
  Sex 19
  Work 10
la Rochefoucauld,
Duc de (1613–80)
  Absence 5
  Hypocrisy 6
  Misfortune 9
Latimer, Hugh
(c.1485–1555)
  Determination 12
Laurier, Wilfrid
(1841–1919)
  Canada 6
Lawrence, D. H.
(1885–1930)
  Australia 5
  Literature 10
  Seasons 12
  Sex 20
  Shakespeare 7
  Sorrow 13
  Writing 18

Lawrence, T. E.
(1888–1935)
  Life 27
Lazarus, Emma
(1849–87)
  America 10
Leach, Edmund
(1910–)
  Family 6
Leacock, Stephen
(1869–1944)
  Advertising 5
Leary, Timothy
(1920–96)
  Computers 8
  Living 9
Leavis, F. R.
(1895–1978)
  Poets 17
Lebowitz, Fran
(1946–)
  Conversation 9
  Fame 10
  Women 13
Lec, Stanislaw
(1909–66)
  Censorship 5
  Progress 11
Le Corbusier
(1887–1965)
  Architecture 3
Lee, Nathaniel
(c.1653–92)
  Madness 8
Lee, Robert E.
(1807–70)
  War 22
Lehrer, Tom (1928–)
  Achievement 13
  Life 28
  Words 13
LeMay, Curtis E.
(1906–90)
  Wars 19
Lenin (1870–1924)
  Democracy 7
  Liberty 11

Lenin (*cont.*)
People 17
Politics 16
Progress 12
Technology 12
Lennon, John
(1940–80)
Fame 11
Happiness 10
Wealth 11
Lennon, John
(1940–80) and
McCartney, Paul
(1942–)
Friendship 11
Money 15
Old Age 16
Past 10
Peace 10
Solitude 10
Leonardo da Vinci
(1452–1519)
Life 29
Nature 10
Lerner, Alan Jay
(1918–86)
Charm 4
Men 12
Temptation 5
Lessing, Doris
(1919–)
Seasons 13
Lessing, G. E.
(1729–81)
Prayer 10
Lever, Harold
(1914–95)
Law 15
**Leverhulme,
Viscount** (1851–1925)
Advertising 6
Leverson, Ada
(1865–1936)
People 18
Levi, Primo (1919–87)
Cruelty 5

Levin, Bernard
(1928–)
Bureaucracy 7
Politicians 27
Lévis, Duc de
(1764–1830)
Government 17
Lewis, C. S.
(1898–1963)
Courage 7
Future 9
Poetry 15
Prayer 11
Sorrow 14
Temptation 6
Women 14
Lewis, Sinclair
(1885–1951)
Literature 11
Liberace (1919–87)
Critics 9
Musicians 7
**Lichtenberg, Georg
Christoph** (1742–99)
News 16
Lincoln, Abraham
(1809–65)
Beauty 15
Change 13
Critics 10
Democracy 8
Fools 10
Political Comment 14
Voting 8
Lin Yutang (1895–1976)
Travel 7
Lippmann, Walter
(1889–1974)
Leadership 7
Lively, Penelope
(1933–)
Language 16
Languages 7
Livingstone, Ken
(1945–)
Economics 8
Politics 17

Voting 9
Livy (59 BC–AD 17)
Success 18
Lloyd George, David
(1863–1945)
Britain 7
Diplomacy 6
Political Comment 15
Politics 18
Speech 18
Titles 4
Wars 20
Locke, John
(1632–1704)
Mistakes 11
Opinion 8
Truth 23
Lodge, David (1935–)
Children 12
Long, H. Kingsley
see McArthur,
Alexander and Long,
H. Kingsley
**Longfellow, Henry
Wadsworth** (1807–82)
Biography 8
Day 7
God 13
Life 30
Solitude 11
Youth 4
Longford, Lord
(1905–)
Old Age 17
Pride 9
Loos, Anita
(1893–1981)
Practicality 9
Women 15
Lorenz, Edward N.
Chance 12
Lorenz, Konrad
(1903–89)
Science 17
Louis XIV (1638–1715)
Management 9
Royalty 15

Louis XVIII
(1755–1824)
  Army 6
  Manners 10

Lovelace, Ada
(1815–52)
  Computers 9

Lovelace, Richard
(1618–58)
  Honour 3
  Liberty 12

Lovell, Bernard
(1913–)
  Youth 5

**Lowell, James
Russell** (1819–91)
  Work 11

Lowell, Robert
(1917–77)
  Middle Age 8
  Optimism 9

Lowndes, William
(1652–1724)
  Money 16

Lowry, Malcolm
(1909–57)
  Love 24

Luce, Clare Booth
(1903–)
  Woman's Role 12

Lucretius (c.94–55 BC)
  Life 31
  Religion 18

Luther, Martin
(1483–1546)
  God 14
  Good 15
  Pleasure 10

Luxemburg, Rosa
(1871–1919)
  Liberty 13

Lydgate, John
(c.1370–c.1451)
  Words 14

Lyte, Henry Francis
(1793–1847)
  Change 14

**McArthur, Alexander
and Long, H.
Kingsley**
  Poverty 15

Macaulay, Lord
(1800–59)
  Bible 4
  Imagination 8
  Liberty 14
  Morality 10
  Pleasure 11
  Praise 6
  Suffering 8
  War 23

McCaig, Norman
(1910–96)
  Scotland 9

McCarthy, Cormac
(1933–)
  Suffering 7

McCarthy, Mary
(1912–89)
  America 11
  People 19

McCartney, Paul
(1942–)
  Musicians 8

McCartney, Paul
(1942–) see Lennon,
John and McCartney,
Paul

**McClellan, General
George B.** (1826–85)
  Wars 21

McCrae, John
(1872–1918)
  Wars 22

MacDiarmid, Hugh
(1892–1978)
  Flowers 5

McDowell, Malcolm
(1943–)
  Acting 8

McEwan, Ian (1948–)
  Argument 5

McGoohan, Patrick
(1928–) et al.
  Self 8

McGough, Roger
(1937–)
  Death 28

McGregor, Jimmy
  Sport 20

McGregor, Lord
(1921–)
  News 17

Machiavelli, Niccolò
(1469–1527)
  Government 19
  Revenge 9

Maclaren, Alexander
(1826–1910)
  Church 11

MacLeish, Archibald
(1892–1982)
  Poetry 16

McLuhan, Marshall
(1911–80)
  Broadcasting 4
  Technology 13, 14, 15
  Transport 12
  Twentieth Century 7

Macmillan, Harold
(1894–1986)
  Morality 11
  *Political
    Comment* 16, 17,
    18, 19, 20
  Politicians 28
  Politics 19
  Power 10

MacNeice, Louis
(1907–63)
  Birth 5
  Marriage 27
  Music 16
  Religion 19
  Time 17

McWilliam, Candia
(1955–)
  Friendship 12

Madan, Geoffrey
(1895–1947)
 Belief 9
**Magee, John
Gillespie** (1922–41)
 Skies 6
Magna Carta (1215)
 Human Rights 6
**Mahaffy, John
Pentland** (1839–1919)
 Ireland 8
Mahler, Gustav
(1860–1911)
 Music 17, 18
Mailer, Norman
(1923–)
 Heroes 8
 Presidency 5
Major, John (1943–)
 Britain 8
 Crime 19
 Economics 9
Malcolm X (1925–65)
 Peace 11
**Mallory, George
Leigh** (1886–1924)
 Achievement 14
Mancroft, Lord
(1914–87)
 Sport 19
Mandela, Nelson
(1918–)
 Diplomacy 7
 Forgiveness 5
 Hatred 9
 Idealism 5
 Twentieth Century 8
Mann, Thomas
(1875–1955)
 Death 27
 Speech 15
Mansfield, Katherine
(1888–1923)
 Travel 8
Mao Tse-tung
(1893–1976)
 Politics 20

 Power 11
Marie-Antoinette
(1755–93)
 Indifference 4
**Marlborough, Sarah,
Duchess of**
(1660–1744)
 Sex 21
**Marlowe,
Christopher** (1564–93)
 Love 25
 Religion 20
Marquis, Don
(1878–1937)
 Idleness 10
 Misfortune 10
 Optimism 10
 Poetry 17
Marshall, Arthur
(1910–89)
 Life 32
Martial (AD c.40–c.104)
 Hatred 10
 Health 8
 Love 26
Martin, Dean
(1917–95)
 Alcohol 10
Marvell, Andrew
(1621–78)
 Gardens 12
 Love 27
 Time 18
Marvell, Holt
(1901–69)
 Memory 12
Marx, Groucho
(1895–1977)
 Pride 10
Marx, Karl (1818–83)
 Custom 8
 History 10
 Philosophy 8
 Religion 21
 Society 8

Marx, Karl (1818–83)
and **Engels, Friedrich**
(1820–95)
 Class 8, 9
**Mary, Queen of
Scots** (1542–87)
 Beginnings 12
Masefield, John
(1878–1967)
 Sea 10
Massinger, Philip
(1583–1640)
 Action 6
Mathew, James
(1830–1908)
 Justice 18
Matlovich, Leonard
(d. 1988)
 Army 7
**Maugham, W.
Somerset** (1874–1965)
 Censorship 6
 Fate 7
 Love 28
 Men and Women 13
 Money 17
 Morality 12
 Parents 12
 Suffering 9
 Women 16
 Writers 10
 Writing 19
Maurois, André
(1885–1967)
 Old Age 18
**Mayakovsky,
Vladimir** (1893–1930)
 Poets 18
Medici, Cosimo de'
(1389–1464)
 Forgiveness 6
Melba, Dame Nellie
(1861–1931)
 Singing 10
Melbourne, Lord
(1779–1848)
 Art 16

Certainty 9
Government 20
Politicians 29
Religion 22
Menander
(342–*c*.292 BC)
Life 33
Youth 6
Mencken, H. L.
(1880–1956)
Conscience 5
Intelligence 10
Men and Women 14
Menuhin, Yehudi
(1916–99)
Civilization 7
**Menzies, Robert
Gordon** (1894–1978)
Australia 6
Meredith, George
(1828–1909)
Certainty 10
Food 15
Meredith, Owen
(1831–91)
Genius 7
Merritt, Dixon Lanier
(1879–1972)
Birds 7
Metternich, Prince
(1773–1859)
Places 19
Michelangelo
(1475–1564)
Art 17
Mies van der Rohe
(1886–1969)
Architecture 4, 5
Mill, John Stuart
(1806–73)
Happiness 11
Liberty 15
Miller, Arthur (1915–)
Business 13
Death 29
News 18

Miller, Jonathan
(1934–)
Sickness 8
Milligan, Spike
(1918–)
Money 18
Thinking 9
Twentieth Century 9
Milne, A. A.
(1882–1956)
Education 15
Food 16
Ideas 6
Weather 12
Milton, John (1608–74)
Action 7
Books 12
Change 15
Dance 7
England 9
Fame 12
Good 16
Heart 4
Heaven 5
Hypocrisy 7
Men and Women 15
Mind 3
Music 19
Opening Lines 13
Opinion 9
Peace 12
Philosophy 9
Poetry 18
Skies 7
Sleep 11
Speech 16
Sport 21
Violence 6
Wealth 12
Writing 20, 21
Mitchell, Adrian
(1932–)
Poetry 19
Mitchell, Joni
(1945–)
Life 34

Mitchell, Margaret
(1900–49)
Birth 6
Hope 13
Indifference 5
Mitford, Nancy
(1904–73)
Titles 5
Mitterrand, François
(1916–96)
Politicians 30
Mizner, Wilson
(1876–1933)
Certainty 11
Places 20
Success 19
Writing 22
Molière (1622–73)
Critics 11
Food 17
Fools 11
Justice 19
Language 17, 18
Medicine 12
Secrets 13
**Montagu, Lady Mary
Wortley** (1689–1762)
Enemies 9
Montague, C. E.
(1867–1928)
War 24
Montaigne (1533–92)
Belief 10
Cats 4
Children 13
Home 9
Ideas 7
Life 35
Living 10
Love 29
Solitude 12
Montesquieu
(1689–1755)
Birth 7
God 15
History 11

Montessori, Maria
(1870–1952)
　Teaching 6
**Montgomery, Field
Marshal** (1887–1976)
　War 25
Moore, George
(1852–1933)
　Travel 9
Moore, Thomas
(1779–1852)
　Love 30
　Memory 13
More, Sir Thomas
(1478–1535)
　Last Words 11
　Meeting 7
**Morgan, John
Pierpont** (1837–1913)
　Law 16
Morris, Desmond
(1928–)
　Cruelty 6
　Society 9
Morris, William
(1834–96)
　Home 10
　Wealth 13
Morrison, Toni
(1931–)
　Beauty 16
　Choice 6
　Old Age 19
　Race 13
Morrison, Van
(1945–)
　Music 20
Mortimer, John
(1923–)
　Ambition 10
　Beauty 17
　Law 17
Mowlam, Mo (1949–)
　Peace 13
**Mozart, Wolfgang
Amadeus** (1756–91)
　Music 21

**Muggeridge,
Malcolm** (1903–90)
　Minorities 6
　Sex 22
　Virtue 10
Muller, Herbert J.
(1905–)
　Business 14
Muller, H. J.
(1890–1967)
　Human Race 12
Mumford, Lewis
(1895–1982)
　Generation Gap 4
Munch, Edvard
(1863–1944)
　Painting 11
Murdoch, Iris
(1919–99)
　Flowers 6
　Hope 14
　Marriage 28
Murrow, Ed (1908–65)
　Broadcasting 5
　Speech 17
　Wars 23
Muste, Rev. A. J.
(1885–1967)
　Love 31

Nabokov, Vladimir
(1899–1977)
　Opening Lines 14
　Reading 8
　Travel 10
　Writers 11
Napoleon I
(1769–1821)
　Army 8
　Courage 8
　England 10
　Europe 9
　Past 11
　Sex 23
　Success 20

Nash, Ogden
(1902–71)
　Advertising 7
　Alcohol 11
　Animals 14
　Careers 6
　Cats 5
　Dogs 3
　Family 7
　Middle Age 9
　Parents 13
　Transport 13
Nehru, Jawaharlal
(1889–1964)
　Temptation 7
**Nelson, Horatio,
Lord** (1758–1805)
　England 11
　Last Words 12
　Wars 24
Nemerov, Howard
(1920–91)
　Inventions 12
Nesbit, Edith
(1858–1924)
　Children 14
　Pleasure 12
Neumann, John von
(1903–57)
　Mathematics 14
Newbolt, Henry
(1862–1938)
　Sport 22, 23
Newman, Cardinal
(1801–90)
　Belief 11
　Religion 23
Newton, Isaac
(1642–1727)
　Inventions 13
　Progress 13
　Science 18
**Nicholas I, Emperor
of Russia** (1796–1855)
　Places 21

Nicholson, Vivian
(1936–)
  Money 19
Nicolson, Harold
(1886–1968)
  Diaries 3
  Royalty 16
Niebuhr, Reinhold
(1892–1971)
  Change 16
  Democracy 9
  Twentieth
    Century 10
Niemöller, Martin
(1892–1984)
  Cooperation 9
  Liberty 16
Nietzsche, Friedrich
(1844–1900)
  Human Race 13
  Humour 14
  Living 11
  Morality 13
  Suffering 10
  Women 17
Nightingale,
Florence (1820–1910)
  Medicine 13
Nixon, Richard
(1913–94)
  Hatred 11
  Presidency 6
Norris, Steven
(1945–)
  Transport 14
North, Christopher
(1785–1854)
  Law 18
Northcliffe, Lord
(1865–1922)
  Censorship 7
  Titles 6
Norton, Caroline
(1808–77)
  Death 30

Norworth, Jack
(1879–1959)
  Sport 24
Nye, Bill
  Musicians 9

Oates, Captain
Lawrence (1880–1912)
  Last Words 13
O'Casey, Sean
(1880–1964)
  Writers 12
Occam, William of
(c.1285–1349)
  Philosophy 10
Ochs, Adolph S.
(1858–1935)
  News 19
Ogilvy, David (1911–)
  Advertising 8
Ogilvy, James, 1st
Earl of Seafield
(1664–1730)
  Scotland 10
O'Kelly, Dennis
(c.1720–87)
  Sport 25
Okpik, Abraham
  Race 14
Olivier, Laurence
(1907–89)
  Acting 9
Omar, Caliph (d. 644)
  Censorship 8
Onassis, Jacqueline
Kennedy (1929–94)
  Parents 14
Ondaatje, Michael
(1943–)
  Heart 5
O'Neill, Eugene
(1888–1953)
  Crime 20
  Sea 11
Ono, Yoko (1933–)
  Women 18

Oppenheimer, J.
Robert (1904–67)
  Inventions 14
  Science 19
  Technology 16
O'Rourke, P. J.
(1947–)
  Political Parties 11
Ortega y Gasset,
José (1883–1955)
  Environment 13
Orwell, George
(1903–50)
  Advertising 9
  Argument 6
  Body 10, 11
  Censorship 9
  Class 10
  England 12
  Equality 7
  Future 10
  Government 22
  Liberty 17
  Opening Lines 15
  Poets 19
  Politics 21
  Power 12
  Prejudice 12
  Sport 26
  Thinking 10
  War 26
Osborne, Dorothy
(1627–95)
  Letters 7
Osborne, John
(1929–)
  Royalty 17
  Women 19
Osler, Mirabel
  Gardens 13
Osler, William
(1849–1919)
  Medicine 14
O'Sullivan, John L.
(1813–95)
  Government 21

Otis, James (1725–83)
  Taxes 7
O'Toole, Peter
(1932–)
  Health 9
Ovid (43 BC–AD c.17)
  Character 11
  Moderation 8
  Religion 24
  Time 19
Owen, Wilfred
(1893–1918)
  Army 9
  Poetry 20
  War 27
Oxenstierna, Count
(1583–1654)
  Government 23

Paget, Reginald
(1908–90)
  Bible 5
Paglia, Camille
(1947–)
  Broadcasting 6
  Civilization 8
Paine, Thomas
(1737–1809)
  Belief 12
  Government 24
  Patriotism 15
  People 20
  Religion 25
  Revolution 15
Palafox, José de
(1780–1847)
  Wars 25
Paley, William
(1743–1805)
  Argument 7
Palmerston, Lord
(1784–1865)
  Last Words 14
  Meeting 8
  Political Comment 21

**Pankhurst,
Emmeline** (1858–1928)
  Argument 8
Parker, Charlie
(1920–55)
  Music 22
Parker, Dorothy
(1893–1967)
  Acting 10
  Birth 8
  Cinema 12
  Death 31
  Dress 8
  Gifts 7
Parker, Ross (1914–74)
and **Charles, Hugh**
(1907–)
  Meeting 9
Parkes, Henry
(1815–95)
  Australia 7
**Parkinson, C.
Northcote** (1909–93)
  Bureaucracy 8
  Management 10
  Money 20
  Work 12
Parks, Rosa (1913–)
  Race 15
**Parnell, Charles
Stewart** (1846–91)
  Advice 4
Parsons, Tony
(1953–)
  Poverty 16
Pascal, Blaise
(1623–62)
  Body 12
  Death 32
  God 16
  Heart 6
  Human Race 14, 15
  Letters 8
  Self 9
  Skies 8
  Style 8
  Writing 23

Pasternak, Boris
(1890–1960)
  Life 36
Pasteur, Louis
(1822–95)
  Science 20
Patrick, St (fl. 5th
cent.)
  Prayer 12
Pauli, Wolfgang
(1900–58)
  Thinking 11
Payn, James
(1830–98)
  Misfortune 11
Payne, J. H.
(1791–1852)
  Home 11
**Peacock, Thomas
Love** (1785–1866)
  Humour 15
  Marriage 29
Peake, Mervyn
(1911–68)
  Living 12
Pearson, Hesketh
(1887–1964)
  Titles 7
Péguy, Charles
(1873–1914)
  Liberty 18
Pelé (1940–)
  Sport 27
**Pembroke, 2nd Earl
of** (c.1534–1601)
  Government 25
Penn, William
(1644–1718)
  Children 15
Penrose, Roger
(1931–)
  Mind 4
Pepys, Samuel
(1633–1703)
  Crime 21
  Marriage 30
  Money 21

Sleep 12

Peres, Shimon
(1923–)
Broadcasting 7

Pericles (*c.*495–429 BC)
Fame 13
Women 20

Persons, Ted
Past 12

Pétain, Marshal
(1856–1951)
Biography 9

Peter, Laurence
(1919–)
Management 11

Petronius (d. AD 65)
Death 33
Sex 24

**Phelps, Edward
John** (1822–1900)
Mistakes 13

Philby, Kim (1912–88)
Trust 10

**Philip, Duke of
Edinburgh, Prince**
(1921–)
Food 18
Sea 12

Picasso, Pablo
(1881–1973)
Genius 8
God 17
Painting 12

Pirsig, Robert M.
(1928–)
God 18
Mind 5

Pitt, William (1708–78)
Environment 14
Youth 7

Pitt, William
(1759–1806)
Europe 10
Last Words 15

Pius VII, Pope
(1742–1823)
Diplomacy 8

Pius XII, Pope
(1876–1958)
Mistakes 13

Planck, Max
(1858–1947)
Science 21

Plath, Sylvia (1932–63)
Birth 9
Madness 9
Women 21

Plato (429–347 BC)
Justice 20
Religion 26

Pliny the Elder
(AD 23–79)
Inventions 15

Poincaré, Henri
(1854–1912)
Science 22

**Pompadour, Madame
de** (1721–64)
Revolution 16

Pompidou, Georges
(1911–74)
Politicians 31

Pope, Alexander
(1688–1744)
Children 16
Dogs 4
Education 16
Environment 15
Food 19
Fools 12
Forgiveness 7
Good 17
Government 26
Happiness 12
Heart 7
Hope 15
Human Race 16
Intelligence 11
Knowledge 19
Law 19
Meeting 10
Mistakes 14
Old Age 20

Opinion 10
Poets 20
Political Parties 12
Praise 7
Reading 9
Royalty 18
Science 23
Self 10
Self-Knowledge 9
Style 9
Teaching 7
Virtue 11
Writing 24

Popper, Karl (1902–94)
Prejudice 13

Porter, Cole
(1891–1964)
Change 17
Love 32
Trust 11

Portillo, Michael
(1953–)
Careers 7

Potter, Dennis
(1935–94)
Present 8
Religion 27
Transport 15

Pound, Ezra
(1885–1972)
Literature 12
Middle Age 10
Music 23
Seasons 14

Poussin, Nicolas
(1594–1665)
Painting 13

Powell, Anthony
(1905–2000)
Character 12
Old Age 21

Powell, Enoch
(1912–98)
Politicians 32
War 28

**Power, John
O'Connor** (1848–1919)
  Political Parties 13
Pratchett, Terry
(1948–)
  Advice 5
  Imagination 9
  Self 11
Preston, Keith
(1884–1927)
  Poetry 21
Priestley, J. B.
(1894–1984)
  Class 11
  Sport 28
  Weather 13
Prior, Matthew
(1664–1721)
  Sickness 9
Pritchett, V. S.
(1900–97)
  Books 13
Protagoras
(b. *c.*485 BC)
  Human Race 17
**Proudhon, Pierre-
Joseph** (1809–65)
  Society 10
Proust, Marcel
(1871–1922)
  Day 8
  Heaven 6
  Memory 14
Publilius Syrus (1st
century BC)
  Beauty 18
  Gifts 8
Pulitzer, Joseph
(1847–1911)
  News 20
Punch
  Choice 7
  Diplomacy 9
  Prejudice 14
Puzo, Mario (1920–)
  Choice 8
  Law 20

Quant, Mary (1934–)
  *Twentieth
    Century* 11
  Wealth 14
  Youth 8
Quarles, Francis
(1592–1644)
  Work 13
Quennell, Peter
(1905–93)
  People 21
**Quiller-Couch,
Arthur** (1863–1944)
  Perfection 5

Rabelais, François
(*c.*1494–*c.*1553)
  Children 17
  Food 20
  Last Words 16
  Living 13
Rabin, Yitzhak
(1922–95)
  Peace 14
Racine, Jean
(1639–99)
  Women 22
**Rainborowe,
Thomas** (d. 1648)
  Human Rights 7
Ralegh, Walter
(*c.*1552–1618)
  Ambition 11
  Death 34
  Last Words 17
  Time 20
Raleigh, Walter
(1861–1922)
  Quotations 6
Rantzen, Esther
(1940–)
  Family 8
Ratner, Gerald
(1949–)
  Business 15

Raymond, Derek
(1931–94)
  Madness 10
Rayner, Claire
(1931–)
  Happiness 13
Reade, Charles
(1814–84)
  Custom 9
Reagan, Ronald
(1911–)
  Character 13
  Leadership 8
  Sickness 10
  Work 14
Reger, Max
(1873–1916)
  Critics 12
Reith, Lord
(1889–1971)
  Prejudice 15
**Rendall, Montague
John** (1862–1950)
  Broadcasting 8
Renoir, Jean
(1894–1979)
  Letters 9
Reynolds, Joshua
(1723–92)
  Work 15
Reynolds, Malvina
(1900–78)
  Environment 16
Rhodes, Cecil
(1853–1902)
  England 13
  Last Words 18
Rhys, Jean
(*c.*1890–1979)
  People 22
Rice, Grantland
(1880–1954)
  Sport 29
Rice-Davies, Mandy
(1944–)
  Lies 12

Richards, Keith
(1943–)
  Drugs 9
Richardson, Joely
(1965–)
  Success 21
Richardson, Ralph
(1902–83)
  Acting 11
Rimbaud, Arthur
(1854–91)
  Europe 11
Ritz, César
(1850–1918)
  Business 16
Rivarol, Antoine de
(1753–1801)
  France 5
**Robespierre,
Maximilien** (1758–94)
  Human Rights 8
Robin, Leo (1900–)
  Wealth 15
**Rochester, John
Wilmot, Earl of**
(1647–80)
  Courage 9
  Epitaphs 14
Roddick, Anita
(1942–)
  Business 17
Rogers, Richard
(1933–)
  Architecture 6
Rogers, Samuel
(1763–1855)
  Action 8
  Marriage 31
  Solitude 13
Rogers, Will
(1879–1935)
  Civilization 9
  Heroes 9
  Humour 16
  Ignorance 6
  Political Parties 14
  Taxes 8

  Time 21
Roland, Mme
(1754–93)
  Liberty 19
**Rolle, Richard de
Hampole** (c.1290–1349)
  Class 12
Roosevelt, Eleanor
(1884–1962)
  Pride 11
**Roosevelt, Franklin
D.** (1882–1945)
  Censorship 10
  Fear 8
  Human Rights 9
  Wars 26
Roosevelt, Theodore
(1858–1919)
  America 12
  Diplomacy 10
  News 21
  Presidency 7
  War 29
Rootes, Lord
(1894–1964)
  Transport 16
Ross, Eric
  Life 37
Rossetti, Christina
(1830–94)
  Memory 15
  Seasons 15
Rossini, Gioacchino
(1792–1868)
  Musicians 10
Rostand, Jean
(1894–1977)
  Life Sciences 12
  Murder 6
Rosten, Leo (1908–97)
  Children 18
Roth, Philip (1933–)
  Parents 15
Rotten, Johnny
(1957–)
  Sex 25

Roupell, Charles
  Sport 30
**Rousseau, Jean-
Jacques** (1712–78)
  Liberty 20
Rowland, Helen
(1875–1950)
  Fools 13
  Men 13
Rowland, Richard
(c.1881–1947)
  Cinema 13
Royden, Maude
(1876–1956)
  Church 12
Rumbold, Richard
(c.1622–85)
  Democracy 10
Runcie, Robert
(1921–2000)
  Travel 11
Runyon, Damon
(1884–1946)
  Money 22
Rushdie, Salman
(1947–)
  Absence 6
  Liberty 21
Rusk, Dean (1909–)
  Crises 8
Ruskin, John
(1819–1900)
  Beauty 19
  Cooperation 10
  Ignorance 7
  Painting 14
  Work 16
Russell, Bertrand
(1872–1970)
  Belief 13
  Bores 9
  Censorship 11
  Cruelty 7
  Leisure 3
  Mathematics 15, 16
  Minorities 7
  Opinion 11

Russell, Bertrand
(*cont.*)
    Parents 16
    Progress 14
    Religion 28
    Science 24
    Work 17
**Russell, William
Howard** (1820–1907)
    Army 10
Rutherford, Ernest
(1871–1937)
    Science 25, 26
    Statistics 7

Sagan, Carl (1934–96)
    Universe 11
Sagan, Françoise
(1935–)
    Envy 5
**Saint-Exupéry,
Antoine de** (1900–44)
    Children 19
    Love 33
Saki (H. H. Munro)
(1870–1916)
    Beauty 20
    Dress 9
    Food 21
    Politicians 33
Salisbury, Lord
(1830–1903)
    Gifts 9
Salisbury, Lord
(1893–1972)
    Politicians 34
Samuel, Lord
(1870–1963)
    Libraries 5
Sandburg, Carl
(1878–1967)
    Language 19
    Past 13
    Places 22
    War 30
    Weather 14

**Sanders, Henry
'Red'**
    Sport 31
Santayana, George
(1863–1952)
    Past 14
**Sargent, John
Singer** (1856–1925)
    Painting 15
Sartre, Jean-Paul
(1905–80)
    Heaven 7
    Hope 16
    Liberty 22
    Optimism 11
    Time 22
Sassoon, Siegfried
(1886–1967)
    Army 11
Sayers, Dorothy L.
(1893–1957)
    Men and Women 16
    Quotations 7
Scalpone, Al
    Prayer 13
Scanlon, Hugh
(1913–)
    Liberty 23
**Schelling, Friedrich
von** (1775–1854)
    Architecture 7
**Schiller, Friedrich
von** (1759–1805)
    Happiness 14
    Intelligence 12
**Schlesinger, Arthur
M. Jr.** (1917–)
    Presidency 8
    *Twentieth
    Century* 12
Schnabel, Artur
(1882–1951)
    Music 24
    Musicians 11
Schroeder, Patricia
(1940–)
    Presidency 9

Schumacher, E. F.
(1911–77)
    Economics 10
    Environment 17
Schumann, Robert
(1810–56)
    Musicians 12
**Schumpeter, Joseph
Alois** (1883–1950)
    Technology 17
Schurz, Carl
(1829–1906)
    Patriotism 16
Schwitters, Kurt
(1887–1948)
    Painting 16
Scott, C. P.
(1846–1932)
    News 22
Scott, Robert Falcon
(1868–1912)
    Experience 7
    Last Words 19
    Places 23
Scott, Sir Walter
(1771–1832)
    Chance 13
    Indifference 6
    Lies 13
    Patriotism 17
    Scotland 11
    Style 10
    Women 23
**Scott-Maxwell,
Florida**
    Parents 17
Searle, Ronald
(1920–) see Willans,
Geoffrey and Searle,
Ronald
Seeger, Pete (1919–)
    Experience 8
Segal, Erich (1937–)
    Love 34
Sei Shōnagon
(*c.*966–*c.*1013)
    Enemies 10

Selden, John
(1584–1654)
  Law 21
  Pleasure 13
  Words 15
Self, Will (1961–)
  Idleness 11
  People 23
Sellar, W. C.
(1898–1951) and
Yeatman, R. J.
(1898–1968)
  History 12
  Teaching 8
**Seneca ('the
Younger')**
(*c*.4 BC–AD 65)
  Death 35
  Ignorance 8
  Teaching 9
Service, Robert W.
(1874–1958)
  Time 23
Sewell, Brian
  Art 18
Sexby, Edward
(d. 1658)
  Murder 7
Sexton, Anne
(1928–74)
  Old Age 22
**Shaftesbury, 1st
Earl of** (1621–83)
  Religion 29
**Shaftesbury, 3rd
Earl of** (1671–1713)
  Thinking 12
**Shakespeare,
William** (1564–1616)
  Achievement 15
  Acting 12
  Action 9
  Ambition 12
  Army 12
  Beauty 21
  Bible 6
  Body 13

Business 18
Careers 8
Certainty 12
Chance 14
Character 14
Children 20
Choice 9
Conscience 6
Courage 10
Cruelty 8, 9
Custom 10
Day 9
Death 36, 37, 38
Determination 13
Diplomacy 11
Dress 10
Education 17
England 14
Envy 6
Epitaphs 15
Equality 8
Fame 14
Family 9
Fate 8
Fear 9, 10
Flowers 7, 8
Food 22
Friendship 13
Future 11
Generation Gap 5
Gifts 10
Good 18, 19, 20
Greatness 4, 5
Heart 8
Honour 4, 5
Human Race 18, 19,
  20
Humour 17, 18
Hypocrisy 8, 9
Imagination 10
Indifference 7
Justice 21, 22
Language 20
Law 22
Leisure 4
Libraries 6
Lies 14

Life 38, 39
Love 35, 36, 37, 38,
  39, 40
Madness 11, 12
Manners 11
Marriage 32, 33
Meaning 7
Medicine 15
Meeting 11, 12, 13
Memory 16, 17
Men 14
Misfortune 12
Moderation 9
Money 23
Murder 8
Music 25
Nature 11
News 23
Old Age 23, 24
Opening Lines 16
Parents 18
Past 15, 16
Peace 15
Perfection 6
Politicians 35
Pollution 10
Power 13
Praise 8
Prayer 14
Prejudice 16
Present 9
Reading 10
Religion 30
Royalty 19, 20
Satisfaction 6
Scotland 12
Sea 13
Seasons 16
Self 12
Self-Knowledge 10
Sex 26, 27
Sickness 11
Skies 9
Sleep 13, 14
Sorrow 15, 16
Speech 18, 19
Sport 32

Shakespeare,
William (*cont.*)
  Success 22
  Suffering 11, 12, 13
  Supernatural 10
  Temptation 8
  Thinking 13
  Time 24, 25
  Universe 12
  Virtue 12, 13
  Wales 4
  War 31
  Weather 15
  Women 24, 25
  Words 16, 17
  Work 18
  Writing 25
  Youth 9
Shankly, Bill (1914–81)
  Sport 33
Shaw, George
Bernard (1856–1950)
  Action 10
  Alcohol 12
  Army 13, 14
  Art 19
  Beauty 22
  Choice 10
  Cinema 14
  Dance 8
  Democracy 11
  Determination 14
  England 15
  Forgiveness 8
  Generation Gap 6
  Happiness 15
  Heaven 8
  Home 12
  Hope 17
  Ideas 8
  Imagination 11
  Indifference 8
  Languages 8
  Liberty 24
  Love 41
  Marriage 34
  Medicine 16

  Men and Women 17
  Music 26
  Parents 19, 20
  Patriotism 18
  Photography 8
  Poverty 17
  Progress 15
  Self 13
  Shakespeare 8
  Speech 20
  Teaching 10
  Titles 8
  Violence 7
  Virtue 14
  Women 26
Shelley, Percy
Bysshe (1792–1822)
  Birds 8
  Heaven 9
  Hope 18
  Memory 18
  Places 24
  Poetry 22
  Religion 31
  Royalty 21
  Seasons 17
  Skies 10
  Sleep 15
Sheridan, Philip
Henry (1831–88)
  Prejudice 17
Sheridan, Richard
Brinsley (1751–1816)
  Manners 12
  Speech 21
  Women 27
Sherman, General
(1820–91)
  War 32
Sibelius, Jean
(1865–1957)
  Critics 13
Sidney, Philip
(1554–86)
  France 6
  Gifts 11
  Humour 19

  Poetry 23
Sieyès, Abbé
Emmanuel Joseph
(1748–1836)
  Revolution 17
Signoret, Simone
(1921–85)
  Marriage 35
Simenon, Georges
(1903–89)
  Writing 26
Simon, Paul (1942–)
  Music 27
  Silence 5
  Suffering 14
Simonides
(*c*.556–468 BC)
  Epitaphs 16
Simpson, N. F.
(1919–)
  Management 12
Simpson, O. J.
(1947–)
  Character 15
Sinatra, Frank
(1915–98)
  Living 14
Skinner, B. F.
(1904–90)
  Education 18
  Thinking 14
Smart, Christopher
(1722–71)
  Cats 6
Smiles, Samuel
(1812–1904)
  Food 23
  Management 13
Smith, Adam
(1723–90)
  Business 19, 20
  Taxes 9
  Wealth 16
Smith, Delia
  Food 24

Smith, F. E.
(1872–1930)
  Ambition 13
  Manners 13
Smith, Godfrey
(1926–)
  Words 18
**Smith, Logan
Pearsall** (1865–1946)
  Books 14
  Careers 9
  Hypocrisy 10
  Reading 11
  Youth 10
Smith, Stevie
(1902–71)
  Death 40
  England 16
  Indifference 9
  Past 17
Smith, Sydney
(1771–1845)
  Books 15
  Conversation 10
  Country 10
  Critics 14
  Death 39
  Food 25
  Heaven 10
  Intelligence 13
  Ireland 9
  Letters 10
  Living 15
  Marriage 36
  Mathematics 17
  Minorities 8
  Poverty 18
  Prayer 15
Socrates (469–399 BC)
  Knowledge 20
  Last Words 20
  Philosophy 11
  Truth 24
  Wealth 17
Solon (*c*.640–after
556 BC)
  Happiness 16

**Solzhenitsyn,
Alexander** (1918–)
  Censorship 12
  Power 14
  Work 19
Sondheim, Stephen
(1930–)
  America 13
Sontag, Susan
(1933–)
  Critics 15
  Reality 6
Soper, Donald
(1903–98)
  Church 13
Soper, Lord (1903–98)
  Politicians 36
Sophocles
(*c*.496–406 BC)
  Human Race 21
  Life 40
  Sex 28
Spark, Muriel (1918–)
  Life 41
  Teaching 11
Sparrow, John
(1906–92)
  Dogs 5
Spencer, Herbert
(1820–1903)
  Crime 22
  Fools 14
  Life Sciences 13
  Perfection 7
Spencer, Lord
(1964–)
  Titles 9
Spencer, Stanley
(1891–1959)
  Painting 17
Spender, Stephen
(1909–)
  Transport 17
Spenser, Edmund
(*c*.1552–99)
  Languages 9

Spielberg, Steven
(1947–)
  Past 18
Spring-Rice, Cecil
(1859–1918)
  Patriotism 19
Springsteen, Bruce
(1949–)
  Success 23
Spurgeon, C. H.
(1834–92)
  Lies 15
Squire, J. C.
(1884–1958)
  Alcohol 13
  Science 27
Staël, Mme de
(1766–1817)
  Behaviour 13
  Opinion 12
Stalin, Joseph
(1879–1953)
  Class 13
  Death 41
  Gifts 12
  Power 15
**Stanley, Henry
Morton** (1841–1904)
  Meeting 14
Stark, Freya
(1893–1993)
  Women 28
Steele, Richard
(1672–1729)
  Letters 11
  Reading 12
  Wealth 18
Steffens, Lincoln
(1866–1936)
  Revolution 18
Stein, Gertrude
(1874–1946)
  Self 14
Steinbeck, John
(1902–68)
  Greatness 6
  Human Race 22

Steinem, Gloria
(1934–)
  Men and Women 18
  Women 29
Steiner, George
(1926–)
  Morality 14
Stendhal (1783–1842)
  Literature 13
Stephens, James
(1882–1950)
  Perfection 8
Sterne, Laurence
(1713–68)
  Determination 15
  France 7
  Ideas 9
Stevens, Anthony
  Men and Women 19
Stevens, Wallace
(1879–1955)
  Music 28
  Reality 7
Stevenson, Adlai
(1900–65)
  Liberty 25
  People 24
  Political Parties 15
  Praise 9
  Speech 22
Stevenson, Anne
(1933–)
  Birds 9
**Stevenson, Robert
Louis** (1850–94)
  Epitaphs 17
  Lies 16
  Marriage 37
  Seasons 18
  Travel 12
Stewart, Ian (1945–)
  Life Sciences 14
Sting (1951–)
  Environment 18
Stone, Oliver (1946–)
see Weiser, Stanley
and Stone, Oliver

Stoppard, Tom
(1937–)
  Bureaucracy 9
  Knowledge 21
  Life 42
  News 24
  Poets 21
  Voting 10
  War 33
Stowell, Lord
(1745–1836)
  Law 23
Strachey, Lytton
(1880–1932)
  Biography 10
  Last Words 21
  People 25, 26
Stravinsky, Igor
(1882–1971)
  Music 29
  Musicians 13
Straw, Jack (1946–)
  Britain 9
Street-Porter, Janet
(1946–)
  Broadcasting 9
Strindberg, August
(1849–1912)
  Family 10
Strunsky, Simeon
(1879–1948)
  Quotations 8
Suckling, John
(1609–42)
  Love 42
Sullivan, J. W. N.
(1886–1937)
  Science 28
Sullivan, Louis Henri
(1856–1924)
  Architecture 8
**Sully, Maximilien de
Béthune, Duc de**
(1559–1641)
  England 17
  France 8

Surtees, R. S.
(1805–64)
  Animals 15
  Dance 9
  Pleasure 14
Swenson, May
(1919–89)
  Children 21
Swift, Jonathan
(1667–1745)
  Church 14
  Critics 16
  Epitaphs 18
  Genius 9
  Lies 17
  Life Sciences 15
  Old Age 25
  Progress 16
  Religion 32
  Science 29
  Style 11
  Travel 13
**Swinburne,
Algernon Charles**
(1837–1909)
  Virtue 15
Szasz, Thomas
(1920–)
  Forgiveness 9
  Happiness 17
  Justice 23
  Medicine 17
**Szent-Györgyi,
Albert von** (1893–1986)
  Inventions 16
  Life Sciences 16

Tacitus (AD c.56–after
117)
  Peace 16
  Success 24
**Tagore,
Rabindranath**
(1861–1941)
  Prejudice 18
  Solitude 14

**Talleyrand, Charles-
Maurice de**
(1754–1838)
  Moderation 10
Tally, Ted (1952–) see
Harris, Thomas and
Tally, Ted
Tangye, Derek
(1912–96)
  Twentieth
    Century 13
Taupin, Bernie
(1950–) see John,
Elton and Taupin,
Bernie
Tawney, R. H.
(1880–1962)
  Titles 10
Taylor, A. J. P.
(1906–90)
  History 13
  Mistakes 15
  Wars 27
Tebbit, Norman
(1931–)
  Patriotism 20
Tecumseh (1768–1813)
  Race 16
**Tennyson, Alfred,
Lord** (1809–92)
  Army 15
  Beginnings 13
  Belief 14
  Birds 10, 11
  Change 18
  Day 10
  Death 42
  Determination 16
  Europe 12
  Fate 9
  Gardens 14
  Honour 6
  Love 43
  Meeting 15
  Mistakes 16
  Nature 12
  Perfection 9

  Prayer 16
  Sorrow 17
  Time 26
  Titles 11
Terence (c.190–159 BC)
  Human Race 23
Teresa, Mother
(1910–97)
  Sickness 12
Teresa, St of Ávila
(1512–82)
  God 19
Teresa, St of Lisieux
(1873–97)
  Heaven 11
Tertullian
(AD c.160–c.225)
  Belief 15
  Church 15
**Thackeray, William
Makepeace** (1811–63)
  Family 11
  Men and Women 20
Thatcher, Margaret
(1925–)
  Choice 11
  Europe 13
  Gifts 13
  Home 13
  Leadership 9
  Money 24
  News 25
  Political Comment 22
  Society 15
Theroux, Paul
(1941–)
  Manners 14
Thomas, Dylan
(1914–53)
  Death 43
  Home 14
  Life 43
  Old Age 26
  Power 16
  Wales 5
  Youth 11

Thomas, Edward
(1878–1917)
  Past 19
Thomas, Gwyn
(1913–81)
  Wales 6
Thomas, R. S.
(1913–)
  Wales 7
Thomas à Kempis
(c.1380–1471)
  God 20
  Virtue 16
Thompson, Francis
(1859–1907)
  Religion 33
  Suffering 15
Thomson, James
(1700–48)
  Britain 10
  Teaching 12
Thomson, Roy
(1894–1976)
  Broadcasting 10
**Thoreau, Henry
David** (1817–62)
  Dress 11
  Life 44, 45
  Pollution 11
  Self 15
  Time 27
  Writing 11
Thorne, Robert
(d. 1527)
  Travel 14
Thorpe, Jeremy
(1929–)
  Political Comment 23
Thurber, James
(1894–1961)
  Alcohol 14
  Health 10
  Humour 20
  Technology 18
**Thurlow, Edward,
1st Baron** (1731–1806)
  Conscience 7

Tipu Sultan
(*c.*1750–99)
Heroes 10

**Tocqueville, Alexis
de** (1805–59)
England 18
France 9
History 14
Places 25

Tolstoy, Leo
(1828–1910)
Body 14
Family 12
Hypocrisy 11

Torke, Michael
(1961–)
Mind 6

Toussenel, A.
(1803–85)
Dogs 6

Townshend, Pete
(1945–)
Generation Gap 7

Toynbee, Arnold
(1889–1975)
*Twentieth
Century* 14

Toynbee, Polly
(1946–)
Woman's Role 13

Travis, Merle
(1917–83)
Poverty 19

Tremain, Rose
(1943–)
Crime 23

Trevelyan, G. M.
(1876–1962)
France 10

Trillin, Calvin (1935–)
Writers 13

Trinder, Tommy
(1909–89)
America 14

Trollope, Anthony
(1815–82)
Equality 9
Ideas 10
Pride 12
Suffering 16

Trotsky, Leon
(1879–1940)
Civilization 10
Old Age 27
Violence 8

Truman, Harry S.
(1884–1972)
Censorship 13
Economics 11
Government 27
Leadership 10
Politicians 37

Trump, Donald
(1946–)
Business 21

Truth, Sojourner
(*c.*1797–1883)
Human Rights 10

Tucker, Sophie
(1884–1966)
Wealth 19
Women 30

Tupper, Martin
(1810–89)
Books 16

Turgenev, Ivan
(1818–83)
Nature 13
Prayer 17

Turgot, A. R. J.
(1727–81)
People 27

Turing, Alan (1912–54)
Mind 7

Tusa, John (1936–)
Management 14

Twain, Mark
(1835–1910)
Anger 6
Books 17

Certainty 13
Fools 15
Generation Gap 8
Gossip 10
Human Race 24
Inventions 17
Lies 18
News 26
Prayer 18
Quotations 9
Success 25
Temptation 9
Truth 25

Tynan, Kenneth
(1927–80)
Civilization 11
Critics 28
People 28

Tyutchev, F. I.
(1803–73)
Places 26

Unamuno, Miguel de
(1864–1937)
Certainty 14

**Universal
Declaration of
Human Rights** (1948)
Human Rights 11

Updike, John (1932–)
America 15
Bores 10
England 19
Fame 15
Science 30

Ustinov, Peter
(1921–)
Computers 10
Friendship 14

Valéry, Paul
(1871–1945)
Politics 22
Science 31
Solitude 15

Vanbrugh, John
(1664–1726)
  Women 31
**Vanderbilt, William
H.** (1821–85)
  Business 22
**van der Post,
Laurens** (1906–96)
  Murder 9
Van Dyke, Henry
(1852–1933)
  Time 28
Vaneigem, Raoul
(1934–)
  Work 20
Vaughan, Harry
  Character 16
**Vaughan Williams,
Ralph** (1872–1958)
  Musicians 14
Veblen, Thorstein
(1857–1929)
  Leisure 5
  Science 32
Vegetius (fourth
century AD)
  Peace 17
Vespasian, Emperor
(AD 9–79)
  Taxes 10
Vicious, Sid (1957–79)
  Music 30
Victoria, Queen
(1819–1901)
  Birth 10
  Children 22
  Conversation 11
  Humour 21
  Royalty 22
  Success 26
  Woman's Role 14
Vidal, Gore (1925–)
  Business 23
  Lies 19
  People 29
  Politicians 38
  Success 27

  Technology 19
Vidor, King
(1895–1982)
  Marriage 38
**Viera Gallo, José
Antonio** (1943–)
  Politics 23
Villon, François
(b. 1431)
  Past 20
Virgil (70–19 BC)
  Achievement 16
  Courage 11
  Experience 9
  Love 44
  Money 25
  Opening Lines 17
  Pleasure 15
  Science 33
  Sorrow 18
  Success 28
  Suffering 17
  Time 29
  Trust 12
  Women 32
Voltaire (1694–1778)
  Bores 11
  Canada 7
  Censorship 14
  Change 19
  Democracy 12
  God 21, 22
  Government 28
  Last Words 22
  Management 15
  Optimism 12
  Perfection 10
  Practicality 10
  Supernatural 11
  Taxes 11
  Writing 28

Walcott, Derek
(1930–)
  Idleness 12
  Writing 29

Walker, Alice (1944–)
  Life 46
  Violence 9
**Wallace, William
Ross** (d. 1881)
  Parents 21
Wallas, Graham
(1858–1932)
  Meaning 8
Walpole, Horace
(1717–97)
  Life 47
  Seasons 19
  Virtue 17
  Weather 16
Walpole, Robert
(1676–1745)
  Politicians 39
  Wars 28
Walton, Izaak
(1593–1683)
  Food 26
  Health 11
  Sport 34
**Warburton, Bishop
William** (1698–1779)
  Religion 34
Warhol, Andy
(1927–87)
  Fame 16
**Warner, Sylvia
Townsend** (1893–1978)
  Diaries 4
  Food 27
  Hatred 12
  Misfortune 13
  Sorrow 19
Washington, George
(1732–99)
  Truth 26
Waterhouse, Keith
(1929–)
  Manners 15
**Watson, Thomas
Snr.** (1874–1956)
  Business 24

Watts, Isaac
(1674–1748)
  God 23
  Idleness 13
  Time 30
Waugh, Evelyn
(1903–66)
  Britain 11
  Charm 5
  Class 14
  Crime 24
  England 20
  Manners 16
  News 27
  Style 12
Webb, Sidney
(1859–1947)
  Marriage 39
Webster, Daniel
(1782–1852)
  Ambition 14
Webster, John
(c.1580–c.1625)
  Death 44
  Fate 10
  Satisfaction 7
Wedgwood, Josiah
(1730–95)
  Prejudice 19
Weil, Simone
(1909–43)
  Economics 12
Weinreich, Max
(1894–1969)
  Language 21
Weiser, Stanley and Stone, Oliver (1946–)
  Economics 13
Weissmuller, Johnny
(1904–84)
  Men and Women 21
Weldon, Fay (1931–)
  Parents 22
  Titles 12
  Violence 10

Welles, Orson
(1915–85)
  Broadcasting 11
  Cinema 15
  Civilization 12
  Transport 18
Wellington, Duke of
(1769–1852)
  Army 16
  Books 18
  Life 48
  War 34
  Wars 29, 30, 31
Wells, H. G.
(1866–1946)
  Epitaphs 19
  History 15
  Morality 15
  Shakespeare 9
  Society 12
Wells, John (1936–)
  Self-Knowledge 11
Welsh, Irvine (1957–)
  Scotland 13
Wesker, Arnold
(1932–)
  Censorship 15
Wesley, John
(1703–91)
  Church 16
  Old Age 28
  Religion 35
West, Mae (1892–1980)
  Choice 12
  Diaries 5
  Good 21
  Meeting 16
  Men 15
  Sex 29
West, Rebecca
(1892–1983)
  Conversation 12
  Home 15
  Trust 13
Wetherell, Charles
(1770–1846)
  Biography 11

Wharton, Edith
(1862–1937)
  Singing 11
Whately, Richard
(1787–1863)
  Economics 14
Whistler, James McNeill (1834–1903)
  Argument 9
  Critics 18
  Painting 18
  Quotations 10
White, E. B.
(1899–1985)
  Statistics 8
  Transport 19
White, T. H. (1906–64)
  Education 19
  Law 24
Whitehead, Alfred North (1861–1947)
  Civilization 13
  Ideas 11
  Intelligence 14
  Philosophy 12
Whitehorn, Katharine (1928–)
  Cinema 16
Whitman, Walt
(1819–92)
  America 16
  Gifts 14
  Self 16
Whittier, John Greenleaf (1807–92)
  Sorrow 20
Whittington, Robert
  People 30
Whitton, Charlotte
(1896–1975)
  Men and Women 22
Wiesel, Elie (1928–)
  Forgiveness 10
  Indifference 10
Wilberforce, Bishop Samuel (1805–73)
  Life Sciences 17

Wilbur, Richard
(1921–)
　Mind 8
　Universe 13
Wilcox, Ella Wheeler
(1855–1919)
　Religion 36
　Solitude 16
Wilde, Oscar
(1854–1900)
　Advice 6
　Bible 7
　Biography 12
　Books 19
　Cynicism 8
　Diaries 6
　England 21
　Experience 10
　Genius 10
　Gossip 11
　Idealism 6
　Literature 14
　Love 45
　Marriage 40
　Men and Women 23
　Mistakes 17
　Parents 23
　People 31
　Reality 8
　Style 13
　Temptation 10
　Truth 27, 28
　Work 21
Wilder, Billy (1906–)
see Brackett, Charles
and Wilder, Billy
Wilensky, Robert
(1951–)
　Computers 11
Willans, Geoffrey
(1911–58) and **Searle,
Ronald** (1920–)
　Christmas 7
　Ignorance 9
Willard, Emma Hart
(1787–1870)
　Sea 14

William III (1650–1702)
　Fate 11
Williams, Kenneth
(1926–88)
　Quotations 11
Williams, R. J. P.
(1926–)
　Life Sciences 18
Williams, Shirley
(1930–)
　Church 17
Williams, Tennessee
(1911–83)
　Determination 17
　Human Race 25
　Living 16
　Reality 9
**Williams, William
Carlos** (1883–1963)
　Certainty 15
**Williamson,
Marianne** (1953–)
　Fear 11
Williamson, Roy
(1936–90)
　Scotland 14
Willmot, Eric Paul
(1936–)
　Australia 8
Wilson, A. N. (1950–)
　Wales 8
Wilson, Edward O.
(1929–)
　Mind 9
Wilson, Harold
(1916–95)
　Crises 9, 10
　Money 26
　Political Comment 24
　Political Parties 16
　Technology 20
**Wilson,
McLandburgh**
(1892–)
　Optimism 13

Wilson, Woodrow
(1856–1924)
　Cinema 17
　Democracy 13
Windsor, Duchess of
(1896–1986)
　Body 15
Winters, Shelley
(1922–)
　Acting 13
**Wittgenstein,
Ludwig** (1889–1951)
　Language 22
　Philosophy 13
　Speech 23
　Universe 14
Wodehouse, P. G.
(1881–1975)
　Apology 7
　Family 13
　Marriage 41
　Satisfaction 8
Wogan, Terry (1938–)
　Broadcasting 12
Wolf, Naomi (1962–)
　Beauty 23
Wollstonecraft, Mary
(1759–97)
　Mind 10
　Parents 24
　Woman's Role 15
Wolsey, Cardinal
(c.1475–1530)
　Last Words 23
**Wolstenholme,
Kenneth**
　Beginnings 14
Woods, Tiger (1975–)
　Race 17
Woolf, Virginia
(1882–1941)
　Books 20
　Life 49
　Men and Women 24
　Misfortune 14
　Writers 14

Woollcott,
Alexander (1887–1943)
  Pleasure 16
Wordsworth, William
(1770–1850)
  Birds 12
  Birth 11
  Children 23
  Death 45
  Flowers 9
  Good 22
  Imagination 12
  Knowledge 22
  Leisure 6
  London 7
  Memory 19
  Nature 14, 15
  People 32
  Poetry 24
  Revolution 19
  Satisfaction 9
  Writing 30
  Youth 12
Worrall, Terry
  Weather 17
Wotton, Henry
(1568–1639)
  Architecture 9
  Diplomacy 12

  Sorrow 21
Wright, Frank Lloyd
(1867–1959)
  Architecture 10
  Civilization 14

Yeatman, R. J.
(1898–1968) see Sellar,
W. C. and Yeatman,
R. J.
Yeats, W. B.
(1865–1939)
  Change 20
  Day 11
  Death 46
  Generation Gap 9
  Heart 9
  Idealism 7
  Indifference 11
  Ireland 10
  Life 50
  Love 46
  Old Age 29, 30
  Perfection 11
  Poetry 25
  Suffering 18
York, Sarah,
Duchess of (1959–)
  Royalty 23

Young, Edward
(1683–1765)
  Critics 19
  Fools 16
  Idleness 14
  Quotations 12
  Sleep 16
Young, George W.
(1846–1919)
  Alcohol 15
Young, Neil (1945–)
  Living 17

Zamyatin, Yevgeny
(1884–1937)
  Thinking 15
Zangwill, Israel
(1864–1926)
  America 17
  Religion 37
Zappa, Frank
(1940–93)
  News 28
Zeno (333–261 BC)
  Speech 24
Zobel, Hiller B.
(1932–)
  Law 25